Mini 1959-76 Autobook

By Kenneth Ball
and the Autobooks Team of Technical Writers

Mini 1, 2, 1959-69
Mini Traveller, Countryman, 1960-69
Mini 850, 1000, 1275 GT, 1967-76
Mini Clubman 1969-76
Riley Elf 1, 2, 3, 1961-69
Wolseley Hornet 1, 2, 3, 1961-69

Autobooks Ltd. Golden Lane Brighton BN1 2QJ England

The AUTOBOOK series of Workshop Manuals is the largest in the world and covers the majority of British and Continental motor cars, as well as all major Japanese and Australian models. For a full list see the back of this manual.

CONTENTS

ISBN 0 85147 606 6

First Edition 1968
Second Edition, fully revised 1968
Third Edition, fully revised 1969
Fourth Edition, fully revised 1969
Fifth Edition, fully revised 1970
Sixth Edition, fully revised 1970
Seventh Edition, fully revised 1970
Reprinted 1971
Reprinted 1971
Reprinted 1971
Eighth Edition, fully revised 1972
Reprinted 1972
Ninth Edition, fully revised 1973
Reprinted 1973
Tenth Edition, fully revised 1974
Reprinted 1974
Eleventh Edition, fully revised 1975
Reprinted 1975
Twelfth Edition, fully revised 1976

777

Printed and bound in Brighton England for Autobooks Ltd by G. Beard & Son Ltd D

ACKNOWLEDGEMENT

We wish to thank British Leyland Motor Corporation Limited for their co-operation and also for supplying data and illustrations. Considerable assistance has also been given by owners, who have discussed their cars in detail, and we would like to express our gratitude for this invaluable advice and help.

INTRODUCTION

This do-it-yourself Workshop Manual has been specially written for the owner who wishes to maintain his car in first class condition and to carry out his own servicing and repairs. Considerable savings on garage charges can be made, and one can drive in safety and confidence knowing the work has been done properly.

Comprehensive step-by-step instructions and illustrations are given on all dismantling, overhauling and assembling operations. Certain assemblies require the use of expensive special tools, the purchase of which would be unjustified. In these cases information is included but the reader is recommended to hand the unit to the agent for attention.

Throughout the Manual hints and tips are included which will be found invaluable, and there is an easy to follow fault diagnosis at the end of each chapter.

Whilst every care has been taken to ensure correctness of information it is obviously not possible to guarantee complete freedom from errors or to accept liability arising from such errors or omissions.

Instructions may refer to the righthand or lefthand sides of the vehicle or the components. These are the same as the righthand or lefthand of an observer standing behind the car and looking forward.

CHAPTER 1

THE ENGINE

1:1 Types, features, models and capacities

This manual deals with the well-known Mini series of cars, which features a number of alternative models with the same basic transverse engine design and front wheel drive. In some cars automatic transmission is fitted instead of the usual fourspeed manual gearbox, but in general operations for dismantling and overhaul are the same for all models. Any differences are covered in the following instructions by a reference to the particular car concerned. The following table shows the cylinder bores, strokes and compression ratios which compose the series:

It should be noted that references in this manual to the righthand or lefthand side of the car mean that it is viewed as from the driving seat looking forward. As the engines in these cars are fitted transversely, the cylinders are numbered from the lefthand side, the number 1 cylinder being next to the radiator.

The power unit, a part-sectioned view of which is shown in **FIG 1:1** comprises a four cylinder engine having pushrod operated overhead valves. The pushrods are positioned over a set of eight tappets actuated by a three bearing camshaft which is driven by a roller chain

	Capacity (cc)	*Bore (mm)*	*Stroke (mm)*	*Compression ratio*
Morris Mini, Austin Mini and Moke ..	848	62.94	68.26	8.3:1
Mini Automatic	848	62.94	68.26	8.9:1
Wolseley Hornet Mk I and Riley Elf Mk I	848	62.94	68.26	8.3:1
Mini Mk II	998	64.588	76.2	8.3:1
Mini Mk II Automatic	998	64.588	76.2	8.9:1
Wolseley Hornet Mk II and III, Riley Elf Mk II and III	998	64.588	76.2	8.3:1
Wolseley Hornet and Riley Elf Mk III Automatic	998	64.588	76.2	9.0:1
Mini Clubman, Automatic ..	998	64.588	76.2	8.3 or 7.6:1
Manual to 1976	998	64.588	76.2	8.3 or 7.6:1
Manual 1976	1098	64.588	83.73	8.5:1
Mini 1275 GT	1275	70.61	81.28	8.8 or 8.0:1

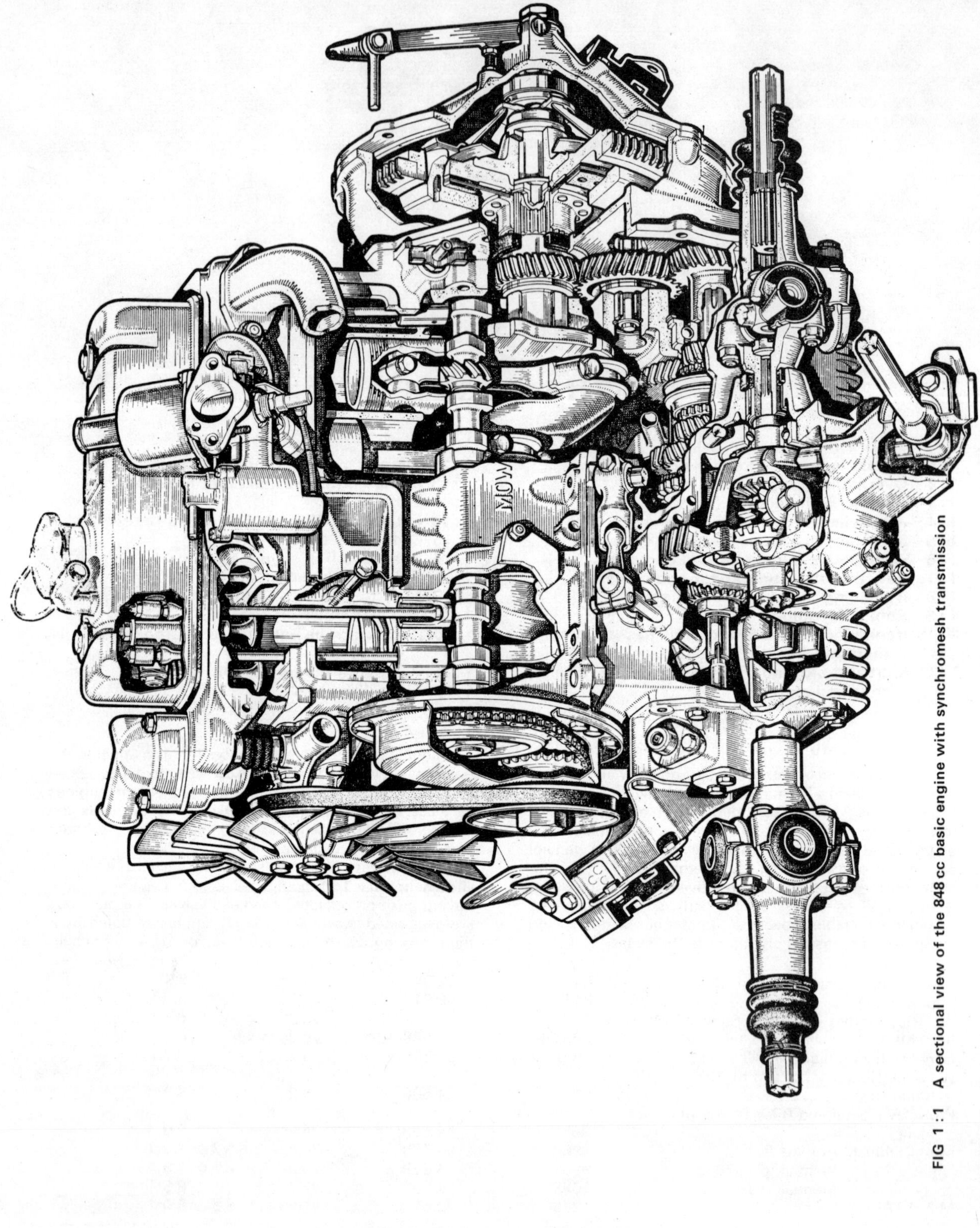

FIG 1 : 1 A sectional view of the 848 cc basic engine with synchromesh transmission from the crankshaft. Most standard models have one steel-backed whitemetal lined bearing at the front end of the camshaft, the remaining camshaft journals running in the crankcase recesses as bearings. Others have three detachable whitemetal lined bearings. The oil pump and distributor are both driven from the camshaft.

A single dry-plate clutch is incorporated in the flywheel in such a manner as to convey the drive forwards and downwards through an idler gear to the first-motion shaft of the transmission gears. The main (third motion) shaft of the gear system is in constant mesh with the large driving gear of the differential unit, which is designed as an integral assembly mounted on the side of the transmission casing. There is no conventional right-angle drive crown wheel and pinion in the differential unit. Two detachable output shafts terminate in universal couplings for the front wheel drive shafts which extend laterally outwards to the constant-speed universal couplings on the front wheels.

The power unit is mounted in a detachable subframe on which are also mounted the front suspension and wheels. There is no mechanical power connection between the engine and the rear wheels.

One oil control and three compression rings are fitted to each piston. In some engines the gudgeon pins are clamped in the connecting rod little-ends, in others the gudgeon pins are fully floating.

The big-ends have steel-backed bearings shells with alloy running surfaces. Mini, Hornet and Elf Mk 1 models have either lead/bronze linings with a lead/indium plated surface or copper/lead with a lead/tin plated surface. Mini Mk II, Hornet, Elf Mk II and III, and Clubman have copper/lead linings.

Steel-backed shells are also used for the main bearings. Mini, Hornet and Elf Mk I have white-metal linings. Mk II and III models, have copper/lead linings. A common oil supply lubricates the engine, gear system and differential unit, and for this reason it is doubly important to ensure always that the oil quality and quantity, and the lubrication system generally are in good order. The lubricating oil is pressure fed to the engine via a fullflow oil filter at the front of the engine as illustrated in **FIG 1 : 2** which shows the complete power unit, subframe and front suspension removed from the car. Oil at reduced pressure is conveyed from the front camshaft bearing to the rocker gear and the oil returning from here to the crankcase lubricates the eight tappets.

Some of the following operations may be performed with the engine still in the chassis, but if extensive work is contemplated it will be convenient to remove the power unit and mount it on a suitably constructed work-bench or cradle. **Section 1 : 3** describes how to remove the power unit when manual transmission is fitted, to remove the power unit incorporating automatic transmission refer to **Chapter 6a, Section 6a : 5.**

1 : 2 Overhauling methods

Generally the work can be divided into four stages; dismantling, cleaning, inspection, reassembly. Cleanliness, orderliness and good workmanship should be cultivated throughout, coupled with a willingness to seek advice if in doubt about any particular point. Some useful hints are given at the end of this manual. Make full use of the Technical Data when assessing the condition of components.

The lateral arrangement of the engine in these vehicles results in the 'front' of the engine being on the lefthand side of the car viewed from the driver's seat. The cylinders are numbered 1 to 4 starting at the 'front' of the engine on the lefthand side. The firing order is 1, 3, 4, 2.

Before attempting to remove a component, clean off all road dirt and oil so that a clear view of the component is presented. Paper is useful for initial cleaning, followed with paraffin and finally with petrol, taking due account of any possible fire risk. If there is any likelihood of fluff or dirt entering oil passages or other small holes, plug them before dismantling with material which can easily be removed later and remember to remove the plugging on final reassembly.

Penetrating fluids and rust removers are very useful for aiding the release of tight nuts and bolts. If hammers have to be used provide some support behind the assembly where necessary to prevent damage or distortion. As a last resort the careful application of heat may be useful.

A large magnifying glass will often facilitate the detection of a joint, not otherwise visible, between two mating parts. It will also be found useful during inspection procedures.

If any component is found to be bent, it is good policy not to attempt to straighten it as cracking and subsequent failure might result. This particularly applies to engine and chassis parts. Distortion itself may mean that a part is well on the way to fatigue failure.

The only really accurate method of measuring precise dimensions is to use precision instruments such as a micrometer or vernier gauge. Shafts can be checked for distortion by setting them up on vee-blocks on a surface plate and using a surface gauge or accurately machined gauge blocks. In general however, it will be found more convenient for the owner to consult a BMC Service agent on these matters.

If no identifying marks are visible on parts which might present some difficulty in reassembly, mark the parts by light centre popping, scratching a number or by tying on small labels. Lay the parts out in the order of dismantling if unfamiliarity is likely to lead to errors.

Clean joint faces with special care to ensure fluid-tightness. Joint washers cannot always be relied on to compensate for high spots on joint faces. When scraping off old material try to do it with scrapers slightly softer than the component material to avoid gouging the surface.

When checking clearances make sure it is the actual clearance which is being measured and not an apparent clearance due to wear.

Always use good quality spanners correctly designed for the thread size stamped on them and do not lengthen them artificially by fitting pieces of pipe over the arms or tommy bars.

Great damage can be caused during the initial moments of running reassembled parts if no lubricant is present, therefore apply some engine oil, or if this is likely to drain away, a little soft clear grease to rubbing surfaces during assembly. This will afford protection until the engine lubrication system becomes effective.

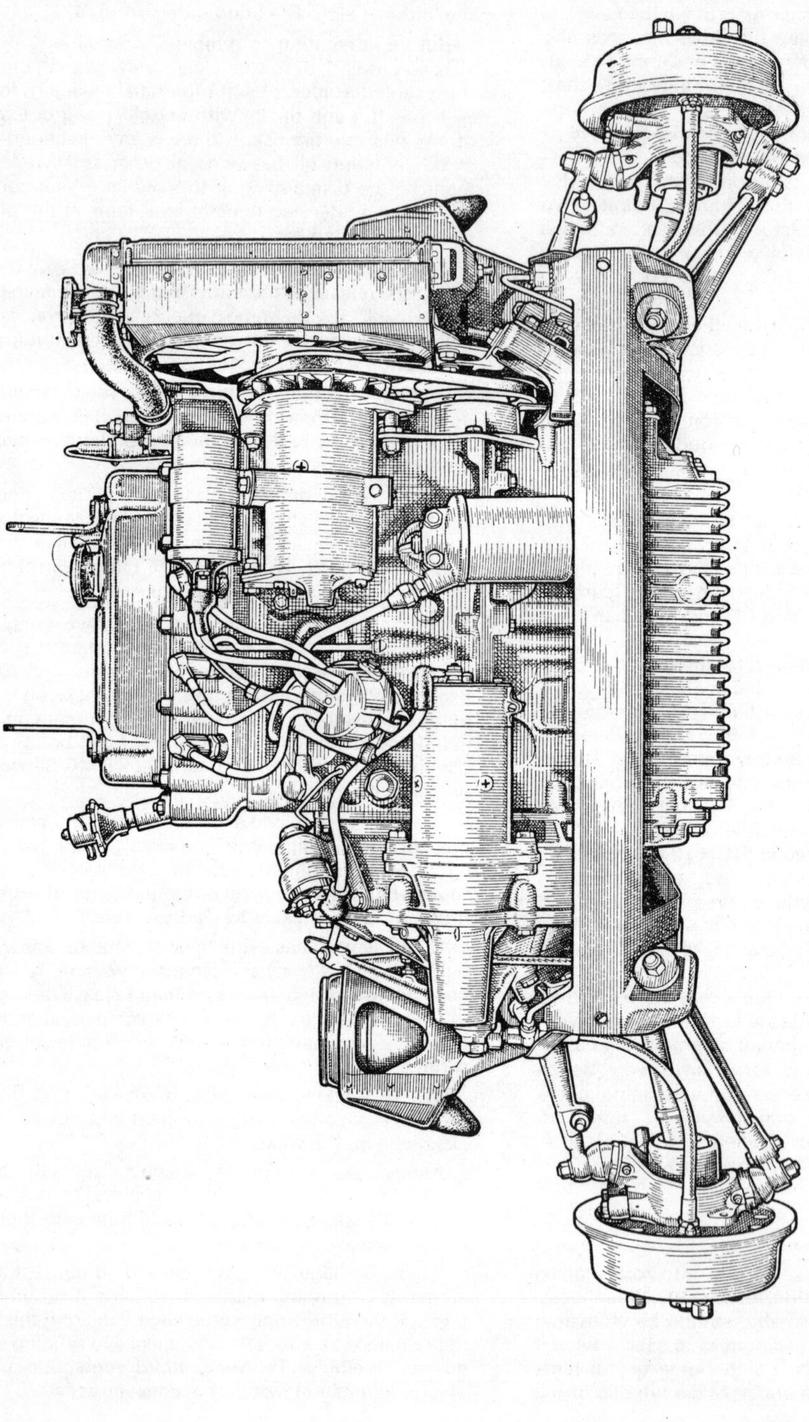

FIG 1 : 2 View of the power unit and front subframe complete with front suspension

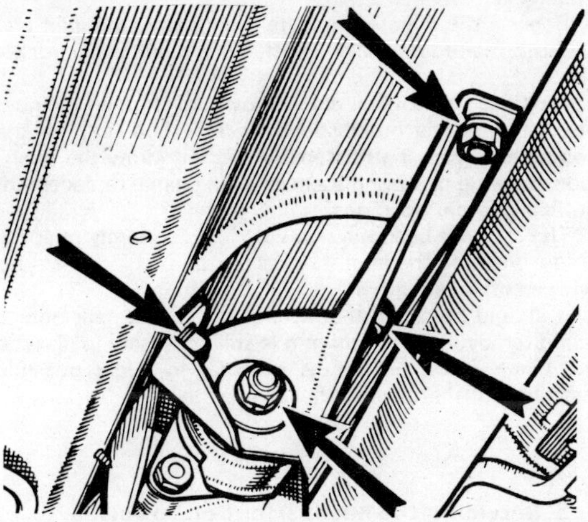

FIG 1:3 Remote control gearchange extension attachment bolts

1:3 Removing the engine up to 1974

There are two methods of removing the engine, either by removing the engine and subframe complete, or by detaching the engine from the subframe and lifting the engine out through the bonnet aperture. The first method requires heavy lifting tackle to raise the body of the car and release the engine and subframe for removal. It also has the disadvantage that the disconnection of the front suspension will require the assistance of a service agent possessing the necessary equipment. The operations described below, therefore, are those concerned with removing the engine through the bonnet aperture. They are as follows:

1 Drain off the coolant by opening the tap or removing the plug at the bottom of the radiator.
2 Drain off the lubricating oil by removing the magnetic plug at the bottom righthand side of the transmission casing. Clean off any metallic residue from the magnetic drain plug.
3 Remove the bonnet.
4 Take off the grille.
5 Disconnect the battery.
6 Remove the windscreen washer bottle and bracket.
7 Take off the distributor cap, disconnect the low tension lead, mark the distributor and clamp, to ensure correct reassembly, undo the clamp bolt and remove the distributor.
8 Disconnect the earthing strap at the righthand wing valance. Disconnect the pipes at the three-way union.
9 Disconnect the speedometer cable at the instrument. Elf: Pull back the glove box trim at the snap fastener located at the top rear corner adjacent to the instrument panel, remove the cross-head screws retaining the speedometer to its bracket on either side of the instrument panel, press the instrument forwards and unscrew the knurled cable retaining nut from under the bonnet. Hornet models: Unscrew the knurled cable retaining nut accessible from under the bonnet.
10 Disconnect the heater hoses at the engine ends.
11 Remove the fresh air heater motor (if fitted) and remove the heater.
12 Disconnect the engine tie rod at the cylinder block.
13 Disconnect the breather hose (if fitted) from the rocker cover, remove the air cleaner(s) by unscrewing the wingnut (Mini), or the retaining butterfly nut (Hornet and Elf). Disconnect the mixture and throttle control cables, the fuel supply pipe(s), the suction advance pipe (where fitted), remove the carburetter securing nuts and washers and lift off the carburetter. Lift off the cable plate and two gaskets.
14 Disconnect the exhaust system at the manifold clamp and release the pipe at the transmission casing. Tie the exhaust pipe back for support. Also release the steering balljoint from the lever with Tool 18G. 1063. Disconnect the inner ends of the drive shafts (4 outer U-bolts only). Disconnect RH brake hose from backplate. Remove RH upper suspension arm retaining nut and release with same Tool. Disconnect steering tie rod and also tie rod from lower arm. Part hub from arm. Withdraw RH hub and shaft.
15 Where oil pressure gauges are installed, disconnect the rubber pipe connector.
16 Mini, Hornet and Elf: Unscrew and remove the hexagon plug and remove the anti-rattle spring and plunger from the gearchange extension casing. Take out two setscrews, remove the changespeed lever retaining plate and pull the lever out of the casing from inside the car. On the Mini II and Elf and Hornet III, remove three bolts securing the rear gearchange extension mounting to the floor. Unscrew the gearlever knob, take off the rubber cover plate and remove the gearchange extension. The three bolts can be seen in **FIG 1:3**.
17 Remove the clutch operating lever return spring, take out two slave cylinder securing screws, leave the pushrod on the lever, withdraw the cylinder and tie it back to the bulkhead out of the way.
18 Disconnect the electrical leads to the coil, generator, temperature gauge element (where applicable) and the starter cable at the starter motor terminal. Remove the screws securing the starter solenoid switch bracket to the flywheel housing and lower the switch and cables clear of the engine. Disconnect the electrical lead and remove the horn.
19 On all cars lift front at middle of front subframe member. Remove RH wheel and disconnect tie rod from steering lever on Elf and Hornet. Remove the radiator as described in **Chapter 4, Section 4:3** and the clutch cover as described in **Section 1:8.**
20 On Mini, Hornet and Elf, remove U-bolts from inner universal joints. On Elf and Hornet only, disconnect top and bottom swivels from suspension arms and partially withdraw the RH hub and drive shaft. Support hub to prevent damage to brake hose.

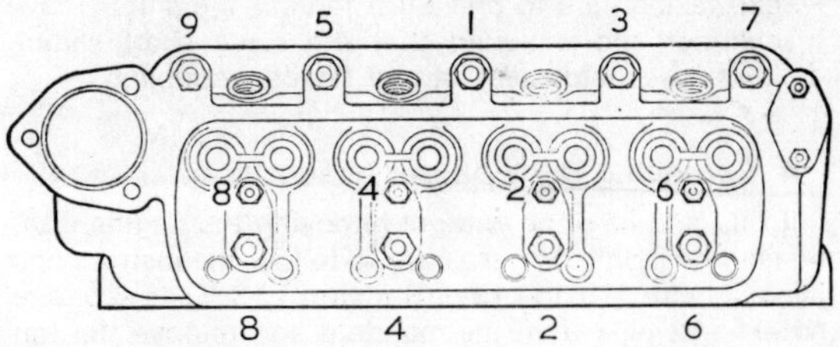

FIG 1:4 The order of slackening and tightening the cylinder head nuts

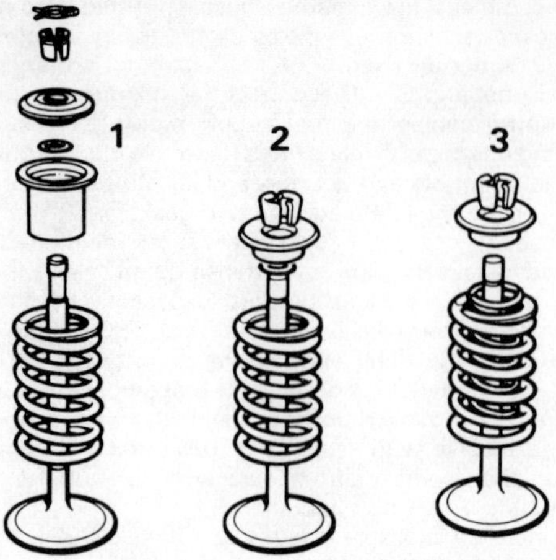

FIG 1:5 Component parts of typical valve assemblies

Key to Fig 1:5 1 Early Mini 2 Later Mini 3 Cooper and Cooper S

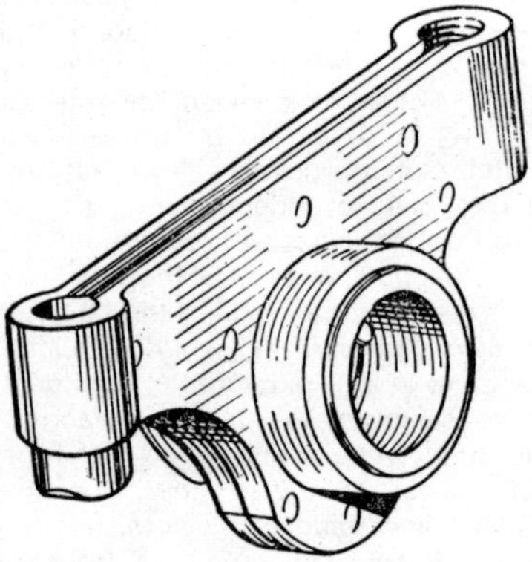

FIG 1:6 The pressed steel type of valve rocker

21 Remove the overhead valve rocker cover and gasket. Fit lifting eyes to the second and fourth cylinder head studs, making use of the existing cylinder head nuts. Take the weight of the engine on a suitable sling and remove the two setscrews securing each engine mounting to the subframe. Lift the engine from the car, taking care to prevent it fouling the clutch slave cylinder and ensuring that the drive shaft sliding joints are held clear of the flexible couplings.

1:4 Removing the cylinder head

If this is to be done without removing the engine from the car it will only be necessary to follow the instructions given in items 1, 5 and 13 of **Section 1:3**. Then separate the exhaust pipe from the manifold and remove the top radiator hose. Take out the sparking plugs. Disconnect heater hose from water valve. Slacken the bypass hose.

Release the radiator tie plate and remove the inlet and exhaust manifolds. Take off the overhead valve rocker cover.

Progressively loosen and remove the thirteen cylinder head nuts in the order shown in **FIG 1:4**. Lift off the complete rocker shaft assembly and withdraw the push-rods, marking or storing them so as to ensure replacement in their original positions.

The cylinder head may now be lifted squarely over the studs, breaking the joint if necessary by tapping the sides with a soft-headed hammer.

It should be noted that even if the rocker gear only is being removed for attention it is still necessary to slacken the five outside head nuts in order to avoid possible distortion of the cylinder head.

1:5 Servicing the head, attention to valves

Leaving the valves in place at this stage, clean up the cylinder head by washing away as much deposit as possible from the interior of the combustion chambers and valve passages, then scrape away any hard deposits, preferably using a scraper of softer material than the cylinder head, e.g. aluminium alloy strip. Carefully clean off all old jointing material. Inspect the head casting for any superficial damage.

The component parts of the valve assemblies are shown in **FIG 1:5.** Using a valve spring compressor, remove the valve assemblies, keeping them in sets, as follows: Withdraw the cotter clip, compress the spring, take out the two cotter halves, release the spring slowly. Lift off the retainer, shroud, spring and rubber seal.

Clean all parts and inspect the valves, particularly the exhaust valves, for cracks, burning, pitting of the seating surfaces and stem wear. Hard deposits should be removed by scraping down the stem and outwards across the back of the valve head. If only slight damage to the seating surfaces is visible, the valves may be refaced by a service agent.

Continuing with the head, clean out the induction and exhaust passages thoroughly, if possible finally polishing with a rotary brush. Slight damage to the valve seats may be rectified by refacing to an angle of 45 deg., for which special tools have to be used and the assistance of a service agent is advised. Other special tools are used for reducing the width of the seating surfaces if necessary. Remember that wide seating surfaces reduce the valve-to-seat sealing pressure. If the seats are beyond repair they may be renewed by fitting inserts after machining out the head recesses. New inserts are pressed into position, which is a job for a service agent to perform.

Worn valve guides may be renewed by driving them downwards through the cylinder head using a special drifting tool 4 inch long, $\frac{7}{16}$ inch dia., and having a locating spigot $\frac{9}{32}$ inch dia. and 1.0 inch long at one end. Drive the new guide into the cylinder head from the top. Inlet valve guides have the large chamfer at the top, exhaust valve guides have the counterbore at the lower end. All guides should be positioned with $\frac{19}{32}$ inch standing above the machined surface of the valve spring seating on the head.

When grinding the valve to its seat use only a light application of medium or fine grinding paste. Place a light spring under the valve to lift it occasionally so that it may be turned to a different position (about a third of a turn). Semi-rotary movements using a suction tool are most suitable and the aim should be an even dull matt surface free from any blemishes on the valve and the seat. Carefully clean away all abrasive on completing this operation. Refit the valve assemblies by reversing the removal sequence, making sure they are in their correct positions.

Inspect the rocker gear, checking the rockers and support brackets for cracks. Check the shaft and rocker bushes for excessive wear. If possible set the shaft up on vee-blocks on a surface plate to check for distortion. The plug at the front end of the rocker shaft can be removed for cleaning the shaft oilways.

Two types of rockers have been fitted to these models. The pressed steel rocker shown in **FIG 1 : 6** is not suitable for rebushing if the bush is worn. Worn bushes in the forged steel rockers, **FIG 1 : 7** may be renewed by the following method:

1 Press out the old bush and press in a new one with the split at the top.
2 Remove the adjusting screw and drill out the plug in the end of the rocker using a number 43 drill, continuing the oilway through the bush. Cut off a mild steel rivet of suitable dia. to a length which will not allow the shank to interfere with the adjusting screw, when refitted; place the rivet in the rocker end hole and weld in position.
3 Continue the hole in the rocker barrel (on the opposite side to the hole just drilled) with a number 47 drill and finally burnish-ream the bush bore to the correct dimension given in the Technical Data Section. Clean off all swarf.

When reassembling the rocker gear do not forget to insert the grub screw locating the shaft in the front bracket. Fit a new splitpin. Reassemble all parts on the shaft in exactly the reverse order to the removal sequence.

The piston crowns may be cleaned at this stage by turning the crankshaft to bring each piston to the top of its cylinder in turn and, using a scraping device preferably a little softer than the alloy pistons, scraping the carbon from the crown except for a narrow line round the outer edge. The carbon round the inside top edges of the cylinder bores should also be removed.

Remove the tappet covers from the cylinder block and lift out the tappets, keeping them in their correct order. The fit of the tappets in their guides should be such that they just fall under their own weight when clean and lubricated with normal engine lubricating oil. Inspect for scoring and in the top end for signs of damage. New tappets are chosen by selective assembly for fit as described.

Clean and examine the pushrods for wear or damage to the ends. Check for any bending. Retain in the correct order for reassembly.

Reassembly of the tappets, pushrods, cylinder head and rocker gear will follow broadly the reverse of instructions for removal. Lubricate the tappets and position the pushrods after the head has been placed into position, but before the rocker gear is replaced. Leave the tappet covers off so that the correct positioning of the pushrods can be ascertained. When refitting the covers fit new gaskets and tighten the securing bolts to a torque of 2 lb ft. (early type) or 5 lb ft. (later deep-pressed type) to ensure oil-tightness.

When refitting the cylinder head, clean and dry the head and cylinder block joint surfaces. Place a new cylinder head gasket, marked 'front' and 'top', correctly over the cylinder head studs and lower the head squarely into position. Replace the five outside nuts and washers finger tight only. Then position the pushrods as described, carefully lower the complete rocker gear over the studs and replace the remaining nuts and washers finger tight. Make sure all rocker adjusting screws are screwed well back. Tighten all cylinder head nuts a turn at a time in the correct order as shown in **FIG 1 : 4** to a torque of 40 lb ft for the nine cylinder head stud nuts and 25 lb ft for the rocker shaft bracket nuts.

Valve rocker adjustment is necessary whenever disturbance of the cylinder head or rocker gear has occurred. To save much crankshaft turning and possible doubt as to the correct rocker position for adjustment, follow this order:

Adjust No. 1 rocker with No. 8 valve fully open.
Adjust No. 3 rocker with No. 6 valve fully open.
Adjust No. 5 rocker with No. 4 valve fully open.
Adjust No. 2 rocker with No. 7 valve fully open.
Adjust No. 8 rocker with No. 1 valve fully open.
Adjust No. 6 rocker with No. 3 valve fully open.
Adjust No. 4 rocker with No. 5 valve fully open.
Adjust No. 7 rocker with No. 2 valve fully open.

Insert a feeler gauge .012 inch thick between the valve stem and the rocker screw, adjust the screw until the feeler gauge is just firm in the gap (a sliding fit) and tighten the locknut. Recheck after tightening the locknut.

Where applicable, this operation must be followed by an exhaust emission check.

1 : 6 Removing timing gear and camshaft

For this work the engine must be taken out of the car and it suggested therefore that the work be planned only as part of a major overhaul. A suitable time is after removal of the cylinder head and valve gear. The camshaft

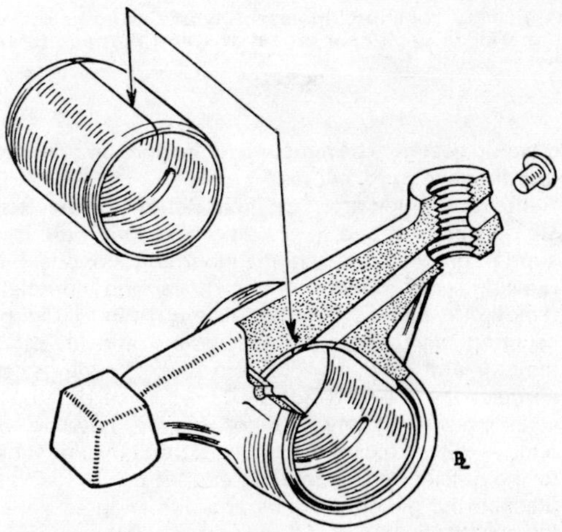

FIG 1 : 7 The forged steel type of valve rocker

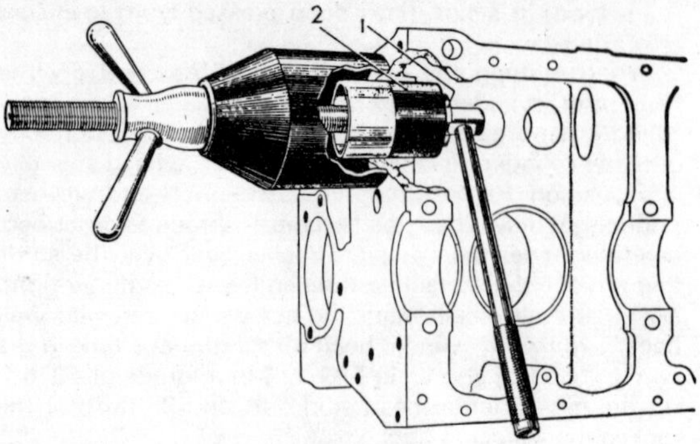

FIG 1:8 Removing a camshaft front bearing liner with the basic removing and replacing tool

Key to Fig 1:8 1 Washer 2 Adaptor 18G.124K

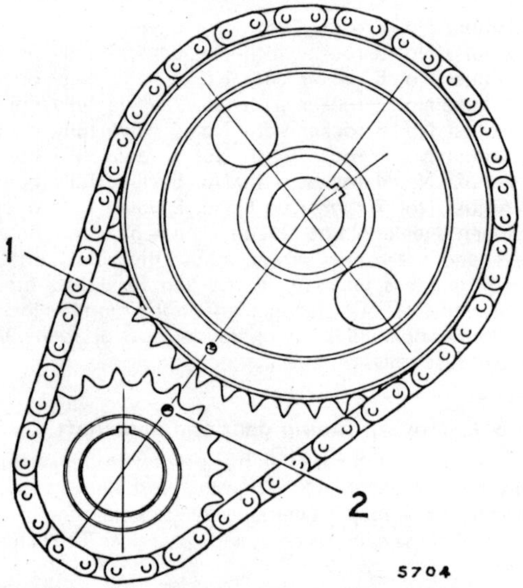

FIG 1:9 View showing assembly of timing gears with the marks on each gear wheel at 1 and 2 opposite each other

and timing gear may be removed for inspection or renewal by the following procedures:

1 Remove the radiator, by first removing the upper support bracket and the two bolts securing the lower support bracket to the engine mounting. For one-piece cowlings disconnect the top hose and completely remove the lower hose, then take out the four screws securing the radiator to the cowling and lift off the radiator and cowling. For two-piece cowlings, disconnect the top and bottom hoses, take out the six screws securing the radiator to the cowling and remove the top half of the cowling. Bend the lower hose to the outside of the cowling and lift out the radiator.

2 Slacken the generator bolts and adjusting screw and remove the fan belt. Bend back the tab of the crankshaft pulley locking washer, remove the pulley securing screw and very carefully lever off the pulley. Discard the tab washer.

3 Take out the ten timing cover securing screws and remove the timing cover, taking care not to damage the oil seal. Take off the oil thrower, noting which way round it is fitted to the crankshaft (concave face forwards). Note also that this early type front cover and oil thrower must only be used together. Where the later type front cover and oil thrower are used, the oil thrower must be fitted with the face marked 'F' away from the engine.

4 Unlock the camshaft chainwheel nut, remove the nut and discard the lockwasher. Lever off gently both chainwheels and remove them complete with the chain. Remove and store the keys. Notice the positioning marks on the chainwheels and the packing washers behind the crankshaft wheel. Take off the chain.

5 Remove one screw and take out the distributor housing, being careful not to damage the oil seal O-ring on later models, insert a $\frac{5}{16}$ inch UNF bolt about $3\frac{1}{2}$ inches long into the threaded end of the distributor drive spindle and pull out the spindle, turning slightly to disengage the drive gears.

6 Behind the camshaft chainwheel is a camshaft locating plate. Having made quite certain first that all the tappets are out, remove the three setscrews and lockwashers and then withdraw the locating plate and camshaft.

7 Inspect the camshaft journals and cam surfaces for obvious damage such as scoring. Check the journal diameters with the dimensions given in the Technical Data Section and measure and compare the overall dimensions across all inlet cams and exhaust cams. If any inlet or exhaust cams differ from the others, the camshaft should be offered to a service agent for a critical check of all dimensions with a view to possible renewal. The camshaft may be set up on vee-blocks on a surface plate if available for bending or distortion checks. If any journal wear is recorded, it may be advisable to make or borrow some form of 'go/no-go' gauge to check the camshaft bearing diameters.

8 If the front camshaft bearing is worn a new bearing liner can be fitted. The operation requires the use of a special service tool and adaptor, shown in **FIG 1:8**, to remove the old and fit the new liner, thus avoiding the probability of damage caused by improvised drifts. Line reaming with special equipment is essential after renewing this or the centre and rear bearings fitted to Mk II Mini and Mk II and III Elf and Hornet engines. This is work for a Service agent. Access to centre and rear bearings calls for removal of the flywheel housing, transmission casing and oil pump as covered in **Sections 1:8, 1:9** and **1:10**.

If at any time renewal of the camshaft bearings is undertaken, make sure that all reaming swarf is cleaned away from the cylinder block afterwards.

1:7 Refitting the timing gear and camshaft

Lubricate the camshaft journals and bearings with a fairly viscous engine oil (about SAE 40 or 50 will not drain away too quickly), or soft clear grease to provide initial lubrication. Enter the camshaft gently into position in the cylinder block, being very careful not to damage the bearings, and insert the three setscrews with new shakeproof washers through the camshaft locating plate. Tighten the setscrews.

Refit the timing gear as follows:

1 Refit the washers behind the crankshaft gear, of which mention was made during removal, if no crankshaft or camshaft items have been renewed. If renewals have been made, fit the camshaft and crankshaft gears without the washers and without the chain, place a straightedge across the camshaft gear and press the crankshaft chainwheel hard back. With feeler gauges check the gap between the crankshaft gear and the straightedge. This measurement will indicate the thickness of washers required. Remove the chainwheels.

2 Set the crankshaft keyway at TDC, fit packing washers to the determined thickness and set the camshaft keyway to approximately the one o'clock position as shown in **FIG 1 : 9.** Position the keys and assemble the chain and wheels with the two marks, mentioned during removal, opposite each other.

3 With the gears and chain thus assembled, engage the crankshaft gear keyway with the key, align the camshaft gear with the key by turning the camshaft a little either way and then push the gears on to the shafts as far as possible. Fit a new lockwasher, then tighten and securely lock the camshaft gear nut, making sure that the two marks still coincide.

4 Refit the early type oil thrower to the crankshaft, concave side forwards, or the later type with the 'F' marking forwards.

5 Inspect the timing cover oil seal for wear or defects. If a new seal is to be fitted, a service tool 18G.134 and adaptor 18G.134BD are best used for this purpose. Fill the annular groove between the lips with a soft grease.

6 Fit a new timing cover joint washer and centralize the seal when fitting the cover, using if possible the service tool 18G.138 for the early type of cover. Use service tool 18G.1044 on the later cover. In its absence the crankshaft pulley can be used by lubricating the pulley hub, pushing it into the seal and turning it at the same time to avoid damaging the sealing edge. Slide the pulley with the cover on to the crankshaft, lining up the keyway with the key and turning the cover to line up the setscrew holes with those in the crankcase. Take care not to strain the cover against the flexibility of the seal. Fit a new lockwasher and the pulley securing screw, tighten to a 70 lb ft. torque and lock securely. Insert the timing cover bolts and tighten to a 6 lb ft. torque for $\frac{1}{4}$ inch UNF bolts, or 14 lb ft. torque for $\frac{5}{16}$ inch UNF bolts.

7 To check the valve timing, or the relationship between crankshaft position and valve operation, increase No. 1 inlet rocker clearance to .019 inch and turn the crankshaft until the valve is about to open. This point may be somewhat indeterminate if much oil is present on the rocker and tappet/pushrod system. If so, insert a strip of very thin foil such as cigarette foil in the rocker gap and turn the crankshaft until the foil is gripped firmly but not crushed. Take off the flywheel inspection hole cover shown in **FIG 1 : 10** and note if the 5° BTDC mark on the flywheel is just about opposite the pointer in the inspection aperture. If this is so, the valve timing is correct. Reset the rocker clearance to .012 inch with the engine cold.

8 To restore the distributor driving spindle to its correct position in relation to the camshaft, first set the crankshaft with No. 1 piston at TDC on compression stroke (both valves fully closed). Adjust the position of the flywheel so that the 1/4 mark is in line with the mark on the pointer. Using a $\frac{5}{16}$ inch UNF by $3\frac{1}{2}$ inch long bolt screwed into the distributor drive gear, position the gear so that the slot is just below horizontal and has the large offset uppermost. Insert the gear, noting that as it engages with the camshaft gear it turns a little anticlockwise, finishing with the slot in the two o'clock position when fully home. The correct final position can be seen in **FIG 1 : 11.**

Remove the $\frac{5}{16}$ inch UNF bolt and insert the distributor, making sure that the sealing O-ring has

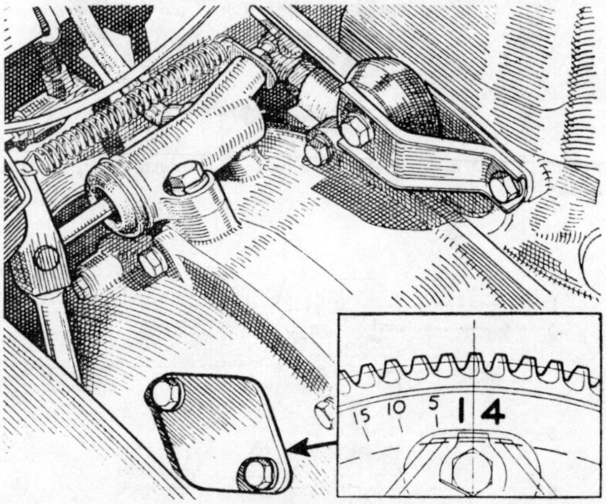

FIG 1 : 10 The flywheel inspection hole cover. Inset, the timing indicator marks on the flywheel may be seen with the aid of a mirror after removing the cover. 1/4 indicates the TDC position. Marks indicating the 5, 10 and 15 deg. BTDC positions are also provided

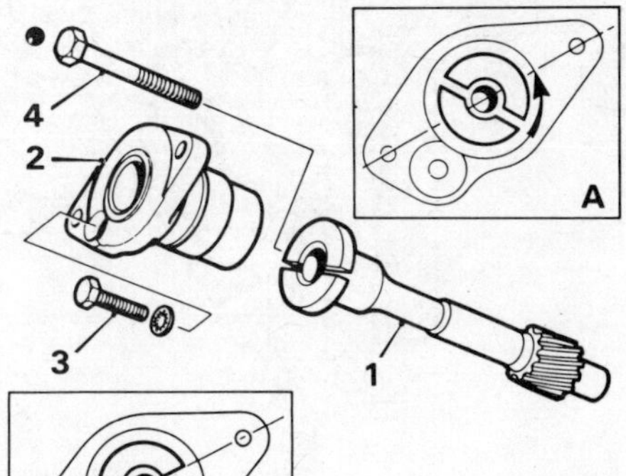

FIG 1 : 11 Fitting the distributor drive shaft. Inset A shows the preliminary engagement position. Inset B shows the final engaged position

Key to Fig 1 : 11 1 Drive shaft 2 Housing 3 Attachment screw 4 Bolt—$\frac{5}{16}$ inch UNF

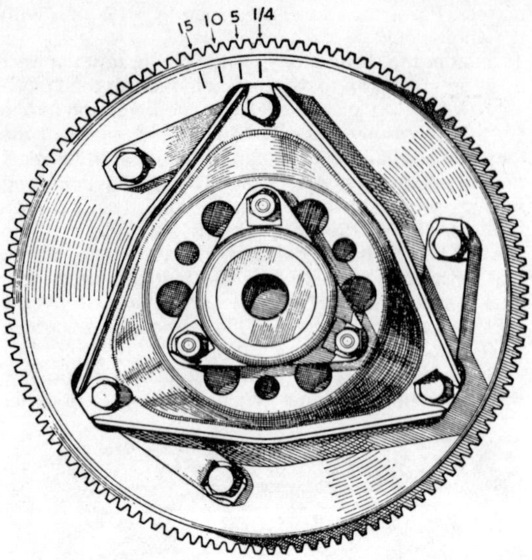

FIG 1 : 12 View of the flywheel and coil spring clutch assembly

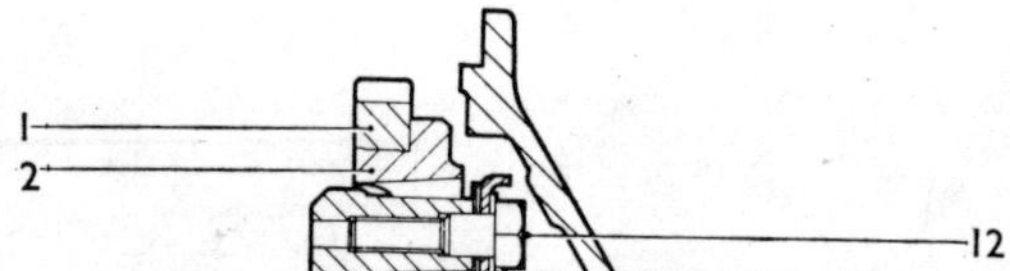

FIG 1 : 13 A sectional view of the flywheel and diaphragm spring clutch assembly

Key to Fig 1 : 13 1 Starter ring 2 Flywheel 3 Pressure plate 4 Driven plate 5 Driven plate hub 6 Circlip 7 Crankshaft 8 Crankshaft primary gear 9 Primary gear bearing 10 Thrust washer 11 Flywheel hub bolt 12 Driving pin 13 Lock washer 14 Driving strap 15 Flywheel hub 16 Thrust plate 17 Plate retaining spring 18 Thrust bearing 19 Flywheel screw 20 Keyed washer 21 Cover 22 Diaphragm spring

not been damaged. If doubtful, renew it. Secure the distributor housing in this position with the special screw and washer and finally check that the screw head does not protrude above the face of the housing. If the distributor clamp bolt has been loosened or removed and the distributor setting is in doubt, information on resetting will be found in Chapter 3.

Where applicable, this operation must be followed by an exhaust emission check.

1 : 8 Removing clutch and flywheel

Two types of clutch have been fitted, the early one being of fairly orthodox design using six coil springs but without the usual toggle levers to operate the pressure plate. The later clutch uses a circular diaphragm spring instead of the coil springs. To remove the clutch:

1 Remove the starter motor and switch, slave cylinder and lever, exhaust pipe clamp, top radiator bracket and two nuts and setscrews from the RH engine mounting. Disconnect the tie bar and raise the engine slightly, being careful not to let the fan damage the radiator.

2 Remove the clutch cover by taking out the nine setscrews securing it to the flywheel housing. Referring to **FIG 1 : 12,** unlock three tab washers, detach three nuts and remove the clutch thrust plate from the pressure spring housing. Note that two clutch to flywheel driving straps are fitted to each of the three driving points. Mark all components, including both straps and driving pins, for refitting.

3 To remove diaphragm spring clutches the engine must be disconnected from the subframe, as described in **Section 1 : 3,** to give access to the flywheel housing bolts. Remove the retaining circlip 17 **(FIG 1 : 13),** and the thrust plate 16. Slacken evenly the three clutch driving pins 12 to release the pressure of the clutch spring 22. As each pin is removed, replace it with a $\frac{5}{16}$ inch UNF by 2 inch stud to prevent the pressure plate 3 from moving out of alignment, then remove the cover and spring assembly.

4 For both types of clutch, turn the crankshaft until the 1/4 mark on the flywheel is at the top to prevent the 'C' washer locating the primary gear from falling and wedging behind the flywheel. This may damage the flywheel oil seal when the flywheel is withdrawn.

5 Prise up the locking tab and slacken the flywheel retaining screw three or four turns.

6 The flywheel has now to be drawn off its taper seating on the end of the crankshaft, for which operation service agents use a puller plate with a centre screw, service tool 18G.304, and an adaptor set of three screwed studs, nuts and washers (service tool 18G.304M, plain, for coil spring clutches; or 18G.304N, cadmium-plated, for diaphragm spring clutches). It is possible that some owners may be able to make up a similar device of their own with a little ingenuity. It is essential to keep the flywheel upright when removing it from the crankshaft, otherwise oil from the back of the flywheel oil seal may flow down the flywheel face and contaminate the clutch linings.

7 When the grip of the taper has been broken, remove the tool and adaptor set and take out the flywheel retaining screw and keyed washer 20 **(FIG 1 : 13).** Notice the manner of assembly of the washer and withdraw the flywheel assembly. It is possible to

remove coil spring clutches in this manner with the engine still in the car.

The flywheel starter gear ring should be inspected for wear and chipping of the teeth. If renewal is considered necessary it would be advisable to make use of the special facilities at the disposal of a service agent for removing the old and shrinking on a new gear ring.

On diaphragm spring clutches inspect the cover for elongation of the driving pin holes, the driving pins for ridging or wear, and the driving straps for wear or distortion. Renew as necessary.

Remove the flywheel housing (with the engine out of the car) by unlocking and removing the six setscrews and nine stud nuts securing the housing to the cylinder block and transmission casing, noting the positions of the screws for correct reassembly. The housing may then be withdrawn, care being taken to avoid damaging the lips of the oil seal on the clutch plate splines of the crankshaft primary gear. Service agents use a protector sleeve 18G.570, as shown in **FIG 1 : 14**, positioned and held firmly over the splines. Use service tool 18G.1043 if a red oil seal is fitted.

With removal of the flywheel housing, access is obtained to the crankshaft primary gear shown in **FIG 1 : 15**, which can be withdrawn for inspection after extracting the retaining 'C' washer. The bushes fitted to the bore of the gear should be examined for wear. If necessary they can be removed and new bushes pressed into position, then burnish reamed to the dimensions shown in **FIG 1 : 16**. It should be noted that two types of crankshaft primary gears have been fitted to these engines. The early type had lubricated bushes at each end of the bore and received oil through drillings from the crankshaft rear end just behind the rear main bearing. End float of the lubricated gear is extremely important apart from mechanical considerations, as a means of controlling the quantity of oil exuding from the rear bearing and finding its way into the clutch. The longitudinal running clearance must be between .003 and .006 inch. Measure the gap indicated in **FIG 1 : 15**. The table indicates washer thicknesses required for a selection of measured gaps.

FIG 1 : 17 shows how to provide the correct running clearance for crankshaft primary gears with non-lubricated bushes. Note that the lubricated gear has a

FIG 1 : 14 Crankshaft primary gear with the oil seal protector sleeve 18G.1043 in position

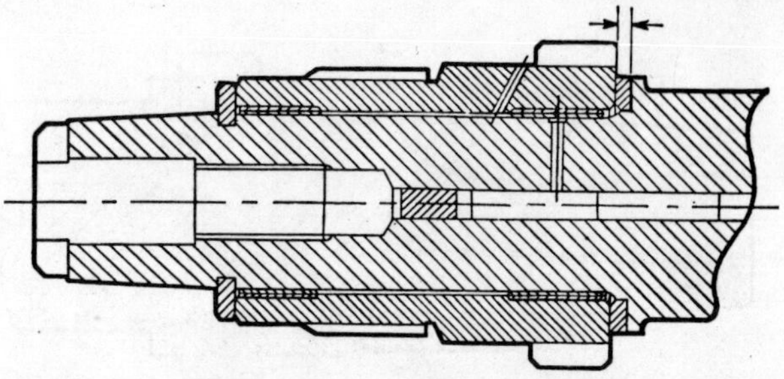

FIG 1 : 15 Sectional view of the crankshaft primary gear with lubricated bushes. Measure the gap indicated to obtain the correct running clearance of .003 to .006 inch and use the table below to determine the correct thickness of thrust washer

Gap	*Washer thickness*
.1295 to .1315 inch	.125 to .127 inch
.1315 to .1335 inch	.127 to .129 inch
.1335 to .1345 inch	.129 to .131 inch

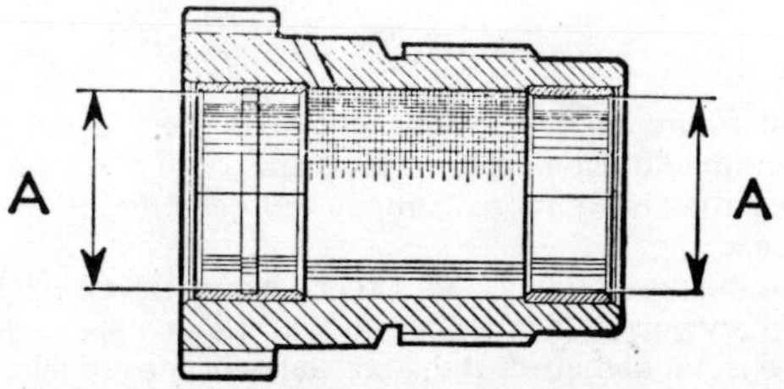

FIG 1 : 16 A section through the crankshaft primary gear. When new bushes are fitted the bores at A must be line-reamed to 1.3775 to 1.3780 inch after fitting (lubricated bushes only)

thrust washer at the front end only, whereas the unlubricated gear has a washer at each end. The front thrust washer is assembled with the chamfered bore against the flywheel flange.

The crankshaft primary gear oil seal can be renewed if it shows damage or there are signs of oil leaking into the clutch. This seal can also be renewed without removing the flywheel housing or draining the engine/transmission unit. For both operations however, special tools are required and the work should be undertaken by a service agent.

When lubricated crankshaft primary gears were fitted, there was also an oil seal fitted into the bore in the front face of the flywheel. This seal is not fitted to engines with non-lubricated primary gears. If fitted, the seal can only be renewed by removing the flywheel.

Early Mini engines had a rubber plug fitted into the end of the crankshaft in case of oil leakage past the normal brass taper plug. This practice is now discontinued in favour of an improved taper plug.

When refitting the flywheel housing, attend carefully to the following details while reversing the removal sequence:

1 The idler gear end float should be within the limits of .003 to .008 inch, for which a range of thrust washers of various thicknesses are available.

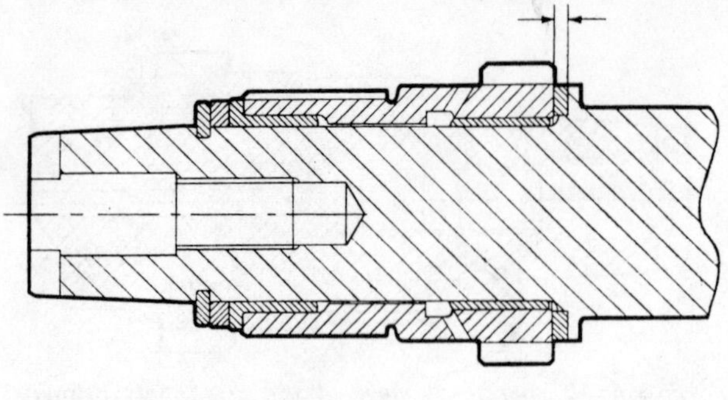

FIG 1 : 17 Sectional view of later type crankshaft primary gear with unlubricated bushes. Measure the gap indicated to obtain the correct running clearance. The table below lists correct thicknesses of thrust washers for various gaps

Gap	*Washer thickness*
.1175 to .119 inch	.112 to .114 inch
.119 to .121 inch	.114 to .116 inch
.121 to .123 inch	.116 to .118 inch
.123 to .125 inch	.118 to .120 inch

2 Make sure all joint faces are absolutely clean and smooth and use new joint washers.
3 Pack the first-motion shaft rear roller bearing with soft grease.
4 Use the protecting sleeve 18G.570 over the crankshaft primary gear clutch splines so that the primary gear oil seal is not damaged. If the oil seal is of the red silicone rubber type, use the protecting sleeve 18G.1043. Lubricate the oil seal liberally.
5 Two pilot bars are available if needed for screwing into the two bottom tapped holes in the crankcase face to pilot the flywheel housing into position, and so protect the primary gear oil seal from receiving the full weight of the housing during fitting.
6 Make sure the first motion shaft bearing rollers are retained correctly by the grease when finally closing the flywheel housing on to the crankcase and transmission casing.
7 Use new locking washers and fasten all nuts and bolts firmly but finger tight only at this stage.
8 Finally tighten the fasteners, turning all nuts and bolts one turn at a time to ensure even pressure all round, to a torque of 18 lb ft.
9 The compressed thickness of the flywheel housing joint, should be .030 inch. There is a small cutaway opening in the jointing material which enables a feeler gauge to be inserted for checking purposes.

Inspect the clutch superficially for elongation of the driving pin holes, ridging or wear of the driving pins and wear or distortion of the driving straps. More detailed information about the clutch is contained in **Chapter 5.**

The following operations are undertaken to refit the clutch and flywheel:

1 Use the compression tool to ensure that the holes in the pressure spring housing and the driving straps are lined up with the tapped holes of the clutch pressure plate lugs.
2 Screw the driving pins into position, making certain that the shoulders of the driving pins are through the driving straps, also that the straps and pins are returned to their original positions.
3 Turn the crankshaft to bring Nos. 1 and 4 pistons to TDC and check that the primary shaft 'C' washer is fitted with the gap at the bottom.
4 Lubricate the flywheel oil seal if fitted, and the primary gear splines lightly with Duckham's MB grease.
5 Clean and degrease the crankshaft male and flywheel female tapers.
6 Refit the diaphragm spring clutch cover and spring assembly with the clutch balance mark A, shown in **FIG 5 : 6 Chapter 5,** adjacent to the 1/4 mark on the flywheel.
7 Fit the clutch and flywheel to the crankshaft, using a new locking washer, and tighten up the retaining screw to a torque of 110 to 115 lb ft. If it is necessary to clean up the flywheel retaining screw thread, the operation must be confined to cleaning only with no metal removal. The thread is highly stressed and must always be up to full size.
8 Refit the coil spring clutch thrust plate using the three retaining nuts and new lockwashers. Refit the clutch cover to the flywheel housing.

1 : 9 Removing the sump

On these engines the sump is combined with the transmission casing and, in effect, removing the sump is also the first operation required for removing the transmission for overhaul. Following the removal of the flywheel housing described in the previous section, further operations are as follows:

1 Remove the two screws securing the lower radiator mounting bracket to the engine mounting.
2 Take out the ten setscrews and remove the two nuts securing the transmission casing, noting the different lengths and positions of these for reassembly.
3 Lift the cylinder block off the transmission casing using suitable equipment. Refer to **Chapter 6** for servicing the transmission and oil strainer.

1 : 10 Removing, dismantling and reassembling oil pump

One of two different types of oil pump may be found fitted to these engines, manufactured by Hobourn Eaton Ltd., or Concentric (Engineering) Ltd.

To remove the oil pump it is necessary first to remove the flywheel/clutch assembly and flywheel housing as described in **Section 1 : 8.** With the pump accessible, bend back the locking washers, remove the three $\frac{1}{4}$ inch UNF screws (or the bolts) securing the pump to the crankcase and withdraw the pump. Note the relative positions of the slot in the driving shaft and the pin in the end of the camshaft in order to assist refitting.

The Concentric (Engineering) Ltd. pump is serviced as an assembly and should be exchanged for a new or reconditioned unit if defective. The Hobourn-Eaton pump may be dismantled by removing one screw in the front face. Notice the two dowels locating the pump outer portions. Inspection, overhaul and refitting is undertaken as follows:

1 Position the rotors 2 in the pump body 1 in **FIG 1 : 18.** Using a straightedge across the body joint face, check the clearance between the rotor top faces and the straightedge, which should not exceed .005 inch.

Excessive clearance may be reduced by removing the two dowel pins and lapping the cover/body joint faces. As this is likely to be a very tedious performance for the owner, it is advised that the unit be exchanged or taken to a service agent for attention.

2 Tip clearance of the inner rotor in the positions indicated in **FIG 1 :18**, at A must be less than .006 inch. Clearance in excess of this figure calls for renewal of the rotors.

3 Reassemble the pump and check for freedom by spinning the rotor shaft by hand. Fill with oil before refitting, using a new joint washer, and checking finally that the inlet and outlet passages are not obstructed when the pump is refitted to the engine crankcase.

1 :11 Splitting big-ends, removing connecting rods and pistons

With the engine out of the car and suitably stripped, unlock and remove the big-end setscrews 14 in **FIG 1 : 19**, also remove the bearing caps 12, locking washers 13 and lower shells 11. Separate the connecting rods 8, lift out the upper bearing shells and move the crankshaft as necessary so that the pistons and connecting rods can be removed from the top of the cylinder block. Make sure there is no ring of hard carbon at the upper end of the bore to obstruct the piston as it is pushed upwards and out. Discard the big-end screw locking washers.

1 Number the connecting rods, caps and shells so that they may be refitted in their original positions.

2 Inspect the bearing shells for wear and damage. Wear may be caused by lack of adequate oil pressure and, equally, inadequate oil pressure may result from worn bearings. It is possible for a vicious circle of cause and effect to be set up if bearing wear is allowed to proceed beyond certain limits. Inspect for scratching and scoring especially round the position of the oil supply holes, also for flaking of the surface material. If severe score marks are evident it will be advisable to renew the bearing shells. Bearing diametrical clearances may be checked against the figures given in the Technical Data Section using Plastigage calibrated plastic thread. Place the thread along the journal and refit the bearing cap, tightening the setscrews to the correct torque. On removal the width of the thread is compared with a scale supplied with the thread and the clearance is read off directly. It will be appreciated that any absence of normal bearing surface due to flaking or deep scoring will result in increased loading of the remaining surface material. A rule of thumb guide for the amount of scoring permissible would be to estimate the total loss of bearing surface due to the deep scores. If this is estimated at more than about five per cent of the original surface the bearings should be renewed. Change the shells if any flaking of the bearing surface is visible. Never file the shells or caps to reduce the bearing clearance.

3 When reassembling the big-ends, replace the used bearing shells in their original positions with the locating tabs correctly positioned. New bearing shells are drilled for cylinder wall lubrication and are therefore interchangeable position-wise.

4 Lubricate with engine oil during assembly, and use new locking washers for the bolts.

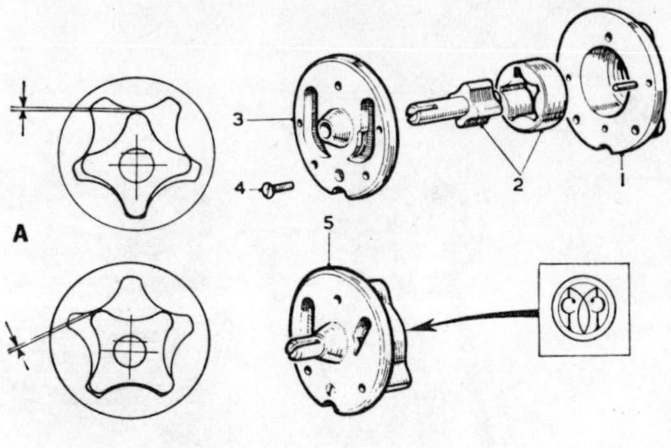

FIG 1 :18 An exploded view of the two types of oil pump. A indicates the positions of the lobes for checking clearances

Key to Fig 1 :18 1 Pump body 2 Shaft and rotor 3 Cover 4 Screw—cover to body 5 Pump by Concentric (Engineering) Ltd—serviced as a unit

1 :12 Pistons, rings and gudgeon pins

When removing piston rings and gudgeon pins, make sure that all parts are adequately marked for correct reassembly, both with reference to assembly number and orientation in the assembly. It is advisable to use separate boxes for the parts of each assembly.

Always remove the piston rings upwards over the piston crown and not downwards over the skirt. Thoroughly clean all parts, if necessary using scrapers of slightly softer material than the parts being cleaned.

Standard Mini, also Elf and Hornet Mk I engines, have the gudgeon pins clamped in the little-end of the connecting rod. To remove the gudgeon pin, hold the assembly by means of the gudgeon pin between two plugs in a vice and unscrew the clamp bolt at the little-end (inside the piston). The gudgeon pin can then be pushed out.

Mini Mk II and cars fitted with 998 and 1098 cc engines have fully floating gudgeon pins retained by two circlips. Connecting rod little ends are bushed. Pistons and gudgeon pins should never be renewed independently but always as sets, and the little-end bush should be renewed only as part of a new connecting rod assembly.

Inspection of piston assemblies should include:

1 Checking for cracking around the skirt, gudgeon pin bosses, under the crown and on the land areas adjacent to the rings.

2 Checking for burning in these areas.

3 Checking for obstruction of oil passages behind the oil control ring.

4 Damage to and wear of piston rings and their fit in their grooves. When new the clearance in the groove is .0015 to .0035 inch and the gap when assembled in the cylinder bore is .007 to .012 inch. The gap may be checked by placing a piston in the cylinder bore with the crown about three inches down from the top of the bore and resting the piston ring squarely on it. Use a feeler gauge to check the gap.

When reassembling the pistons and connecting rods attend carefully to the following points:

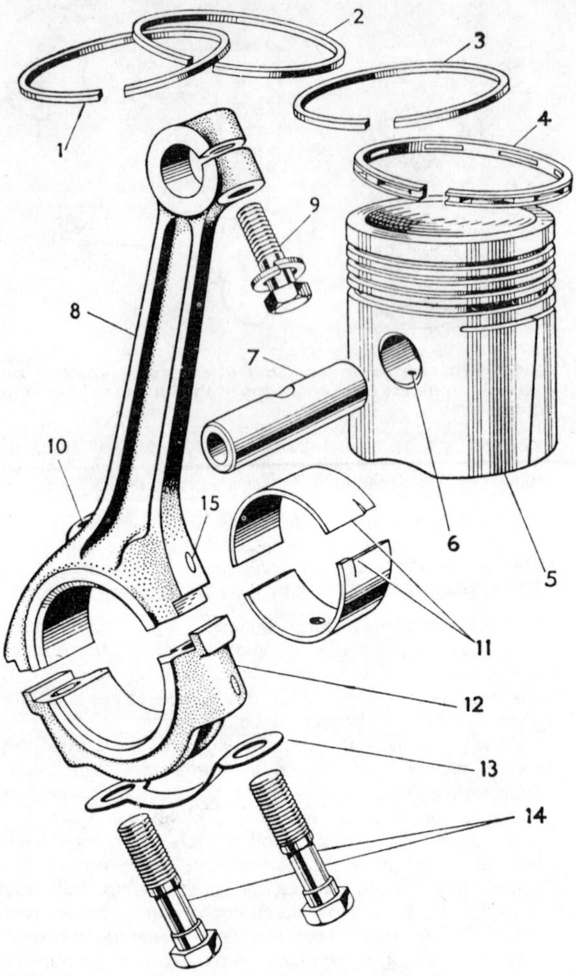

FIG 1 : 19 The parts of a connecting rod and piston assembly (clamped gudgeon pin type)

Key to Fig 1 : 19 1 Piston ring—parallel 2 Piston ring—taper 3 Piston ring—taper 4 Piston ring—scraper 5 Piston 6 Gudgeon pin lubricating hole 7 Gudgeon pin 8 Connecting rod 9 Clamping screw and washer 10 Cylinder wall lubricating jet 11 Connecting rod bearing 12 Bearing cap 13 Lockwasher 14 Setscrews 15 Identification mark

1 Where clamped gudgeon pins are used, it may be necessary to select one of several in order to obtain the correct fit in the piston as described. These gudgeon pins must be a thumb push fit in the piston for three-quarters of their length at room temperature, finally being tapped home with a hide mallet.
2 The gudgeon pin is positioned in the little-end of the connecting rod so that the clamp bolt groove is in line with the clamp bolt.
3 The clamp bolt passes freely in its hole and screws freely into its thread sufficiently to ensure effective use of the spring washer. The clamp bolt is tightened to a torque of 25 lb ft.
4 A new spring washer is used for the clamp bolt.
5 The piston is fitted the same way round as before dismantling. The crown of the piston is marked 'front'.
6 The piston and connecting rod are assembled with the gudgeon pin clamp bolt on the camshaft side of the engine.
7 If new piston rings are fitted, note that the second and third rings are tapered. The narrow portion is fitted at the top. T is stamped on the narrow face to facilitate identification. Space the ring gaps at 180 deg. to each other.

On the piston crowns will be found a number enclosed in a diamond. This number is the piston grade size used during initial assembly of the engine to obtain an accurate fit.

Excessive wear of pistons, rings and cylinder bores can be rectified by reboring the cylinders and fitting oversize pistons. Oversize pistons are marked on the crown with the oversize dimension, e.g. .010. The maximum oversize is +.040 inch except for Mini Mk II, Elf, Hornet Mk II and III and Clubman for which the maximum rebore oversize is +.020 inch. Damage in excess of the maximum rebore size is rectified by fitting cylinder liners and new pistons. All these are operations which must be undertaken in service workshops.

1 : 13 Removing crankshaft and main bearing shells

The procedure for the removal of the crankshaft and the three main bearings is similar for all models. The work is undertaken after the flywheel, flywheel housing and transmission have all been removed. It will be helpful to place the cylinder block upside-down on a suitable stand for the following operations to be undertaken:

1 Check the crankshaft end float by means of feeler gauges at the centre main bearing thrust washer position, or by means of a dial test indicator suitably applied to register crankshaft longitudinal movement. The measurement should be between the designed limits of .002 to .003 inch. If it is excessive, the thrust washers must be renewed during reassembly.
2 If the crankshaft primary gear is still in position, remove the retaining circlip and the gear.
3 Release the main bearing cap bolts and withdraw the bearing caps complete with the lower half bearing shells, keeping the caps and shells in sets and noting the numbers on the caps corresponding with similar numbers on the crankcase webs near the bearings. The lower halves of the thrust washers are removed with the centre main bearing cap.
4 Lift out the crankshaft very carefully and remove the remaining halves of the thrust washers and the top main bearing shells. Keep them all in correct order to avoid malpositioning during reassembly. If possible place the crankshaft in a suitable supporting stand for further attention.
5 Thoroughly clean all parts, including the interior of the crankshaft oil passages, by syringing through them with petrol or paraffin under pressure.
6 The crankpins and journals should be checked visually for marking and scoring, and then dimensionally for wear and ovality against the dimensional requirements of a new crankshaft shown in the Technical Data Section. Regrinding to an undersize is permissible in

cases of advanced wear, the limits of regrinding being sufficient to take care of all damage likely to be experienced in a normally cared-for vehicle. Undersize bearings are available if required for this purpose. The work should be undertaken by an authorized service agent.

7 The most likely damage to be observed to the main bearing shells will be scoring, pitting, possibly some breaking away of the bearing liner material and even wearing away of the sound surfaces. Breaking away of the surface material should be regarded as good reason for rejecting the old bearing shells. If slight pitting marks or minor scores are present over areas representing in total not more than about five per cent of the whole bearing area and the clearance on the journals does not appear to have increased substantially, e.g. by more than about ten per cent of the designed clearance, the bearings can safely be used again. Never file caps or shells to reduce bearing clearance. If new bearing shells are considered necessary, they are available finished to the correct size and require no fitting or scraping to size. The new shells should be marked to match the marking of the bearing caps. Worn thrust washers should be renewed to maintain the correct end float.

For refitting the crankshaft and main bearings, particular attention should be given to the following details:

1 Make certain that the thrust washers are correctly installed, that is with the oil grooves facing outwards. The tab of the lower half should register in the slot in the bearing cap.
2 Assemble the main bearing shells with the notches in the housing and cap recesses.
3 Freely lubricate all moving parts as they are put together.
4 Tighten the main bearing setscrews to a torque of 60 lb ft.

1 : 14 External oil filter and oil pressure relief valve

The purpose of the external oil filter is to restrain solid matter entrained in the lubricating oil from entering and recirculating in the engine and gear system. The restrained solids build up on the outside surface of the filter element and accumulate also in the filter bowl. Changing the element at the recommended intervals and cleaning of the filter bowl are essential to the continued efficiency of the power unit.

The external oil filter is situated on the front side of the engine under the generator behind the bonnet grille. Some small variations exist in the appearance and layout according to which model is under consideration, but generally the procedure for servicing filters is as follows, referring to **FIG 1 : 20**.

1 Unscrew the central bolt to release the bowl and element.
2 Clean out the bowl thoroughly, using petrol or solvent.
3 Check that the felt or rubber sealing washer is in good condition and a close fit on the central bolt. If otherwise, fit a new one.
4 Fit a new sealing ring for the bowl into the recess at the filter head attached to the engine.
5 Fit a new element, the seating plate, the seating washer, the steel washer and spring in position in that order in the bowl. Apply the bowl complete to the filter head and tighten up the retaining bolt, while turning the bowl to ensure its correct location and the seating of the sealing washer.
6 When it is possible to start the engine, check immediately for leaks at this point.

Another type of oil filter is of the disposable cartridge type, the complete unit being unscrewed from the filter head when renewal becomes due. When fitting the new cartridge, lubricate the sealing ring and screw the cartridge in by hand only.

On later engines a differential pressure switch is fitted to the filter head. This operates a warning light on the instrument panel. If the light continues to glow when the engine is running at or above idling speed, it is time to change the engine oil and filter element. This should be done before 300 miles at the most has been covered.

To overhaul the oil pressure relief valve shown in **FIG 1 : 21**, the following operations are required:

1 Unscrew and remove the domed hexagon nut adjacent to the distributor, together with the folded copper washer. Under this nut there is a spring and a valve cup which seats in a conical machined seating inside the cylinder block.
2 Check the valve cup for correct seating. Marks on the seating face of the valve will usually indicate if anything is amiss, when the valve must be reground with metal polish. Service agents use a tool 18G.69 for this operation. When complete, carefully clean off any residue.
3 Check the spring for possible distortion, which may be a reason for incorrect seating. If distortion is suspected, fit a new spring. No adjustment of relief valve pressure is provided on these vehicles.
4 When the valve is reassembled make certain that the domed nut fits tightly down on the folded copper washer.

1 : 15 Crankcase emission control

If fitted this will either be a Valve Control or Carburetter Control System. The latter may have fuel evaporative loss control, this is described under 'Carburetter Control System'.

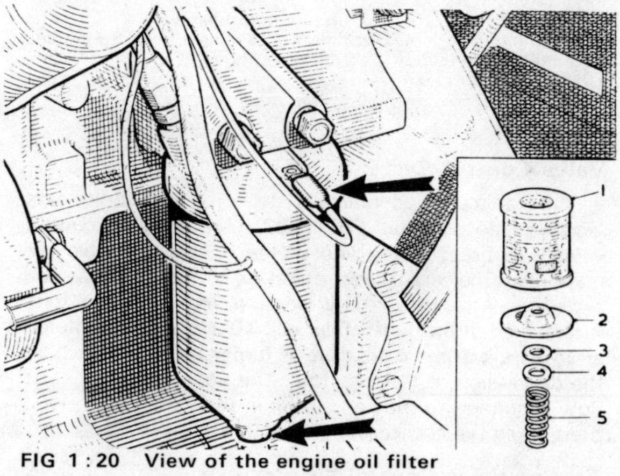

FIG 1 : 20 View of the engine oil filter

Key to Fig 1 : 20 1 Filter element 2 Seating plate 3 Seating washer 4 Steel washer 5 Spring
The arrows indicate the warning light differential pressure switch and the filter retaining bolt

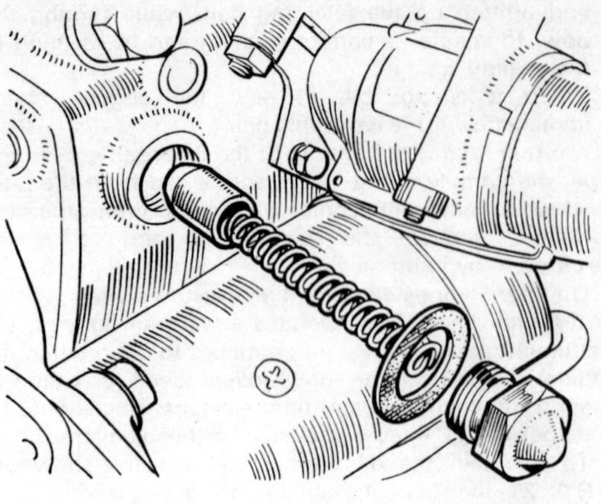

FIG 1:21 The oil pressure relief valve

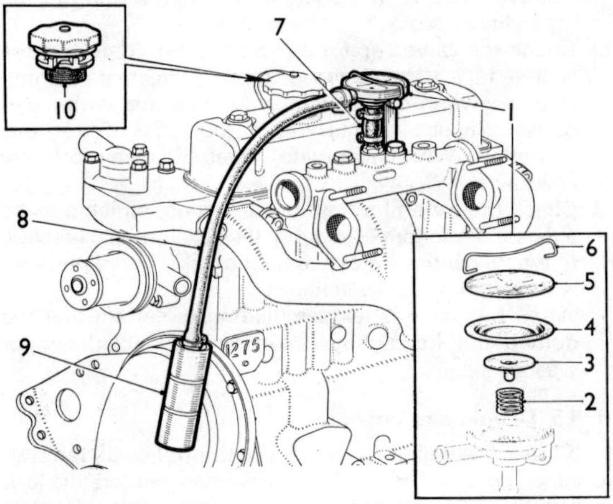

FIG 1:22 Crankcase emission valve control system

Key to Fig 1:22 1 Emission control valve 2 Spring 3 Metering valve 4 Diaphragm 5 Cover 6 Spring clip 7 Manifold connection 8 Breather hose 9 Oil separator 10 Filtered filler cap

Valve Control System:

The crankcase is connected to the inlet manifold via a length of hose 8 (see **FIG 1:22**). An emission control valve 1 is fitted to the end of the hose just above the manifold. The crankcase outlet is fitted with an oil separator 9 to prevent oil passing into the manifold. A restricted orifice in the filler cap 10 allows fresh filtered air to pass into the crankcase as fumes are withdrawn by the depression in the manifold. The valve 1 controls the flow according to the depression in the manifold and the pressure in the crankcase.

Testing Valve Control System:

To test for correct functioning, allow the engine to idle at normal running temperature and remove the oil filler cap 10. If the system is in order the increase in engine speed will be audibly noticeable. If there is no increase in speed the control valve 1 should be serviced as follows:

Servicing valve control system:

1 Disconnect the hoses and remove valve 1. Remove spring clip 6 (see inset **FIG 1:22**) and withdraw cover-plate 5, diaphragm 4, metering valve 3 and valve spring 2.
2 Clean all metal parts in fuel. Obstinate deposits can be removed by immersing in boiling water then cleaning with fuel. Clean the diaphragm with detergent or methylated spirits.
3 Renew any parts that are worn or damaged. Reassemble the valve ensuring that the metering valve 3 is fitted correctly in its guides and that the diaphragm is seated properly. Refit the valve and check that it operates correctly.

Renew the oil filler cap every 12,000 miles or 12 months.

Carburetter control system:

The engine breather outlet is connected to the depression chamber on the carburetter via a length of hose 6 (see **FIG 1:23**). Fumes are drawn out of the crankcase and pass through an oil separator 5 and from there to the inlet manifold. Fresh filtered air passes to the crankcase through a restricted orifice in the oil filler cap 4.

An evaporative loss control may be fitted in conjunction with this system (items 1 to 4 in **FIG 1:23**). Vapour from the fuel tank is fed to and stored in an absorption canister 2 while the engine is not running. The canister is filled with activated charcoal granules. When the engine is started the fuel vapours pass through the crankcase emission control to the combustion chambers. Air for engine breathing passes through an air vent 1 to the absorption canister 2, it then passes through a restricted connection 3 on the rocker cover, this ensures crankcase depression.

An expansion tank is provided to accommodate fuel displaced from the fuel tank when it is full and there is a high temperature rise. The fuel and oil filler caps on this system are sealed and they must be correctly replaced after being removed.

Servicing carburetter control system:

Renew oil filler cap every 12,000 miles or 12 months. If there is a loss of crankcase depression, check the hoses and connections for leaks or blockages.

If fuel evaporative loss control is incorporated, the two intake filter pads should be renewed at intervals of 12,000 miles or sooner if used in dusty conditions.

Renew the complete canister every 50,000 miles or if it has been inadvertently saturated with fuel. **Do not attempt to renovate a saturated canister by passing compressed air through the charcoal granules.**

1:16 Reassembling stripped engine

Generally speaking the reassembly of the stripped engine follows the reverse pattern of the dismantling sequences outlined in the foregoing sections of this Chapter. Many of the individual reassembly sequences have been described in detail and where this is so an appropriate reference is made in the text.

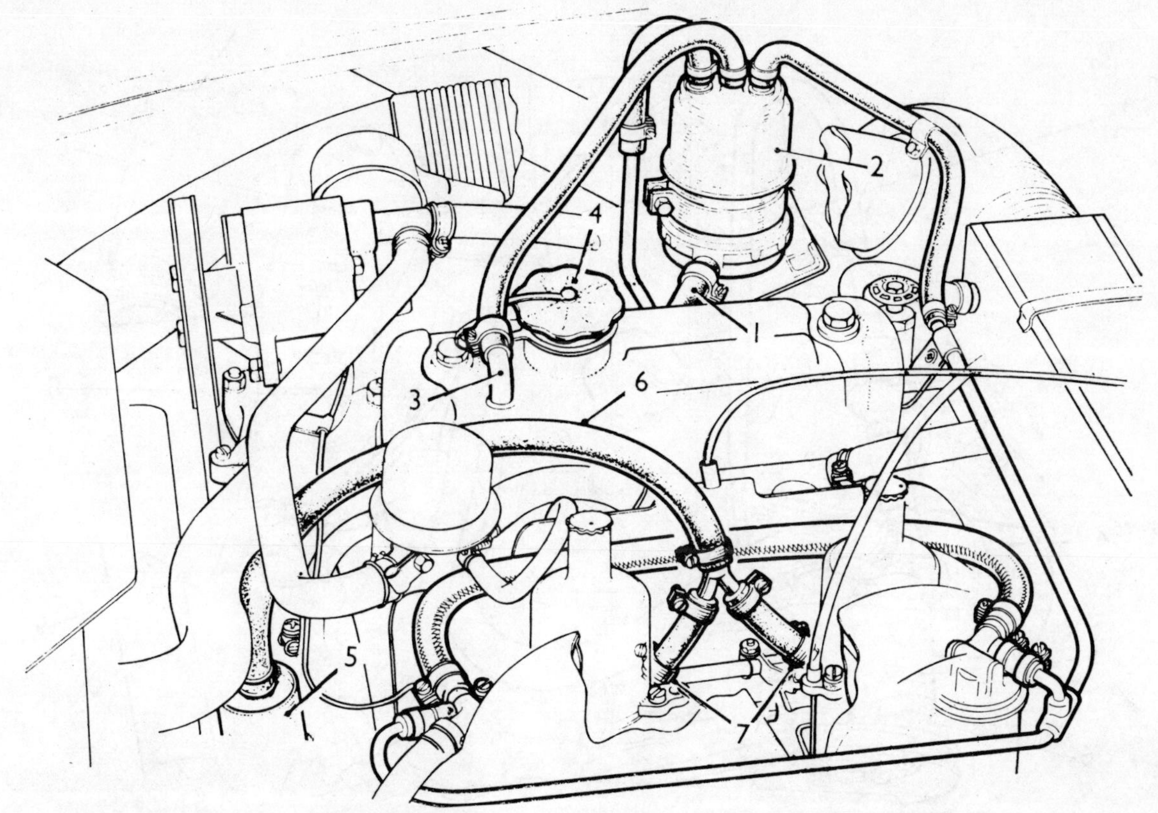

FIG 1:23 Crankcase emission control system with fuel evaporative loss control. If the system is fitted without the latter, items 1 to 3 are not included and item 4 is a filtered filler cap

Key to Fig 1:23 1 Ventilation air intake 2 Absorption canister 3 Restricted connection 4 Sealed oil filler cap 5 Oil separator 6 Breather hose 7 Depression chamber connection

When the engine has been completely dismantled its reassembly will provide a useful opportunity to make a last check of the work already completed on sub-assemblies. For example, have all the split pins, locking washers and tabs been correctly inserted and safely locked? Is sufficient lubricant present on moving parts to provide adequate initial lubrication when the engine is first started?

Cleanliness and orderliness during reassembly operations are essential in order to avoid any possibility of spoiling the careful work already carried out and to enable the work to go forward without difficulty. It will be found useful to have a supply of clean rags, a small quantity of petrol, some clean new and suitable engine lubricating oil and some soft mineral oil grease available as aids to the reassembly work. Suitable spanners and of course, a torque wrench are essential for some of the work. Owners are strongly advised against the practice of improvising with spanners by artificially increasing their effective length with pieces of tubing or using tommy bars of inordinate size. If a nut or bolt will not tighten correctly there is probably some good reason such as dirt, or the absence of a part or washer, which can be found on further examination. The only parts which should require force for assembly are those which are designed with an interference dimension.

It is almost certain that all joint washers will require renewal and owners are advised to obtain a complete new set. Whilst simple joint washers can be made up locally it is modern practice to employ jointing materials to quite precise material and thickness specifications, and as these are not expensive items, it is advisable to use only the approved products.

A wandering lamp with a clamp attachment will be found useful for lighting up areas in shadow.

1 Commence work by placing the cylinder block upside-down on the bench or stand and reassembling the crankshaft and main bearings. The upper bearing

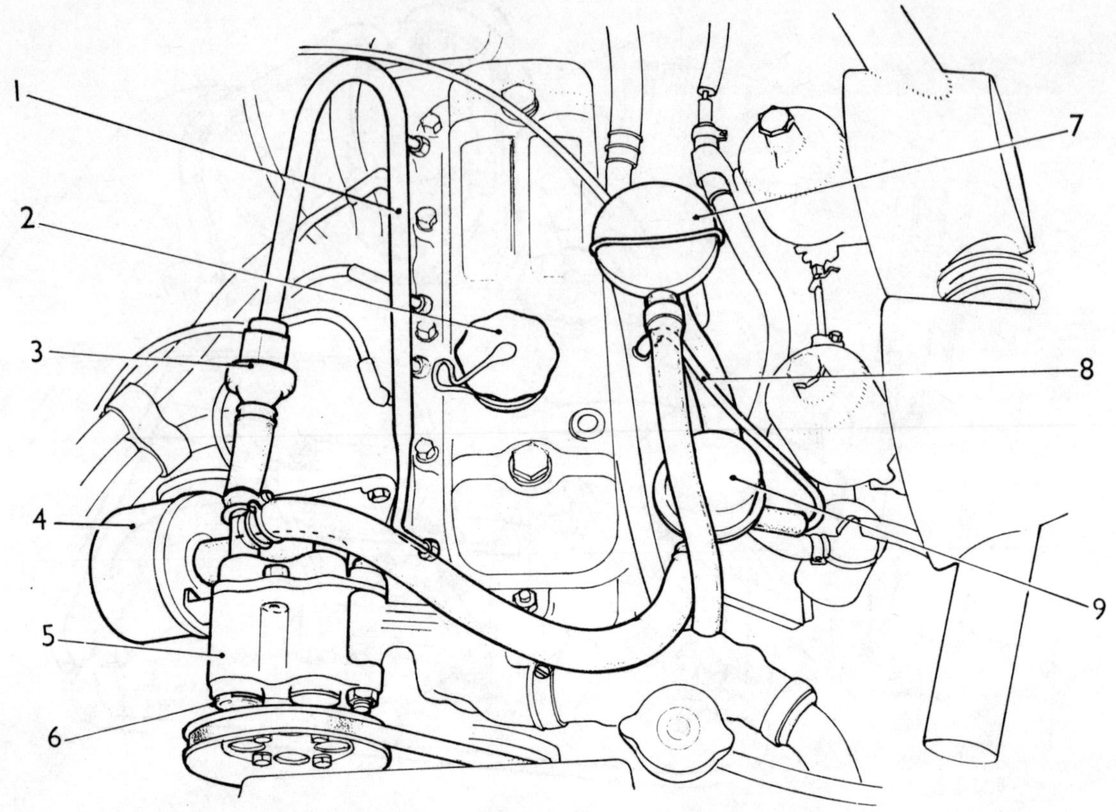

FIG 1:24 Components of engine emission control system

Key to Fig 1:24 1 Air manifold 2 Filtered filler cap 3 Check valve 4 Air cleaner 5 Air pump 6 Relief valve 7 Emission control valve 8 Vacuum sensing tube 9 Gulp valve

shells of the main bearings and the upper halves of the crankshaft thrust washers are fitted, making sure the shell locating tags are correctly positioned and the thrust washer oil grooves are facing outwards. The crankshaft should be lowered gently on to the upper bearing shells without impact.

2 Follow the procedure outlined in **Section 1:13** to ensure correct assembly and positioning of the lower bearing shells and caps. Liberally lubricate the journals and bearings during assembly and be careful to lock the screws safely.

3 The cylinder block assembly must now be turned upright and the piston assemblies and connecting rods prepared for reassembly. Recheck that the piston rings are correctly fitted with the gaps at 180 deg. and apply a little lubricant. Check the assembly of pistons and gudgeon pins for correctness and enter the big-ends of the connecting rods into the cylinder bores first, taking care when entering the pistons to compress each ring in turn as it is entered so that no damage or jamming can occur. Make sure the piston assembly faces the correct side of the engine, i.e. with the split on the camshaft side.

4 When all pistons and connecting rods have been inserted in the cylinders, position them at the tops of the bores and then for convenience turn the engine upside-down again to facilitate the reassembly of the connecting rod big-ends. Be careful not to allow impact between the rods and the cylinder bores as this is being done.

5 Position the crankshaft with two of the crankpins uppermost and draw up the connecting rods and pistons to suit. Position the upper bearing shell, remembering that the engine is upside-down, and pull the big-end on to the crankpin, fit the lower bearing shell and the connecting rod cap, position new lockwashers and insert the big-end screws, tightening them to a torque of 35 lb ft.

6 Follow the same procedure with the remaining three connecting rod and big-end assemblies.

7 The oil pump has to be installed as described in **Section 1:10** before the transmission case is

refitted. Towards the completion of the latter operation the end float of the idler gear should be checked, which necessitates the refitting of the flywheel housing and to which further reference is made in **Chapter 6.** It is suggested that some reminder such as a small label is tied to the idler gear for reference when the flywheel housing and transmission are about to be fitted.

8 Make sure the joint faces are quite clean and place a new joint washer on the transmission casing. Lower the engine carefully on to the transmission casing and insert the small screw as far as possible before finally bringing the two components together. Make sure the front crankshaft bearing oil seal (cork on earlier models, moulded rubber on later models) is correctly positioned. Holding the components together, insert the ten setscrews and two bolts and nuts and tighten them all firmly finger tight only. This is necessary because the final tightening of the transmission casing and the flywheel housing must be carried out as if these parts were one unit. The lower portion of the flywheel housing must be pulled on to the side face of the transmission casing as the transmission casing is pulled on to the lower face of the crankcase and the flywheel casing upper face is pulled on to the cylinder block. Distortion may occur if this is not carefully observed.

9 Position the flywheel housing joint washer, apply some grease to the first motion shaft rear roller bearing to hold the rollers to the centre, lubricate the idler gear with engine oil, and the splined portion of the crankshaft primary gear with a little Duckhams MB grease. Follow through with the remainder of the procedure outlined in **Section 1 : 8** as far as fitting all nuts bolts and washers finger tight, then tighten one turn at a time all nuts, bolts and screws securing the transmission casing and flywheel housing so that the two components are pulled gently into position together. The transmission case stud nuts are tightened to a torque of 25 lb ft. for $\frac{3}{8}$ inch dia. UNF nuts and 18 lb ft. for $\frac{5}{16}$ inch dia. UNF nuts. The flywheel housing bolts and stud nuts are tightened to 18 lb ft. torque. At this point check that the idler gear end float is between .003 and .008 inch. It will be necessary to remove the flywheel housing if any adjustment is required but it is not necessary to loosen the transmission casing fixings for this purpose.

10 When the flywheel housing has been secured in its final position check that the compressed thickness of the flywheel housing joint material is .030 inch as described. This dimension must be preserved throughout to keep the idler gear end float to the correct figure.

11 Full instructions for the assembly of the flywheel and clutch are given in **Section 1 : 8.** Follow these for reassembly when dealing with the stripped engine under the present heading, giving due attention to the crankshaft primary gear as described.

12 The engine should now be returned to its normal upright position for the reassembly of the camshaft, timing gear wheels, timing cover, crankshaft pulley, fan belt, fan and distributor drive spindle in the reverse order of their removal as described in

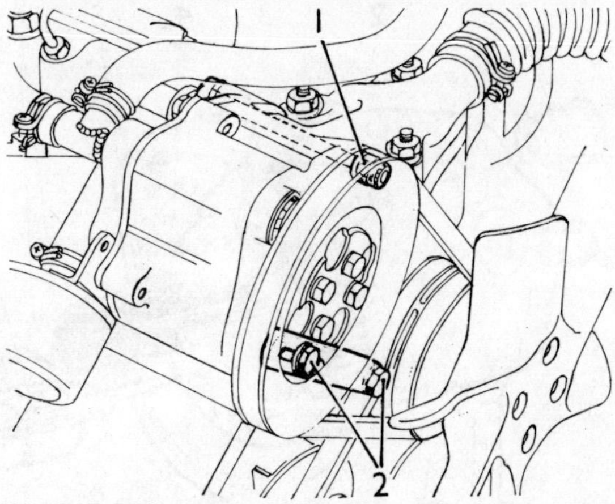

FIG 1 : 25 Adjustment of air pump drive belt tension

Key to Fig 1 : 25 1 Mounting bolt 2 Adjusting-link bolts

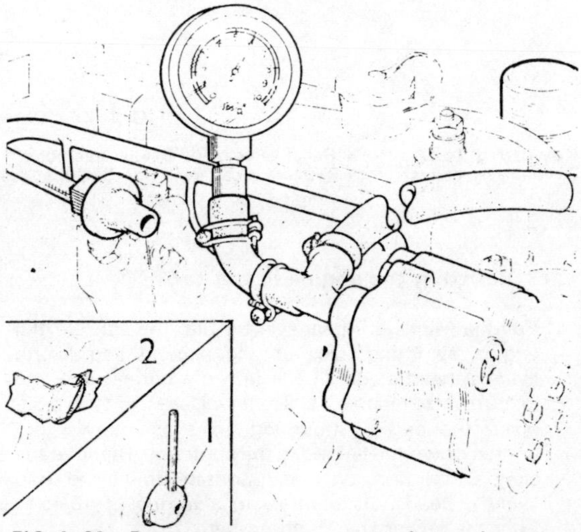

FIG 1 : 26 Pressure gauge connected to air pump. Inset shows adhesive tape over end of relief valve forming a duct

Section 1 : 7. Care must be taken that the slot in the oil pump drive shaft lines up accurately with the pin in the camshaft during assembly, otherwise damage will result when securing it in position. Adjust the tension of the fan belt by moving the generator on its mounting, as described in **Chapter 4, Section 4 : 2,** so as to obtain $\frac{1}{2}$ inch free movement either way on the longest run of the belt.

13 Reassembly follows of the tappets, cylinder head, pushrods, tappet covers and rocker gear as described in **Section 1 : 5.** Refit the starter motor with new locking washers and tighten the nuts securely. Heavy loads are imposed on the motor when starting. The rocker cover cannot be refitted until the engine has been installed in the car as the second and fourth cylinder head studs and nuts are used for lifting. Refit the radiator and reconnect the hoses and induction manifold.

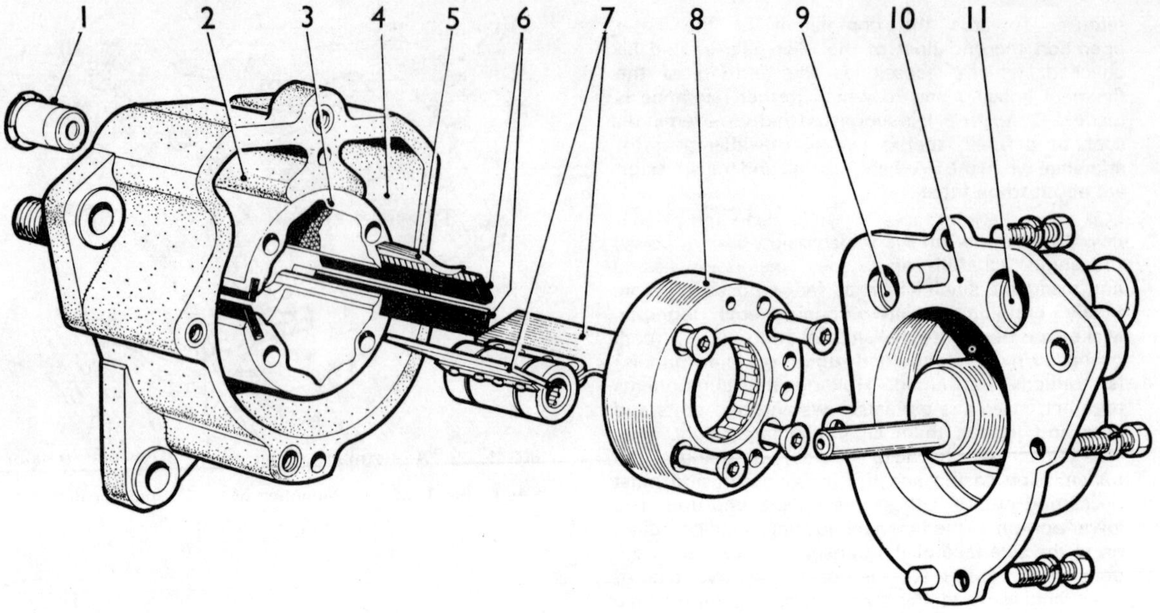

FIG 1:27 Components of air pump

Key to Fig 1:27 1 Relief valve 2 Inlet chamber 3 Rotor 4 Outlet chamber 5 Spring 6 Carbons 7 Vane assemblies 8 Bearing carrier 9 Outlet port 10 End cover 11 Inlet port

1:17 Refitting the engine in the car

1 Pull the Mini Mk I gearlever up into the car. Lift the engine by lifting eyes on the second and fourth cylinder head studs. Lower into the bonnet aperture in the reverse manner of its removal, see **Section 1:3**.

2 Insert the engine mounting securing screws and tighten down the engine to the subframe. Remove the sling and lifting eyes and tighten down the two cylinder head nuts securely to a torque of 40 lb ft. Refit the rocker cover and gasket.

3 Refit the engine tie rod and insert the bolt loosely. Assemble the exhaust system on the car with all securing bolts loose. Wedge the engine forward during this operation. Tighten the engine tie rod bolt and, keeping the engine wedged forwards, insert sufficient slip packings to fill the gap between the transmission casing lug and the pipe support stay. Insert the securing bolt at this point and tighten fully. Then tighten the manifold clamp and the pipe and tail pipe support clips. Remove the wedging device.

4 Release the clutch slave cylinder and position it on the pushrod, secure the cylinder in position with the two screws and refit the return spring.

5 Refit the earthing strap and the speedometer cable at the instrument, reversing the removal instructions.

6 Refit the carburetter(s), the control cables and fuel supply pipes.

7 Reconnect the suspension, steering and drive couplings and refit the road wheel.

8 Refit the starter solenoid switch at the flywheel housing and make good the electrical connections to the ignition coil, generator, temperature gauge (where applicable) and the starter motor. Reconnect the oil pressure gauge pipe where this is fitted.

9 Reconnect the steering rack balljoints.

10 On Mk III Elf and Hornet models, refit the gearchange extension, the rubber cover and plate and the gearlever knob. Secure the rear gearchange extension mounting to the floor by means of the three bolts.

11 On Mini models, refit the gearchange lever into its casing from inside the car, also the changespeed lever retaining plate, securing the latter with the two setscrews. Refit the anti-rattle spring and plunger in the gearchange extension casing. Fit and tighten the hexagon plug.

12 Refit the air cleaner(s) and, where fitted, connect the breather hose to the rocker cover.

13 Attach the fresh air heater and motor, where fitted, and reconnect the heater hoses at the engine end.

14 Refit the distributor and connect the low-tension lead. Fit the distributor cap and the sparking plugs and connect the high-tension leads to the plugs and coil. Retime the ignition as described in **Section 3:6**.

15 Refit the windscreen washer bottle and bracket. Reconnect the battery and refit the grille and bonnet. Bleed the clutch and brake systems.

16 Close the coolant drain taps and fill the cooling system with $5\frac{1}{4}$ pints of coolant or $6\frac{1}{4}$ pints if a heater is fitted.

17 Fill the lubrication system with $8\frac{1}{2}$ pints of approved lubricating oil.

Make a final inspection to ensure that all components have been properly connected, run the engine and carry out any minor adjustments which may be necessary,

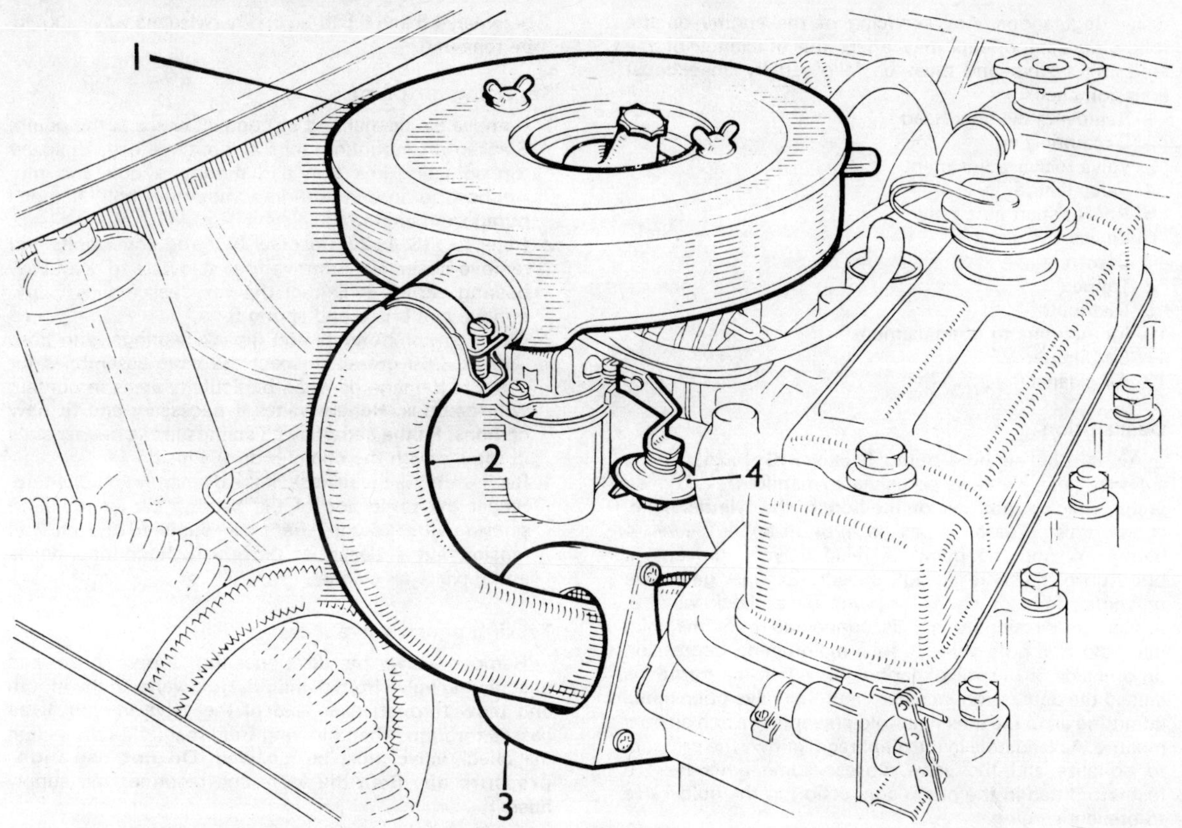

FIG 1:28 Engine modification exhaust emission control system. The air intake is in the low ambient temperature position

Key to Fig 1:28 1 Air cleaner 2 Air intake tube 3 Manifold shroud 4 Throttle damper

including attention to any oil or water leaks. After the car has travelled about 200 miles, tighten the cylinder head bolts to the correct torque and readjust the rocker clearances.

1:18 Automatic transmission modifications

Substantial modifications to the engine, transmission and power unit installation result from the introduction of automatic transmission to these vehicles. The engine is equipped with a torque converter using oil as the power transmission medium in place of the conventional clutch and flywheel. The torque converter drives a converter output gear somewhat similar to the crankshaft primary gear employed on the engines having synchromesh transmission, and from this point the drive is transmitted through an idler gear and a transmission input gear, again somewhat similar in arrangement to the gears on synchromesh models. Beyond this point however there is no similarity between the two types of transmission as the automatic system comprises an assembly of epicyclic trains with associated clutches, all operated by a complicated hydraulic system controlled by a mechanical governor, the accelerator pedal and the hand selector through hydraulic valves.

The engine lubricating oil supply is taken off the main oil supply system feeding the gearchange hydraulics. After the engine lubrication takeoff, oil is fed to the torque converter at reduced pressure.

The differential unit is very similar to that used with synchromesh transmission, but all-metal universal couplings are employed at the inboard ends of the drive shafts to the road wheels.

The carburetter is the SU HS4 model with an additional control rod operating through a spring to regulate the action of the governor in the automatic transmission and adjust the timing of the gearchanges in relation to the throttle position.

From this it will be appreciated that some additional data is necessary for the removal and overhaul of engines equipped with automatic transmission, and the details are given in **Chapter 6A**.

1:19 Exhaust emission control

Models exported to certain countries are fitted with an exhaust emission control system which complies with

State Regulations. Any servicing of the engine on the following components may affect the efficiency of the emission system and must be followed by an exhaust emission check.

1 Removing cylinder head
2 Decarbonizing
3 Valve rocker adjustment
4 Valve timing
5 Rocker shaft assembly
6 Valves and seats
7 Camshaft
8 Tappets
9 Distributor
10 Ignition timing or adjustment
11 Carburetter
12 Air cleaner

Description:

Air is supplied by a pump 5 (see **FIG 1:24**) to the cylinder head exhaust ports via a manifold 1. The air pump, which is mounted on the front of the cylinder head, is belt driven. The air is passed through an air cleaner 4 before entering the pump. A relief valve 6 prevents a build-up of pressure at high speeds. Exhaust gases are prevented from entering the pump by a check valve 3. A vacuum sensing tube 8 is connected from the inlet manifold to a gulp valve 9, thus maintaining depression on one side of the valve diaphragm. When the throttle is closed the depression increases and the valve opens thus admitting air to the inlet manifold preventing a rich air/fuel mixture. A bleed hole in the diaphragm allows the pressure to equalize and the valve closes. Some units have a restrictor fitted in the pump connection to the gulp valve to prevent surging.

Air pump:

The drive belt should deflect ½ inch at the mid-point of the longest belt run. If necessary adjust as follows:

Slacken the mounting bolt 1 (see **FIG 1:25**) and adjusting-links 2.

Move the pump until the correct tension is obtained and tighten the bolts to a torque of 10 lb ft.

Testing air pump:

Check the belt tension as just described and connect a tachometer to the engine. Then proceed as follows:

1 Disconnect air supply hose at the gulp valve 9 and plug the hose. Disconnect air supply hose at the check valve 3 and fit pressure gauge to the hose as shown in **FIG 1:26**.
2 Run the engine at 1200 rev/min and note the gauge reading. If less than 2.75 lb/sq in, remove the pump air cleaner, clean thoroughly and fit new element. Refit air cleaner and repeat test. If the reading is still low, blank-off the relief valve 6 and recheck. Renew the valve if the reading is now correct. If the pressure is still low, remove and service pump.
3 Switch off the engine and use a piece of adhesive tape to form a duct over the face of the relief valve as shown in inset **FIG 1:26. Do not try to check the air flow from the valve using the fingers.**
4 Start the engine and increase speed slowly until air flows from the valve duct, the gauge reading should be between 4.5 and 6.5 lb/sq in otherwise the valve should be renewed.

Servicing air pump:

1 Remove air cleaner and disconnect hoses at the pump. Slacken off mounting bolts and remove belt. Unscrew top adjusting-link bolt and mounting bolt and nut. Support pump and withdraw mounting bolt. Remove pump from engine.
2 Refer to **FIG 1:27**, unscrew four end cover bolts and remove cover 10. Remove four screws and withdraw bearing carrier 8. Extract the vane assemblies 7 and remove carbons 6 and spring 5.
3 Clean all components and repack bearings with Esso 'Andok' 260 grease. Inspect the vane assemblies for signs of damage or wear, particularly areas in contact with carbons. Renew vanes if necessary and fit new carbons. Fit the carbons and springs in the deeper slots in rotor 3 with the chamfer on the inside.
4 Reassembly is the reverse of the dismantling procedure. Smear the underside of the bearing carrier retaining screws with 'Loctite'. Refit the pump to the engine, tension belt as described previously. Reconnect hoses and replace air cleaner.

Testing check valve:

Remove valve by disconnecting supply hose and unscrewing valve from manifold. Hold valve to the mouth and blow through each end of the valve in turn. If air passes through when blowing from manifold connection the check valve must be renewed. **Do not use high-pressure air.** Refit the valve and reconnect air supply hose.

Testing air manifold:

Disconnect manifold from cylinder head. Slacken check valve hose clip and rotate manifold until injector connections are accessible. Tighten hose clip and run engine at idling speed. Check air flow from each end of manifold connections. If the flow is restricted from any of the connections, remove manifold and clear any obstruction using air pressure. Check that exhaust gases blow from each injector on the cylinder head. Ensure that the injectors are not displaced while testing. If any of the injectors are restricted they should be cleared as follows:

Turn the engine until the exhaust valve below the injector is closed. Use a hand drill and pass a ⅛ inch drill through the injector bore. **Ensure that the drill does not touch the exhaust valve stem. Do not use a power drill.** Blow through the injector to clear carbon dust from the exhaust port. Reconnect the manifold.

Testing gulp valve:

Disconnect gulp valve supply hose from air pump. Connect a vacuum gauge using a Tee-connector, to the end of the hose. Run the engine at idling speed. Place thumb over open end of Tee-connector and check that the gauge reading is zero for 15 seconds. If gauge registers a vacuum the gulp valve should be renewed. Do not increase engine speed above idling while carrying out this test. Keep the Tee-connector temporarily sealed and open throttle rapidly, the gauge should register a vacuum. Repeat this test several times, temporarily unsealing Teepiece between each test. If the gauge fails to register a vacuum, renew the gulp valve.

Testing limit valve:

Disconnect vacuum sensing pipe from inlet manifold. Connect a vacuum gauge to the inlet manifold. Connect a tachometer to the engine. Run the engine at fast-idling speed until normal operating temperature is reached. Increase speed to 3000 rev/min and release throttle quickly. The vacuum gauge reading should rise to 20.5 to 22 in Hg. If the reading is outside these limits the limit valve assembly and the carburetter throttle disc must be renewed as described in **Section 2:11** of the Fuel System Chapter. Refit the carburetter and tune as described in **Section 2:11** of the Fuel System Chapter.

Engine modifications:

On certain high compression engines the control of exhaust gases is ensured by using a specially tuned carburetter, as described in **Section 2:11**, which incorporates a limit valve in the throttle disc—to limit the depression in the inlet manifold when the throttle is closed and maintain an otherwise over-rich mixture at a combustible level.

A throttle damper is fitted (see **FIG 1:28** and **Section 2:11**) to prevent an over-rapid shutting of the butterfly valve on releasing the accelerator pedal.

Arrangements are also made for obtaining an air supply at the optimum temperature. When operating at a low ambient temperature the air intake is positioned in a shroud over the exhaust manifold as shown in the illustration. At high ambient temperatures the intake tube is positioned away from the manifold and the air entering the carburetter is at the ambient temperature.

1:20 Removing the engine and gearbox assembly (1974)

With the introduction of the new 'rod-shift' gearchange for the 1974 models, a new procedure for the removal of the power plant assembly is necessary as follows:

Remove the bonnet and disconnect the battery.

From the carburetter remove the air cleaner, petrol feed pipe, vacuum pipe and breather hose, then remove the carburetter.

Disconnect the two hoses from the fuel pump and the two-piece speedometer drive cable at its centre joint.

Drain the cooling system by removing the cylinder block drain plug and remove the heater hose from the radiator bottom hose connection. Remove the heater water control valve from the cylinder head.

Disconnect the exhaust pipe from the manifold and the pipe from the air intake from underneath the righthand front wing. Remove the air intake from the wing valance.

Disconnect and remove the horn.

Disconnect the starter cable from the solenoid and the earthing cable from the clutch cover.

Remove the cap and rotor arm from the distributor then disconnect the leads from the coil, oil pressure switch and the alternator.

Release the clutch return spring, unbolt the slave cylinder and tie it out of the way.

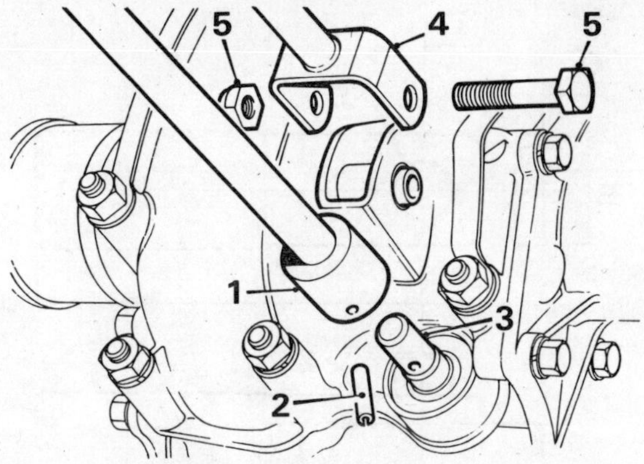

FIG 1:29 Disconnecting the later rod type gearchange remote control from the transmission

Key to Fig 1:29 1 Extension rod 2 Roll pin 3 Selector shaft 4 Fork on steady rod 5 Nut and bolt

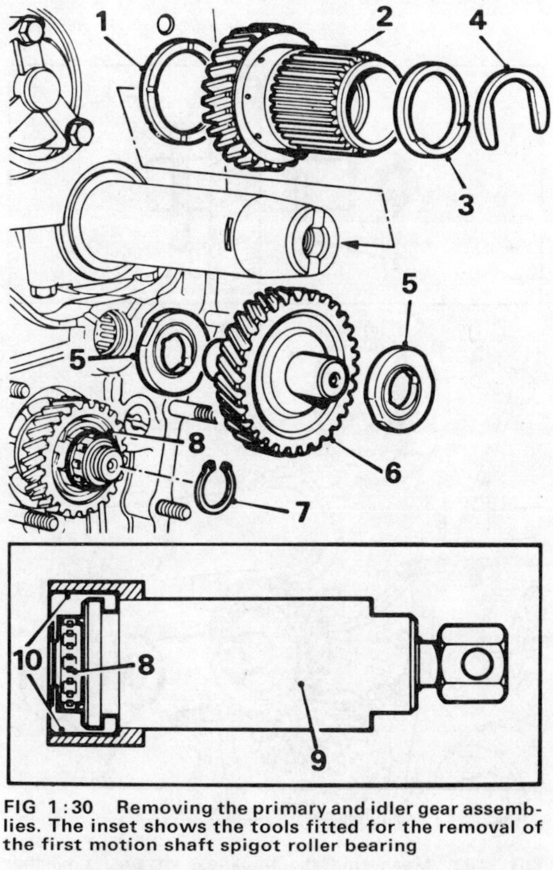

FIG 1:30 Removing the primary and idler gear assemblies. The inset shows the tools fitted for the removal of the first motion shaft spigot roller bearing

Key to Fig 1:30 1 Rear thrust washer 2 Primary gear 3 Backing ring 4 Front thrust washer 5 Idler gear thrust washers 6 Idler gear 7 Circlip 8 Roller bearing first motion shaft 9 18G 705 10 18G 705C

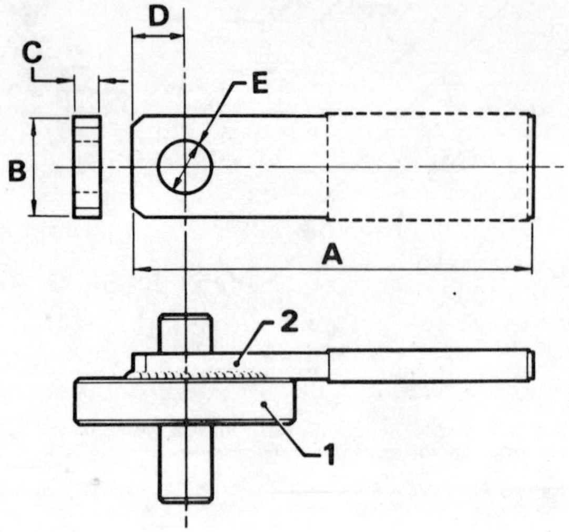

FIG 1:31 Details of the fabricated gear locking tool

Key to Fig 1:31 1 Idler gear 2 Steel bar A=5¼ inch (133 mm) B=1½ inch (38 mm) C=⅜ inch (9.5 mm) D=¾ inch (19.05 mm)=E

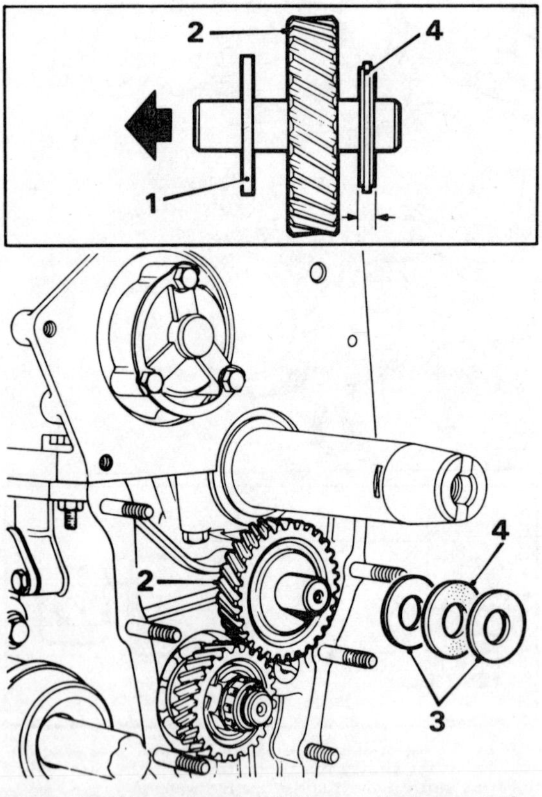

FIG 1:32 Measuring the thickness of thrust washer required for idler gear end-float adjustment

Key to Fig 1:32 1 Thrust washer 2 Idler gear 3 18G 1089 4 Dental wax washer

The engine tie-rod should now be disconnected from the rear of the block. Loosen the other tie-rod bolt and swing the rod out of the way.

The rocker cover should now be removed to permit the attachment of the engine lifting bracket, if available. The front eye of this bracket is used in order to provide an angled lift from the front of the engine. Failing this tool, eyes can be fitted to the cylinder head studs as convenient, using the cylinder head nuts.

Refer to **Chapter 7**, **Section 7:10** for details of the removal of the drive shafts from the inboard joints.

Refer to **FIG 1:29** and drive out the roll-pin 2 securing the extension rod 1 to the selector shaft 3. Remove the nut and bolt 5 from the fork 4 on the remote control steady rod and detach it from the final drive housing.

Disconnect the exhaust steady bracket from the end cover on the final drive. Remove the four bolts and nuts securing the engine mountings to the subframe.

Attach suitable lifting tackle to the lifting eye and raise the power unit out of the car.

Refitting the power unit is carried out in the reverse order to the above, but do not omit to tighten the cylinder head nuts as described in **Section 1:5**.

1:21 Removing the primary drive (1974 models)

First remove the clutch and flywheel assembly as described in **Section 1:8** and then remove the flywheel housing.

Refer to **FIG 1:30**. Remove the rear thrust washer 1, backing ring 3, primary gear 2 and the front thrust washer 4.

Pull off the first motion shaft roller bearing 8, using the service tools 18G 705 and 705C as shown, after first removing the retaining circlip 7.

Remove the idler gear 6 and its two thrust washers 5.

It will now be necessary to make up a tool, to the pattern given in **FIG 1:31**, in order to lock the gear train while the retaining nut for the first motion shaft gear is released. The tool is fabricated using an old idler gear 1 and a piece of steel bar 2 to the dimensions given.

Drill a hole E of diameter ¾ inch (19.05 mm) in the position shown and weld the bar to the gearwheel. Wrap the bar well with tape where it will contact the crankshaft.

Insert the tool into the idler gear bearing with its handle against the crankshaft. Knock back the lock-washer tab and unscrew the retaining nut on the first motion gear. Withdraw the gear.

Carefully inspect all the gears for wear or damage and note that these should be replaced as a complete set if renewal of any part is necessary. Thrust washers must be selected as necessary to obtain the correct end float for the idler and primary gears.

Refitting:

The first motion shaft gear must be fitted with a new lockwasher and the holding tool applied to the opposite side of the crankshaft while the gear retaining nut is tightened to a torque of 150 lb ft (20.7 kgm). Remove the tool and set the primary gear end float as follows:

Fit the primary gear and the front thrust washer with its chamfered side towards the crankshaft, then fit the rear backing ring and thrust washer.

Use feeler gauges between the gearwheel and the rear backing ring to measure the gear end float. This should be between .0035 and .0065 inch (.089 and .165 mm). Any necessary adjustment may be made by selecting the correct thrust washer thickness from the range given below.

.112 to .114 inch	(2.84 to 2.89 mm)
.114 to .116 inch	(2.89 to 2.94 mm)
.116 to .118 inch	(2.94 to 2.99 mm)
.118 to .120 inch	(2.99 to 3.04 mm)

Having confirmed the adjustment, remove the primary gear and adjust the idler gear end float.

Fit the idler gear in place, as shown in **FIG 1:32**, the longer spindle into the transmission and with a nominal washer 1 on the inner side of the gear.

Tool 18G 1089 comprises two thin washers which are now fitted with a dental wax washer between them as shown at 4.

Using a new flywheel housing joint washer, refit the housing and tighten the securing bolts and nuts to a torque of 18 lb ft (2.5 kgm). Remove the housing and discard the joint washer.

Slide off the tool 18G 1089 as one piece and measure the thickness of the three washers together with a micrometer. From the measurement dimension taken, subtract .004 to .007 inch (.102 to .178 mm) and select and fit a thrust washer of this calculated thickness from the four sizes given below.

.132 to .133 inch	(3.35 to 3.37 mm)
.134 to .135 inch	(3.40 to 3.42 mm)
.136 to .137 inch	(3.45 to 3.47 mm)
.138 to .139 inch	(3.50 to 3.53 mm)

Refit the primary gear with its selected front thrust washer, backing ring and rear thrust washer.

Fit the tool 18G 1043 over the primary gear to protect the oil seal and screw the two guides into the two bottom holes in the crankcase.

Using another new joint washer, refit the flywheel housing and then the clutch and flywheel assembly.

1:22 Fault diagnosis

(a) Engine will not start

1 Defective coil
2 Faulty distributor capacitor
3 Dirty, pitted or incorrectly set contact breaker points
4 Ignition wires loose or insulation faulty
5 Water on sparking plug leads
6 Corrosion of battery terminals or battery in discharged condition
7 Faulty or jammed starter
8 Sparking plug leads wrongly connected
9 Vapour lock in fuel pipes
10 Defective fuel pump
11 Overchoking
12 Underchoking
13 Blocked petrol filter or carburetter jets
14 Leaking valves
15 Sticking valves
16 Valve timing incorrect
17 Ignition timing incorrect

(b) Engine stalls

Check 1 2 3 4 10 11 12 13 14 and 15 in (a)

1 Sparking plugs defective or gap incorrect
2 Retarded ignition
3 Mixture too weak
4 Water in fuel system
5 Petrol tank breather choked
6 Incorrect valve rocker clearance

(c) Engine idles badly

Check 1 and 6 in (b)

1 Air leak at manifold joints
2 Slow-running adjustment incorrect
3 Air leak in carburetter
4 Worn piston rings
5 Worn valve stems or guides
6 Weak exhaust valve springs

(d) Engine misfires

Check 1 2 3 4 5 8 10 13 14 15 16 17 in (a), and 1 2 3 and 6 in (b)

1 Weak or broken valve springs

(e) Engine overheats, see Chapter 4

(f) Compression low

Check 14 and 15 in (a), 5 and 6 in (c) and 1 in (d)

1 Worn piston ring grooves
2 Scored or worn cylinder bores

(g) Engine lacks power

Check 3 10 11 13 14 15 and 16 in (a), 1 2 3 and 6 in (b), 5 and 6 in (c), and 1 in (d). Also check (e) and (f)

1 Leaking joint washers
2 Fouled sparking plugs
3 Automatic advance not operating

(h) Burnt valves or seats

Check 14 and 15 in (a), 6 in (b), and 1 in (d). Also check (e)

1 Excessive carbon around valve seat and head

(j) Sticking valves

Check 1 in (d)

1 Bent valve stem
2 Scored valve stem or guide
3 Incorrect valve clearance

(k) Excessive cylinder wear

Check 11 in (a) and see Chapter 4

1 Lack of oil
2 Dirty oil
3 Piston rings gummed up or broken
4 Badly fitting piston rings
5 Connecting rods bent

(l) Excessive oil consumption

Check 5 and 6 in (c) and check (k)

1 Ring gaps too wide
2 Oil return holes in piston choked with carbon
3 Scored cylinders
4 Oil level too high
5 External oil leaks
6 Ineffective valve stem oil seals

(m) Crankshaft and connecting rod bearing failure

Check 1 in (k)

1 Restricted oilways
2 Worn journals or crankpins
3 Loose bearing caps
4 Extremely low oil pressure
5 Bent connecting rod

(n) Internal water leakage, see Chapter 4

(o) Poor circulation, see Chapter 4

(p) Corrosion, see Chapter 4

(q) High fuel consumption, see Chapter 2

(r) Engine vibration

1 Loose generator bolts
2 Fan blades out of balance
3 Badly fitted or defective engine mountings
4 Exhaust pipe mountings too tight or exhaust system incorrectly fitted
5 Defective or incorrectly fitted universal drive couplings

The following items apply only to cars fitted with exhaust emission control.

(s) Backfire in exhaust system

1 Leak in exhaust system
2 Leak in hoses or connections to gulp valve or vacuum sensing pipe
3 Leak in intake system
4 Faulty gulp valve
5 Faulty carburetter limit valve

(t) Hesitation when accelerating after sudden throttle closure

1 Check 1, 2, 3 and 4 in (s)

(u) Engine surges

1 Check 2 and 4 in (s)
2 Air supply to absorption canister restricted (if fitted)

(v) Erratic idling or stalling

1 Check 2 and 4 in (s)
2 Carburetter limit valve not seating

(w) Burned or baked hose between air pump and check valve

1 Faulty check valve
2 Faulty air pump

(x) Noisy air pump

1 Belt tension incorrect
2 Pulleys loose or misaligned
3 Damaged air pump

(y) High exhaust system temperature

1 Incorrect ignition timing
2 Air injector missing
3 Faulty air pump relief valve
4 Choke valve not fully returned

(z) Mixture needs enriching to obtain correct exhaust emission reading

1 Air leak in crankcase
2 Faulty crankcase control valve on early cars
3 Leaks in crankcase breather hose or carburetter connections on later cars

CHAPTER 2

THE FUEL SYSTEM

2:1 Fuel pump, operating principles

SU fuel pumps are fitted to all vehicles in the Mini range, but whereas the earlier cars, which had a positive earth electrical system, used an electrical pump, later cars on which a negative earth system is employed have a mechanical fuel pump as standard.

The electric pump is either the type PD which is shown in **FIG 2:1** or either of the types SP or AUF which are fully illustrated in **FIG 2:2**. The mechanical fuel pump may be either the type AUF 705 which is shown in **FIG 2:7** or the similar, but non-serviceable, type AUF 800.

Each of the electric types has the basic principle of a reciprocating diaphragm, actuated by a solenoid, drawing fuel from the tank through a non-return valve on one stroke and pumping it through another one-way valve to the carburetter on the return stroke.

The mechanical pump is driven from the camshaft which actuates a diaphragm by means of a rocking lever, drawing the fuel in on one stroke and forcing it to the carburetter on the return stroke under the influence of a spring.

In each type of pump provision is made for preventing the diaphragm from working when a full float chamber has caused its needle valve to close.

2:2 Routine maintenance

Electric pump:

1 A periodical inspection should be carried out to check the security of the pump on its mounting bracket. Check also the secure attachment of the fuel and electrical connections, and for cleanliness and weeping at the fuel pipe unions. Check the fuel and electrical lines for chafing or cracks.

2 The fuel pump gauze filters should be cleaned periodically to avoid any troubles due to fuel starvation. About 8000 miles is a suitable interval for this operation.

3 The location of the pump on all models except the Moke is on a mounting bracket attached to the vehicle's rear subframe under the car body and close to the fuel tank. On the Moke the pump is located on its mounting bracket in the pannier of the lefthand sidemember. Disconnect the battery before starting work.

4 **FIG 2:1** illustrates the PD-type pump. To clean the filter first clean off all external road dirt, then disconnect the electrical lead, slacken the fuel hose clamp screws and pull off the fuel pipes. Blank off the pipe from the fuel tank. Unscrew the pump mounting bracket screws and remove the pump and bracket complete. To expose the small gauze filter, take off the domed bottom cover-

FIG 2 : 1 The PD-type fuel pump showing (inset) access to the fuel filter

plate secured by one nut and a plain and spring washer. Clean the filter by brushing lightly in a solvent or fuel.

As the bottom coverplate is replaced, rotate it a little to ensure correct bedding on to the pump body.

Dirty contact points are cleaned by lifting off the top cover. This is only a push-fit. Then draw a piece of clean paper between the contact points. Check that there is a gap of at least .015 inch between the upper end of the outer contact blade and its stop face.

5 **FIG 2 : 2** illustrates the component parts of the SP and AUF-type pumps. To remove these, first disconnect the electrical lead, slacken the flexible fuel pipe hose clips and pull off the pipes. Plug the supply pipe from the fuel tank with a $\frac{5}{16}$ inch dia. bolt to prevent loss of fuel.

Remove the nut and spring washer securing the fuel pump clamp to the subframe bracket and lift out the pump.

The filters on these pumps are located by reference to No. 49 **FIG 2 : 2** for the SP-type pump, and No. 40 for the AUF pump.

6 The Moke pump is removed complete with mounting bracket by removing two nuts.

Mechanical pump:

The only maintenance required is a periodical inspection of the gauze filter (4 in **FIG 2 : 7**). Clean the outside of the pump and remove the outlet cover 1 and the

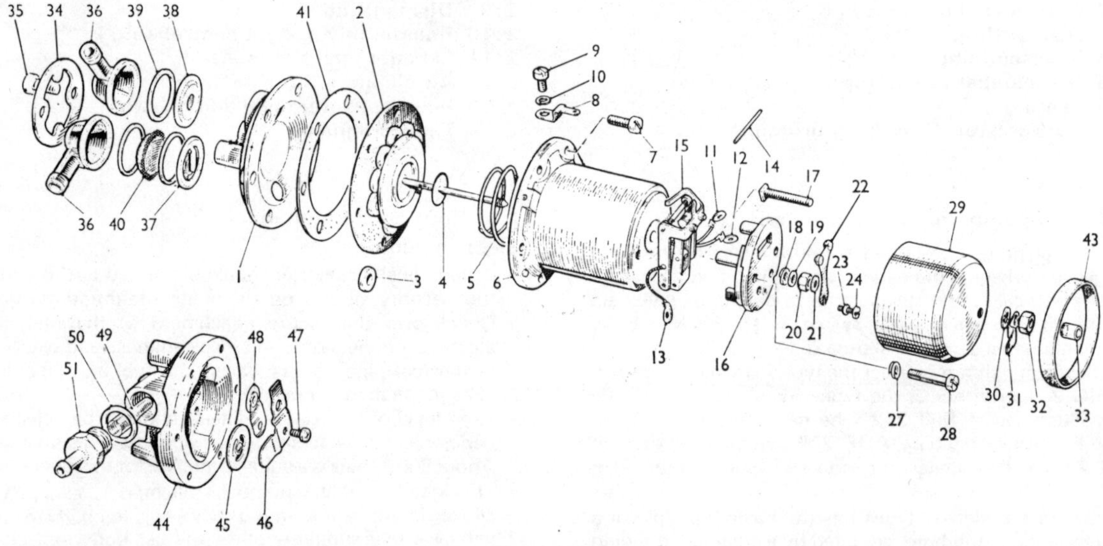

FIG 2 : 2 An exploded view of the AUF and SP type fuel pumps

Key to Fig 2 : 2 1 Pump body (AUF only) 2 Diaphragm and spindle assembly 3 Armature centralizing roller 4 Impact washer 5 Armature spring 6 Coil housing 7 Setscrew 8 Earth connector 9 Setscrew 10 Spring washer 11 Terminal tag 12 Terminal tag 13 Earth tag 14 Rocker pivot pin 15 Rocker mechanism 16 Pedestal 17 Terminal stud 18 Spring washer 19 Lead washer 20 Terminal nut 21 End-cover seal washer 22 Contact blade 23 Washer 24 Contact blade screw 27 Spring washer 28 Screw 29 End-cover 30 Shakeproof washer 31 Connector 32 Nut 33 Insulating sleeve
AUF: 34 Clamp plate 35 Setscrew 36 Inlet and outlet nozzles 37 Inlet valve 38 Outlet valve 39 Sealing washer 40 Filter 41 Gasket
SP: 43 Sealing band 44 Pump body 45 Outlet valve 46 Valve retainer 47 Screw 48 Inlet valve 49 Filter 50 Washer 51 Inlet nozzle

sealing ring 3 after marking it to ensure correct replacement. Wash the filter in petrol and clean out the filter chamber.

When refitting the cover, use a new sealing ring if the old one shows signs of damage or deterioration.

2 : 3 Dismantling

The PD-type pump is serviced as a unit, and apart from the maintenance operations described in **Section 2 : 2**, should not be dismantled. If the pump fails to operate satisfactorily, it should be exchanged for a new or reconditioned pump, taking into account that if a later type pump is fitted it will have a higher pressure and delivery rate. This may cause flooding of the carburetter, and a later type float chamber lid complete with needle valve and float will then have to be fitted.

Referring to **FIG 2 : 2**, dismantle the SP and AUF pumps as follows:

1 For the SP-type pump, unscrew and remove the inlet nozzle 51.
2 Remove the fibre washer 50 and filter 49 from the pump body
3 Clean the filter and replace if no further work is planned.
4 For the AUF-type pump, take out two screws 35 securing the spring clamp plate 34 holding the inlet and outlet nozzles 36.
5 Remove the nozzles, valve assemblies 37, 38 and washers 39, and take out the filter 40, noting carefully the order of assembly of these parts.
6 For both types of pump, proceed by separating the pump body 1 or 44 from the diaphragm 2 and coil housing 6 by taking out the six setscrews 7. If desired, remove the earthing screw and connector 9 and 8.
7 Remove from the SP-type pump body the valve retainer screw 47, retainer 46 and valves 45 and 48.
8 It is now possible to remove the diaphragm and armature spindle assembly 2 and impact washer 4 by unscrewing the diaphragm and allowing the armature spring 5 to push these parts away from the coil housing. Take great care when separating these parts not to tear the diaphragm as if the pump has been in use for a long period the diaphragm may be adhering firmly to the pump body washer 41 or coil housing. Notice the assembly of the eleven brass positioning rollers under the diaphragm.
9 Remove the insulated sleeve 33, terminal nut 32, connector 31, spring washer 30 and, if fitted, the sealing band 43.
10 Take off the end cover 29.
11 Remove the contact blade screw 24 and washer 23, lift off the coil lead connector and contact blade 22. Notice that the longer of the two leads goes to the contact blade.
12 The pedestal is secured by two 2BA screws. Before attempting to remove these, take off the sealing washer 21, terminal nut 20 and lead washer 19 which may have to be cut away with a knife. Remove the spring washer 18 and the terminal tag connector 11.
13 Take out the two pedestals securing screws 28 and remove them with the spring washers 27, remove the earthing terminal tag 13, tip the pedestal to remove the terminal stud 17 and lift off the pedestal. The hardened steel pin 14 can now be extracted to release the rocker mechanism from the pedestal. Do not attempt to remove the toggle spring from the rocker mechanism.
14 Thoroughly clean all parts of the pump but do not use strong solvents on rubber or plastic parts. Gum formation from low grade fuels can be removed from steel or brass parts by boiling them in 20 per cent caustic soda solution, and then if necessary, dipping in weak nitric acid solution, followed by a boiling water rinse. Do not use this treatment on light alloy parts, but soak them in methylated spirits.
15 Visually check the valves and valve retainers. After assembly, the operation of the valves may be checked by blowing and sucking at the inlet and outlet ports in the pump body. Scratches or marks on the sealing faces may cause slight leakage inefficiencies. Corrosion may be present on the pump body, and if severe the body should be renewed.
16 If the main feed spring appears to be in good condition, the most practical method of checking it for loss of compression strength is to check the operating pressure of the pump under working conditions.
17 Badly burnt or pitted contact points call for renewal of the rocker assembly and/or the contact blade. Check also the pedestal for cracks and wear at the ridge where the contact blade rests.
18 Check the diaphragm for cracks in rubber surfaces, separation, or undue distortion.
19 Examine the rollers for wear around the peripheries and renew if necessary, making sure that the correct number are available for reassembly.
20 Finally obtain a complete set of washers, gaskets and sealing rings, and make sure that all screw threads are in good order.
21 In addition check the outlet valve in the SP-type pump for tightness of the centre rivet and correct operation of the lift spring. The spring should not have become unwound so that it does not hold the plastic valve disc on its seating. Make sure the valve is free to lift at least $\frac{1}{16}$ inch. If the inlet valve is slightly discoloured but otherwise satisfactory, it need not be renewed. Severe corrosion on and around the valve seating faces in the pump body calls for a new body.

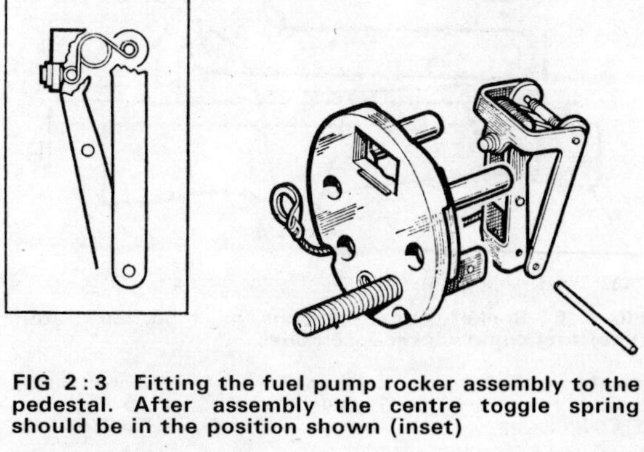

FIG 2 : 3 Fitting the fuel pump rocker assembly to the pedestal. After assembly the centre toggle spring should be in the position shown (inset)

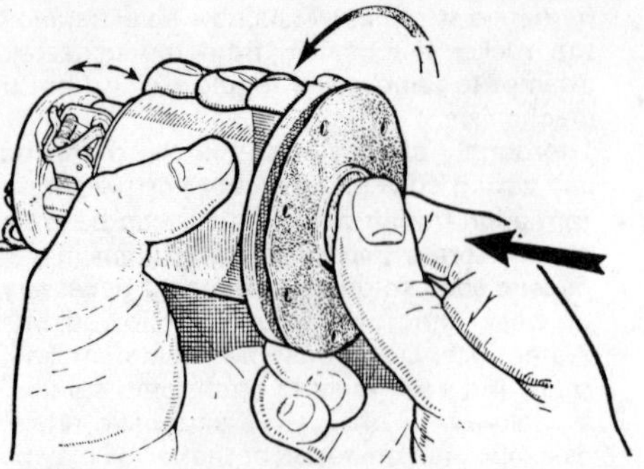

FIG 2:4 Adjusting the position of the fuel pump diaphragm/armature assembly. The diaphragm is unscrewed until the rocker just throws over

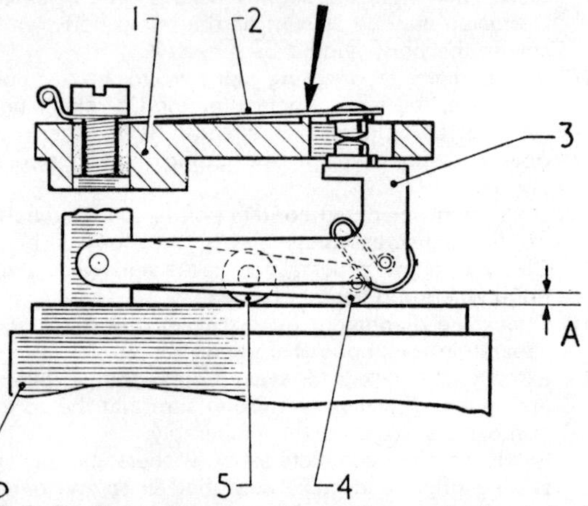

FIG 2:5 Contact gap settings for early type fuel pump rocker assemblies

Key to Fig 2:5 1 Pedestal 2 Contact blade 3 Outer rocker 4 Inner rocker 5 Trunnion 6 Coil housing A=.030 inch

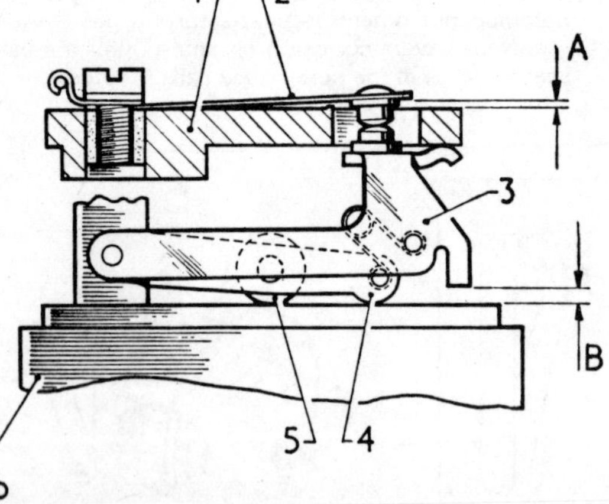

FIG 2:6 Rocker finger settings on modified (later type) fuel pump rocker assemblies

Key to Fig 2:6 1 Pedestal 2 Contact blade 3 Outer rocker 4 Inner rocker 5 Trunnion 6 Coil housing A=.035 inch B=.070 inch

2:4 Reassembling

Reassembly of all pumps is generally the reverse of dismantling with special attention given to the following:

1 Never replace the special pin securing the rocker mechanism with anything but a genuine part, as it is of specially hardened steel.
2 Note that **FIG 2:3** shows the method of assembly of the rocker mechanism to the pedestal, and **FIG 2:4** illustrates the best way to hold the coil housing when adjusting the position of the armature and the diaphragm.
3 When the contact breaker and pedestal have all been assembled together securely, make sure that the spring blade is so adjusted that a 'wiping' action takes place at the two contact points as they meet and part. Tighten the blade screw firmly when this condition has been achieved. When the points make contact, check that the blade is deflected sufficiently to leave a small gap between itself and the small rib on which it rests in the open position.
4 On early type rocker assemblies there should be a gap of .030 inch at A **FIG 2:5** when the contact blade 2 is held gently against the rib, indicated by the arrow. On modified rocker assemblies check that the gap A between the end of the contact blade and the pedestal face is .035 inch when the outer rocker 3 **FIG 2:6** is touching the underside of the pedestal face. The stop-finger at the centre of the outer rocker bridgepiece can be bent slightly to correct this clearance. On these assemblies it is also necessary to adjust the gap B **FIG 2:6** to .070 inch by the same method.
5 When refitting the armature and diaphragm assembly, first refit the main diaphragm return spring, larger diameter towards the coil. Fit the neoprene impact washer over the armature spindle, insert the spindle through the spring centre and then the coil and screw the spindle into the rocker trunnion until the rocker does not quite 'throw over'. Position the eleven rollers under the diaphragm while the pump is held vertically, diaphragm uppermost. At this point it is recommended that the contact blade of later type pumps, i.e. those with the adjustable finger, should be removed.
6 The diaphragm and armature spindle are now screwed forwards into the rocker trunnion until a steady pressure on the armature just fails to cause the outer rocker to 'throw over'. The diaphragm assembly is then unscrewed as far as the nearest body securing screw hole and beyond this for a further four holes totalling two-thirds of a complete turn.
7 When refitting the pump body to the coil housing, make sure that the relative positioning is correct, i.e. with the coil housing cast lugs to the bottom. Line up the six securing screw holes and insert the 2BA screws finger tight, checking throughout that the rollers are not falling out of position, as a misplaced roller may cut the diaphragm. The six screws should be tightened up progressively in diametrically opposite pairs until they are all fully tightened. Refit the contact blade correctly and make a final check of rocker adjustment.

2:5 Mechanical fuel pump

Removal:

Disconnect the battery and remove the air cleaner. Disconnect the two fuel pipes.

Remove the two securing nuts and partially pull the pump away from the engine. Carefully prise apart the pump and the insulating block and pull out the pump and the block with its two joint washers.

Dismantling (type AUF 705 only):

See **FIG 2:7**. Mark the outlet cover 1 and the upper 6 and lower 12 bodies as arrowed for later alignment and remove the outlet cover, seal 3 and filter 4.

Remove three screws 5 and lift off the upper body. Remove the combined inlet/outlet valve 7. This is a press fit and care must be taken not to damage it. Hold the diaphragm 8 and rocker lever 14 against the pressure of the spring and tap out the pivot pin 15. Remove the rocker lever 14 and spring 13 and apply a drop of oil to the crankcase seal 11 before pulling out the diaphragm and stirrup assembly.

The crankcase seal and cup 10 need to be removed only if a new seal is to be fitted. This may be done by screwing in the service tool 18G.1119 to the retaining cup and pulling it out of the lower body.

Carefully examine all parts and renew any showing wear or damage.

Reassembling:

This is the reverse of the dismantling procedure with attention to the following points.

Remove any sharp edges from the diaphragm spindle and stirrup and oil lightly before engaging the rocker lever.

Ensure that the inlet/outlet valve groove registers in the housing and that the fine edge contacts its sealing evenly.

Line up the screw holes in the lower body with the holes in the diaphragm, depress the rocker lever so that the diaphragm lies flat, fit the short screws 5 and leave slack. Fit the filter, sealing ring and outer cover. Tighten all screws evenly.

Refitting:

Use new joints on the insulating block, noting that the total thickness of block and washers must not be changed from the original.

Switch on the ignition and use the starter for 20 seconds to prime the pump.

2:6 Testing

Testing an electrical pump:

Testing of fuel pumps is undertaken on special test equipment which is held by service agents. Five tests are generally carried out to establish the all-round operating efficiency of SU pumps. These are a flow test at a predetermined delivery head, a test for leaks on suction side of pump, a test for valve leakage, a test for minimum delivery and finally a reduced voltage test. The contact breaker is also checked for sparking, which if severe may indicate that the solenoid is faulty and requires renewal.

When refitting the pump in the car, reverse the removal procedure and make sure that the outlet port is vertically above the inlet port, that is, with the two nozzles horizontal as shown in **FIG 2:8**.

Testing a mechanical pump:

A reasonable indication of the condition of a mechanical pump can be obtained by using the following procedure:

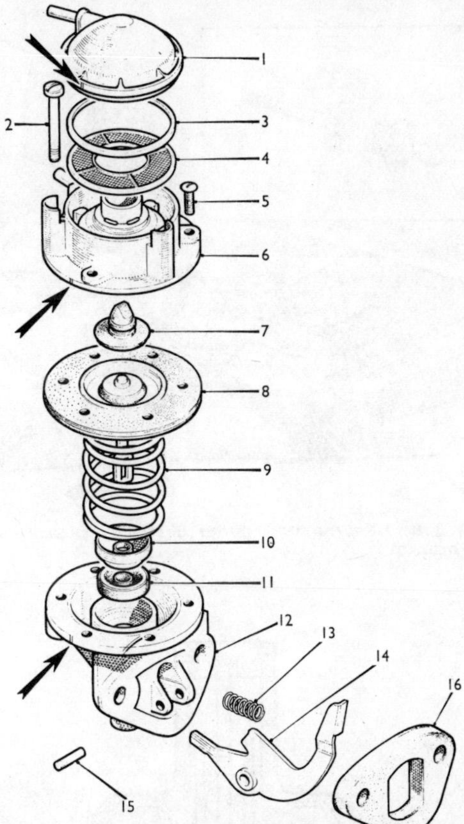

FIG 2:7 Components of fuel pump type AUF.705

Key to Fig 2:7 1 Outlet cover 2 Cover retaining screws 3 Sealing ring 4 Filter 5 Body securing screws 6 Upper body 7 Combined inlet/outlet valve 8 Diaphragm/stirrup assembly 9 Diaphragm spring 10 Crankcase seal cup 11 Crankcase seal 12 Lower body 13 Rocker lever return spring 14 Rocker lever 15 Rocker lever pivot pin 16 Insulating block assembly

Hold a finger over the inlet port and operate the rocker lever through three full strokes. Release the finger when a distinct noise caused by the suction should be heard.

Hold a finger over the outlet port and depress the rocker arm fully. Pressure should hold for up to 15 seconds.

CARBURETTER

2:7 Operating principles

All early cars covered by this manual are fitted with an SU carburetter type HS2 except automatic transmission models and the 1275 GT which have type HS4 carburetters. Later cars, on which carburetters designed to comply with the European emission control requirements are required, are equipped with HS4 carburetters irrespective of engine size or type of transmission. The earlier type will be described first and operation of the later type is covered under the heading 'Exhaust emission control' in **Section 2:11**.

The SU carburetter provides the engine with the correct fuel/air mixture for all conditions of engine speed and load by mechanical control of the factors affecting air and fuel flow through the choke and single jet respectively.

FIG 2:8 SP-type fuel pump correctly positioned on its bracket

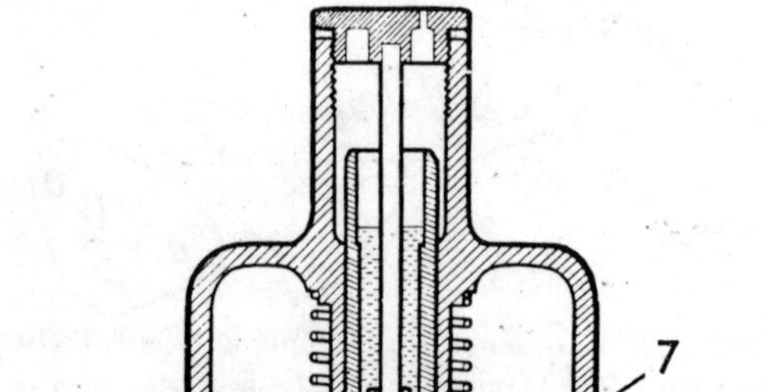

FIG 2:9 Sectional view of SU carburetter

Key to Fig 2:9 1 Jet locking nut 2 Jet adjusting nut 3 Jet head 4 Nylon fuel pipe 5 Piston lifting pin 6 Needle securing screw 7 Piston damper oilwell

Entry of air into the engine is determined by the position of a rising and falling piston assembly which increases or decreases the effective choke area when up or down. Its position under any particular running conditions is dependent entirely on the pressure conditions in the space between the choke and the throttle butterfly. The pressure at this point is conveyed to the space above the suction disc attached to the piston which moves in the suction chamber located above the choke and jet. A compression spring and oil damper piston control the rate of movement up and down, and any rapid movements of the main piston assembly. Note that the main piston is not in contact with the bore of the suction chamber. A simplified section of the carburetter is illustrated in **FIG 2:9** in which the features so far described can be seen.

Continuing to refer to **FIG 2:9** it will be seen that the single jet orifice is positioned in the centre of the lower face of the choke opening. Fuel is caused to flow upwards through the jet orifice by virtue of the depression created by venturi effect arising from the air flow through the choke. A tapered needle is fitted to the centre of the lower face of the piston. The needle extends downwards into the jet orifice and tube and therefore determines by its position the quantity of fuel flowing through the jet according to the throttle opening, the position of the piston, the rate of air flow through the choke and the resultant depression operating over the jet orifice. The jet may be lowered by the mixture control so that a larger effective orifice area is presented to the choke depression for conditions such as cold starting, when, temporarily, a richer mixture is required. Adjustment of the mixture for normal running conditions is achieved by adjusting the position of the jet adjusting nut 2 in **FIG 2:9**. This nut determines the maximum upward movement of the jet when the mixture control is returned to normal.

2:8 Routine maintenance and tuning for slow-running

Carburetters are not normally the cause of much trouble, but it is occasionally advisable to inspect for general cleanliness, condition of the pins and screws in the control mechanisms, and for weeping joints or fractures of flexible pipes near their ends. Apply a spot of high temperature grease or 'thick' oil to moving parts for lubrication. Air leaks at the main carburetter-to-manifold joint can cause weak mixture and consequent damage to the engine if allowed to continue.

Unsatisfactory running may be due to the piston sticking or dirt in the jet. To check for piston sticking, remove the piston damper assembly 7 in **FIG 2:10** and lift the piston by raising the piston lifting pin 5 in **FIG 2:9**. If the piston does not rise and fall quite freely, remove the vacuum chamber and piston assembly complete and carefully clean these parts, leaving no dust or fluff on them. When refitting them lubricate the piston rod only, which is the only part in actual physical contact with other parts, with no more than a drop or two of light spindle oil along its length. When assembled, top-up the damper with normal engine lubricating oil, SAE.20 grade.

If a choked or partially choked jet is suspected as a result of power loss, failure to accelerate properly, blowing back through the carburetter or possibly overheating, start the engine and open the throttle. Immediately

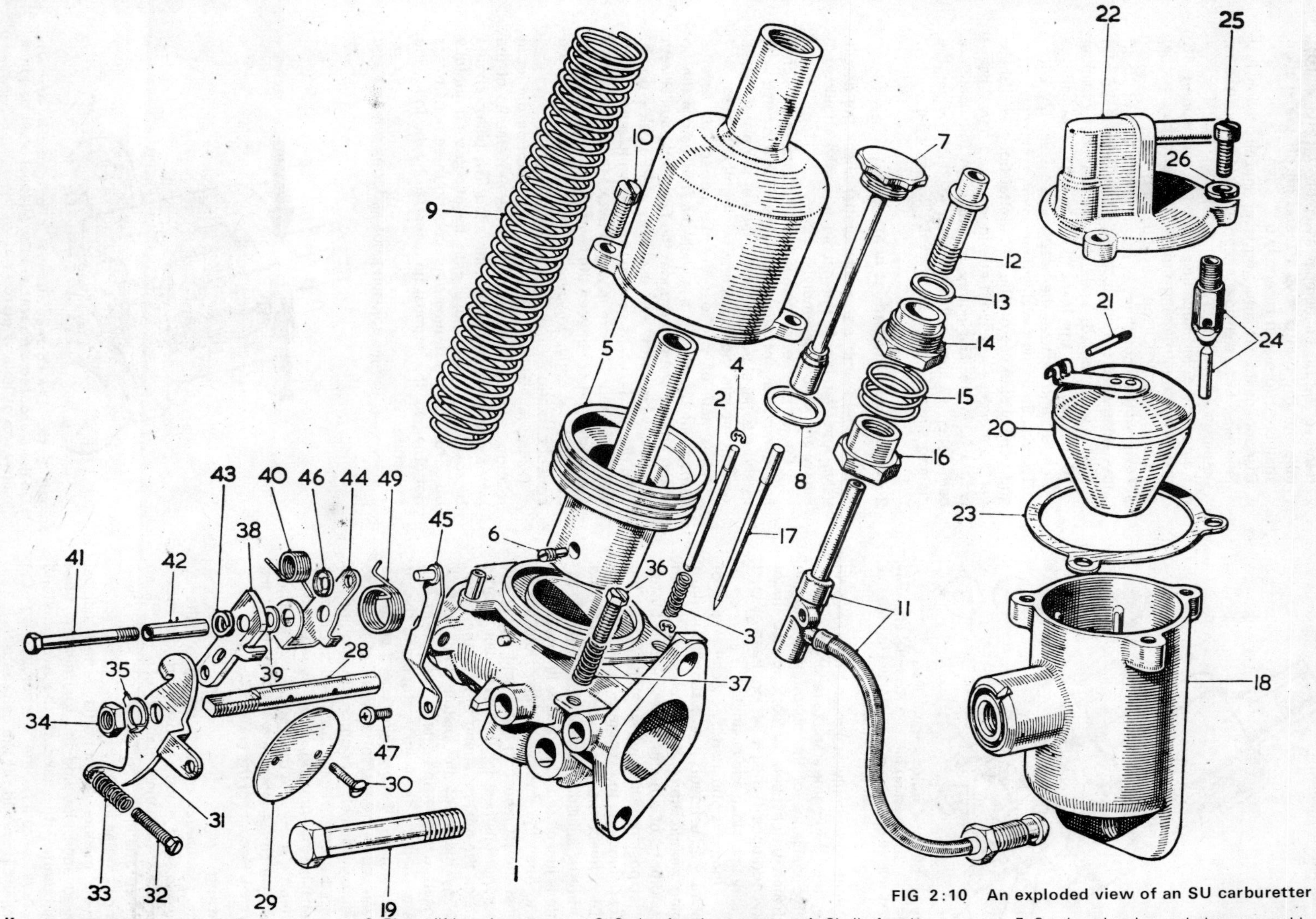

FIG 2:10 An exploded view of an SU carburetter

Key to FIG 2:10 1 Body 2 Piston lifting pin 3 Spring for pin 4 Circlip for pin 5 Suction chamber and piston assembly 6 Needle locking screw 7 Piston damper assembly 8 Washer for damper cap (fibre) 9 Piston spring 10 Screw—suction chamber to body 11 Jet assembly 12 Jet bearing 13 Washer for jet bearing (brass) 14 Lockscrew for jet bearing 15 Lock spring 16 Jet adjusting screw 17 Jet needle 18 Float chamber body 19 Float chamber retaining bolt 20 Float and lever assembly 21 Lever hinge pin 22 Float chamber lid assembly 23 Washer for lid 24 Needle and seat assembly 25 Screw—float chamber lid to body 26 Spring washer 28 Throttle spindle 29 Throttle disc 30 Screw—throttle disc 31 Throttle lever 32 Cam stop screw 33 Spring for stop screw 34 Throttle spindle nut 35 Tab washer for nut 36 Idling stop screw 37 Spring for stop screw 38 Cam lever 39 Washer 40 Cam lever spring 41 Cam lever pivot bolt 42 Pivot bolt tube 43 Spring washer 44 Pickup lever assembly 45 Jet link 46 Jet link retaining clip 47 Jet link securing screw 49 Spring for pickup lever

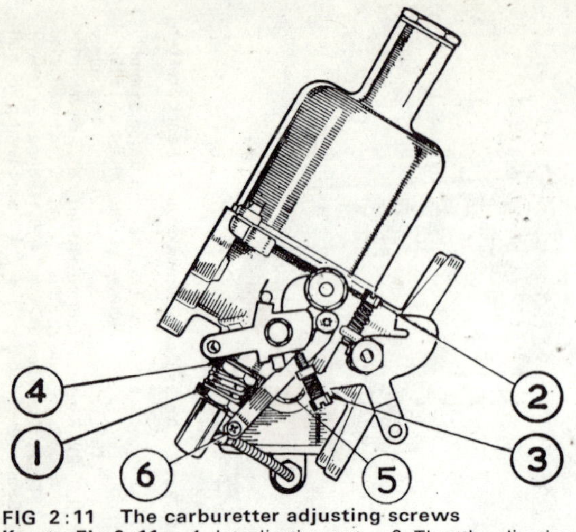

FIG 2:11 The carburetter adjusting screws
Key to Fig 2:11 1 Jet adjusting nut 2 Throttle adjusting screw 3 Fast-idle adjusting screw 4 Jet locking nut 5 Float chamber bolt 6 Jet link securing screw

close off the air inlet momentarily, at the same time keeping the throttle open until the engine starts to race. Racing will indicate probable clearance of the obstruction and the engine should then be checked for performance under normal running conditions. If the jet has not been cleared it will be necessary to remove and clean it.

Correct slow-running is obtained by a combination of throttle and mixture adjustment. It is essential to adjust the slow-running mixture correctly as mixture strength for all other conditions of running is determined by the setting of the jet position for slow-running. Adjust the mixture by first running the engine up to normal temperature. Disconnect the choke control cable and unscrew the throttle adjusting screw 2 in **FIG 2:11** until the throttle is just closed, then screw it forward one complete turn to open the throttle slightly. Hold the jet firmly up against the jet adjusting nut 1 and adjust the nut until the engine runs best for that particular throttle opening. To check the mixture strength, raise the piston about $\frac{1}{32}$ inch by means of the piston lifting pin. A momentary speed increase indicates correct mixture. The mixture is too weak if the engine stops and the jet must be lowered slightly. If the engine speed continues to increase, even when the piston is raised as much as $\frac{1}{4}$ inch, the mixture is too rich for normal running and the jet must be raised a little. Having obtained the best jet adjustment, set the slow-running speed as required by adjusting the throttle screw. Set the fast idle screw to give a clearance of $\frac{1}{64}$ inch (.4 mm) between the end of the screw and the cam. Reconnect the choke cable.

2:9 Dismantling

Remove the carburetter by first taking off the air cleaner. Disconnect the breather hose from the rocker cover and slacken the cleaner retaining clip on the air intake pipe before attempting to lift off the air cleaner. Further operations are as follows:

1 Disconnect the mixture and throttle control cables, the suction advance pipe and the fuel delivery hose from the carburetter, then take off the two nuts and spring washers securing the carburetter to the induction manifold and lift off the carburetter(s).
2 Remove the piston damper assembly 7 (**FIG 2:10**), take out the two screws 10, and lift off the suction chamber and piston assembly 5.
3 Disconnect the jet actuating lever, and the nylon fuel feed pipe from the float chamber 18. Pull out the jet assembly 11.
4 Remove the jet adjusting nut 16 and spring 15, unscrew the jet bearing nut 14, take out the brass jet bearing washer 13 and the jet bearing 12.
5 Take out the float chamber securing bolt 19 and lift off the float chamber, remove the three screws 25 and spring washers 26, and take off the float chamber lid 22, remove the lever hinge pin 21, take off the float 20 and remove the needle valve assembly 24.

There is little point in dismantling the remaining levers and control spindles on the carburetter body as if these parts are excessively worn due to long and heavy use it would be more satisfactory to exchange the complete carburetter. A light dab of grease or thick oil on the moving surfaces will help minimize future wear.

2:10 Reassembly and jet centralizing

Before reassembling the carburetter check the needle valve and seating. If the needle is badly 'shouldered' renew the whole assembly.

If the jet needle is damaged or bent, renew it with a correct replacement needle. The new needle is fitted with its shoulder level with the lower face of the piston. Make sure the needle locking screw 6 is tightly secured.

Adjustment of the float lever for correct fuel level is carried out by placing a $\frac{1}{8}$ inch dia. rod across the lip of the float chamber lid, under the float and parallel with the hinge pin, with the assembly held upside-down. With the needle on its seating the lever should just touch the $\frac{1}{8}$ inch rod. If there is a gap between the lever and the needle end or between the lever and the rod, the lever may be set slightly, adjacent to the hinge, to obtain the correct condition.

During reassembly it is essential to position the jet in relation to the jet needle so that the movements of the piston and jet needle are not inhibited. The piston should be absolutely free to move, with the jet adjusting nut fully up or fully down. If, after reassembling these parts this is not obtained, the jet must be recentred by the following procedures:

1 Screw up the jet adjusting nut as far as possible and

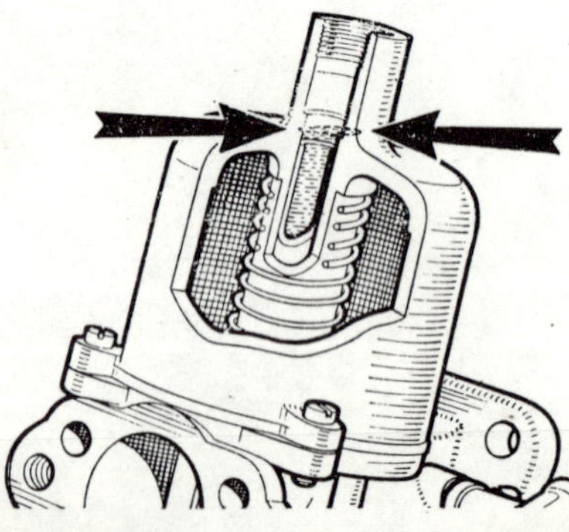

FIG 2:12 The correct oil level is indicated by arrows. On dust-proofed carburetters the oil level must be $\frac{1}{2}$ inch below top of hollow piston rod

slacken the jet bearing locking nut so that the bearing is free to turn.

2 Remove the piston damper and move the piston down so that it rests on the bridge across the choke passage. Tighten up the jet bearing locking nut.

3 Lift the piston and check if it falls quite freely on to the bridge. If the piston is quite free unscrew the jet nut to its lowest position and check the piston fall again. If it is still free the centring is satisfactory. If the piston is not quite free in its movement, repeat the centring process until it is free in all jet positions.

4 Refit all parts removed during dismantling in the reverse order of their dismantling and finally top-up the oil well with SAE.20 grade engine lubricating oil to within $\frac{1}{2}$ inch of the top of the piston rod before replacing the damper.

5 Use a new set of joint washers throughout when reassembling and refitting the carburetter. Note that the cable abutment plate fitted between the carburetter and induction manifold flange has two joint washers, both of which should be in excellent condition.

2:11 Exhaust emission control system

The HS4 carburetters used with exhaust emission control are balanced to give maximum pollution control with maximum performance. These carburetters must not be interchanged with carburetters manufactured for engines without emission control. Carburetter tuning must only be carried out with the exhaust emission control equipment connected and functioning correctly.

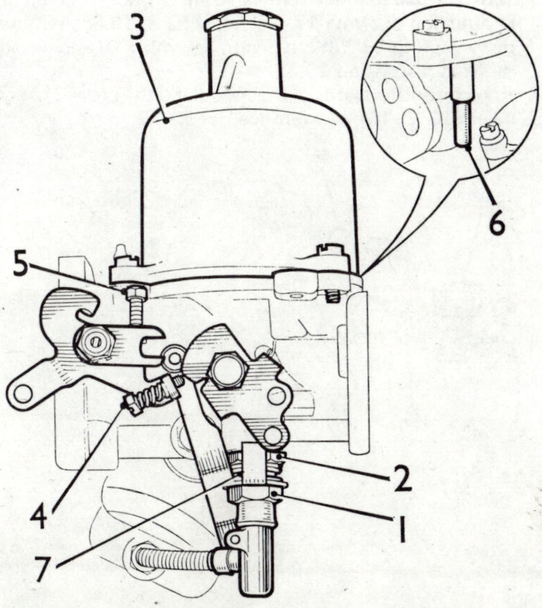

FIG 2:13 The SU carburetter type HS used with exhaust emission control system

Key to Fig 2:13 1 Jet adjusting nut 2 Jet locking nut 3 Depression chamber 4 Fast-idle adjusting screw 5 Throttle adjusting screw 6 Piston lifting pin 7 Jet adjustment restrictor

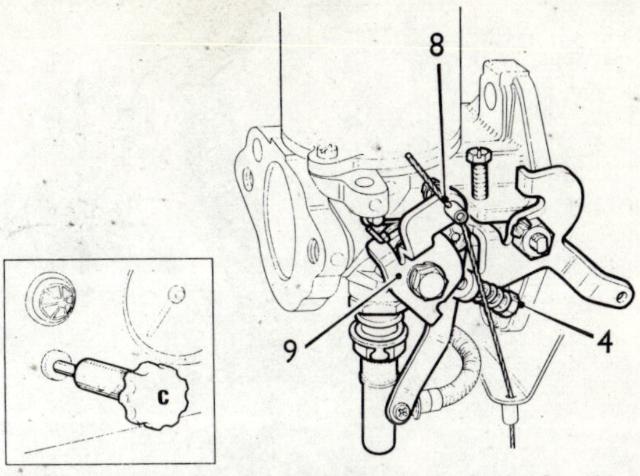

FIG 2:14 Details of the mixture control wire 8 and jet lever 9. The fast-idle screw 4 is also shown

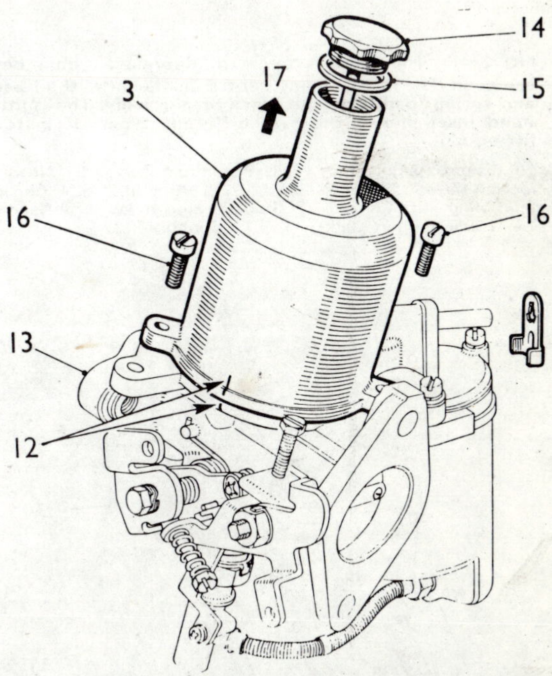

FIG 2:15 Before removing depression chamber, mark the carburetter body and chamber flange as shown at 12. Remove the chamber in direction of arrow 17 without tilting

Key to Fig 2:15 3 Depression chamber 13 Carburetter body 14 Damper 15 Washer 16 Retaining screws

Tuning carburetter:

Top up the piston damper (see **FIG 2:12**) to $\frac{1}{2}$ inch above top of hollow piston rod. If the carburetter has a drilled hole in the suction chamber neck, the oil level must be $\frac{1}{2}$ inch below the top of the piston rod. Check that the throttle control linkage has no tendency to stick. Connect a tachometer to the engine. Start the engine and run it at fast-idling speed for five minutes after the thermostat has

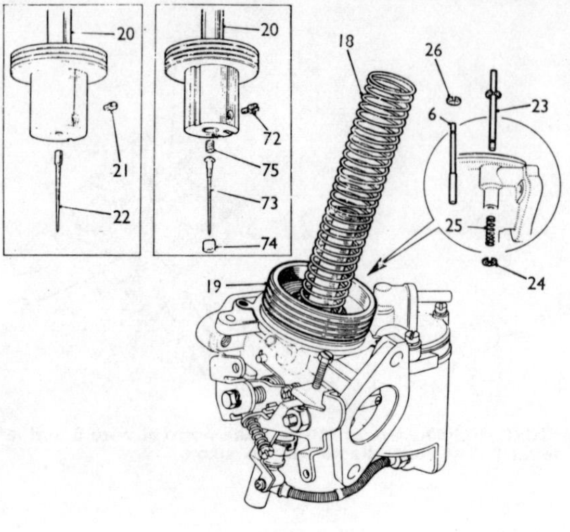

FIG 2:16 The carburetter with depression chamber removed. The lefthand and centre insets show the fixed and spring-loaded needle types respectively. The right-hand inset shows the two different types of piston lifting pin

19 Piston assembly 20 Piston rod 21 Needle locking screw 22 Needle 23 Lifting pin 24 Circlip 25 Spring 26 Circlip 72 Guide locking screw 73 Needle 74 Needle support guide 75 Spring

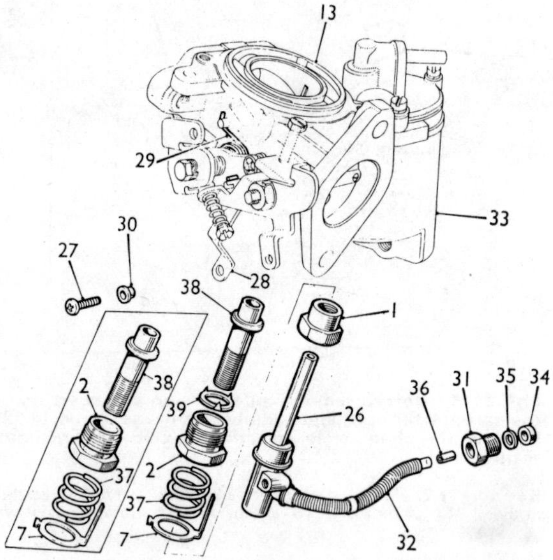

FIG 2:17 Details of jet assembly. Inset shows jet bearing details for spring-loaded needle type

Key to Fig 2:17 1 Jet adjusting nut 2 Jet locking nut 7 Restrictor 13 Carburetter body 26 Jet assembly 27 Screw 28 Jet pick-up link 29 Return spring 30 Brass bush (if fitted) 31 Sleeve nut 32 Flexible jet tube 33 Float chamber 34 Gland 35 Washer 36 Ferrule 37 Spring 38 Jet bearing 39 Locking washer (fixed needle type)

opened. This will be indicated by a sudden rise in temperature of the radiator header tank. Run the engine under no-load at 2500 rev/min for one minute. Carry out the tuning procedure as quickly as possible, every three minutes run the engine at 2500 rev/min for one minute. **Do not remove the jet adjustment restrictor.**

Use the throttle adjusting screw to obtain the correct idle speed as specified in **Technical Data** and with the engine running smoothly.

If unable to obtain a smooth idling, stop the engine and check that the piston falls freely when the lifting pin 6 (see **FIG 2:13**) is released, a distinct 'click' should be heard. Turn the jet adjusting nut 1 through the full range within the limits of the restrictor 7. The correct setting is when the engine runs smoothly with maximum speed obtained on the tachometer. Readjust the throttle adjusting screw 5 to give correct idling speed.

Adjust the mixture control wire 8 (see **FIG 2:14**) to give $\frac{1}{16}$ inch free movement before it operates the jet lever 9. Pull out the mixture control knob until the carburetter jet is about to move, adjust the fast-idle screw 4 to give a speed of 1050 to 1200 rev/min.

Dismantling carburetter:

Remove the carburetter as described in **Section 2:9**, disconnecting the depression chamber hose connection if this type of crankcase emission control is fitted.

If the car has an automatic transmission, it will be necessary also to disconnect the governor control rod fork end from the throttle lever, see **Section 6a:4** and **FIG 6a:6**.

1 Refer to **FIG 2:15** and remove damper 14 and washer 15. Mark the top chamber 3 and carburetter body 13 as shown at 12. Remove screws 16 and withdraw chamber in direction of arrow 17. Refer to **FIG 2:16** and remove piston spring 18. Lift out piston assembly 19 and empty oil from piston rod 20.

2 **Fixed needle type:** Unscrew locking screw 21 (see inset **FIG 2:16**) and remove needle 22.

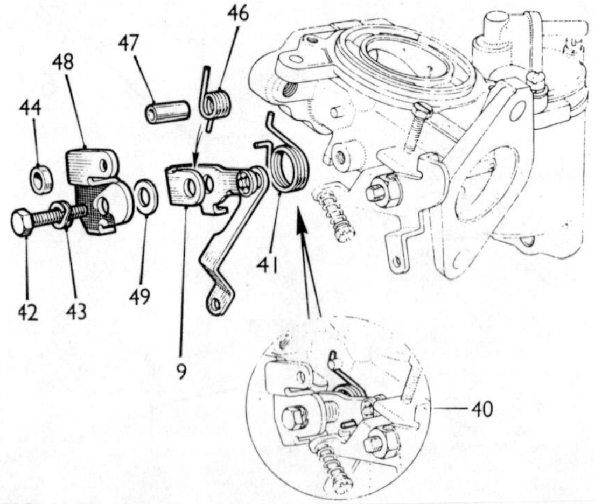

FIG 2:18 Details of pick-up lever assembly. The return spring is shown correctly fitted in inset

Key to Fig 2:18 9 Pick-up lever assembly 41 Pick-up lever return spring 42 Pivot bolt 43 Spring washer 44 Spacer 46 Cam lever spring 47 Pivot bolt tube(s) 48 Cam lever 49 Skid washer

Spring-loaded needle type: Unscrew locking screw 72 and remove needle assembly 73, needle support guide 74 and spring 75. Remove needle from guide together with spring.

3 **Both types:** Extract circlip 24 and spring 25, push the piston lifting pin 23 up and remove from body. If the lifting pin is of the concealed spring type 6 (see inset **FIG 2:16**), press the pin upwards, remove circlip 26 and withdraw pin and spring from the body.

4 Hold the base of the jet 26 (see **FIG 2:17**) and slacken screw 27. Disconnect spring 29 and remove screw together with brass bush 30, if fitted. Unscrew sleeve nut 31 and withdraw jet assembly 26 together with gland 34, washer 35 and ferrule 36.

5 Bend tag on restrictor 7 clear of jet adjusting nut 1 and remove nut, restrictor and spring 37. Unscrew jet locking nut 2 and remove jet bearing 38. Note that on fixed needle carburetters only, a locking washer 39 is fitted under the bearing flange.

6 Refer to **FIG 2:18** and note location of lever return spring 41 shown in inset 40. Unscrew bolt 42 and remove lever assembly 9 and return spring. Extract pivot bolt tube 47 taking care not to lose spring 46. Remove cam lever 48 and washer 49. Unscrew bolt 50 (see **FIG 2:19**) and remove float chamber 33 and flexible mounting 51.

7 Mark the float chamber 33 and lid 53 as shown at 52. Remove screws 54 and withdraw lid, gasket 55 and float assembly 56. Push out float hinge pin and remove float together with float needle 58. Unscrew seating 59 from lid.

8 Close throttle and mark throttle disc 61 and flange 62 as shown at 60 in **FIG 2:20 Do not mark disc near the limit valve 63.** Remove two screws 64, open throttle and ease disc from slot in the spindle 65. Knock down ears of tabwasher 66 and unscrew nut 67.

9 Inspect all parts including float needle and seating for signs of damage or wear. Renew any suspect components. Check for excessive play of the throttle spindle in the carburetter body. Clean all parts using fuel or methylated spirits. Allow to dry before reassembling.

Reassembly is the reverse of the preceding dismantling instructions. The heads of the countersunk screws 64 should face outwards when the throttle is closed. Centralize the throttle disc in the bore before tightening screws. The throttle limit valve must be below the spindle with the head of the valve facing the engine.

Check that the clearance between the float lever and lid is between $\frac{1}{8}$ and $\frac{3}{16}$ inch. If the carburetter is of the fixed needle type centralize the jet as described in **Section 2:10**, this is not necessary with the spring-loaded needle type. Screw in the jet adjusting nut until the top face of the jet is level with the carburetter bridge. Unscrew the adjusting nut eleven flats. Refit the carburetter to the engine as described in **Section 2:10**. Reconnect the depression chamber hose, if fitted. Tune the carburetter as follows:

Complete carburetter tuning:

The following procedure should be carried out when a new carburetter has been fitted or if the carburetter has been dismantled as described previously. Tuning must only be carried out with the exhaust emission control

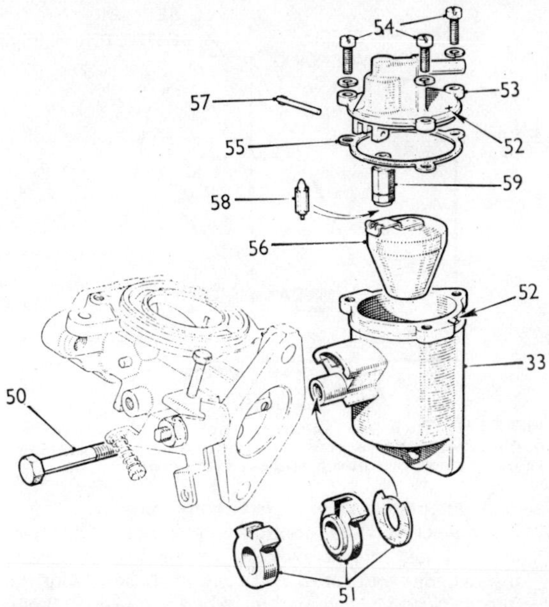

FIG 2:19 Components of float chamber assembly. Mark the float chamber and lid as shown at 52 before dismantling

Key to Fig 2:19 33 Float chamber 50 Retaining bolt 51 Flexible mounting 53 Float chamber lid 54 Retaining screws 55 Gasket 56 Float assembly 57 Float hinge pin 58 Float needle 59 Needle seating

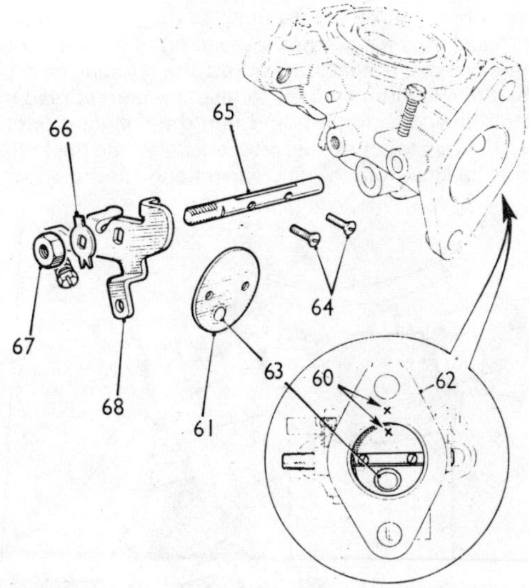

FIG 2:20 Components of throttle assembly. Mark the carburetter flange and throttle disc as shown at 60 before dismantling

Key to Fig 2:20 61 Throttle disc 62 Carburetter flange 63 Limit valve 64 Screws 65 Throttle spindle 66 Tabwasher 67 Spindle nut 68 Lever arm

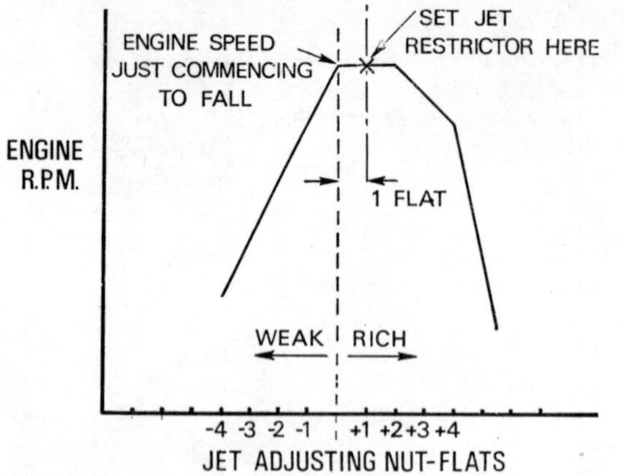

FIG 2:21 Turn jet adjusting nut to obtain fastest engine speed then screw in nut until speed just starts to fall. Turn one flat down and set restrictor

equipment connected and functioning correctly.

1 Disconnect mixture control wire (choke) if fitted, unscrew fast-idle screw clear of the cam. Unscrew throttle adjusting screw just clear of its stop with the throttle closed. Unscrew throttle adjusting screw 5 one turn. Do not alter jet adjusting nut 1 at this stage. Connect an exhaust gas analyser in accordance with the manufacturers instructions.
2 Carry out the procedure described previously under 'Tuning carburetter'.
3 Turn the jet adjusting nut until the fastest engine speed is obtained then screw the nut slowly in until the speed starts to fall. Screw the nut out one flat as shown in **FIG 2:21**. Lightly tap the neck of the depression chamber with the plastic handle of a screwdriver. Check that the idling speed is as specified, if necessary adjust by turning throttle adjusting screw. Check that the exhaust gas analyser gives a reading of 4.5 per cent CO (maximum). If necessary adjust the jet adjustment nut by the minimum amount to give the correct reading.
4 Hold the adjusting nut and turn the restrictor until the vertical tag touches the carburetter body on the lefthand side looking from the air cleaner flange. Bend down the small tag so that the restrictor is locked to the nut. Identify this position by painting the small tag and its adjacent flat on the nut. Reconnect the mixture control wire and adjust the fast-idle screw as previously described under **Tuning carburetter.**

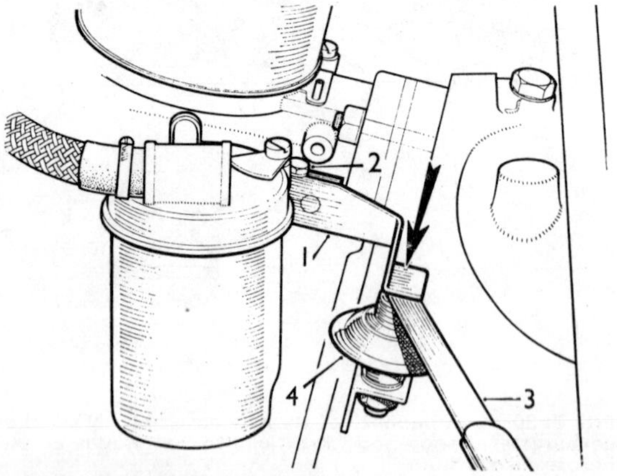

FIG 2:22 Adjusting the throttle damper

Key to Fig 2:22 1 Throttle lever 2 Clamp screw 3 Feeler gauge 4 Throttle damper

Check and adjust, if necessary, the throttle damper setting (if fitted) as follows:

Adjusting throttle damper:

Refer to **FIG 2:22** and slacken clamp screw 2 on damper operating lever 1. Insert an .08 inch feeler gauge between the damper plunger and the operating arm. With the throttle disc fully closed, press the operating lever down until the plunger is fully depressed. Hold the lever in this position, tighten the clamp and remove feeler gauge.

Automatic transmission models:

The method to be used for adjusting the idle speed and mixture for these cars is similar to that already described with the following exceptions:

1 Connect a reliable tachometer according to the manufacturer's instructions.
2 Apply the handbrake and select N on the transmission selector quadrant.
3 Run the engine until it is fully warmed up and adjust the jet position as just described.
4 Use the throttle stop screw, 5 in **FIG 2:13**, until a maximum speed of 650 rev/min is obtained.
5 Pull out the choke control to the maximum fast-idle position and then use the fast-idle adjusting screw 4 to obtain a maximum fast-idle speed of 1050 rev/min.
6 Push the choke control fully in and recheck the idle speed.
7 Check the adjustment of the governor control rod as detailed in **Section 6a:4** of **Chapter 6a**.

2:12 Air cleaners, routine maintenance

Disposable paper air filter elements are fitted to air cleaners in Mini, Elf and Hornet models. Such filters present a very large area of fine mesh paper to the air stream before it enters the carburetter. The large area permits of a very slow rate of air flow through the actual paper mesh and the very slight pressure drop thus created results in a high degree of filtration efficiency rather on the lines of a dust collector bag on a vacuum cleaner. For this reason it is essential to clear the dirt away from the air stream path at regular intervals of not less than 12,000 miles. Otherwise inefficiencies in carburation and resulting engine performance will be experienced. The only method of restoring full induction efficiency is to renew the element.

To change single paper elements unscrew the wingnut on top of the air filter body. Make sure the inside of the body is clean and dry before the new element is fitted.

If at any time air cleaner bodies or parts are removed for servicing, make quite sure that all air manifold rubber joints and other sealing points are in fact airtight and secure. It is advisable to use new joint washers if permanent distortion or any other form of deterioration is apparent.

Where applicable, this operation must be followed by an exhaust emission check.

2:13 Fuel tanks, removal and refitting

Fuel tank installations vary according to model. If any repairs to a fuel tank become necessary it is essential to remove the tank from the car as it is otherwise impossible to clear it of fuel and fumes. There is the serious risk of fire if every vestige of fuel is not first removed from the tank. Recent research has shown that even with qualified professional mechanics using service equipment it is very difficult to ensure the complete cleansing of a fuel tank and the home operator is strongly advised not to attempt any repairs on a tank involving the use of cutting or heated tools. The following instructions should be followed to remove the fuel tank from the car and any such repairs entrusted to a service station.

Removal of the fuel tank in the Mini saloon models is undertaken as follows:

1 Drain off the fuel by removing the flexible hose at the pump connection, on later models by unscrewing the drain plug three turns.
2 Take off the filler cap, disconnect the fuel gauge unit lead, unscrew the bolt on the securing strap and release the vent pipe clip.
3 Lift out the tank, at the same time carefully withdrawing the vent and fuel pipes upwards through the floor. Notice the positioning of the locating plate under the tank, which must be correctly repositioned when the tank is refitted.

To refit the tank reverse the removal procedure. The vent pipe and wiring harness pass through the same hole. The seal between the drain pipe housing and the body must be watertight and the locating plate fitted before the securing strap is tightened.

To remove the fuel tank in the Van, Pickup and later Traveller models, drain off the fuel, disconnect the electrical and fuel lines, remove the filler cap and then remove six flange screws and spacers and lower the tank. To refit the fuel tank reverse this procedure.

To remove the fuel tank from the earlier Traveller model proceed as follows:

1 Remove the trim liner from the body above the tank and the metal finishers from the rear seat squab support.
2 Lift out the luggage platform, disconnect the battery and ease the trim panel away from the tank.
3 Drain the tank and disconnect the drain and fuel delivery pipes.
4 Take off the filler cap, disconnect the fuel gauge unit lead and pull the breather pipe from the tank, then unscrew the support bracket screws and lift the tank from the car. To refit the tank reverse these instructions.

The Moke tank is located inside the lefthand sidemember. Remove the tank as follows:

1 Remove the forward pannier side cover and disconnect the lead from the fuel gauge unit. Drain the tank by means of the drain plug accessible through the underside of the floor on the lefthand side.
2 Disconnect the suction hose from the fuel pump in the pannier of the lefthand sidemember, then remove the bottom coverplate.
3 Extract the tank retaining screw from the top face of the sidemember, remove the support bracket and lower the tank. To replace the tank reverse the removal procedure.

2:14 Fault diagnosis

(a) Leakage or insufficient fuel delivered

1 Air vent in tank restricted
2 Petrol pipes blocked
3 Air leaks at pipe connections
4 Pump or carburetter filters blocked
5 Pump gaskets faulty
6 Pump diaphragm defective
7 Pump valves sticking or seating badly
8 Fuel vapourising in pipelines due to heat

(b) Excessive fuel consumption

1 Carburetter(s) need adjusting
2 Fuel leakage
3 Sticking controls or choke device
4 Dirty air cleaner(s)
5 Excessive engine temperature
6 Brakes binding
7 Tyres under-inflated
8 Idling speed too high
9 Car overloaded

(c) Idling speed too high

1 Rich fuel mixture
2 Carburetter controls sticking
3 Slow-running screws incorrectly adjusted
4 Worn carburetter butterfly valves

(d) Noisy fuel pump

1 Loose mountings
2 Air leaks on suction side and at diaphragm
3 Obstruction in fuel pipes
4 Choked pump filter

(e) No fuel delivery

1 No fuel in tank
2 Float needle stuck in closed position
3 Vent in tank blocked
4 Electric pump connections faulty
5 Electric pump contacts dirty
6 Pipeline obstructed
7 Pump diaphragms stiff or damaged
8 Pump inlet valve stuck open
9 Bad air leak on suction side of pump

The following items apply only if a carburetter control system with evaporative loss control is fitted.

(f) Fuel leakage

1 Fracture in fuel pipe or fuel vapour ventilation system
2 Fuel filler cap not sealing
3 Leak in fuel filler tube or tank unit

(g) Engine stops after short running periods (fuel starvation)

1 Obstructed vapour line to absorption canister
2 Air supply to absorption canister restricted

NOTES

CHAPTER 3

THE IGNITION SYSTEM

3:1 Operating principles of automatic timing controls

The ignition system is generally quite orthodox, comprising the battery, ignition switch, distributor and contact breaker, ignition coil, high tension cables and sparking plugs. A capacitor is connected in parallel with the contact points to prevent sparking and burning.

Some early cars were fitted with a Lucas DM2 distributor, but the most common type is the 25D4. This is shown in **FIG 3:1** and is described comprehensively in the next five sections. From 1974 a Lucas 45D4 distributor may be fitted and, where the servicing procedures differ from the earlier type, is described in **Section 3:10**.

Automatic correction of timing for all engine speeds and loads is provided by a centrifugal weight assembly, 13 in **FIG 3:1** for advancing the ignition point with increasing engine speed, and a vacuum operated diaphragm 16 which varies the timing according to engine load, each acting independently of the other. In the centrifugal control the weights are pivoted so that they move outwards as the rotational speed of the distributor driving spindle increases and advance the position of the cam 11, so advancing the ignition. The diaphragm in the vacuum control moves the contact breaker plate 9 relative to the distributor body, retarding the ignition under heavy engine load conditions and advancing it under light loads.

3:2 Distributor maintenance, contact point adjustment

Efficient maintenance of the ignition system will save many petty little troubles. Keep all parts free from dust, dampness and oil and occasionally clean the inside of the distributor cover with a clean dry soft cloth. Make sure all electrical leads are secure and the terminals and connections are clean and tight. Check that the sparking plugs are tightly secured and that the copper washers are serviceable. Renew them if they have become compressed to less than half their original thickness.

Lubrication of the distributor involves the application of a few drops of engine lubricating oil down the centre of the cam and also down the space between the cam spindle and the distributor centre hole to lubricate the centrifugal advance mechanism and the distributor drive spindle. Occasionally, it is also advisable to apply a drop of oil to the moving contact pivot pin and a light smear of soft grease to the cam surfaces.

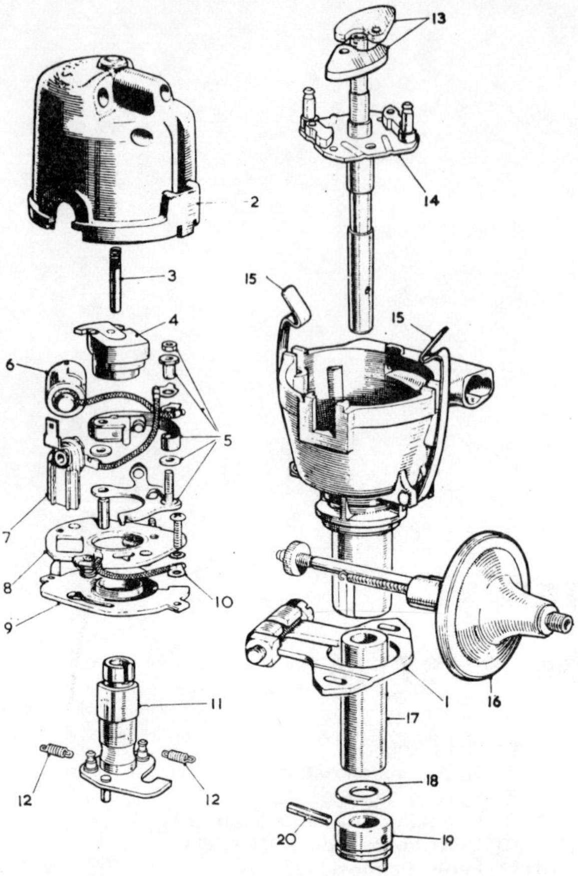

FIG 3 : 1 The component parts of the distributor

Key to Fig 3 : 1 1 Clamping plate 2 Moulded cap 3 Brush and spring 4 Rotor arm 5 Contacts (set) 6 Capacitor 7 Terminal and lead (low tension) 8 Moving contact breaker plate 9 Contact breaker base plate 10 Earth lead 11 Cam assembly 12 Automatic advance springs 13 Weight assembly 14 Shaft and action plate 15 Cap retaining clips 16 Vacuum unit 17 Bush 18 Thrust washer 19 Driving dog 20 Taper pin

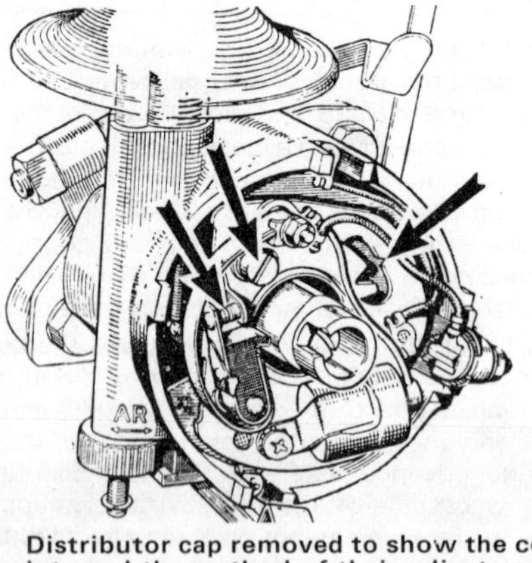

FIG 3 : 2 Distributor cap removed to show the contact breaker points and the method of their adjustment

The contact breaker points indicated by the lefthand arrow in **FIG 3 : 2** should be clean and properly adjusted to the correct gap of .014 to .016 inch. To adjust the gap, remove the distributor cover by releasing the two spring clips 15 in **FIG 3 : 1** and turn the engine so that one cam lobe is holding the points apart to their fullest extent. Slacken the locking screw shown by the centre arrow in **FIG 3 : 2,** securing the fixed contact plate, and using a screwdriver in the notched hole indicated by the right-hand arrow, adjust the gap so that a .014 to .016 inch thick feeler gauge is a sliding fit between the contact points. If the contacts are dirty or burnt they may be cleaned with very fine carborundum stone or very fine emery cloth. The moving contact should be removed for this purpose. Do not forget to tighten the securing screws afterwards.

3 : 3 Removing the distributor

1 Note that if the distributor is removed without disturbing the clamp bolt some of the retiming work will be avoided on refitting.
2 Lift the distributor cover, taking care of the centre brush and spring.
3 Turn the crankshaft until Nos. 1 and 4 pistons are at TDC and the distributor rotor arm is opposite the segment feeding No. 1 cylinder. Notice the position of the vacuum advance unit and its screw adjustment.
4 Disconnect the vacuum pipe and the low tension lead, remove the two screws securing the distributor clamp plate 1, **FIG 3 : 1** and lift off the distributor. Notice the position of the driving dog and, if an O-ring oil seal is fitted, take care not to damage it.

3 : 4 Dismantling the distributor

During dismantling it is advisable to study carefully the positions of the components as they are removed in order to assist correct refitting. Referring to **FIG 3 : 1,** operations for dismantling are as follows. Note, however, that for access to the centrifugal weights it is only necessary to remove the contact breaker plate as an assembly.

1 Take off the cover 2 and brush 3, then lift off the rotor arm 4. If it is a tight fit lever it off gently with a screwdriver.
2 Remove the nut and washer from the moving contact anchor pin 5 and take off the insulating sleeves from the capacitor and low tension lead connectors. Note the order in which they are fitted.
3 Lift the moving contact from the pivot pin and remove the insulating washers from the pivot pin and anchor pin. Note that the larger insulating washer is on the pivot pin. Take out the screw, spring washer and plain washer securing the fixed contact plate 8 and lift off the plate.
4 Remove the capacitor 6 by taking out the securing screw, then take out the two screws securing the base plate 9 to the distributor body. One of these also carries the earth lead. Lift out the base plate.
5 Unhook the vacuum advance flexible actuating link connecting the diaphragm of the vacuum advance unit Take out the cam retaining screw, disconnect the toggle springs and remove the cam assembly 11.

6 At this point note carefully the relative positions of the drive slot in the cam spindle for the rotor arm and the offset drive dog 19 at the driving end of the spindle, for correct reassembly.
7 Lift out the assemblies of centrifugal weights and their springs. Remove the circlip, knurled adjusting nut and friction spring. Withdraw the vacuum unit.
8 If required, drive out the spring pin passing through the driving dog collar and withdraw the spindle from the distributor body.

Before inspection, clean all parts thoroughly using solvent or petrol with care. Do not use such cleaning materials on the capacitor or insulation.

Check the distributor cover for cracks and 'tracking' and for condition and freedom of the carbon brush 3. Clean the metal end of the rotor moulding and if it is badly burned, renew the whole rotor.

Clean or renew the contact breaker points as required. Check all moving parts for wear and freedom of action. The spindle bush 17 can be pressed out for renewal if slack or otherwise unserviceable. The new bush, of porous bronze, should be soaked in engine lubricating oil for 24 hours, or two hours if heated to 100°C, before being pressed into the distributor body.

3 : 5 Reassembly and refitting

Reassembly is generally the reverse of the dismantling procedure but special attention is required to the following matters.

1 Lubricate all moving parts as described in **Section 3 : 2.**
2 The knurled nut of the vacuum advance mechanism should be in the mid-position when this assembly is refitted.
3 Make sure the centrifugal weights are correctly replaced when engaging the cam driving pins.
4 Viewed from above, the small offset of the driving dog must be on the right and the rotor driving slot in the cam at the six o'clock position.
5 Renew the O-ring oil seal on the mounting shank if necessary.
6 The capacitor (.2 microfarad), if suspect, is best tested by substituting a new one and noting if there is any difference in the engine performance. If it is necessary to solder a capacitor to its bracket, use only the minimum of heat.

Where applicable, this operation must be followed by an exhaust emission check.

3 : 6 Retiming

If the timing has been lost altogether, the following procedure should be adopted:

1 Make sure the distributor has been correctly assembled.
2 Turn the engine in the direction of rotation until No. 1 piston is at the TDC position, compression stroke (both valves closed) see **FIG 1 : 10.**
3 Check that the 1/4 mark on the flywheel is in line with the pointer and that the distributor drive shaft is correctly meshed with the camshaft gear as outlined in **Chapter 1**. Note that Mini II, Elf, Hornet II and III and Clubman models are not timed at the TDC position. Static timing positions are given in the **Technical Data** section.
4 Set the contact breaker gap to .014 to .016 inch at the point of maximum opening.
5 Insert the distributor being careful not to damage the O-ring oil seal, if fitted and engage the drive by slightly moving the cam spindle in one direction or the other.
6 Insert and tighten the two setscrews securing the clamp to the distributor housing, tighten the clamp bolt, then tighten down the two setscrews securing the clamp plate to the engine so that they are in the centre of the slots.
7 Undo the clamp bolt and turn the distributor bodily anticlockwise until the points are fully closed. Connect the low tension lead to the distributor terminal and connect a 12-volt lamp across the contact breaker points, i.e. in parallel with them. Then rotate the distributor clockwise until the lamp just lights, showing the contact points to be just open. Tighten up the clamp bolt.
8 Check that the rotor arm is still opposite the correct segment serving No. 1 sparking plug.

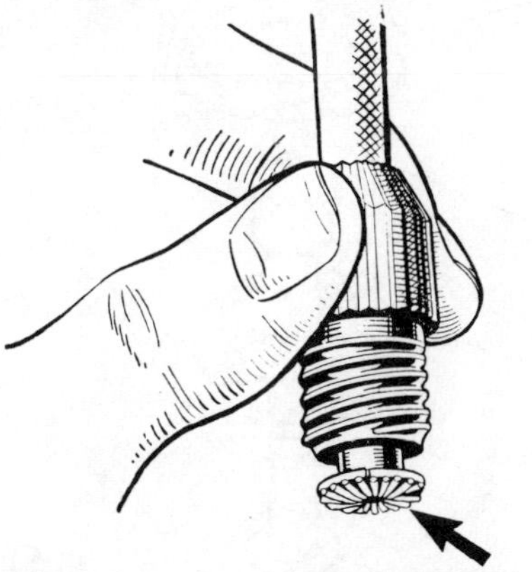

FIG 3 : 3 The correct method of fitting the high tension cable to ignition coil terminal nut

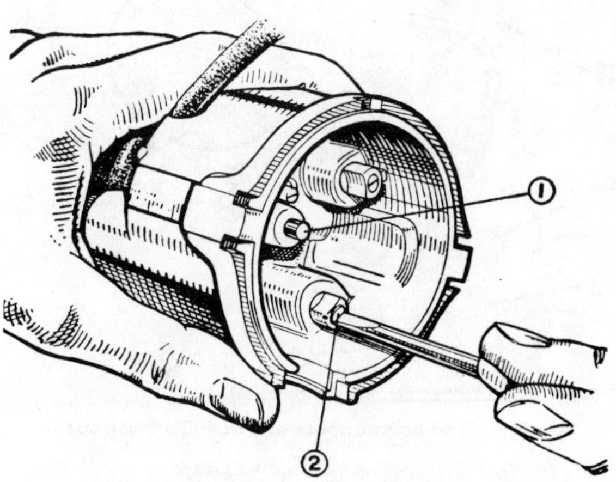

FIG 3 : 4 The method of fitting the high tension leads in the distributor cap

Key to Fig 3 : 4 1 Carbon brush 2 Cable securing screw

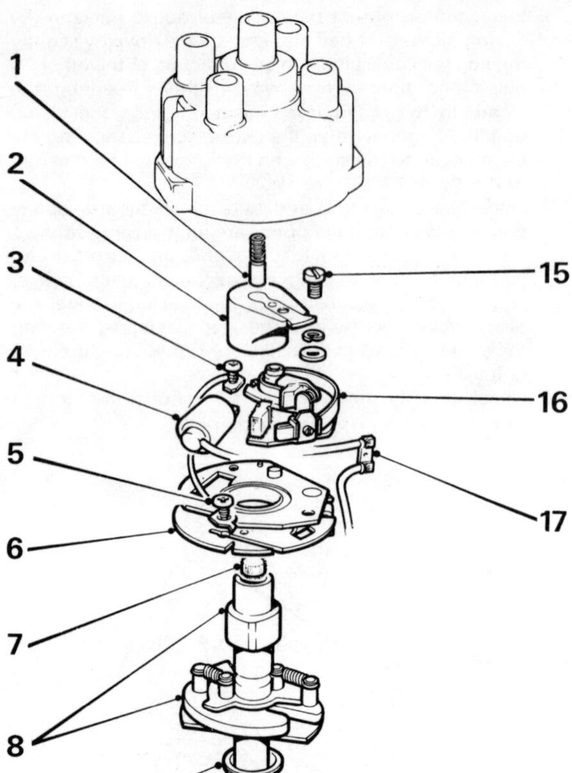

FIG 3:5 The components of the 45D4 distributor

Key to Fig 3:5 1 Pick-up brush and spring 2 Rotor 3 Screw for 4 Capacitor 5 Screw for 6 Baseplate 7 Felt pad 8 Cam and weights assembly 9 Spacer 10 Steel washer 11 Low-tension lead 12 Thrust washer 13 Drive dog 14 Pin 15 Screw for 16 Contact set 17 LT connector 18 Retaining screws for 19 Vacuum unit

9 When the car is running, fine adjustment of the ignition to suit a selected fuel is obtained by adjusting the knurled nut on the vacuum advance unit. Each graduation on the barrel represents 5 deg. alteration to the timing and requires 55 'clicks' of the knurled nut. Where applicable, this operation must be followed by an exhaust emission check.

3:7 High tension cables

The high tension cables work under great electrical stress and should be periodically inspected for cracked or perished insulation and unserviceable terminations. If cables are renewed use only the correct type.

To fit the cable to the ignition coil terminal, thread the moulded terminal over the cable, bare the end of the cable wire for about $\frac{1}{4}$ inch and thread the wire through the brass washer removed from the old cable. Bend back the wire strands evenly round the face of the washer as shown in **FIG 3:3** and screw the terminal and new cable end firmly into position.

The high tension cables are fitted to the distributor cover by slackening the screws inside the cover, removing all remnants of old cable, inserting the new cable ends through the waterproof cover and into the holes in the distributor cover. As the screws are tightened (see **FIG 3:4**), they will pierce the cable insulation and make contact with the wire core. Make sure ample cable is allowed to avoid any mechanical strain when the cables are connected to the sparking plugs and maintain the cables clean and free from grease.

3:8 Sparking plugs

The correct types of sparking plugs should always be used as specified by the manufacturers. Models in the Mini series use Champion N5 or N9Y plugs.

Sparking plug condition has a marked effect on the general behaviour of the vehicle, and therefore regular attention to these items is well worth the time spent. Cleanliness, particularly of the area around the electrodes and the centre electrode insulation, is most important. First of all, however, inspect the plugs for their appearance at the time of removal from the engine.

In their normal condition, they should exhibit a greyish brown powdery deposit with slight erosion of the electrodes, in which case cleaning and gap setting is all that need be undertaken. Abrasive blasting at the service agent's workshop is a most effective treatment. A fine file may be used to brighten up the electrode working surfaces. Make sure all abrasive is removed afterwards.

Sludgy oil deposits indicate excessive oil entering the combustion chambers. In this case attention to the engine is the only real cure but the use of suitable hotter-running plugs may be a temporary palliative.

Excessive fuel, giving an over-rich mixture, causes sooty deposits. This may be due to incorrect carburetter adjustment, excessive motoring under stop-start conditions preventing the plugs becoming hot enough to burn away the deposits, or excessive use of the mixture control (choke).

Overheated and burnt plugs usually exhibit a whiteish burnt or blistered appearance on the insulator nose and heavily eroded electrodes. Weak mixture, inefficient cooling or excessive motoring at or near full throttle may be the cause.

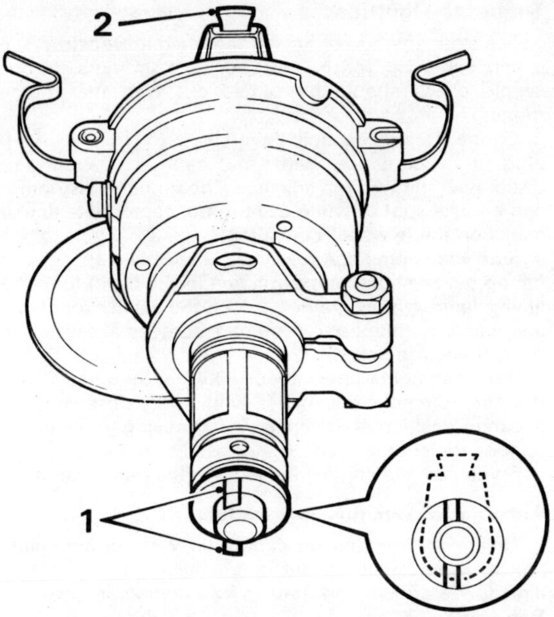

FIG 3:6 Fitting the drive dog to the distributor, note the position of the driving tongues 1 relative to the rotor arm electrode 2

After cleaning the plugs, the gaps should be set to .025 inch by bending the side electrode only, for which a special gap-setting tool is made by the plug manufacturers. If the plugs cannot be seated by hand, clean out the threads in the cylinder head by using a suitable tap or an old sparking plug with three or four saw-cuts down the threads, fit new gaskets and tighten the plugs to 30 lb ft. torque.

When connecting the high tension cables to the plugs, observe the correct firing order which is: 1 3 4 2.

3:9 Checking low tension circuit

If there appears to be a fault in the low tension circuitry, check for continuity as follows. No reading indicates a fault in the specified section of the wiring:

1 Battery to starter solenoid switch. Connect the voltmeter between the starter terminal and a good earthing point.
2 Starter solenoid switch to control box terminal A (brown lead). Voltmeter connected to control box terminal A and earth.
3 Control box. Voltmeter connected to control box terminal A1 and earth.
4 Control box terminal A1 and feed terminal of ignition switch (brown with blue lead). Voltmeter connected to switch feed terminal and earth.
5 Ignition switch. Voltmeter connected to switch terminal marked 2 and earth.
6 Ignition switch to fusebox terminal A3 (white lead). Voltmeter connected to terminal A3 and earth.
7 Fusebox terminal A3 to ignition coil terminal SW (white lead). Voltmeter connected to terminal SW and earth.
8 Ignition coil. Disconnect the cable at terminal CB. Voltmeter connected to terminal CB and earth.
9 Ignition coil to distributor (white with black lead). Disconnect the distributor low tension lead. Voltmeter connected to end of this cable and earth.

All the above tests are carried out with the ignition switch on and the contact breaker points open.

3:10 Distributor type 45D4 (1974)

This distributor type differs only slightly from that described earlier in this chapter, the most noticeable points are the absence of a vernier adjustment and the provision of a one-piece contact breaker set. Removal is similar to that already detailed, overhaul is carried out as follows (see **FIG 3:5**).

Dismantling:

Remove the distributor cap, rotor arm 2 and the felt pad 7 from inside the cam spindle 8.

Remove the two screws 18, tilt the vacuum unit to release the operating arm and withdraw it.

Push the low-tension lead 11 and grommet inside the body.

Remove the screw 5 and lever the slotted segment of the base plate 6 from its retaining groove and lift out the base plate assembly.

Drive out the retaining pin 14 and remove the drive dog 13 and thrust washer 12. The shaft, complete with the advance mechanism, can now be withdrawn. Do not unnecessarily dismantle this any further.

Press in the moving contact spring and detach the LT connector 17 from the spring loop.

Remove screw 3 to release the earth lead and capacitor, remove screw 15 and lift out the contact set 16.

If any of the moving parts or the cam are worn or damaged, renew the complete shaft assembly.

If the shaft is loose in its bearing, the complete distributor must be renewed.

If the spring between the plates of the base plate assembly is damaged or if the plates cannot move freely, renew the assembly.

Carry out the usual checks on the distributor cap and rotor and renew if necessary.

Reassembling:

This is a reversal of the dismantling procedure, but note the following points.

Lubricate the moving parts as described in **Section 3:2**.

Fit the thrust washer 12 with the raised pips towards the drive dog. Fit the drive dog, as shown in **FIG 3:6**, with the driving tongues parallel with the rotor arm and to the left of its centre line. Secure the pin in the dog by ring punching the holes.

Refer to **FIG 3:7**. Fit in the base plate assembly with the two prongs 4 straddling the screw hole 3 below the cap clip. Press the plate in until it engages the undercut.

Carefully measure the diameter A at right angles to the slot in the base plate. Position the earth lead, fit and tighten the base plate securing screw and then re-measure the diameter across the register. If the measurement has not increased by at least .006 inch (.15 mm), the base plate assembly must be renewed.

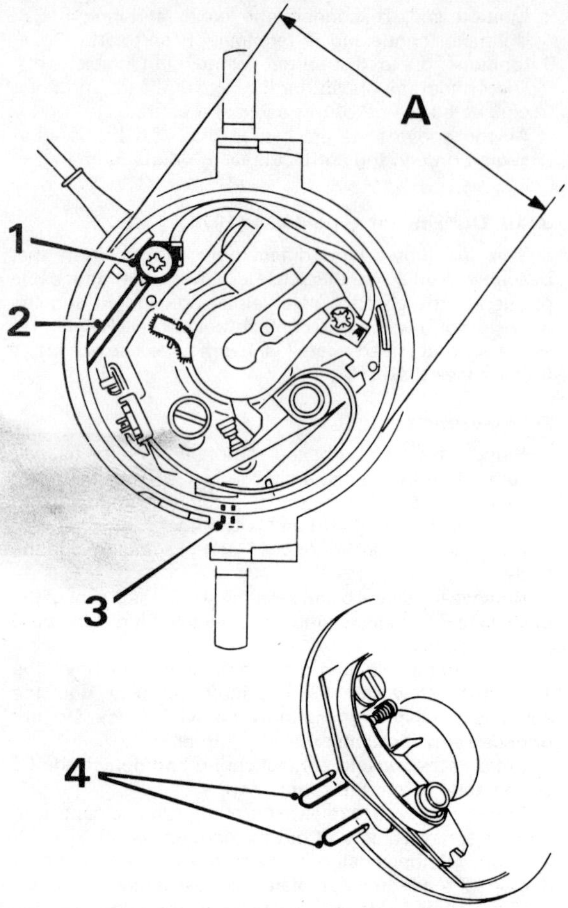

FIG 3:7 Fitting the baseplate assembly

Key to Fig 3:7 1 Securing screw 2 Slot in baseplate 3 Screw hole 4 Prongs A Position for diameter check

Check that the prongs in the base plate still straddle the screw hole and fit the vacuum unit, engaging the arm with the moving plate pin.

Set the contact points to .014 to .016 inch (.36 to .40 mm).

Timing the ignition:

The static method of timing described in **Section 3:6** is applicable, but for the most accurate setting a stroboscopic check should be carried out with the engine running.

Connect a stroboscopic timing lamp to No. 1 sparking plug in accordance with the maker's instructions, disconnect the vacuum advance pipe from the distributor and apply a spot of white paint to the appropriate timing marks on the flywheel/convertor.

Start the engine and run it at the specified speed. The timing marks should appear in line in the beam from the timing lamp. If they are not, loosen the distributor clamp and carefully rotate the distributor body as necessary to bring them into line.

Run the engine up to about 2000 rev/min and check that the automatic advance is working by observing the apparent position of the timing mark moving to the left or right as the engine speed is increased or reduced.

Switch off the engine and remove the timing lamp.

Automatic transmission models:

Timing the ignition on cars fitted with an automatic transmission is carried out in a similar manner to that already described and further information is given in **Section 6a:3**.

3:11 Fault diagnosis

(a) Engine will not fire

1 Battery discharged
2 Contact breaker points dirty, pitted or out of adjustment
3 Distributor cap dirty, cracked or 'tracking'
4 Carbon brush inside distributor cap not in contact with rotor
5 Faulty cable or loose connection in low tension circuit. Check circuit as outlined in **Section 3:9**
6 Distributor rotor arm cracked
7 Faulty coil
8 Broken contact breaker spring
9 Contact breaker points stuck open

(b) Misfiring

Check 1 2 3 5 and 7 in (a)
1 Weak contact breaker spring
2 High tension coil and plug leads cracked or perished
3 Sparking plug loose
4 Sparking plug insulation cracked
5 Sparking plug gap incorrect
6 Ignition timing too far advanced

CHAPTER 4

THE COOLING SYSTEM

4 : 1 Principle of system

The engine is cooled by the circulation of coolant through passages in the cylinder block, the coolant itself being cooled during its flow through the radiator. The coolant circulates by thermosyphon action assisted by a coolant pump. The system works under slight pressure imposed by a spring-loaded radiator cap, which allows a higher temperature to be reached before the coolant boils. Heat generated by the engine raises the temperature of the coolant in the cylinder block. The hot coolant then rises and passes through the thermostat to the radiator header tank, where cooling begins as the coolant passes downwards through the radiator core. External air flow through the radiator core, assisted by a fan, causes the surplus heat to be dispersed.

The coolant returns to the lower end of the jacket to be reheated and recirculated. The centrifugal coolant pump assists in quick circulation of the coolant, thus enabling a comparatively small radiator to be employed. The thermostat restricts circulation until the coolant reaches its designed running temperature thus reducing the time required for the engine to warm up.

4 : 2 Maintenance, flushing, belt tension, antifreeze

The system is drained by opening the taps shown in **FIGS 4 : 1** and **4 : 2** at the base of the radiator and on the lefthand side of the cylinder block at the rear, looking towards the radiator although on later cars the radiator tap may be omitted and removal of a hose is necessary. When draining the system make sure the car is standing level.

Before draining the system allow the engine to cool right down. If it becomes necessary to remove the filler cap when the engine is at full running temperature, take care to turn the cap gradually until the retaining tongues are felt to engage the lobes on the end of the filler spout cam. Allow the pressure to subside before removing the cap further, and protect the hand from steam.

The radiator should be flushed out twice annually to remove loose solids by running clean water through it until the water comes out clear. Once a year the radiator should be back-flushed by forcing clean water through the bottom outlet. If desired, a flushing adaptor 18G.187, shown in **FIG 4 : 3** can be obtained to assist this operation.

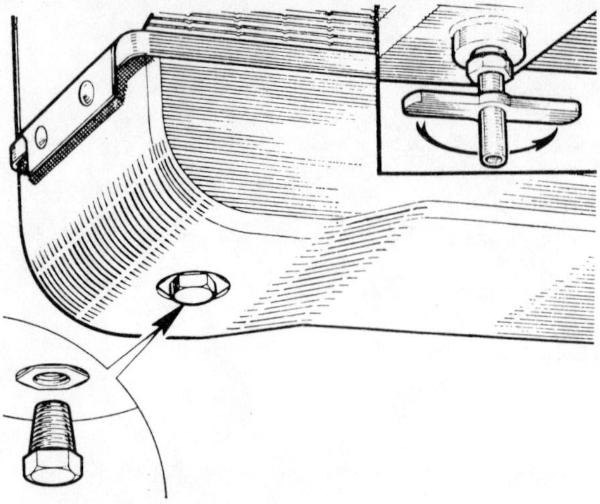

FIG 4:1 Radiator drain plug or tap. Turn anticlockwise, viewed from below, to open

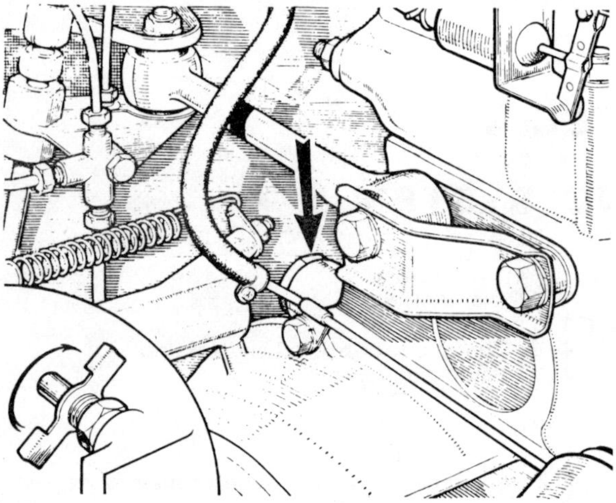

FIG 4:2 Cylinder block drain plug or tap

FIG 4:3 Radiator reverse flush adaptor, 18G.187

To minimize the deposition of mineral solids in the radiator and cylinder block passages, it is advisable to use only soft or clean rainwater when filling or topping-up the system. After refilling the system, inspect all round for leaks at connections and security of the hose clips.

Adjustment of the fan belt to its correct tension is important. If it is too loose it will slip on the pulleys and cause engine overheating and the generator failing to charge the battery. If too tight, excessive wear will occur in the generator and coolant pump bearings. Adjustment is carried out by slackening the four generator attachment points shown in **FIG 4:4**, and moving the generator bodily by hand until the correct tension is obtained, which is at the point where it is possible to move the belt about ½ inch each way at the centre of its longest run.

If the belt has stretched too much to achieve this condition, a new one must be fitted. Remove the old one by slackening the generator pivot and adjusting link bolts. Lift the generator, release the belt from the crankshaft pulley and manoeuvre it out between the fan blades and the radiator, as shown in **FIG 4:5.** The knack is to feed the belt between each blade tip and the cutout in the cowling flange for withdrawal. Fit the new belt by reversing these operations. Adjust the tension correctly and tighten up the generator fixings securely.

It is advisable to add an antifreeze liquid to the coolant water during winter months to protect the engine and radiator from damage due to frozen coolant. Draining, to prevent freezing does not protect the heater matrix, therefore always use antifreeze coolant in cars with heaters. Use only solutions of the ethylene-glycol type. Any solutions conforming to BS.3151 or BS.3152 are recommended by the car manufacturers. The correct proportions of antifreeze for various degrees of frost protection are as follows:

Solution	*Commences to freeze*	*Frozen solid*	*Quantity of antifreeze*
25%	9°F (—13°C)	—15°F (—26°C)	1½ pints
33⅓%	—2°F (—19°C)	—33°F (—36°C)	2 pints
50%	—33°F (—36°C)	—53°F (—48°C)	3¼ pints

4:3 Coolant pump removal

To remove the coolant or water pump proceed as follows:

1 Disconnect battery, drain cooling system, remove bonnet. Remove fan belt and disconnect generator electrical connections. Remove outer bolt attaching adjusting slide to generator and remove generator by taking out two top mounting bolts. See **FIG 4:4**.

2 Remove cowling upper support bracket and the two bolts securing cowling lower support bracket to the engine mounting.

3 For cars fitted with one-piece cowling, disconnect top radiator hose and completely remove lower radiator hose. Remove the four screws securing the cowling to the radiator and lift out the radiator followed by the cowling.

4 For cars fitted with two-piece cowlings, disconnect top and bottom radiator hoses from the engine. Remove the six screws securing the cowling to the radiator, remove cowling top half. Bend lower hose outside of lower cowling half and lift out radiator.

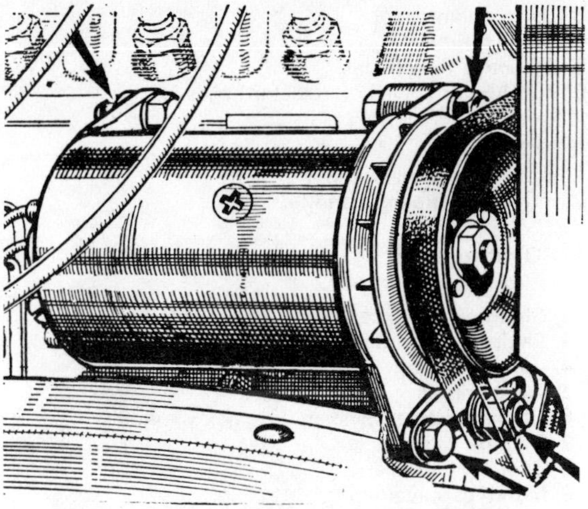

FIG 4 : 4 Bolts for adjusting fan belt tension

5 Slacken the bypass hose clips, remove the four set-screws securing the pump to the cylinder block and remove pump.

4 : 4 Dismantling

The operations required to dismantle the coolant pump are as follows:

1 Withdraw the bearing locating wire through the hole in the top of the pump body, then tap the spindle rearwards to extract the spindle and bearing assembly.
2 Using a suitable extractor, pull off the vane and remove the pump seal assembly.

Inspect all parts for wear, damage and especially for corrosion. Slight corrosion can be contained by applying a reliable anti-corrosive paint on parts subject to the coolant.

If the bearing is worn a new spindle and bearing assembly complete must be fitted. The carbon seal is also renewed as a complete assembly if defective.

4 : 5 Reassembly

Reassembly and refitting are the reverse of dismantling, but particular attention should be given to the following matters:

1 The hole in the bearing shown at A in **FIG 4 : 6** must line up with the lubricating hole in the pump body, under the oblique screw head.
2 Ensure that the interference fit of the fan hub was not impaired when withdrawing the hub from the spindle. If this has occurred, fit a new hub.
3 The bearing should be adequately lubricated with the correct grease, of one of the grades recommended by the manufacturers. Do not over-lubricate.
4 Referring to **FIG 4 : 6,** when reassembling the fan hub, the face of the hub shown at B must be flush with the end of the spindle. The clearance at C must be .020 to .030 inch.
5 Refit by reversing the removal instructions.

On later pumps the provision for adding lubricant is omitted; it is sufficient to apply a silicon-based grease to the impeller sealing face when assembling.

4 : 6 Thermostat removal and testing

Access to the thermostat is obtained by draining the cooling system, disconnecting the top hose and removing the cowling upper support bracket. The thermostat cover is then detached from its securing studs, spring washers and nuts, the paper joint washer removed and the thermostat lifted out.

The thermostat opening temperature is tested by placing the unit in water and raising the temperature of the water to 180°F (82°C). If the valve then fails to open

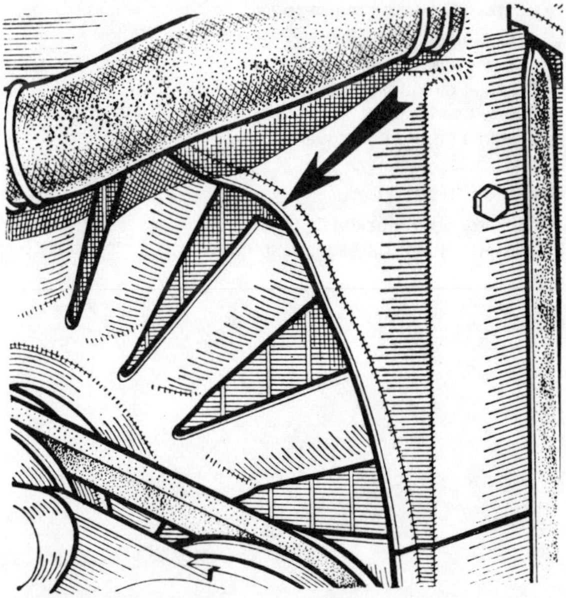

FIG 4 : 5 To fit a new fan belt, manoeuvre it over the fan blade tips and through the recess provided in the radiator cowling

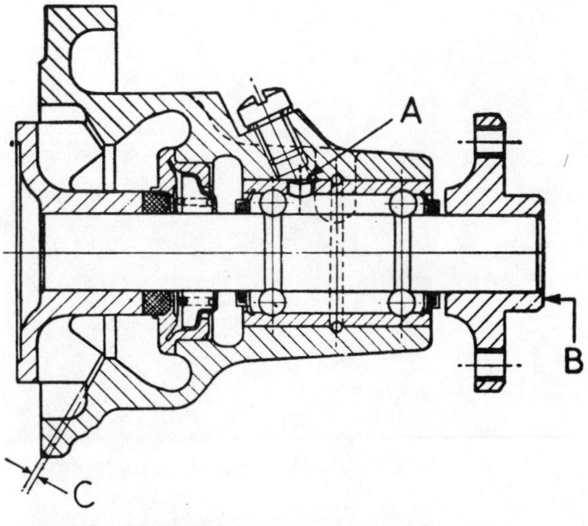

FIG 4 : 6 A sectional view of the coolant pump

Key to Fig 4 : 6 A Holes to coincide for insertion of lubricant B Face of hub flush with end of spindle C .020 to .030 inch or sticks in the fully or partially open positions as the unit cools, the thermostat should be renewed. Repair should not be attempted.

Use a new paper joint when refitting the thermostat in the reverse manner of its removal. Some later cars have a wax-element type thermostat fitted, with a modified thermostat outlet cover. When refitting this type of thermostat, it is essential that the threaded stem faces upwards.

4:7 Fault diagnosis

(a) Internal water leakage

1 Cracked cylinder wall
2 Loose cylinder head nuts
3 Cracked cylinder head
4 Faulty head gasket
5 Cracked tappet chest wall

(b) Poor circulation

1 Radiator core blocked
2 Engine coolant passages restricted
3 Low coolant level
4 Loose fan belt
5 Defective thermostat
6 Perished or collapsed radiator hoses

(c) Corrosion

1 Impurities in the coolant
2 Infrequent draining and flushing

(d) Overheating

1 Check (b)
2 Sludge in crankcase
3 Faulty ignition timing
4 Low oil level in sump
5 Tight engine
6 Choked exhaust system
7 Binding brakes
8 Slipping clutch
9 Incorrect valve timing
10 Retarded ignition
11 Mixture too weak.
12 Faulty radiator cap

CHAPTER 5

THE CLUTCH

5 : 1 Construction and operation

The clutches fitted to the BMC Mini series of cars are orthodox in principle but a little unusual in application in that the friction surface of the flywheel is the front surface and not the rear face. Consequently the driven plate 20 in **FIG 5 : 1** is also in front of the flywheel and the moving pressure plate 19 in front of the driven plate. This arrangement disposes of the need for the three arm toggle mechanism commonly employed for clutch actuation and permits release of the pressure plate by direct forward motion of the pressure spring housing 13 which is bolted to three rearward facing bosses on the pressure plate. These protrude through suitably positioned holes in the flywheel disc 17. Location of the pressure plate and pressure spring housing is by means of three flexible leaf springs or straps 16 bolted to the flywheel rear face and additionally secured by the three bolts attaching the pressure plate bosses to the pressure spring housing.

Outward movement of the slave cylinder pushrod causes the lower end of the clutch operating lever to move forwards with its pressure pad or thrust bearing, so compressing the springs and forcing the pressure plate away from the driven plate. The driven plate is thereby released from the flywheel and is able to rotate freely with the crankshaft primary gear 22 on the crankshaft.

Earlier type clutches employed six coil springs 4 to hold the clutch in engagement. Later type clutches use a single circular shaped diaphragm spring as in **FIG 5 : 2**.

Generally, the instructions which follow apply to both types of clutch, but any alterations to procedure required by virtue of this modification will be mentioned as necessary.

5 : 2 Maintenance

Very little maintenance is possible on the clutch proper while it is still installed in the power unit. However, one adjustment should not be neglected. As clutch wear takes place, the pressure plate 19 moves further rearwards, so allowing the pressure spring housing 13 to approach more closely to the operating lever pressure pad or thrust bearing and reduce the clearance at this point. If neglected, this may subsequently cause clutch slip. The correct method of maintaining the clearance is to pull the operating lever as far back as possible away from the engine and using a feeler gauge, check that there is a clearance of .060 inch between the operating lever and the head of the adjustment bolt. If this clearance is less than .060 inch slacken the locknut and adjust the stop (adjustment) bolt accordingly. For later clutches with the 'throw-out' stop', this clearance must be .020 inch.

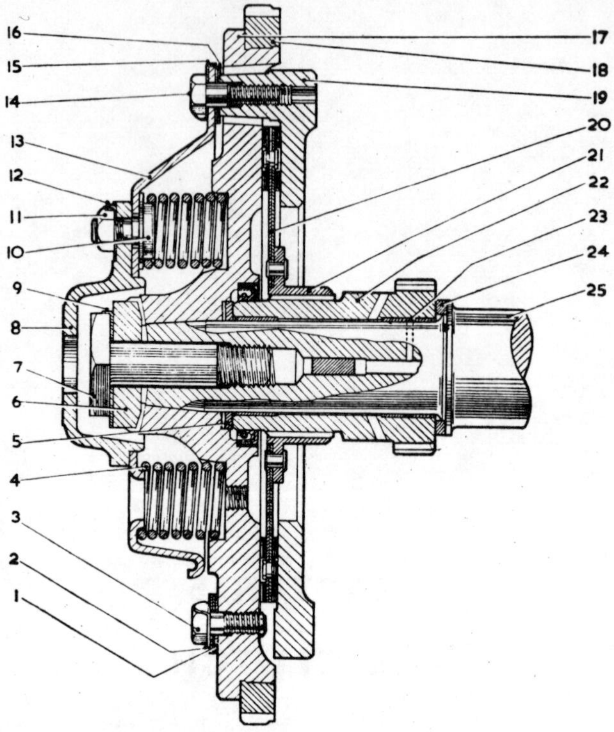

FIG 5 : 1 Section through the coil spring clutch showing the component parts

Key to Fig 5 : 1 1 Driving strap 2 Lockwasher 3 Driving pin 4 Pressure spring 5 Circlip 6 Keyed washer 7 Flywheel screw 8 Thrust plate 9 Locking washer 10 Pressure spring guides 11 Guide nut 12 Lockwasher 13 Pressure spring housing 14 Driving pin 15 Lockwasher 16 Driving strap 17 Flywheel 18 Starter ring 19 Pressure plate 20 Driven plate 21 Driven plate hub 22 Crankshaft primary gear 23 Primary gear bearing 24 Thrust washer 25 Crankshaft

The clutch 'throw-out' stop shown in **FIG 5 : 3** is a device fitted to later models to prevent excessive movement of the pressure plate during clutch disengagement. No adjustment is normally required unless the stop has been removed for any reason during overhaul or servicing in order to attend to the clutch thrust bearing or plunger.

If necessary, adjust as follows:

1 Release the locknut and unscrew the stop away from the clutch cover boss to the limit of its travel.
2 Have an assistant to depress the clutch pedal to the full extent of its travel and hold it in this position.
3 Screw the 'throw-out' stop forwards against the clutch cover boss.
4 Release the clutch pedal to fully engage the clutch and screw the 'throw-out' stop a further .007 to .010 inch towards the boss, equivalent to approximately one flat of the hexagon locknut.
5 Securely tighten the locknut and check the clearance at the lever stop bolt. If necessary, readjust it to .020 inch.

A condition known as clutch overthrow may arise in certain circumstances, which can be damaging to the crankshaft thrust washers. This may result in the possibility of their disintegration and further damage to the transmission from metal particles carried in the lubricating oil.

The two likely causes of this condition are:

1 Stiffness in the clutch operating mechanism preventing the operating lever returning fully to its disengaged position.
2 Incorrect clutch pressure springs being unable to compress to the full amount.

To test for this condition, run the engine up to full running temperature and allow it to idle at not more than 500 rev/min. Depress and release the clutch pedal three or four times in succession without pausing, and notice if the engine slows down appreciably or stops. If this happens, overthrow is occurring.

Examine the external operating mechanism for stiffness at any or all points and fit a new operating lever return spring. Apply a drop of lubricating oil to the pivot pin, clevis pin and operating plunger to ensure freedom of movement. Repeat the stalling test. If there is no apparent improvement, increase the clearance between the lever and the stop bolt to .075 inch and test again. If there is still no improvement the clutch must be dismantled and

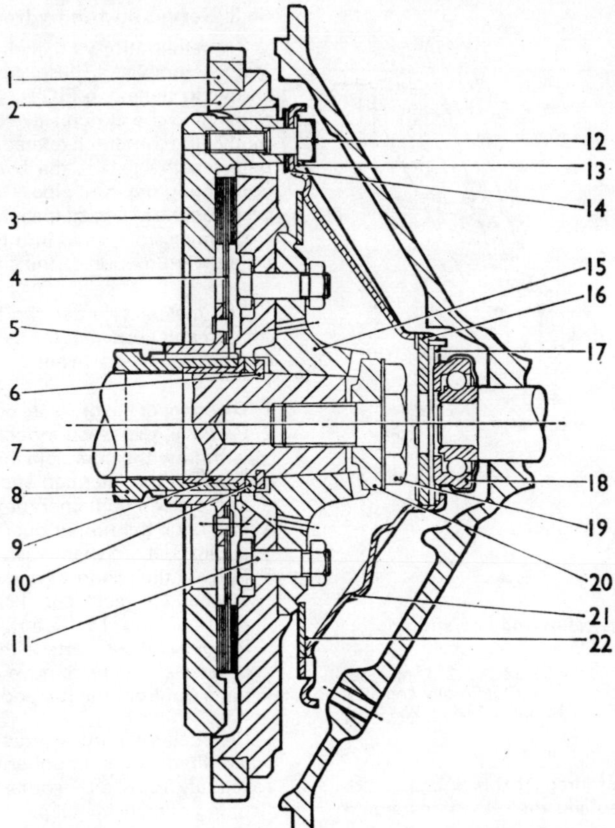

FIG 5 : 2 Section through the diaphragm spring clutch showing the component parts

Key to Fig 5 : 2 1 Starter ring 2 Flywheel 3 Pressure plate 4 Driven plate 5 Driven plate hub 6 Circlip 7 Crankshaft 8 Crankshaft primary gear 9 Primary gear bearing 10 Thrust washer 11 Flywheel hub bolt 12 Driving pin 13 Lockwasher 14 Driving strap 15 Flywheel hub 16 Thrust plate 17 Plate retaining spring 18 Thrust bearing 19 Flywheel screw 20 Keyed washer 21 Cover 22 Diaphragm spring

the pressure springs investigated. It is probable that an incorrect set of springs has been fitted at some time past. Correct identification of springs for each model is given in the Technical Data Section.

Clutch drag is a condition in which there appears to be the partial transmission of torque through the clutch in the disengaged state. It may arise particularly in power units having the lubricated crankshaft primary gear. If it is only due to cold or congealed oil between the crankshaft primary gear bushes and the crankshaft, it can be overcome quickly by running the engine with the clutch disengaged and one of the gears selected with the car stationary. It will be observed that this causes the crankshaft to rotate in the crankshaft primary gear bushes.

Drag may also be caused by air in the hydraulic system preventing the correct release of the clutch operating mechanism. In this event check the hydraulic system, rectify any defects and carefully bleed the system to rid it of any air bubbles.

If drag is apparently due to incorrect adjustment of the operating lever stop and/or somewhat excessive crankshaft end float the clearance of the operating lever stop can be adjusted, taking into account the crankshaft end float, by the following method:

1 Mount a dial test indicator with its probe on the pulley at the crankshaft front end.

2 By any suitable and safe means prise the crankshaft rearwards (towards the flywheel) and set the indicator to zero reading.

3 Operate the clutch pedal, thereby applying a forward thrust to the crankshaft and read the new gauge reading. This represents the crankshaft end float and if it is excessive some attention to the crankshaft thrust washers is required. When adjusting the clutch operating lever stop bolt, hold the crankshaft in the forward position to take account of the end float.

It is possible but most unlikely that the crankshaft oil seal when fitted, may become displaced, and in this

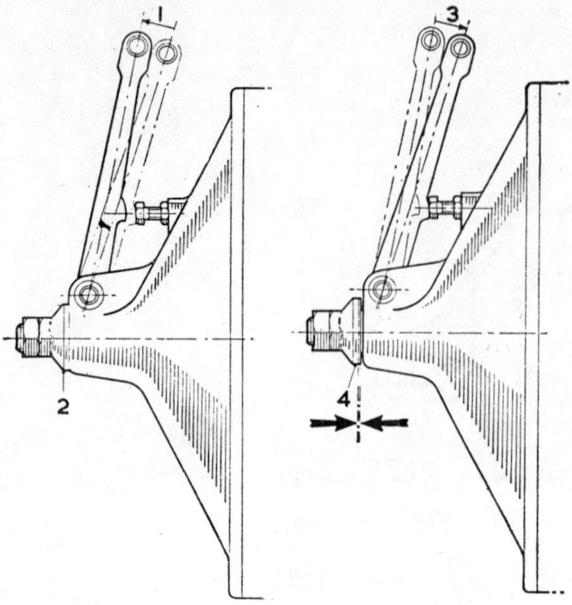

FIG 5 : 3 The release plunger showing the shouldered (throw-out) stop

Key to Fig 5 : 3 1 Clutch fully released 2 Throw-out stop screwed up to the cover boss 3 Clutch fully engaged 4 Stop screwed up a further .007 to .010 inch (.178 to .254 mm) towards the cover boss

condition, contribute to clutch drag. If this is suspected, the clutch must be dismantled and the oil seal inspected and if necessary, renewed. Only fit a replacement having a metal outer casing and apply a light smear of jointing compound to the interior of the seal housing before inserting the seal. This should lock the new seal safely in position.

5 : 3 Servicing the hydraulic system

The straightforward hydraulic system comprises two main assemblies. These are the clutch master cylinder shown in section in **FIG 5 : 4**, and operated by the clutch pedal; and the clutch slave cylinder, shown in **FIG 5 : 5**, motivating the clutch operating lever. The only connection between the two is the hydraulic fluid enclosed in the connecting pressure pipe. The force exerted by the clutch pedal on the piston of the master cylinder causes a flow of (incompressible) fluid into the slave cylinder resulting in an outward motion of the slave piston.

The master cylinder can be removed by taking out a splitpin and removing the clevis pin securing the pushrod 1 to the pedal lever. Then:

1 Disconnect the pressure pipe union from the end plug 7.
2 Remove two securing bolts from the flange 3 and withdraw the complete master cylinder assembly.
3 Take off the filler cap and drain off the hydraulic fluid into a clean container for future use.
4 Pull back the rubber dust cover 2, remove the internal circlip 8, the dished washer 9, the pushrod 1.
5 Pull out the piston 11 and secondary cup 10, the piston washer 12, main cup 13, spring retainer 14 and the return spring 15. If any difficulty is experienced in removing these parts without using sharp implements or pieces of wire, remove the end plug 7 and push the parts out from the top end of the cylinder.

Clean all the parts as much as possible with Lockheed brake fluid. It is important that all parts should be absolutely free of dirt or other foreign matter and additional cleaning of some metal parts using petrol or solvents may be necessary. If these are used make sure they do not come into contact with the rubbers and that all parts are free of such materials before reassembly. Also make sure all traces of dirt and other foreign matter are removed from the interior of the reservoir tank.

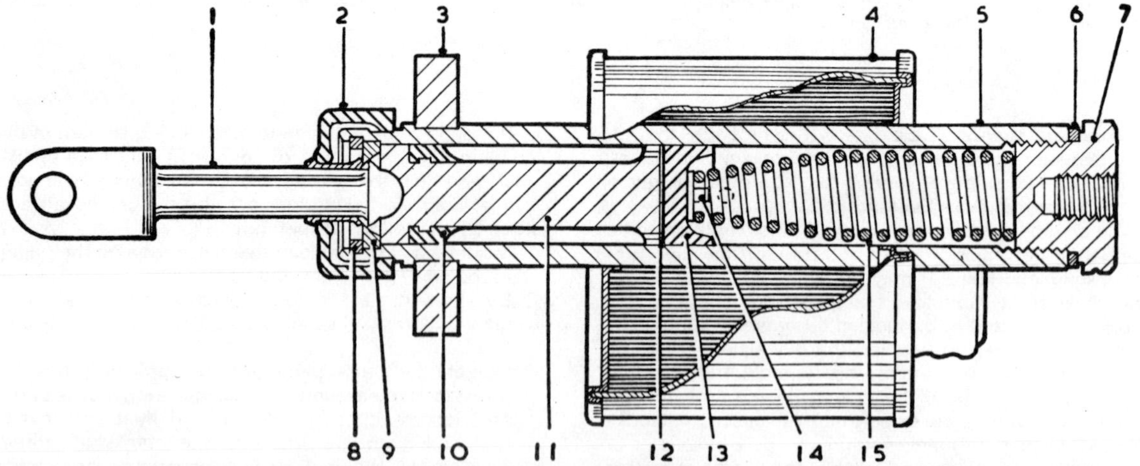

FIG 5 : 4 Section through the clutch master cylinder showing the component parts

Key to Fig 5 : 4 1 Pushrod 2 Rubber boot 3 Mounting flange 4 Supply tank 5 Body 6 Washer 7 End plug 8 Circlip 9 Stop washer 10 Secondary cup 11 Piston 12 Piston washer 13 Main cup 14 Spring retainer 15 Return spring

Carefully inspect the parts for wear and especially the rubber components for abrasion at the sealing surfaces, cracks or severe permanent distortion. Generally speaking it would not be an extravagance to renew all the rubbers during this service.

When reassembling the unit, wet all parts with hydraulic fluid for lubrication and make sure all the rubbers are fitted the right way round and that they sit correctly in their respective positions. Note that the spring is assembled with the small end towards the piston and do not forget to position the piston washer and spring retainer.

The main cup is entered into the cylinder, lip first. Finally, fit the pushrod, circlip and rubber dust cover.

Refit the unit to the bulkhead crossmember, connect the pressure pipe loosely and fill the reservoir to within $\frac{1}{4}$ inch of the bottom of the filler neck with Lockheed Super Heavy Duty Brake Fluid. Line up the pushrod yoke with the pedal lever, insert the clevis pin and splitpin and lock securely. Do not bleed the system at this stage as the slave cylinder has yet to receive attention.

To remove the slave cylinder, first disconnect the pressure pipe, then remove the splitpin and clevis pin from the clutch operating lever. Unscrew two securing bolts and spring washers and lift the unit off. Thoroughly clean the outside of the unit before dismantling as follows:

1 Remove the pushrod 8 (**FIG 5 : 5**) and notice that this item has no retaining device.

2 Carefully remove the rubber dust cover 7.

3 Take out the internal circlip 6 retaining the piston 4, remove the piston, rubber cup 3, the cup filler 2 and the spring 1.

Inspect and clean all parts as instructed for the master cylinder, giving special attention to the rubber parts. Renew as necessary, lubricate with hydraulic fluid and reassemble in the correct order, noting the manner in which the piston, piston cup and cup filler are assembled. Make sure the circlip is properly fitted after the piston has been inserted in the bore of the cylinder. Replace the rubber dust cover and the pushrod, then refit the slave cylinder to the engine and connect up the pressure pipe.

Connect the pushrod and clutch operating lever, lock the clevis pin in position and tighten the pressure pipe at both ends. Bleed the system as described in **Section 5 : 7.**

5 : 4 Removing the clutch

This operation may require engine removal according to whether a coil spring clutch or diaphragm clutch is fitted. Details of the removal and refitting operations together with a mention of some service tools required are given in **Chapter 1, Section 1 : 8.** The owner is advised to consult a service agent before undertaking further work on the clutch. This may be especially advisable if it is intended to fully dismantle the clutch.

Inspection should include the coil springs for distortion, the pressure spring housing for distortion, checked by placing the housing face downwards on a surface plate and checking round with feeler gauges, and for elongation of the driving pin holes.

Check the driving pins 14 for ridging, wear and distortion, and if any defects exist change all three.

Check the driving straps 16 for distortion and elongation of the holes. If any defects exist, renew all three.

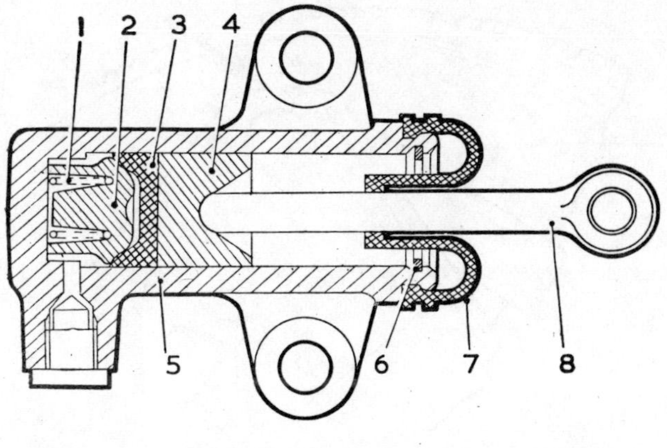

FIG 5 : 5 Section through the clutch slave cylinder showing the component parts

Key to Fig 5 : 5 1 Spring 2 Cup filler 3 Cup 4 Piston 5 Body 6 Circlip 7 Rubber boot 8 Pushrod

If the flywheel or pressure plate surfaces are badly scored, the components concerned should be renewed.

For the diaphragm spring clutch inspect and renew generally to the instructions for coil spring clutches. Additionally, check the diaphragm spring for defects and distortion, and the ball thrust bearing for any wear, looseness or other damage.

5 : 5 Driven plate condition

To ensure further satisfactory service check the clutch driven plate friction liners as follows:

1 A shiny glazed appearance without discolouration of the liners is quite normal.

2 A much darker glazed appearance which obscures the grain of the liner material indicates that oil is finding its way on to them. This calls for a check of the crankshaft primary gear oil seal. The condition may cause clutch slip under load and difficulty in disengagement.

3 Where the liners are fixed with rivets, the overall thickness should be such that there is no imminent danger of the rivets coming into contact with the flywheel or pressure plate surfaces. If the rivets are almost flush with the liner surfaces, exchange the driven plate for one with new linings.

4 Check also that the linings are securely attached to the driven plate disc and that there is no defect in the attachment of the disc to the hub.

5 Inspect the hub splines and the splines on the crankshaft primary gear. These should be a nice sliding fit with no undue slackness.

5 : 6 Reassembly, refitting and plate alignment

For reassembly of the clutch proper, the services of the service agent are best employed as he will have available the essential special tools. Generally reassembly is the reverse of dismantling but the following points are given special attention:

1 The marks A (**FIG 5 : 6**) on the pressure plate and pressure spring housing should be opposite the 1/4 mark on the flywheel.

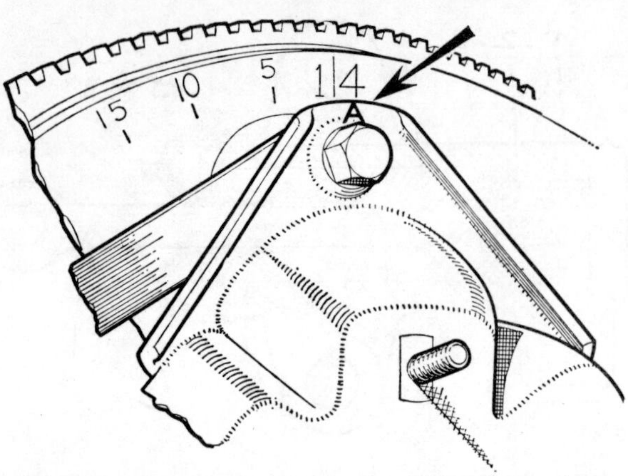

FIG 5 : 6 Fitted position of the clutch pressure spring housing with the balance mark A opposite the 1/4 mark on the flywheel

2 If the driving straps have been removed for inspection or renewal it is essential to ensure that the spacing washers are refitted between them and the flywheel face.

3 The driven plate and flywheel hub should be correctly positioned (centralized) using service tool 18G.571. When applied, assemble the driving straps, springs and pressure spring housing, and using the service tool 18G.304M or 18G.304N (for the diaphragm spring clutch) tighten up the housing nuts evenly. Insert the driving pins and also tighten these up evenly, a turn at a time to a torque of 16 lb ft. Remove the service tools.

4 Before refitting the flywheel and clutch to the crankshaft, check that the crankshaft has not been turned from the TDC position for Nos. 1 and 4 pistons.

Refit the flywheel and clutch to the crankshaft as described in **Chapter 1**, making sure that the keyed washer is correctly fitted and using a new tab washer. Lock securely after tightening the flywheel centre bolt to a torque of 110 lb ft.

Check the operating lever clearance at the clutch return stop and that the lever return spring is not stretched or distorted. Apply a drop of lubricant to the operating lever pivot and the slave cylinder pushrod clevis pin. Make sure the latter is securely fixed with a new splitpin.

5 : 7 Clutch cover alignment

If the operation of the clutch, or the condition of any of its components, suggest a degree of misalignment, the cover assembly can be accurately fitted or corrected as follows.

After removing the engine/transmission assembly from the car, remove the cover retaining screws and pull off the clutch end cover.

Remove the starter motor and the clutch/flywheel assembly as described in **Section 1 : 8**.

Refer to **FIG 5 : 7**. Remove the splitpin and washer 3 and pull out the clevis pin 4. The release lever 5 can now be withdrawn from the release bearing plunger.

Unscrew the plunger stop and locknut 2 and pull out the release bearing assembly 6.

Clean the clutch cover and the crankshaft taper and apply engineers blue to the clutch cover register.

Fit the alignment tool 18G 1247 into the cover and refit the cover, as shown in **FIG 5 : 8** with the tool locating over the tapered end of the crankshaft.

If the cover is pushed fully home and pulled off again, misalignment markings will be apparent on the marking blue. File off the high marked areas of the register.

This procedure should be repeated as necessary, the aim being to bring the cover into full contact with the flywheel housing without any force being required, to ensure correct alignment of the cover with the crankshaft.

When the alignment is satisfactory, secure the cover with two retaining bolts.

Two holes must now be drilled, diametrically opposite each other, through the flanges of the cover and the flywheel housing as shown in inset B of **FIG 5 : 8**. Suitable locating dowels for use in these holes are needle rollers from an old bearing, so use a drill of appropriate size to ensure an interference fit.

Remove the cover and take out the alignment tool.

Lubricate the operating surfaces and refit the release bearing and plunger, release lever and clevis pin and secure with a new splitpin.

Refit the clutch assembly and the clutch cover, fitting the securing bolts loosely. Drive in the two locating dowels to secure the correct alignment of the cover and then tighten the bolts.

Check and, if necessary, adjust the clutch throwout stop and the return stop. Refit the engine/transmission unit in the reverse order of removal as described in **Chapter 1**.

5 : 8 Bleeding the hydraulic system

If for any reason the hydraulic operation of the clutch is ineffective, spongy, or the clutch is difficult to operate into or out of engagement, it is possible that some air has found its way into the hydraulic fluid. This may be due to a slight and very gradual loss of hydraulic fluid and a consequent fall in the level of fluid in the reservoir. Check the hydraulic pipes for leakage at the unions and tighten as necessary. If there is no external leak visible at these points but there is some fluid around the master or slave cylinders, the internal seals may be defective and further investigation and servicing is required as in **Section 5 : 3**. After any rectification of defects, the system must be bled to rid it of any air trapped in the hydraulic fluid or components. First top up the level of hydraulic fluid in the reservoir and bleed the system as follows:

1 Unscrew the bleed valve on the slave cylinder about three-quarters of a turn.

2 Attach a rubber tube to the bleed valve and place the other end of the tube in a clean container having in it about an inch depth of hydraulic fluid.

3 With the help of an assistant, depress the clutch pedal, closing the bleed valve at the end of its stroke and allowing the pedal then to return to its 'up' position.

4 Open the bleed valve again and repeat this operation until clear fluid free from bubbles is delivered from the tube.
5 Close the bleed valve tightly and top-up the level of hydraulic fluid in the reservoir at the master cylinder.
6 Note that if the bleeding process is prolonged for any reason and a considerable quantity of fluid is pumped through the system it may be necessary to replenish the fluid in the reservoir before the operation has been completed in order to ensure that no air enters the system. If this happens it will be necessary to start the bleeding operation over again.

5:9 Fault diagnosis

Some of the major faults possible in these clutches have been described in the foregoing sections. Other possible troubles may occur as follows:

(a) Clutch drag

1 Oil or grease on the friction linings
2 Leaking master cylinder, slave cylinder or pipeline
3 Driven plate hub binding on crankshaft primary gear
4 Crankshaft primary gear bushes dragging on crankshaft
5 Distorted driven plate
6 Damaged linings
7 Fault in hydraulic operation

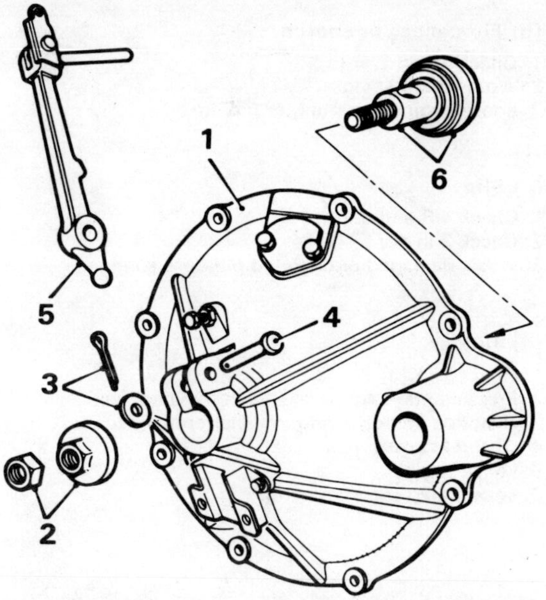

FIG 5:7 Removing, or refitting, the clutch release mechanism

Key to Fig 5:7 1 Clutch cover 2 Plunger stop and locknut 3 Washer and splitpin 4 Clevis pin 5 Release lever 6 Release bearing assembly

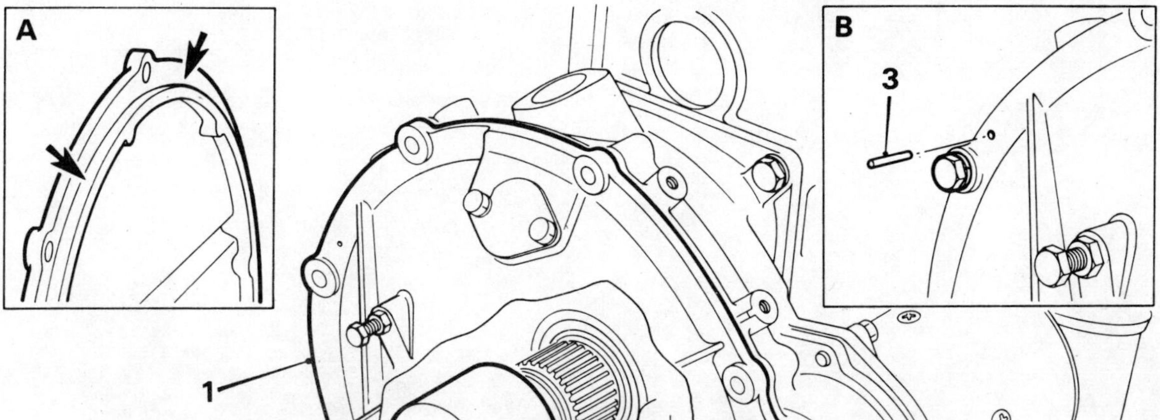

FIG 5:8 Aligning the clutch cover with the crankshaft and flywheel housing. Inset A: File off high spots (arrowed) from the cover register. Inset B: Drilling the cover flange for locating dowel

Key to Fig 5:8 1 Clutch cover 2 18G 1247 3 Locating dowel

(b) Fierceness or snatch

1 Check 1 and 2 in (a)
2 Worn clutch linings
3 Loose engine mounting or tie rod

(c) Slip

1 Check 1 3 and 6 in (a)
2 Check 2 in (b)
3 Weak, damaged or distorted pressure springs

(d) Judder

1 Check 1 in (a) and 3 in (b)
2 Pressure plate not parallel with flywheel face
3 Distorted linings giving irregular contact surface
4 Distorted driven plate
5 Loose engine
6 Loose drive shaft couplings

(e) Rattle

1 Faulty linings presenting uneven contact area
2 Worn release mechanism or loose thrust bearing

(f) Knocking noise at clutch

1 Check 3 in (c)
2 Damaged splines in driven plate hub or on crankshaft primary gear
3 Worn out or damaged thrust bearing or plunger
4 Loose flywheel
5 Faulty Bendix drive on starter motor

(g) Driven plate fracture

1 Check 2 in (d)
2 Contact area of driven plate linings not evenly distributed
3 Careless driving
4 Corrosion weakness in material
5 Incorrect assembly
6 Broken driving straps or damaged driving pins

CHAPTER 6

THE TRANSMISSION

6:1 General description

In these cars the gears and differential assembly are housed in the transmission casing which also forms the lower crankcase and sump. The lateral arrangement of the gears provides for a final drive to the differential unit by means of helical reduction gears direct from the third motion shaft to the differential cage. The cage is enclosed in a small extension casing on the rear face of the transmission casing. The larger of the two final drive gears, that is the gear attached to the differential cage, protrudes into the main transmission casing so that engagement with the smaller gear on the third motion shaft is possible.

It will be observed that no crownwheel and pinion of the type normally used in rear axles to convert longitudinal to lateral drive is necessary. Short final drive shafts complete the transmission of power from the differential gears to the universal couplings which carry the inner ends of the external drive shafts. These shafts terminate in constant velocity universal couplings at the front road wheels and will be described in **Chapter 7** together with the front suspension.

At the engine end of the transmission system power is conveyed from the clutch driven plate, through its centre hub splines, to the crankshaft primary gear. An idler gear is positioned between the crankshaft primary gear and the first motion shaft of the transmission gear train.

Four forward speed and one reverse gears are provided, with synchromesh engagement on second, third and top forward gears on early models. After 1968 all four forward gears are synchronized. Two types of synchronizers are fitted, according to car model and serial number, but these do not affect the procedures to be described in the following pages.

A number of special Service Tools are recommended by BMC for dismantling and reassembly of the transmission unit and therefore owners are advised to consult their local BMC Agent before and during the work. Whilst it will be possible to improvise in some cases, the use of the Service Tools is strongly recommended and in most cases will be found essential if damage is to be avoided.

6:2 Maintenance

Maintenance is concerned mainly with lubrication matters. As the transmission unit is lubricated by the same lubricating oil as that circulating in the engine, it is essential to use only a type and grade of lubricant recommended by BMC and to ensure that this is maintained at the correct level at all times as indicated by the engine oil dipstick. The car manufacturers recommend changing multigrade oils at 6000 miles intervals and monograde oils at 3000 miles intervals. There is also a grease lubricating nipple for the gear change shaft. Relubrication at this point is recommended at major overhaul periods only.

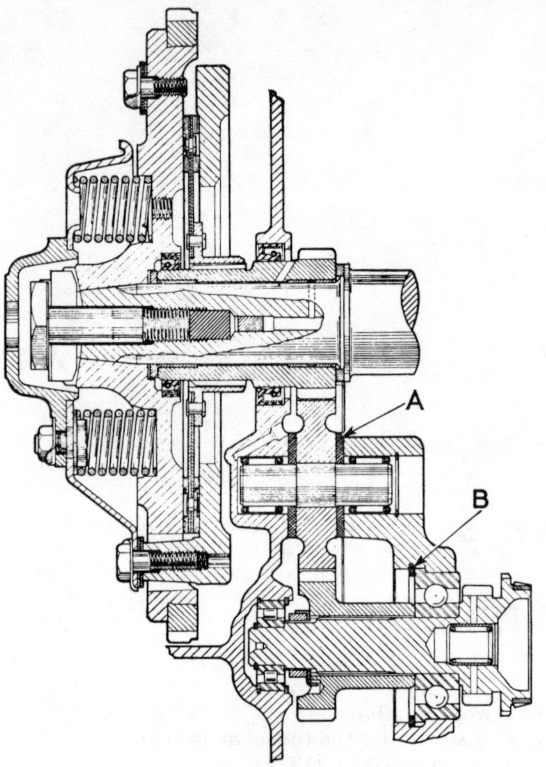

FIG 6 : 1 Section through the idler gear and first motion shaft

A The idler gear must have from .003 to .008 inch end float. **B** Take the measurement between the first motion shaft bearing face and the bearing register. Use Service tool 18G.569 for this purpose.

For measurements (B)	*Use circlip Part No.*
.096 to .098 inch	2A.3710
.098 to .100 inch	2A.3711

Occasionally, the road dirt should be cleaned off the back faces of the inboard universal coupling flanges so that it does not work its way into the final drive oil seals and destroy them by abrasion.

6 : 3 Removing and dismantling

This operation is detailed fully in **Chapter 1, Sections 1 : 8** and **1 : 21**. The location of the idler gear bearings is shared between the transmission casing for the front bearing, and the flywheel housing for the rear bearing. The rear roller bearing of the first motion shaft is also fitted into a recess in the flywheel housing. **FIG 6 : 1** is a section through a portion of the drive showing the arrangement of these gears and shafts. Remove the idler gear and thrust washers, noting the positions of the thrust washers on each side of the idler gear disc and marking them if necessary. A Service Tool 18G.581 shown at **FIG 6 : 9** is used by BMC Agents for removal of the idler gear needle roller bearings if desired.

Remove the differential unit as follows:

1 Take out four setscrews 3 **FIG 6 : 2** and remove the gearchange extension bottom cover plate. Remove the clamp screw securing the lever to the remote control shaft and remove the shaft. Take out the Nylon seating and tension spring from the remote control shaft and the shaft lever.

2 The right and lefthand drive shaft flanges are secured to the final drive shafts in the differential unit by slotted nuts 24 and split pins, see **FIG 6 : 3.** Remove the flanges 23, holding them, if possible with Service Tool 18G.669, shown at **FIG 6 : 10** while undoing the nuts. Do not in any event use a lever against the transmission casing to restrain the flanges during this operation if the Tool is not available.

3 Unscrew five setscrews 21 at each final drive end cover and remove the covers, noting the number of shims 20 under the lefthand cover. Keep the sets of parts together for correct reassembly.

4 Remove the four differential housing stud nuts indicated at 2 **FIG 6 : 2** and remove the differential assembly.

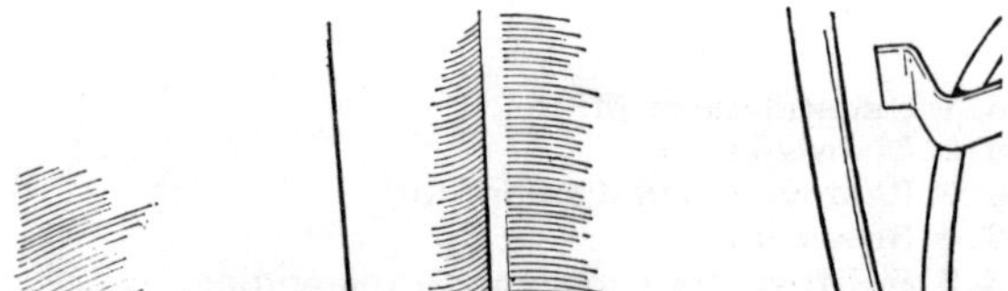

FIG 6 : 2 Rear of the transmission assembly from beneath the car

Key to Fig 6 : 2 1 Change speed lever retaining screws 2 Three of the four differential stud nuts 3 Extension coverplate screws 4 Exhaust pipe front fixing point 5 Plugs, interlocking plungers, and spring

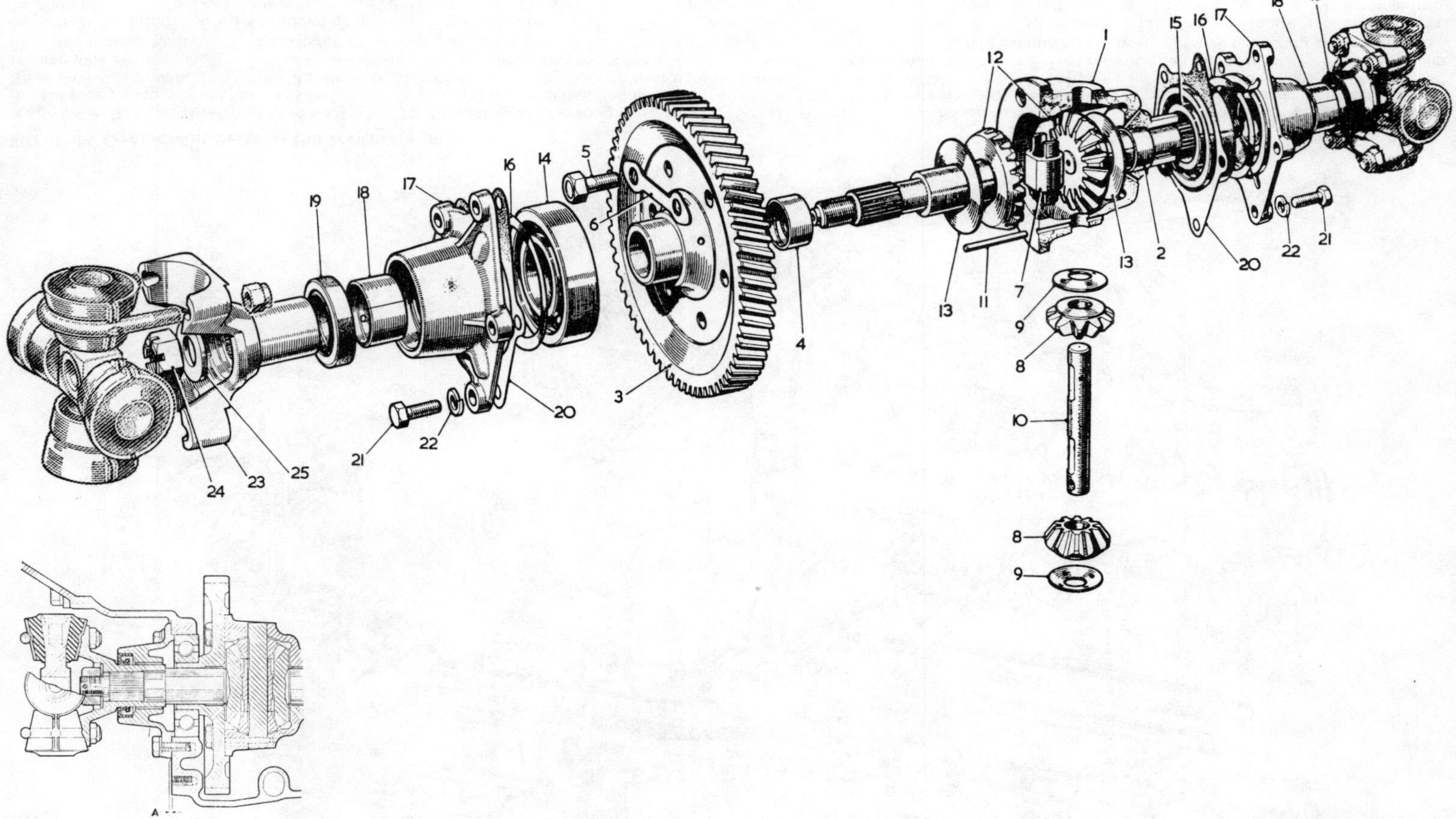

FIG 6:3 Component parts of differential and final drive. A is the point at which feeler gauge measurements should be taken for determination of the thickness of shims for pre-load on the differential bearings.

Key to Fig 6:3 1 Differential case 2 Bush 3 Differential drive gear 4 Drive gear bush 5 Drive gear securing bolts 6 Securing bolt locking washers 7 Thrust block 8 Differential pinion 9 Pinion thrust washer 10 Pinion pin 11 Peg for pinion pin 12 Differential gears 13 Thrust washers 14 Drive gear ballbearing 15 Differential case ballbearing 16 Shims 17 End covers 18 Bush 19 Oil seal 20 End cover joint 21 End cover screws 22 Spring washers 23 Final drive flange 24 Slotted nut for final drive flange 25 Washer

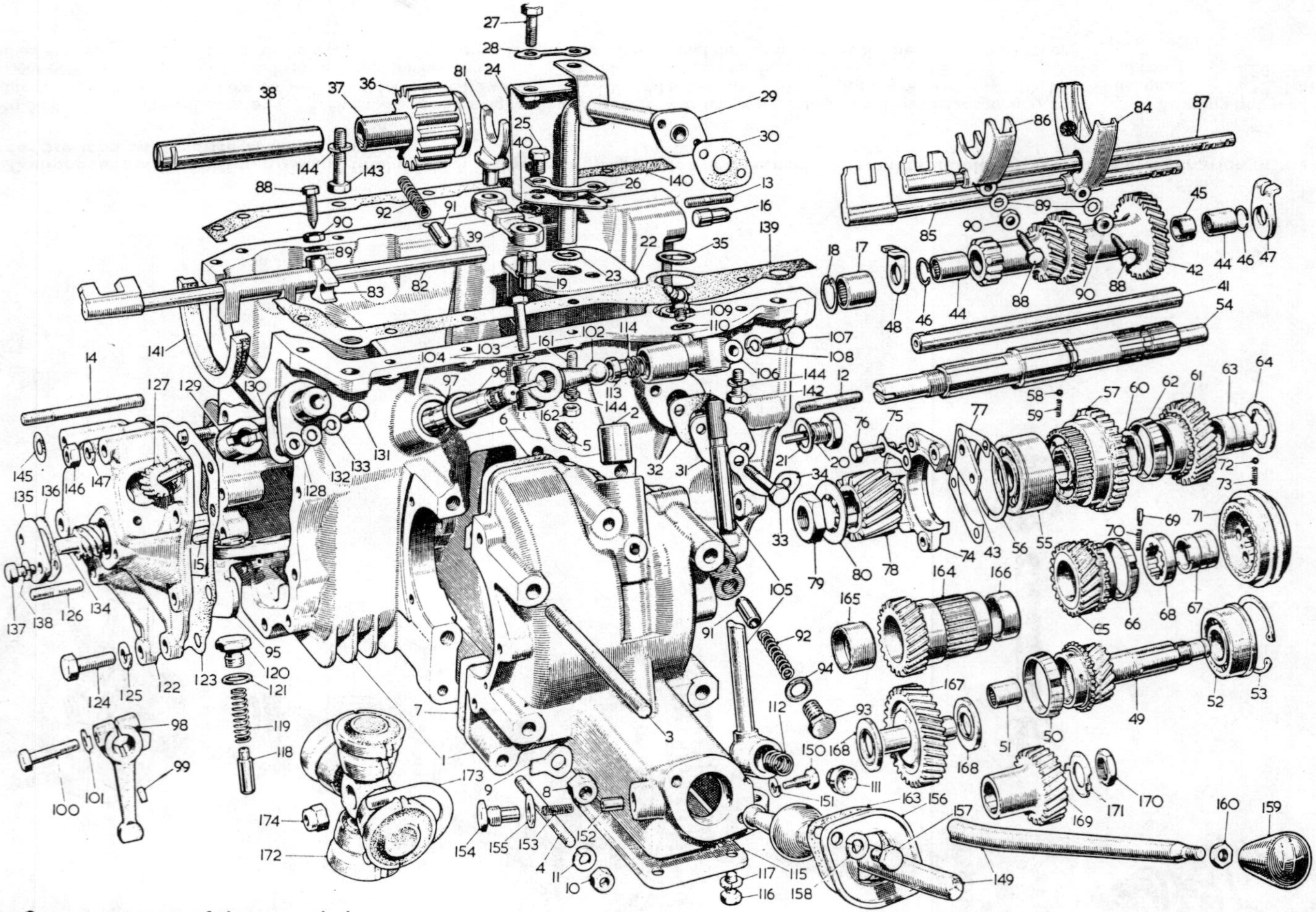

FIG 6:4 Component parts of the transmission.

Key to Fig 6:4 (Parts referred to in text) 19 Reverse gear operating lever pin 22 Oil strainer 27 Bracket screw 28 Locking washer 29 Oil suction pipe 30 Oil pipe flange internal joint washer 31 Oil pipe external flange 32 Oil pipe flange external joint washer 33 Oil pipe flange securing screw 36 Reverse gear with bush 38 Reverse gear shaft 39 Reverse gear operating lever 41 Layshaft 42 Laygear 43 Locating plate for layshaft and reverse gear shaft 47 Rear thrust washer 48 Front thrust washer 49 First motion shaft 52 First motion shaft ballbearing 53 Circlip 54 Third motion shaft 55 Third motion shaft ballbearing 57 First speed gear and synchronizer 61 Second speed gear 63 Second speed gear bush 64 Interlocking ring 65 Third speed gear 67 Third speed gear bush 68 Thrust washer 69 Thrust washer peg 70 Spring 71 Third and fourth gear synchronizer 74 Retainer 75 Locking washer 76 Screw 77 Shim 78 Final drive pinion 79 Pinion retaining nut 80 Lock washer 81 Reverse fork 84 Third/fourth speed fork 85 Third/fourth speed fork rod 86 First/second speed fork 87 First/second speed fork rod 88 Locating screw 90 Locating screw locknut 97 Gear change shaft oil seal 98 Change speed operating lever 99 Key 118 Reverse check plunger 119 Spring 120 Plug 122 Front cover 124 Cover securing screw 127 Speedometer pinion 131 Cover retaining screw 134 Speedometer gear wheel 135 End plate 137 End plate screw 146 Front cover and mounting bracket stud nut 169 First motion shaft drive gear 170 Drive gear securing nut 171 Locking washer 172 Trunnion rubber mounting 173 U-bolt 174 Nut for U-bolt

Continuing to dismantle the separated differential unit:

1 Withdraw the two final drive shaft ballbearings 14. For this operation an extractor or a Service Tool 18G.2, shown in **FIG 6 : 11,** is used by BMC Agents.
2 Unlock and remove the six set bolts 5 securing the large final drive gear 3 to the differential cage 1. Mark the gear and cage for reassembly, and separate the two.
3 Take out the differential gear 12 and thrust washer 13 from the bore of the large gear.
4 Tap out the taper pin 11 to release the pinion spindle 10 and remove the spindle, two pinions 8 and thrust washers 9. Finally remove the second differential gear 12 and thrust washer 13.

The component parts of the transmission are illustrated in **FIG 6 : 4. FIG 6 : 5** shows a section through the third motion shaft main ballbearing and bearing retainer. Dismantle the transmission carefully as follows, making sure the position, orientation and function of each part is properly understood so that there can be no mistake during reassembly. Mark the parts as necessary to ensure this:

1 Take out the plug 120 for the reverse detent plunger and remove the plunger 118 and spring 119.
2 Remove the clamp 98 and key 99 from the inner end of the gearchange operating shaft 96 and pull out the shaft. Take care with the oil seal 97 in the transmission casing.
3 Remove the speedometer housing securing screw 131 and take out the pinion 127. Take out two setscrews 137 and remove the speedometer gear retaining plate 135 from the transmission case front cover. Withdraw the gear 134.
4 Remove the transmission case front end cover 122 by taking out five setscrews 124 and removing four nuts 146.
5 Unlock the tab 28 and remove the screw 27 securing the suction oil pipe 29 bracket to the lug on the transmission casing, slacken the second screw 27 and swing the locking washer 28 clear. Remove the two screws 33 through the pipe flange 29 and the external blanking plate 31, then withdraw the pipe. Notice the paper washers 30 and 32 under the flange and blanking plate. These may require renewal in due course. See **FIG 6 : 4.**
6 Unlock and remove four setscrews 76 and the locking plate 75 securing the third motion shaft bearing retainer 74 to the casing centre web. Take off the retainer and packing shims 77. Unlock and remove the nut 79, locking washer 80 and final drive pinion 78.
7 Remove the circlip and roller bearing from the inside of the end of the first motion shaft 49, then unlock the nut 170 at the other end, take off the nut and washer 171 and withdraw the driving gear 169.
8 Remove the layshaft and reverse shaft locking plate 43, push the layshaft 41 out of the transmission casing. Take out the laygear 42 and thrust washers 47 and 48, noting carefully their positions.
9 Remove the plugs 5 in **FIG 6 : 2** and take out the selector rod interlocking plungers and springs.

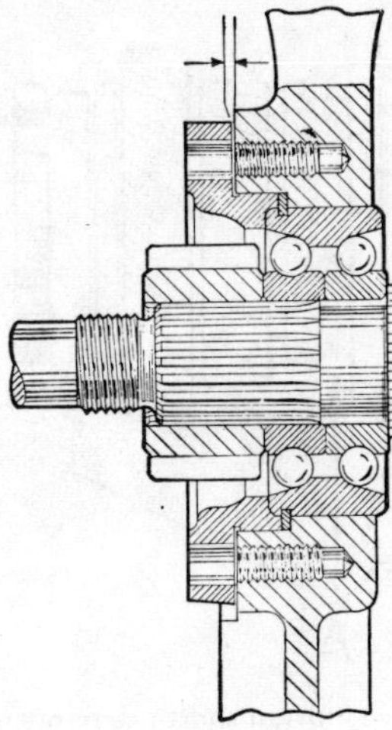

FIG 6 : 5 Section through the third motion shaft bearing and retainer. Use the table below to determine the correct thickness of shims to take up the gap indicated

When the gap is	*Use shims totalling*
.005 to .006 inch	.005 inch
.006 to .008 inch	.007 inch
.008 to .010 inch	.009 inch
.010 to .012 inch	.011 inch
.012 to .014 inch	.013 inch
.014 to .015 inch	.015 inch

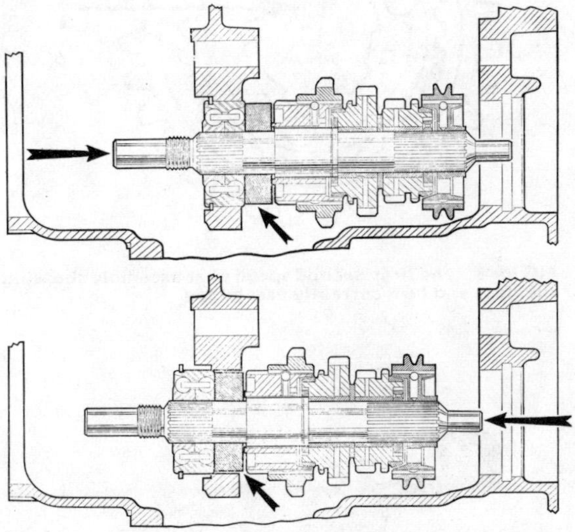

FIG 6 : 6 The correct method of removing the third motion shaft bearing using the Service Tool 18G.613

10 Take out the first motion shaft bearing circlip shown at B **FIG 6 : 1** and 53, **FIG 6 : 4** and withdraw the bearing 52 and shaft 49 from the casing. Service Tool 18G.284 and Adaptor 18G.284B illustrated in **FIG 6 : 12** are required for this operation.
11 Unlock the first and second speed selector fork 86. Withdraw the fork rod 87 and fork from the casing.

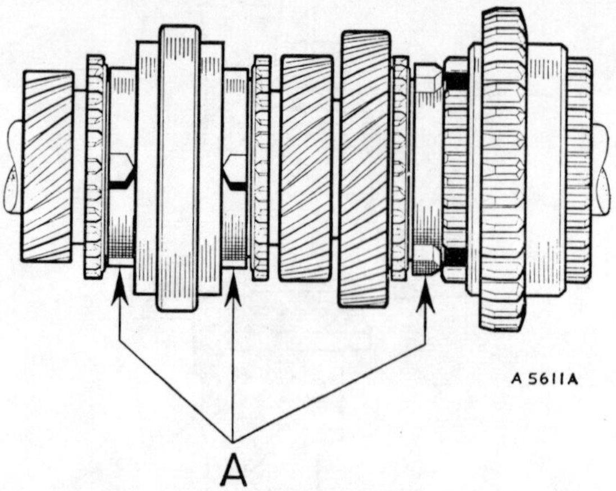

FIG 6 : 7 The third motion shaft assembly indicating at A the position of the baulk rings on later models

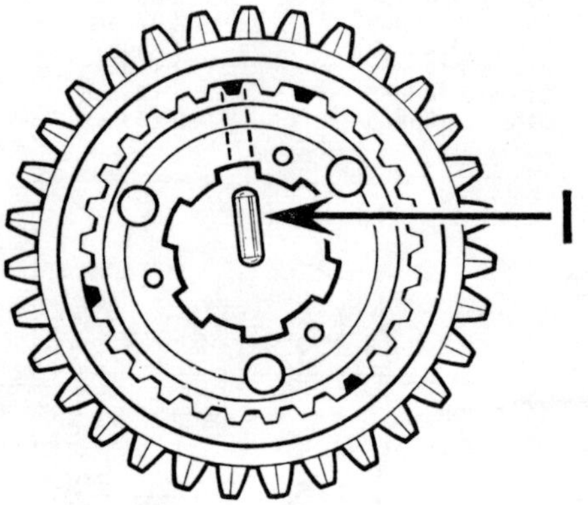

FIG 6 : 8 The first/second speed gear assembly showing the gear and hub correctly assembled

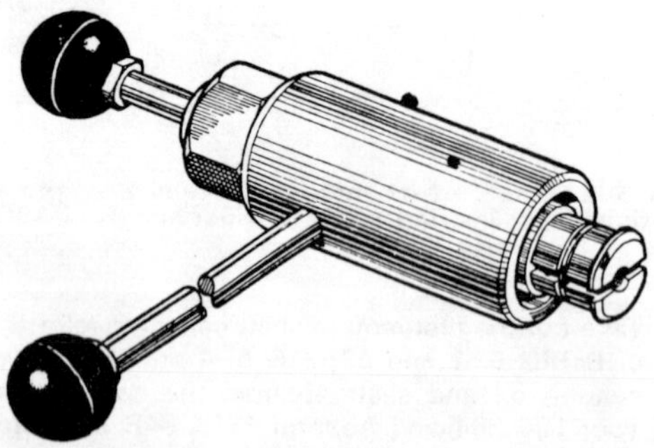

FIG 6 : 9 Service Tool 18G.581. The idler gear needle roller bearing remover

12 Refer now to **FIG 6 : 6.** Carefully drift the third motion shaft 54, **FIG 6 : 4** rearwards lefthand arrow (top) until the Service Tool 18G.613, lower arrow (top) can be placed between the first speed gear 57 and the double ballbearing 55 with the recessed face of the tool towards the bearing see **FIG 6 : 13,** then carefully drift the third motion shaft forwards, until the bearing is almost out of its housing in the casing web. Gently lever the bearing off the shaft and remove it and the shaft from the housing. During this operation take great care not to damage the selector forks.

13 Remove the strainer assembly 22, placing it on one side for future cleaning as mentioned in **Chapter 1,** release the locknut 90 and slacken the third/fourth selector fork locating setscrew 88. Take out the selector rod 85 and fork 84 from the casing.

14 Remove the reverse gear shaft 38, gear 36 and selector fork 81 and finally remove the circlip from the reverse gear shifter lever pivot pin 19 and remove the lever 39.

15 To dismantle the third motion shaft, first withdraw the third/fourth gear synchromesh hub 71 from the rear or flywheel end of the shaft 54.

16 Press down the rear thrust washer spring-loaded plunger 69 and turn the washer 68 until its splines register with those on the shaft. Slide off the washer and remove the plunger and spring 70. Remove third speed gear 65.

17 Withdraw third speed gear bush 67 and interlocking ring 64. Withdraw second speed gear 61 and bush 63, rear thrust washer 60 followed by first speed gear 57 with hub. Heat may be needed to remove the bushes, see **Section 6 : 4.**

18 On later units remove the first-speed gear, baulk ring and needle roller bearing from the opposite end of the shaft. Extract the needle roller bush with tool 18G2. Remove the reverse mainshaft gear and first/second synchronizer and baulk ring. Remove rear thrust washer, second-speed gear and split caged needle roller bearing.

If it is desired to separate the second, third and fourth speed gear striking dogs from the synchromesh hub and cone assemblies take care not to lose the balls and springs. Wrap the assemblies in a cloth to avoid loss when dismantling.

If the synchronising cones are severely worn they can be renewed by shrinking on new ones but the owner is strongly recommended to renew the second, third or fourth gears complete rather than attempt this work as rather special machining is necessary to ensure correct operation after fitting new cones, itself an unsuitable operation for the home workshop.

Baulk ring synchromesh is fitted to the transmission systems of all engines from Nos. 8WR.U.H6288, 8WR.Fa.U.H818 and to all engines of Hornet and Elf Mk II and III cars. Dismantling and reassembly are as detailed except that the second and third/fourth gear synchronizing units are fitted with baulk rings as shown in **FIG 6 : 7.**

Inspect all parts for wear, scoring, pick-up, scuffing of tooth surfaces and pitting. Examine gear bores for enlargement due to wear, shafts for signs of twisting, bushes for looseness in bores and on outside diameters, thrust washers for thickness, ballbearings for deterioration by cleaning and oiling lightly then moving the inner race to observe any slackness, springs for distortion and the transmission casing and differential housing for any signs of cracking or other damage. Make sure to clean out the interior of the transmission casing thoroughly and if metal particles are present endeavour to locate the source for special examination. Renew any defective parts.

6 : 4 Reassembly

Generally reassembly of the main (third motion) shaft is the reverse of dismantling but pay special attention to the following:

1 When reassembling the third-speed gear and bush on early units the rear thrust washer and first-speed gear and synchronizing hub, fit the cone side of the hub on the same side as the plain side of the first-speed gear teeth.

2 On early units it is essential to renew the two bushes 63 and 67 as the necessary interference fit was destroyed on removal. The new bushes are fitted by heating them to 180 to 200°C (356 to 392°F) and sliding them into position on the shaft, then allowing the whole to cool naturally. The interlocking ring follows the second-speed gear. The dogs of each half-bush must engage with the interlocking ring (between the bushes).

3 Position the third speed gear plain side first, insert the spring and plunger, depress the plunger, push the thrust washer over the plunger and turn it until the plunger engages the spline and locks the washer. The correct end float of the second and third speed gears is .0035 inch to .0055 inch. If it is outside these limits check the parts for excessive wear and renew as necessary before proceeding.

4 Refit the third/top speed synchromesh hub, plain side of outer teeth towards the retaining thrust washer, then fit the first/second speed hub ensuring that the cone side of the hub is on the same side of the assembly as the plain side of the first speed gear teeth.

If baulk ring type synchromesh is fitted and the first and second speed gear assembly has been dismantled, make sure when reassembling, that the plunger in the hub aligns with the cut-away tooth in the gear on assembly, otherwise it will not be possible subsequently to select first gear. See **FIG 6 : 8**.

On four-speed synchromesh units ensure that the long bosses on the sleeve and hub of the synchronizers are on the same side.

The third/fourth synchronizer must be fitted with the long boss on the sleeve facing the first motion shaft bearing.

The first/second synchronizer is fitted with the long boss towards the first-speed gear. Drift the needle roller bearing journal onto the third motion shaft with tool 18G.186.

Reassembly of other transmission components is again generally the reverse of dismantling but pay special attention to the following:

1 If removed, the reverse gear shifter lever pivot pin will need pressing into its position in the bottom of the transmission casing. Fit the shifter lever and circlip. Position the reverse gear and fork to engage the shifter lever, then push the reverse gear shaft through the

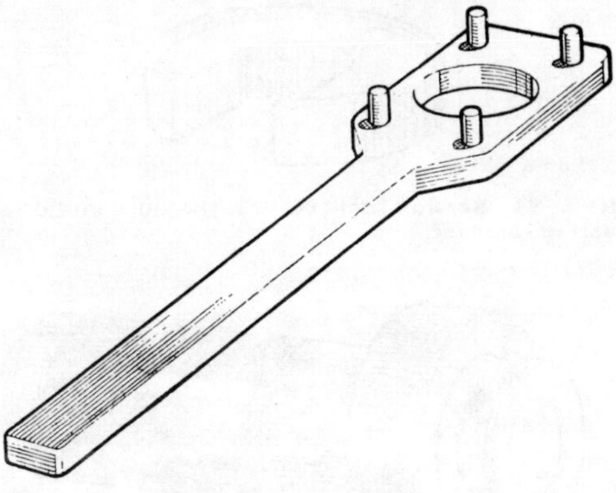

FIG 6 : 10 Service Tool 18G.669. The drive shaft coupling flange wrench

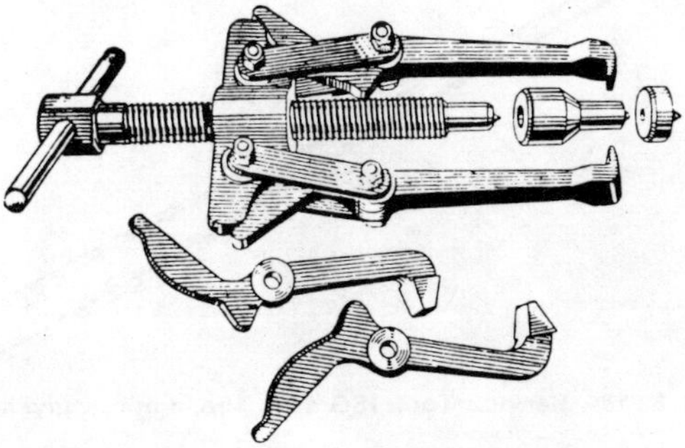

FIG 6 : 11 Service Tool 18G.2. The final drive shaft ballbearing remover

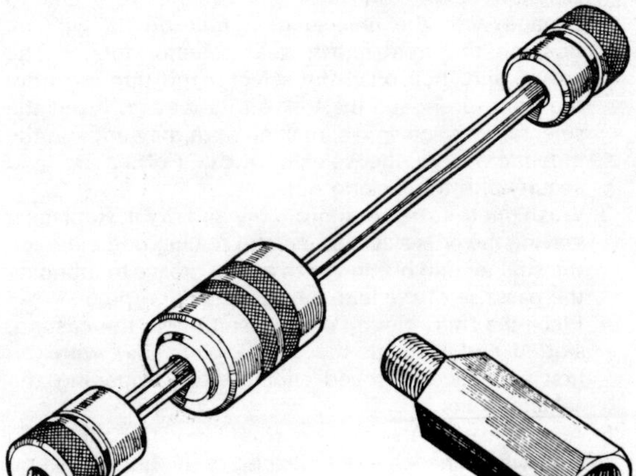

FIG 6 : 12 Service Tool 18G.284 and adaptor 18G.284B. The first motion shaft bearing remover and adaptor

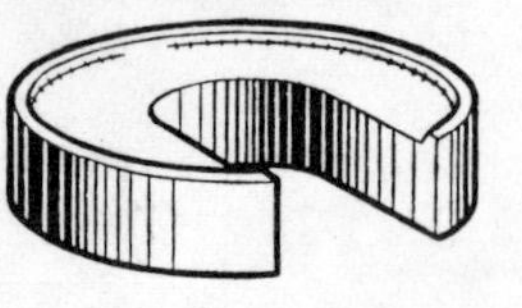

FIG 6 : 13 Service Tool 18G.613. The third motion shaft bearing remover

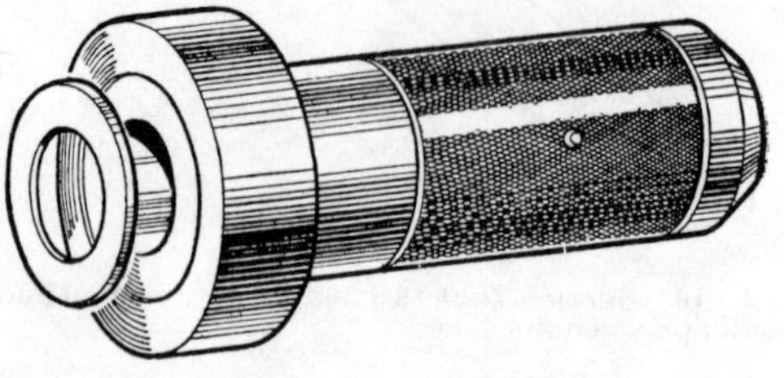

FIG 6 : 14 Service Tool 18G.579. The first and third motion shaft bearing replacer

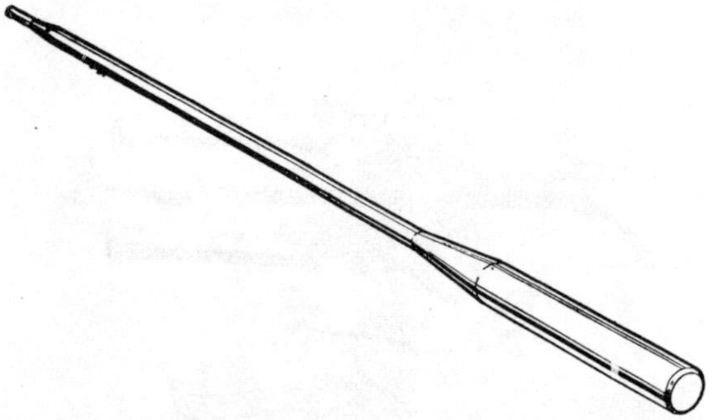

FIG 6 : 15 Service Tool 18G.471. The dummy layshaft

casing centre web and gear, plain end foremost, slotted end exposed. Insert the reverse selector rod interlocking spring and plunger, and the reverse selector rod into the casing from the front end to engage with the reverse gear fork on its way in.

2 Position the third/fourth gear selector fork in the casing and then push the selector rod through from the front to engage the fork on its way in. Insert the selector fork setscrews, making sure they engage the indentations in the selector rods. Tighten up and secure with the locking nuts.

3 Wash out the strainer thoroughly and dry it. Replace it leaving the nuts slack. Smear the sealing ring between the strainer and bracket with a little grease to lubricate the passage of the lubricating oil suction pipe.

4 Place the third motion shaft assembly in the casting, slotted end through the centre web, and with the first and second speed sliding hubs engaging the selector forks.

5 Assemble the first motion shaft and its ballbearing and with its needle roller bearing in the bore. Position the third motion shaft ballbearing in the centre web housing, line up the two shafts and using the Service Tool 18G.579 illustrated in **FIG 6 : 14** and the distance collar, drift both bearings into position in the casing. The collar is placed in the recess at the end of the tool so that the outer race is driven into the housing at the same time as the inner race is driven on to the third motion shaft. The same tool without the distance collar is used to replace the first motion shaft bearing in the casing. This operation would be best entrusted to the BMC Agent.

6 In the following order, refit the first/second speed selector fork and rod securing the fork with the locating screw and locknut; the first, second, third and top gear selector rod detent plungers and springs with new sealing washers under the retaining plug heads; the drive pinion, lock washers and nut at the front of the third motion shaft, not forgetting to lock the nut.

7 Before fitting the first motion shaft drive gear, measure the gap at B **FIG 6 : 1** between the first motion shaft bearing face and the bearing register and fit a suitable circlip to retain the bearing, then fit the first motion shaft drive gear, correctly engaging the tab of the locking washer in the hole in the gear face and finally locking the nut securely when it has been fully tightened.

8 For fitting the laygear and shaft Service Agents use a Service Tool 18G.471 as shown in **FIG 6 : 15.** The procedure is to fit the laygear and shaft with a thrust washer at each end and the slotted end of the shaft to the front. Note that the end clearance when the laygear and thrust washers are fitted should be .002 to .006 inch. This clearance is adjusted by means of thrust washers ranging in thickness from .125 to .134 inch. On three synchromesh boxes the small thrust washer is of a standard size and the large one selective, and vice versa on four synchromesh boxes. The slotted ends of the lay and reverse shafts must now be turned so that the slots face each other and the shaft locking plate can be refitted.

9 Now replace the third motion shaft bearing retainer, fitting sufficient thickness of shims to fill the gap between the bearing outer race and the retainer. See **FIG 6 : 5** and accompanying table for details of shim required and note that the shims must be fitted underneath the reverse shaft and layshaft locking plate. Tighten the setscrews on new locking washers and lock securely.

10 Take out the rear of the two loose strainer bracket securing setscrews, fit the oil suction pipe taking care with the seal, fit new paper joint washers to the pipe flange and outer blanking plate on the opposite side of the transmission casing and tighten the two setscrews at this position. Replace the strainer bracket setscrew and tighten both screws at this position and lock.

11 Refit the selector interlocking arm and then the transmission casing front end cover, using a new joint washer.

12 The speedometer drive gear should now be inserted through the transmission casing front end cover so that it engages in the slot at the end of the third motion shaft. Secure it in position with the cover plate, using a new paper washer, and the two set screws. Check the pinion shaft housing seal for serviceability and renew it if necessary. Carefully refit the housing and seal, then replace the spring plate, if fitted on later engines, and secure it with the one setscrew.

13 Take special care when fitting the gearchange operating shaft as the Woodruff key in the lower half of the shaft can easily damage the oil seal in the casing. If on inspection the oil seal requires renewal it is best replaced using the Special Tool 18G.573 illustrated in **FIG 6:16** to drift the new seal into position to avoid damage. When refitting the selector lever make sure the lower end engages properly with the interlocking arm and push the shaft through the lever boss into its lower bearing point in the casing. Some of these parts can be seen in **FIG 6:4.** Make sure the recess in the shaft lines up with the screw hole in the lever boss before inserting, tightening and locking the setscrew.

14 Lastly, fit the gearchange operating shaft reverse detent plunger, spring and plug, using a new washer under the plug head.

15 During inspection of the differential unit pay particular attention to the gear teeth for scuffing, scoring, flaking or pitting; wear of the thrust washers; any looseness in the ballbearings and bushes for the final drive shafts and the final drive shaft oil seals which may be worn due to ingress of fine abrasive road dirt. Keep the parts in the same order as they were in before dismantling. Note that the differential gear thrust washers must be reassembled with the slightly chamfered bores against the machined faces of the differential gears.

16 Extra care is required when refitting the differential unit as there must be a small pre-load on the differential bearings, which is adjustable by means of shims under the final drive cover on the lefthand side, indicated at A in **FIG 6:3.**

17 Reassemble the differential unit in the reverse order to dismantling and position the assembly in the transmission casing so that it is very slightly towards the righthand side, that is towards the flywheel end of the casing, and using new joint washers replace the differential housing, tightening the nuts sufficiently to hold the bearings firmly but not tight enough to prevent them moving slightly under modest pressure. Refit the righthand final drive cover and a new washer, taking care to tighten the nuts evenly so that the differential assembly is pushed gently to the left as the cover is pulled fully down. Refit the lefthand final drive cover without its joint gasket and pull it down evenly and gently to just grip the lefthand bearing outer race, as shown in **FIG 6:3** (inset).

18 Check the gap between the lefthand final drive cover face and the housing face at A **FIG 6:3** (inset), using feeler gauges at several points and adjust the tightness of the setscrews so that this gap is the same all round the joint face. The preload on the bearings is achieved by placing special shims between the register on the inner face of the lefthand final drive end cover and the lefthand bearing outer race, the degree of preload being .001 to .002 inch. As the compressed thickness of the final drive end cover joint gasket is .007 inch, there must be a measured gap of .008 to .009 inch at A **FIG 6:3** if no shims are fitted. For example, if the measured gap is .005 inch, a shim of .003 inch thickness must be used between the bearing and the register on the inner face of the end cover. Bearings with an increased thrust capacity are fitted to later units. These must be fitted with THRUST towards the end cover. The preload on these bearings is .004 inch so the gap A must be adjusted with shims to .011 inch before the joint washer is fitted.

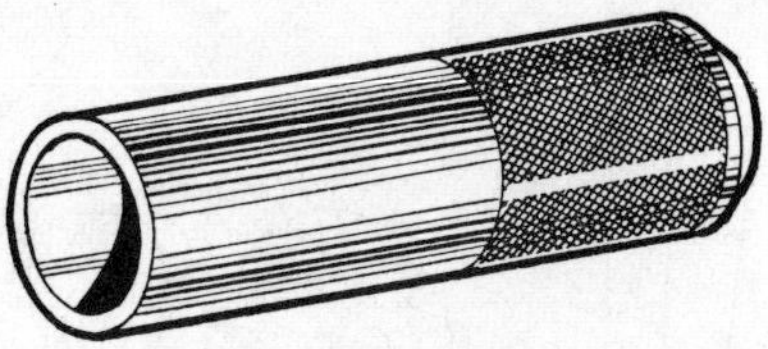

FIG 6:16 Service Tool 18G.573. The change speed shaft oil seal replacer

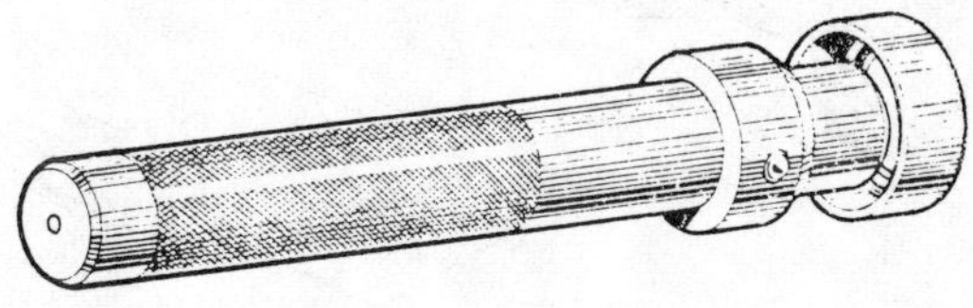

FIG 6:17 Service Tool 18G.582. The idler gear bearing replacer for threespeed synchromesh units

19 When the correct thickness of shims has been determined take off the lefthand end cover, fit the shims in position, fit a new joint gasket, replace the end cover and tighten up the setscrews fully. Tighten up the differential housing nuts and replace the final drive shaft flanges using new splitpins for the slotted nuts and applying a little engine oil or grease to the flange boss sealing surfaces for initial lubrication of the bushes and oil seals. Check freedom of operation of both final drive shafts by turning the driving flanges. If resistance to turning is not approximately the same for both flanges, further investigation is necessary.

20 The remaining parts of the gearchange assembly may now be refitted as required.

21 If the idler gear bearing in the flywheel cover has to be renewed the area around the bearing boss must be adequately supported when the bearing is being pressed home, to prevent distortion of the housing. A Special Tool 18G.582 shown at **FIG 6:17,** is used by BMC Agents to fit both idler gear bearings, with a special distance collar for the flywheel housing bearing to control the depth to which it is pressed so that the oil hole over the bearing is not blanked off. This can be seen in **FIG 6:1.** When the idler gear and flywheel housing are assembled together, the idler gear end float must be checked as instructed in **Chapter 1,** and special thrust washers fitted for adjustment. Note that the idler gear shaft spigot is towards the engine and that the thrust washers must be fitted with the chamfered bores against the gear faces.

22 Do not forget to fit the first motion shaft rear roller bearing circlip into the flywheel housing recess if the bearing has been renewed and be very careful of these two bearings when reassembling the flywheel housing to the engine, greasing them liberally to assist assembly without damage.

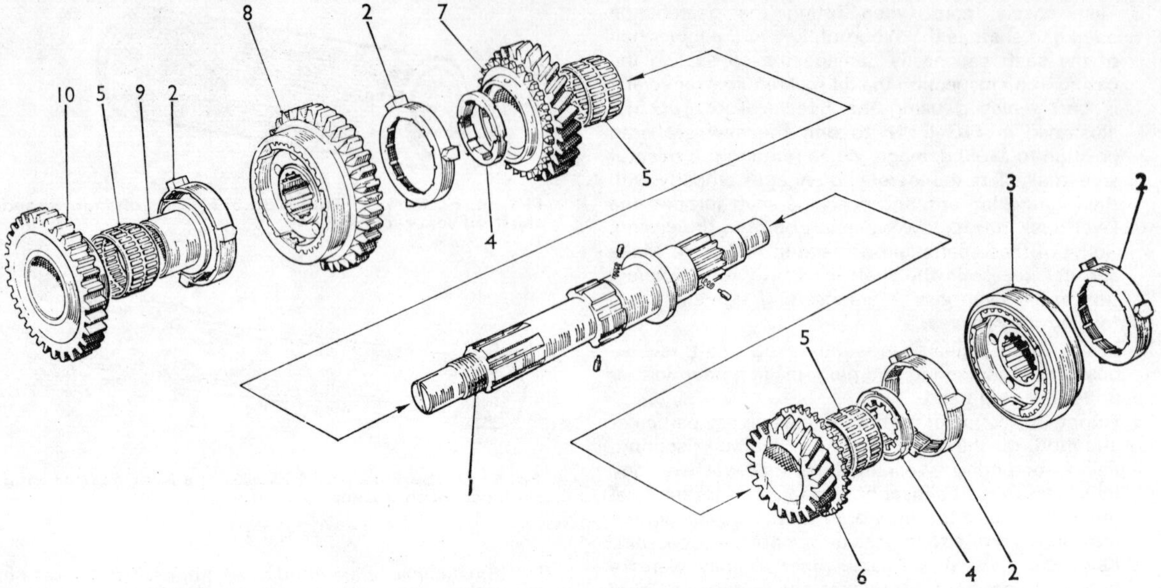

FIG 6:18 Components of the third motion shaft fitted to four speed synchromesh units

Key to Fig 6:18 1 Third motion shaft 2 Baulk ring 3 Third and fourth gear synchronizer 4 Thrust washer 5 Needle roller bearing 6 Third speed gear 7 Second speed gear 8 Reverse gear and first and second speed synchronizer 9 Bearing journal 10 First speed gear

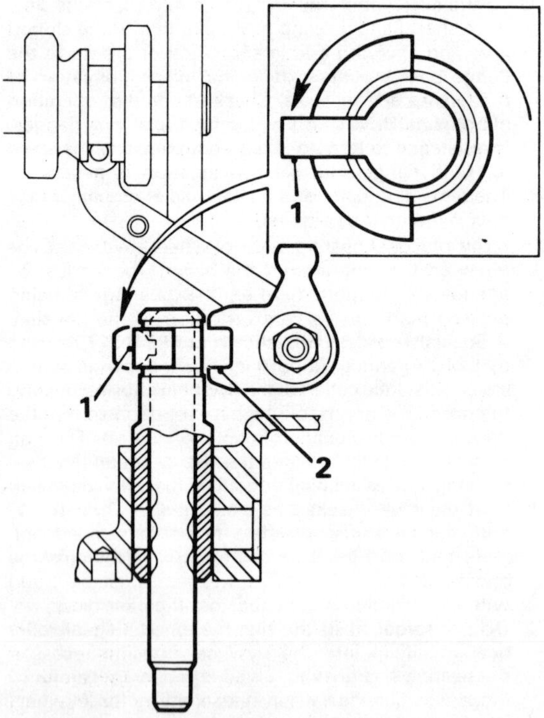

FIG 6:19 Disengaging the stub of the selector shaft 1 and the interlock spool from the bellcrank levers 2

6:5 Refitting the transmission to the engine

These operations are fully described in **Chapter 1**, to which reference should be made.

6:6 Modifications

The fourspeed gearbox with synchromesh on all four forward gears has the baulk ring type of synchronizer assemblies as can be seen in **FIG 6:18** which shows the components of the third motion shaft. Removal and servicing of these units is covered in this chapter. It should be noted that there are two plungers securing the thrust washer 4. This thrust washer is removed in a similar way to that described in **Section 6:3** procedure 16.

6:7 Dismantling the rod-change type transmission (1974)

Remove the complete power unit from the car as described in **Chapter 1** and separate the transmission from the engine.

1 Remove the securing screws and detach the final drive end covers.
2 Extract the selector shaft detent spring, sleeve and ball.
3 Unlock the tab washers and remove the final drive housing nuts and washers. Fit tool 18G 1236 to protect the oil seal and remove the final drive housing.
4 Remove the final drive gear assembly, speedometer drive pinion, engine mounting adaptor housing and speedometer drive housing.
5 Unlock and remove the bolts securing the oil suction pipe to the transmission casing, pull out the pipe.

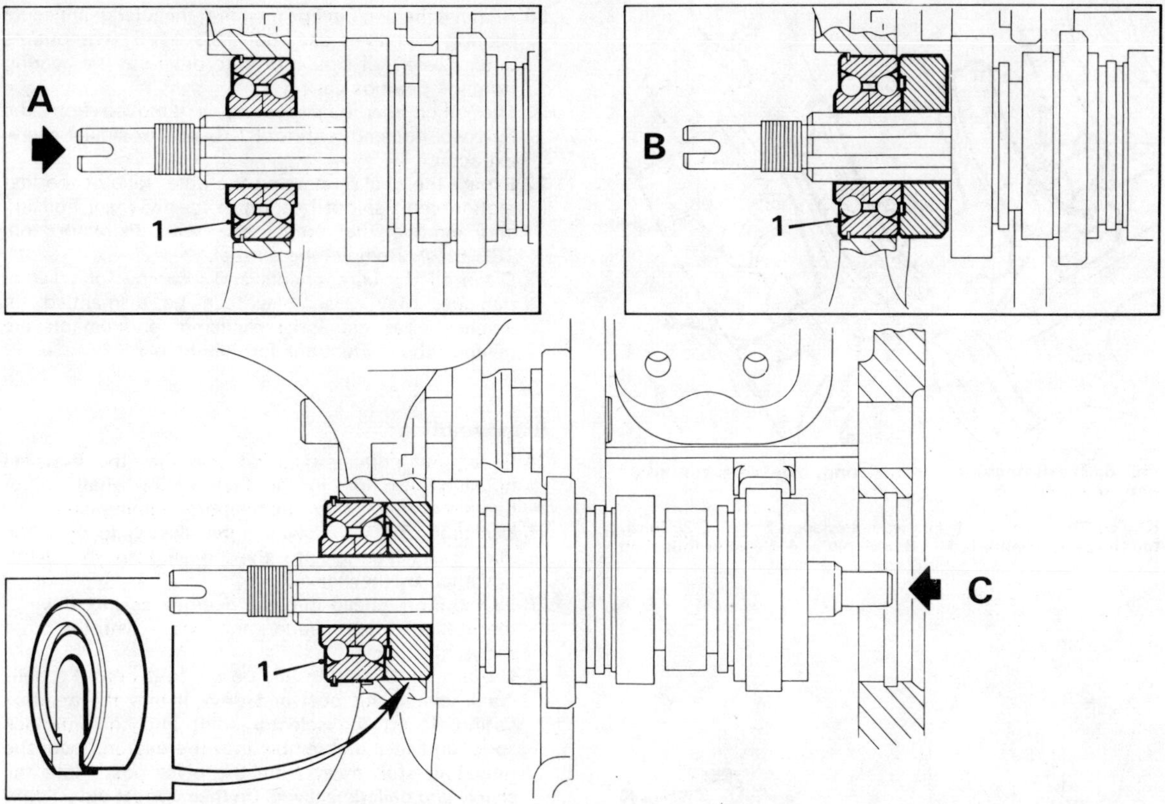

FIG 6:20 Three stages in the removal of the third motion shaft bearing 1

6 Release the circlip retaining the first motion shaft roller bearing and then pull out the bearing with tools 18G 705 and 705C.

7 Unlock the tab washers from the nuts securing the first motion shaft and the third motion shaft final drive gear.

8 Refer to **FIG 6:19**. Rotate the selector shaft anticlockwise to release the operating stub and interlock spool from the bellcrank levers, then engage first and fourth gears together to lock the gear train. Remove the third motion shaft final drive gear nut, using tool 18G 587 if available. Pull off the washer and gear.

9 Remove the first motion shaft gear nut and pull off the lockwasher and gear. Move first and fourth gears to neutral.

10 Unlock the washer tabs on the bolts securing the third motion shaft bearing retainer, remove the bolts and the retainer complete with any adjustment shims.

11 Remove the reverse locking plate and withdraw the layshaft.

12 Take out the small thrust washer from one end of the laygear, remove the laygear and the larger thrust washer.

13 Remove the circlip retaining the first motion shaft bearing and then use 18G 284 and 284B to withdraw the bearing and the shaft from the end casing.

14 For the removal of the third motion shaft bearing, refer to **FIG 6:20** and the three stages illustrated.

A With a soft drift, drive the shaft towards the clutch end, taking care not to disengage the third/fourth speed synchronizer from its hub and so release the the balls and springs.

B Insert the tool 18G 1127 with its relieved side against the bearing.

C Drive the other end of the shaft as shown to remove the bearing from the casing.

If this does not completely expel the bearing, lever it out by careful use of a screwdriver between the casing and the circlip.

15 Remove the whole third motion shaft assembly.

16 Remove the oil strainer and lift out the reverse idler gear and shaft.

17 Refer to **FIG 6:21** and drift out the roll pin 3 securing the third/fourth speed selector fork 2 and remove the selector shaft and forks.

18 Remove the nut and washer securing the bellcrank lever assembly on the pivot post and carefully note the location and marking of the components for later reassembly (see **FIG 6:22**). Withdraw the interlock spool 1 and the selector shaft 2 from the casing.

19 The bellcrank lever pivot post needs to be driven out only if the 'O' ring oil seal is to be renewed.

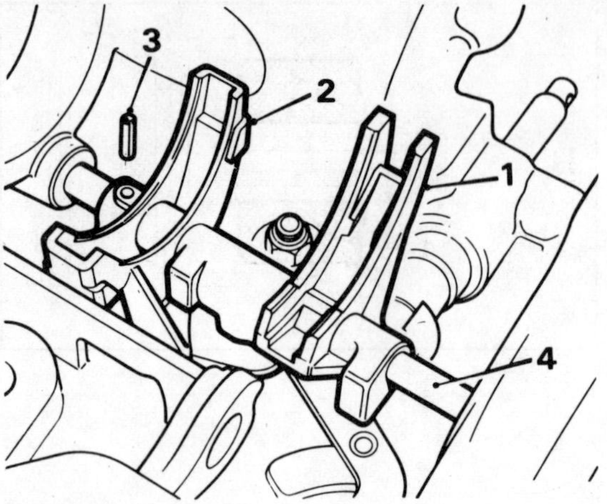

FIG 6:21 Removing, or refitting, the selector shaft and forks

Key to Fig 6:21 1 First speed selector fork 2 Third/fourth speed selector fork 3 Roll pin 4 Selector fork shaft

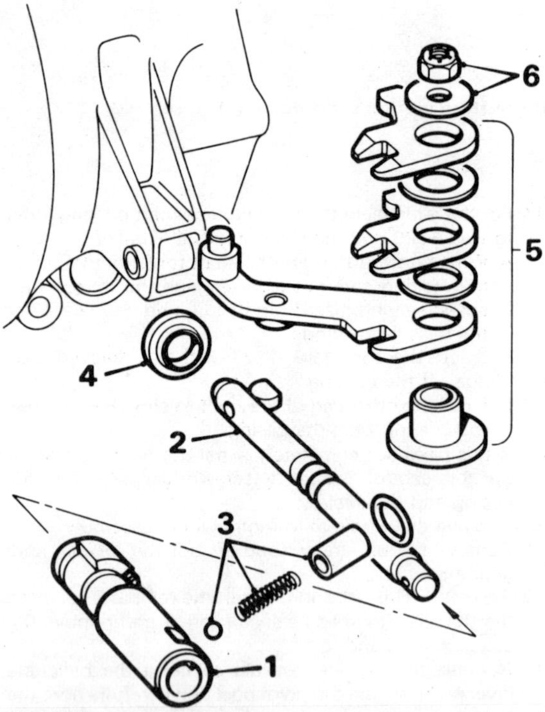

FIG 6:22 The components of the selector shaft and bellcrank lever assemblies

Key to Fig 6:22 1 Interlock spool 2 Selector shaft 3 Detent ball, spring, sleeve and oil seal 4 Oil seal 5 Bellcrank lever assembly 6 Pivot post nut and washer

20 Remove the two circlips retaining the idler gear needle bearing and then use tool 18G 1126 (without its outer sleeve), or similar drift, to drive out the bearing from the gearbox casing.

21 The other idler gear bearing is removed from the flywheel housing with tool 18G 581 or similar screw extractor.

22 Extract the circlip retaining the outer race of the first motion shaft spigot bearing in the flywheel housing and remove the outer race with extractor tool 18G 617A. Remove the oil seal.

23 Clean all the components and examine for wear or damage. Main assemblies can be dismantled for inspection as details of servicing requirements are given in the instructions for reassembly.

Reassembling:

24 Fit a new primary gear oil seal into the flywheel housing and drift in the first motion shaft spigot bearing outer race. Fit the bearing retaining circlip.

25 Use tool 18G 1126 (with outer sleeve) to drive the idler gear bearing into the housing to the depth governed by the sleeve.

26 Fit the inner circlip into the gearbox casing, drive in the new idler gear bearing and secure with the outer circlip.

27 Dip a new 'O' ring in engine oil, fit it onto the bellcrank lever pivot post and drive it into the gearbox casing. Insert the selector shaft into the interlock spool and fit the assembly into the gearbox with the operating stub away from the pivot post. Refit the sleeve and bellcrank levers (in their correct order) onto the pivot post and secure with the self-locking nut (see **FIG 6:22**). DO NOT turn the selector shaft and interlock spool into engagement with the bellcrank levers until the first and third motion shaft gear retaining nuts have been tightened to a torque of 150 lb ft (20.7 kgm).

28 Fit the third/fourth speed selector fork (see **FIG 6:21**). Fit the first speed selector fork and drive the selector rod shaft through both forks and the casing. Line up the pin holes and insert the roll pin as shown, driving it in until it is flush with the fork.

29 Refit the reverse idler gear into engagement with the reverse bellcrank lever pivot and fit the shaft.

30 Fit the oil strainer in place.

31 Dismantle the first and third motion shaft assemblies and check the condition of all components before reassembly.

32 Fit the third motion shaft assembly into the gearbox, locating it in the two selector forks, then use tool 18G 579 to drive the shaft bearing into the centre web of the casing.

33 Locate the needle-roller bearing for the first motion shaft in the gear and drive the assembly into the casing. The correct thickness of circlip required is gauged by means of 18G 569. The sizes are marked on the handle and the thicker side should be tried first.

34 Select the circlip from the details given below and use tool 18G 257 to fit it.

When gap is	*Use circlip No.*
.096 to .098 inch (2.43 to 2.48 mm)	2A 3710
.098 to .100 inch (2.48 to 2.54 mm)	2A 3711

35 Fit the needle-roller bearings into the laygear and refit the laygear and shaft complete with thrust washers. Measure the laygear end float, which should be between .002 and .006 inch (.05 to .15 mm) and select and fit the correct washer from the following:

Washer thickness	*Part No.*
.123 to .124 inch (3.12 to 3.14 mm)	22G 856
.125 to .126 inch (3.17 to 3.20 mm)	22G 857
.127 to .128 inch (3.22 to 3.25 mm)	22G 858
.130 to .131 inch (3.30 to 3.32 mm)	22G 859

36 Refit the reverse and layshaft locking plate, rotating the shafts if necessary to position the slots.

37 Refer to **FIG 6:23** and refit the third motion shaft bearing retainer without the shims. Tighten the bolts lightly and measure the gap as shown. Select and fit the appropriate shims from the table below.

When gap is	*Use shims totalling*
.005 to .006 inch (.13 to .15 mm)	.005 inch (.13 mm)
.006 to .008 inch (.15 to .20 mm)	.007 inch (.18 mm)
.008 to .010 inch (.20 to .25 mm)	.009 inch (.23 mm)
.010 to .012 inch (.25 to .30 mm)	.011 inch (.28 mm)
.012 to .014 inch (.30 to .35 mm)	.013 inch (.33 mm)
.014 to .015 inch (.35 to .38 mm)	.015 inch (.38 mm)

38 Use new lockwashers for the bolts securing the bearing retainer, tighten and lock the bolts.

39 Lock the gear train by engaging first and fourth gears together. Fit the final drive pinion and a new lock-washer on the third motion shaft and tighten the nut to a torque of 150 lb ft (20.7 kgm). Secure with the washer tabs.

40 Fit, tighten to the same torque and lock the first motion shaft gear. Fit the first motion shaft roller bearing and secure with the circlip. Move first and fourth gears back to neutral.

41 Turn the selector shaft and interlock spool to engage the bellcrank levers. Fit the oil suction pipe into the oil strainer.

42 Fit a new joint washer and locking plates. Tighten first the external flange securing screws and then the pipe bracket screws. Lock with the tabs of the locking plates.

43 Refit the speedometer drive housing with a new washer and the drive pinion also with a new joint washer.

44 Refit the engine mounting adaptor housing.

45 Refer to **FIG 6:24**. Protect the oil seal by fitting tool 18G 1236 over the selector shaft and then refit and adjust the final drive gear assembly as described in **Section 6:4**.

46 Refit the selector shaft sleeve, ball and spring before fitting the final drive end covers.

47 Refit the transmission to the engine and the complete unit into the car in the reverse order of removal.

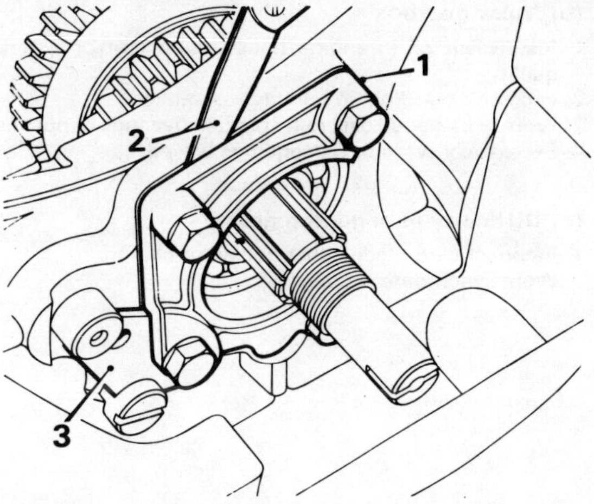

FIG 6:23 Measuring the gap between the third motion shaft bearing retainer and transmission casing. Note the location of the reverse and layshaft locking plate

Key to Fig 6:23 1 Bearing retainer 2 Feeler gauge 3 Locking plate

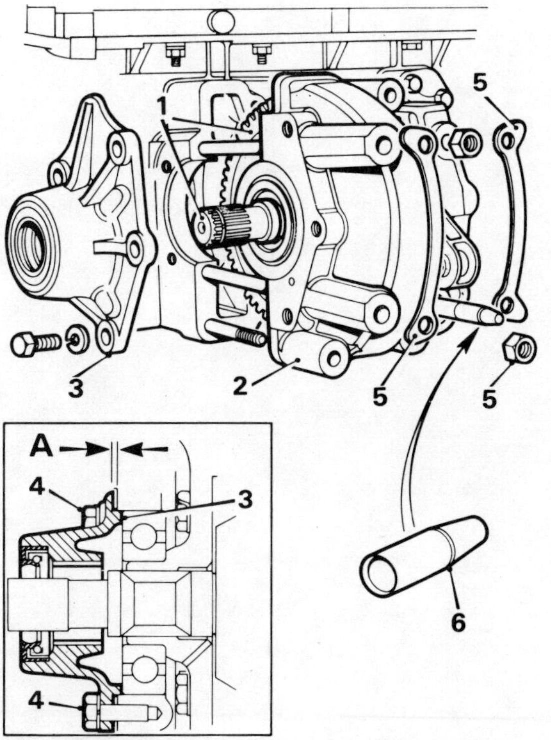

FIG 6:24 Refitting the final drive assembly. Measure the gap at A for the selection of shims to give the necessary bearing preloading

Key to Fig 6:24 1 Final drive assembly 2 Housing 3 End cover 4 Cover retaining screws 5 Retaining nuts and lock plates 6 Oil seal protector 18G 1236

6:8 Fault diagnosis

(a) Jumping out of gear

1 Worn synchromesh units
2 Worn or broken detent plungers and springs
3 Worn coupling teeth
4 Selector fork to selector rod securing screws loose

(b) Noisy gearbox

1 Insufficient oil in engine/transmission unit or wrong quality
2 Excessive end float in various assemblies
3 Worn or damaged ball, roller or plain bearings or bushes
4 Excessively worn or damaged gear teeth

(c) Difficulty in engaging gears

1 Incorrect clutch adjustment or worn clutch
2 Worn synchromesh cones

(d) Oil leaks

1 Damaged joint washers
2 Worn or damaged oil seals
3 Loose or damaged joint faces at transmission casing to engine crankcase, flywheel housing to crankcase or transmission casing, at differential housing or final drive end covers, or at the outer oil pipe blanking plate on the outside of the transmission casing. The latter may also be the cause of oil pressure failure due to a leak on the suction side of the pump. Pay special attention to making this oil and air-tight

CHAPTER 6A

AUTOMATIC TRANSMISSION

6a : 1 General information

The automatic transmission system provides fully automatic gear changing in four forward speeds, and reverse gear by lever selection in the normal way. The system also provides for manual selection of all gears if this is required, it being recognized that no automatic system can be designed to suit all conditions of driving and driver's characteristics. The gear change lever operates in a simple quadrant-type gate having six or seven positions. The first position D on the quadrant selects automatic gear operation and the lever remains in this position all the time the car is being driven with automatic gear changing, even during brief stopping in continuous traffic conditions. For lengthy stops with engine continuing to run, the neutral N position can be temporarily selected to isolate engine torque from the system.

The middle gate positions are the neutral N, first 1, second 2, third 3 and, on some models, fourth 4 for manual gear changing. The reverse gate position is the most forward position to which it is possible to move the gearchange lever, and a stop is provided to prevent inadvertent selection of reverse gear when the car is moving forward. The change lever has to be lifted over the stop in order to engage reverse gear.

The only preliminaries required for driving on automatic gear selection are first to start and warm up the engine for a few minutes in order to circulate the oil and warm up the system, then select the gearchange lever D position. Depression of the accelerator pedal will then cause the car to move smoothly forwards with the gear ratios changing automatically as appropriate road speeds are attained. It is very important not to abuse the manual change facility, and introduce excessive stress to the system and possible driving danger, by changing manually downwards at road speeds in excess of those for which the car is designed to travel in second and third gear. These road speeds are 50 mile/hr for third gear and 40 mile/hr for second gear. First gear is a freewheel gear on over-run and therefore no drive of the engine occurs if the car's road speed is greater than that appropriate to the engine in first gear. For this reason first gear should not be selected as a braking medium for the descent of steep hills. If greater acceleration than that available in the D position is required below road speeds of 43 mile/hr in top gear, 34 mile/hr in third gear, and 22 mile/hr in second gear, this can be achieved by fully depressing the accelerator pedal. Above these road speeds no change will occur.

A tow start can be achieved in emergency by selecting N, switching on the ignition, adjusting the mixture control as required and releasing the handbrake. When a road speed of about 20 mile/hr is reached second gear is selected and the throttle controlled as necessary by the accelerator pedal.

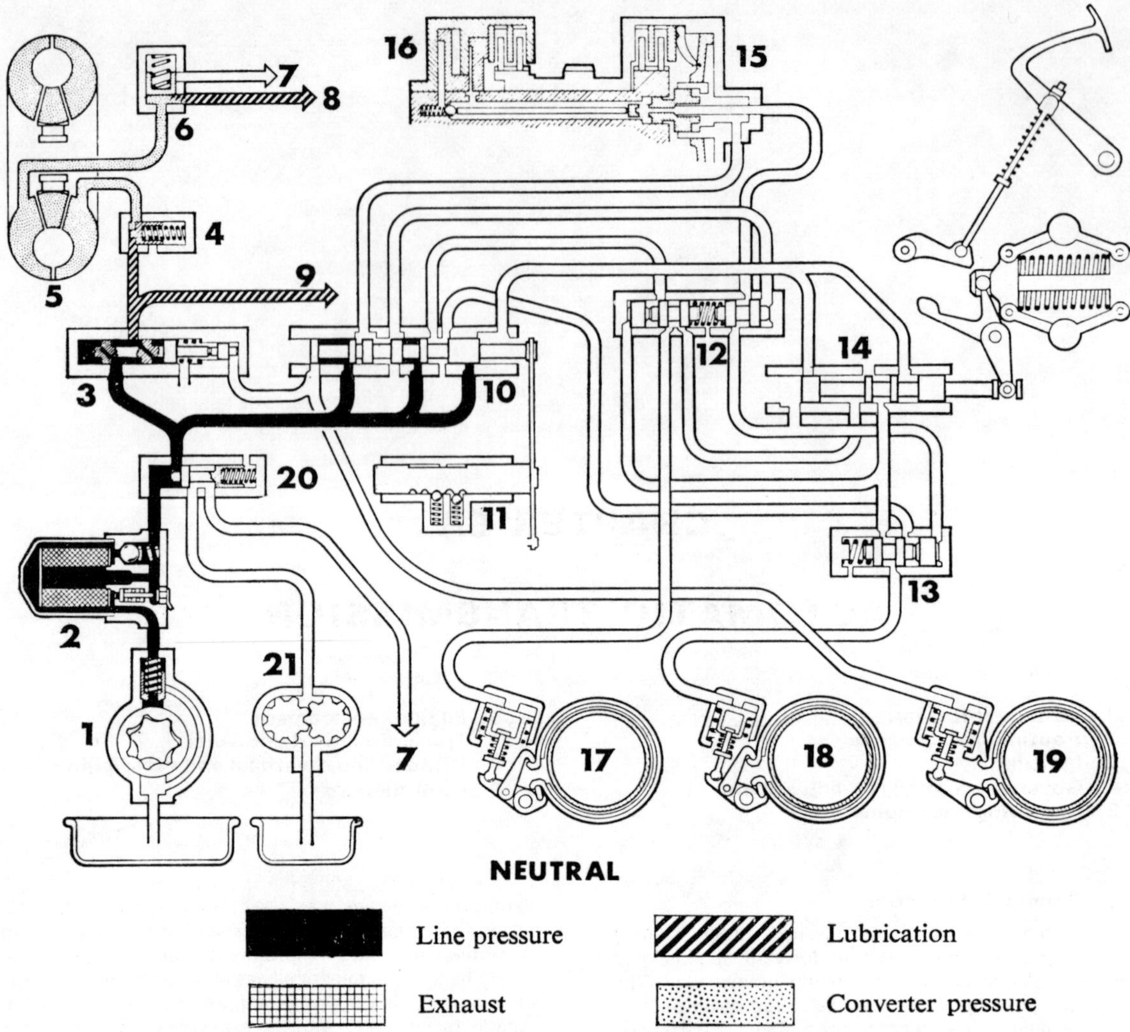

FIG 6a : 1 Line pressure and lubrication diagram with N selected

If the car has to be towed any appreciable distance, have this done with the gearchange lever in the N position. Should a transmission fault be suspected, tow the car with the front wheels off the ground.

Later models are fitted with an engagement control unit which is fitted to eliminate excessive movement of the car when selecting a forward drive range from the rest position. It should be noted that it is not possible to tow start a vehicle fitted with this device.

The automatic transmission system consists of a torque converter instead of the normal flywheel and foot-operated clutch. Drive is transmitted from this unit, through an idler gear to the gearchange system. The three-element fluid torque converter provides a maximum torque conversion ratio of 2:1. It comprises three elements, namely the impeller, the turbine and the stator. The driving (impeller) and driven (turbine) elements are coupled only by the oil contained in the unit. The stator contributes to the variable conversion facility provided by the unit.

The change speed facility is provided by a system of bevel gears with associated brake bands operated hydraulically by means of suitable control valves and servo pistons, and also by means of an associated system of multi-disc clutches. The final drive from the change speed gear system is provided by a final pinion engaging with the large output gear attached to the differential unit similar to that used with synchromesh gearchange systems described in **Chapter 6.**

The hydraulic control system uses oil drawn from the transmission casing, which is also the main lubrication system supply for the power unit. A single main oil pump serves both systems from the common oil supply. All oil is drawn through a strainer in the transmission casing by a pump and passed through an external full-flow filter and regulator valve to the engine's lubrication system as

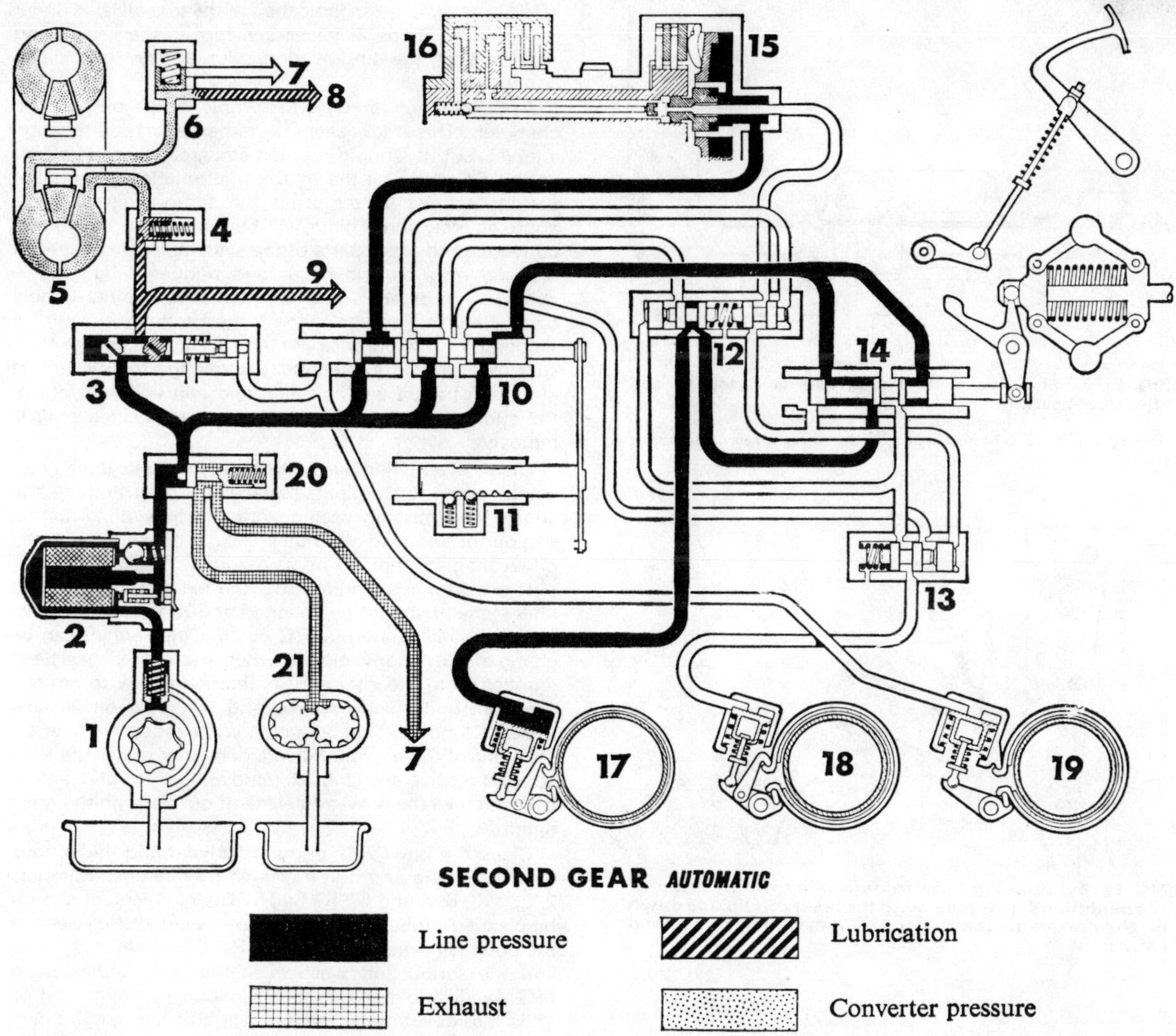

FIG 6a : 2 Line pressure and lubrication diagram with second gear automatic in operation

Key to Figs 6a : 1 and 6a : 2 1 Main oil pump 2 Oil filter 3 Regulator valve 4 Engine lubrication relief valve 5 Converter 6 Low pressure valve 7 Engine lubrication 8 Gear train lubrication 9 Engine lubrication 10 Selector valve 11 Selector valve detent 12 Second and top gear valves 13 Third gear valve 14 Governor valve 15 Forward clutch 16 Top and reverse clutch 17 Second gear brake band 18 Third gear brake band 19 Reverse gear brake band 20 Tow start valve 21 Auxiliary pump

well as the torque converter and transmission, where, in addition to providing lubrication, it also operates the various valves, clutches and brake bands. It may be of interest to study the hydraulic fluid flow diagrams for an idea of the manner in which the brake bands and clutches are used to provide the desired gear selections. See **FIGS 6a : 1** and **6a : 2**.

6a : 2 Routine maintenance

Precision valves such as those employed in the Mini automatic transmission system are very sensitive to foreign matter in the oil and incorrect or low quality oils. Therefore the most important aspect of routine maintenance for these systems concerns attention to the lubricating/hydraulic oil.

The car manufacturers recommend checking the oil level every week no matter what oil consumption the owner believes applicable to his own particular vehicle. **This is a very necessary safety precaution.** Start by running the engine for two minutes to ensure that the torque converter, filter and hydraulic valves and pipelines are full to capacity. Then switch off and after a moment or two check the engine/transmission oil level by means of the dipstick. The indication of oil level will almost certainly differ a little from that shown before the engine

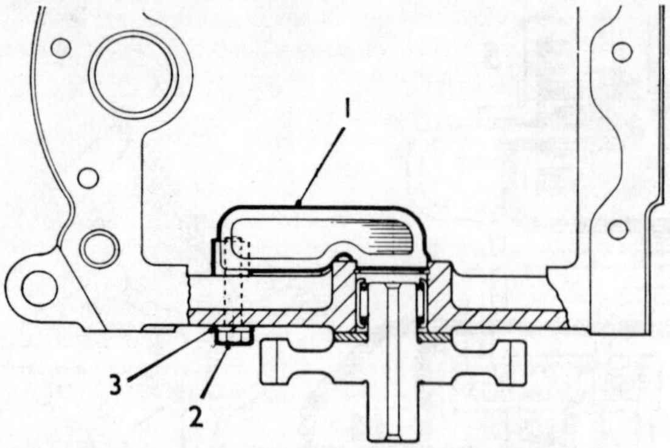

FIG 6a:3 Showing how a reservoir is fitted to the idler gear bearing

Key to Fig 6a:3 1 Reservoir 2 Securing screw 3 Spring washer

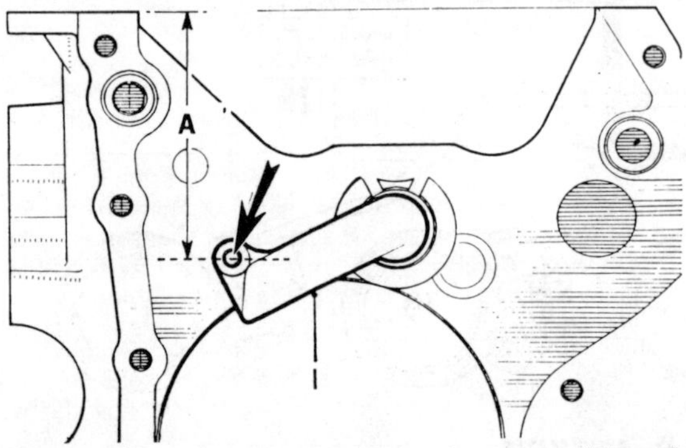

FIG 6a:4 Showing how to determine the position of the mounting screw hole, with the reservoir upside down on the outside of the transmission casing. A = $3\frac{19}{32}$ inch (91.3 mm)

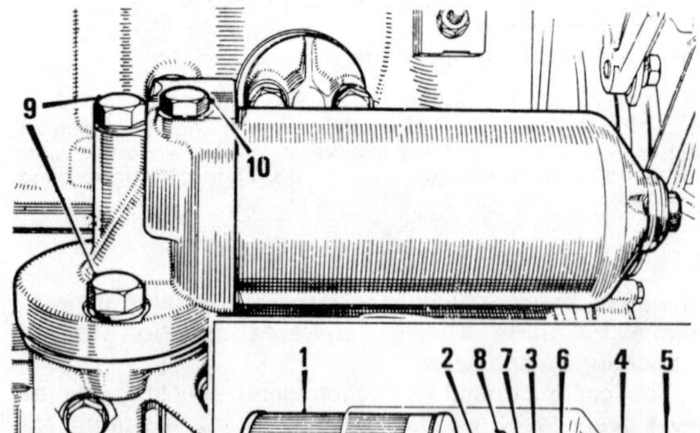

FIG 6a:5 The external full flow filter

Key to Fig 6a:5 1 Filter element 2 Circlip 3 Steel washer 4 Sealing ring 5 Centre bolt 6 Spring 7 Sealing washer 8 Sealing plate 9 Filter head retaining bolts 10 Oil pressure checking plug

was run and will be an indication of the true oil level under running conditions. If necessary, top up the level using only one of the approved oils in a new and clean condition.

At 3000 miles intervals the whole of the oil must be changed. This may seem a rather short oil change interval but it should be remembered that it is not possible to drain all the oil from automatic transmission systems merely by removing the sump drain plug, as approximately three pints will be retained in the torque converter and other parts of the system. Some mixing of old and new oil will occur and frequent changing is necessary in order to maintain permanently a reasonably clean fresh oil charge. Nine pints of fresh oil will be required for this purpose. Preferably run the engine for a short period before attempting to change the oil. In this condition the oil will be fairly fluid and will flow out of the sump quite freely when the magnetic drain plug is removed.

Clean all adhering particles off the magnetic drain plug, using a non-fluffy cloth, replace the plug and fill the engine/transmission casing with the new oil. Run the engine for about two minutes, switch off and check the oil level again, topping up as required.

It is also recommended that the external full-flow oil filter element should be changed at 3000 miles intervals. This unit is illustrated in **FIG 6a : 5.** The element can be changed most conveniently when the old oil has been emptied from the engine. It is first necessary to remove the front grille fixing screws and the grille on all cars except Clubman. This operation will expose the filter on the front of the engine. Place a container under the filter bowl to receive any spilt oil, remove the central retaining bolt and take the bowl and element out through the grille aperture.

Clean the bowl with petrol or solvent and the various washers spring and bolt indicated by reference numbers 2, 8, 7, 3, 6, 4 and 5 **FIG 6a : 5.** The old element cannot be cleaned properly and must be discarded. Reassemble the bowl with the new element, BMC Part No. 12A.1191 and the spring and washers in the order indicated in **FIG 6a : 5** and tighten up the centre retaining bolt to 16 lb ft torque, turning the bowl slightly during tightening to ensure a good fit of the bowl on the new washer in the head and the washer under the bolt head. Check for leaks at both ends of the filter bowl as soon as the engine is started and before replacing the grille.

Lubrication reservoir for the idler gear:

Experience of operating these transmissions has shown that early cars required additional lubrication for the idler gear bearings. **FIG 6a : 3** shows how a separate oil reservoir for this purpose can be fitted to those cars prior to engine numbers 8AH-A-H11338, 99H-143-H5983 and 99H-147-H834 when a cast-in reservoir was included in the specification.

It is necessary to remove the engine/transmission assembly from the car and then separate the transmission from the engine. These operations are described for those home operators with the necessary facilities in **Sections 6a : 5** and **6a : 8**.

Refer to **FIG 6a : 4**. Measure down from the joint face on the outside of the casing the dimension A ($3\frac{19}{32}$ inch or

91.3 mm) and from this point mark a horizontal line as shown. Place the reservoir upside-down on the outside of the casing with its spigot in the bore of the idler gear bearing and the securing lug centrally positioned on the horizontal line. Mark this position (arrowed) and drill a $\frac{9}{32}$ inch (7.14 mm) hole, catching any swarf which may fall inside.

Ensure that the reservoir fits snugly against the casing, filing down if necessary, then smear the spigot with Hylomar jointing compound and fit the reservoir as shown in **FIG 6a:3**. Later reservoirs have a built-up boss around the securing lug, if this is not present, a flat washer may be fitted beneath the lug to ensure that the spigot is square in the bearing bore. Leave the idler gear bearing circlip in position and tighten the securing bolt.

Refit the transmission to the engine and the engine/transmission assembly to the car as described in the appropriate sections.

6a:3 Ignition

The ignition timing checking procedure on the models with automatic transmission is slightly different from the procedure employed on models with normal synchromesh transmission. The timing can be checked with the engine in the car by the following procedure:

1 Remove the large rubber grommet from the top of the converter cover and the small grommet from the converter housing nearest the engine and adjacent to the dipstick.

2 Turn the converter starter ring gear by means of a screwdriver through the smaller opening, in the normal direction of rotation, until the TDC mark on the converter is aligned with the pointer. The TDC mark on early models is similar to the 1/4 mark on manual transmission models. On later cars it takes the form of a zero line with graduations on either side indicating degrees BEFORE and AFTER Top Dead Centre.

3 Check that the contact breaker gap is correctly set to .014 to .016 inch.

4 With the crankshaft and converter in the position set, the contact breaker points should be just opening. If the points are already open, turn the knurled nut on the side of the distributor towards the R until they are clearly seen to be closed, then turn the knurled nut in the opposite direction until the points are just open.

A .001 inch thick feeler gauge or a small strip of cigarette tinfoil between the points will give a sufficiently accurate 'feel' of the open or closed state of the points if visual judgement of the open or closed position is difficult. Alternatively, connect a twelve-volt lamp between the low tension terminal on the side of the distributor and a good 'earth'. When the ignition is switched on the light will go on if the points are open and the knurled nut must be turned towards R, then turned slowly back towards A until the bulb just goes out. If correct adjustment is not possible within the range of adjustment of the knurled nut, it would be advisable to check the ignition timing throughout. See **Chapters 1** and **3**.

6a:4 Governor control rod adjustment

The automatic transmission governor consists basically of two rotating bobweights on spring loaded links which respond to changes in their rotational speed and, by means of a rod linkage, operate the governor valve which in turn controls the timing of the automatic gearchanges.

A spring loaded rod connected to the throttle linkage provides an override device. The spring is compressed by the movement of the accelerator pedal and this load is transferred to the governor and by delaying its movement also delays gearchanges as the pedal is depressed.

FIG 6a:6 shows the attachment of the governor control rod to the throttle control linkage while the lower adjustable connection to the transmission is shown in **FIG 6a:7**. Adjustment is carried out as follows:

1 Check that with the engine fully warmed up the idle speed is 650 rev/min.

2 Disconnect the control rod at the carburetter and insert a $\frac{1}{4}$ inch (6.4 mm) rod 4 through the hole in the bellcrank lever and into the hole in the transmission casing as shown.

3 It should now be possible to line up the holes in the control rod fork end and the carburetter linkage so that the connecting clevis pin is an easy sliding fit. If it is not, adjust the length of the control rod as necessary.

4 Slacken the locknut 3 and rotate the control rod until the correct length is obtained. Secure the locknut.

5 Road test the car and check that automatic gearchanges occur at the speeds given in **Section 6a:9**. If the full throttle change speeds are low the control rod must be shortened, if they are high the rod must be turned anticlockwise to lengthen it slightly.

6a:5 Removing the engine

Engine removal procedure follows generally the pattern outlined for engines with synchromesh transmission with certain procedural alterations. It will be found helpful if a study of the car in conjunction with **FIGS 6a:8** and **9** is first carried out. The following are the operations required:

1 Disconnect the battery earth cable.

2 Remove the bonnet.

3 Raise the front of the car securely until the wheels are free to rotate and remove the inboard drive shaft flange securing nuts.

4 Pull back the rubber sleeve and disconnect the gear selector cable by removing the clevis pin. Slacken the yoke clamp and remove the yoke, nut, rubber ferrules and sleeve. Remove the cable front adjusting nut from the outer cable and pull the cable clear of the transmission.

5 Remove the exhaust pipe bracket from the final drive cover. The larger nut is secured by a locking tab as shown in **FIG 6a:8**.

6 Drain the coolant from the radiator and the cylinder block.

7 Disconnect the heater hoses and the water control valve cable. Slacken the fixing clips on the heater fresh air tube connections on the grille and wing valance and swing the tube clear of the engine compartment.

8 Disconnect the electrical leads to the sparking plugs, high-tension coil, generator, starter, distributor and starter solenoid.

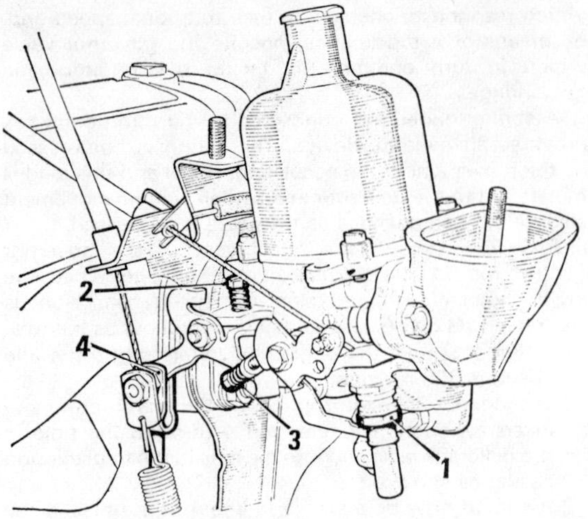

FIG 6a : 6 The SU HS4 carburetter fitted to models with automatic transmission

Key to Fig 6a : 6 1 Jet adjusting nut 2 Throttle adjusting screw 3 Fast idle adjusting screw 4 Governor control rod

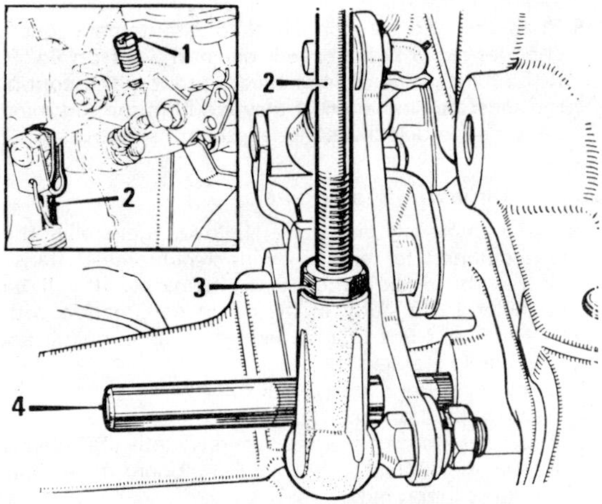

FIG 6a : 7 The governor control rod adjustment

Key to Fig 6a : 7 Inset 1 Carburetter throttle adjustment screw Inset 2 Carburetter governor control rod linkage 3 Locknut 4 $\frac{1}{4}$ inch diameter rod through lever into hole in transmission casing

9 Remove the distributor cover.
10 Remove the air cleaner unit.
11 Disconnect the fuel feed pipe and remove the control connections, then remove the carburetter.
12 Disconnect the speedometer cable from the rear of the instrument.
13 Disconnect the oil pressure gauge hose.
14 Disconnect and remove the horn.
15 Disconnect the exhaust front pipe from the manifold and tie the pipe back to the bulkhead out of the way of the engine.
16 Disconnect the engine tie rod from the cylinder block and swing the rod away from the engine.
17 Disconnect the breather hose if fitted, remove the rocker cover nuts and remove the cover.
18 Undo four cylinder head securing nuts and fit the special lifting attachment to the top of the engine as shown in **FIG 6a : 10.**
19 Remove the setscrews securing each engine mounting to the subframe.
20 Lift the engine, first sufficiently to release the drive shaft flanges from the shafts, then further to remove the engine/transmission unit from the car.

6a : 6 Engine replacement

General replacement is the reverse of removal with special attention to the following:

1 Lower the engine/transmission unit first to a position in which the drive shafts can engage the flanges, bringing them together over the studs and screwing on the nuts about four turns each.
2 Lower the engine further until it is in its final position in the car and then reconnect the engine mountings and secure the drive shafts.
3 On early cars which have an adjustable transverse selector rod, 3 in **FIG 6a : 11**, this is adjusted as follows:
4 Pull back the rubber boot 1 and remove the clevis pin 2. See that the selector rod 3 is screwed in tightly and pushed fully into the casing.
5 Turn the bellcrank lever arm clear of the yoke 4 on the transverse rod and refit the clevis pin. Measure the dimension A and if it is not as specified, slacken the locknut 5 and rotate the yoke until the correct measurement is obtained.
6 Tighten the locknut, ensuring that the yoke is set squarely to the bellcrank lever arm.
7 On later cars the transverse selector rod is not adjustable and a pressed, instead of forged, type bellcrank lever arm is fitted.
8 Proceed to adjust the selector lever cable by first selecting N in the transmission unit. On transmissions with seven selector positions this is done by pulling the transverse selector rod fully out and then pushing it in **one** detent. When the selector has six positions the selector rod must be pushed back **two** detents.
9 On early models, move the selector lever to the N position on the quadrant and use the cable adjuster 6 to adjust the length of the cable until the hole in the cable fork is in line with the hole in the bellcrank lever and the clevis pin can easily be inserted.
10 On later models, proceed as in item 9 above but line up the cable fork with the bore in the spherical joint in the bellcrank lever until the connecting bolt can be easily inserted.
11 Make sure that the yoke end on the selector cable is secured squarely to the bellcrank lever before connecting. Never start the engine with the selector rod disconnected.

Checking the selector adjustment:

12 Apply the handbrake and start the engine. Move the selector lever to R position and check that reverse is engaged. Slowly move the lever towards N and check that the gear disengages as soon as or just before the lever drops into the N position. Repeat this procedure in the 1 position and if necessary make

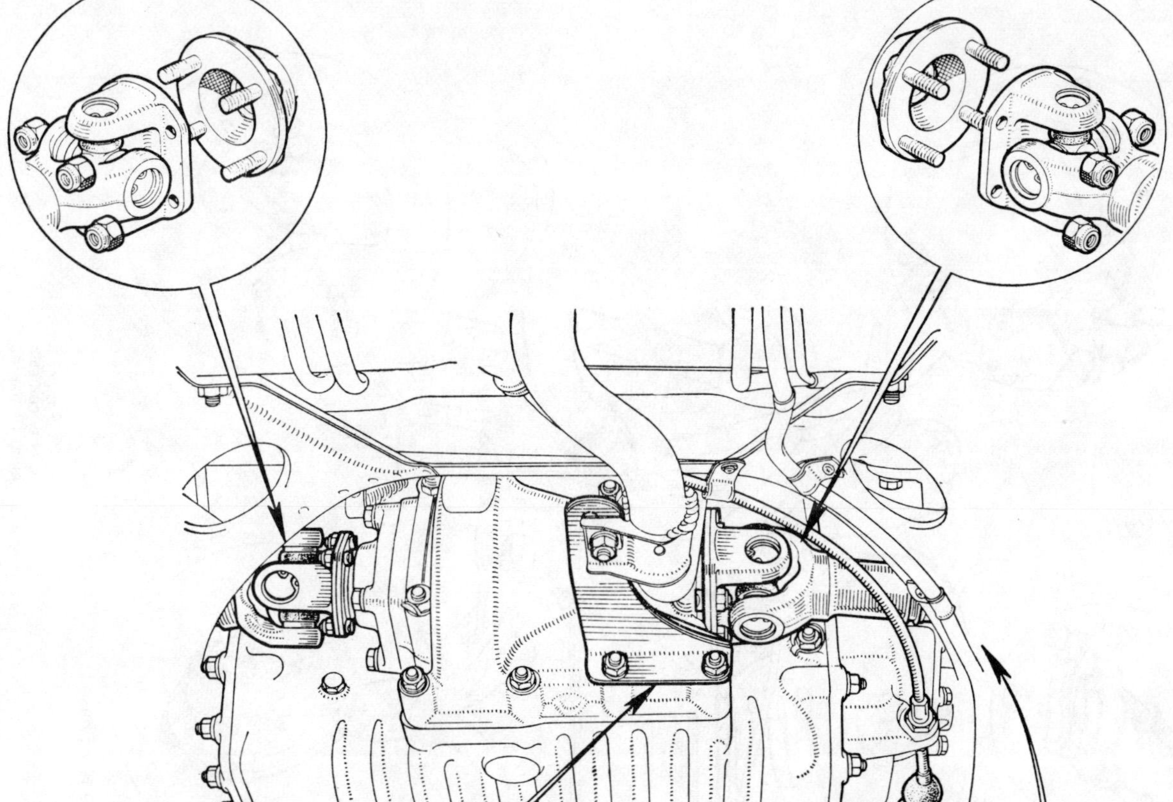

FIG 6a : 8 Components to be disconnected from below the car before engine removal

Key to Fig 6a : 8
Lefthand drive shaft coupling
Exhaust pipe support bracket
Transmission control cable connection
Righthand drive shaft coupling
Righthand engine mounting

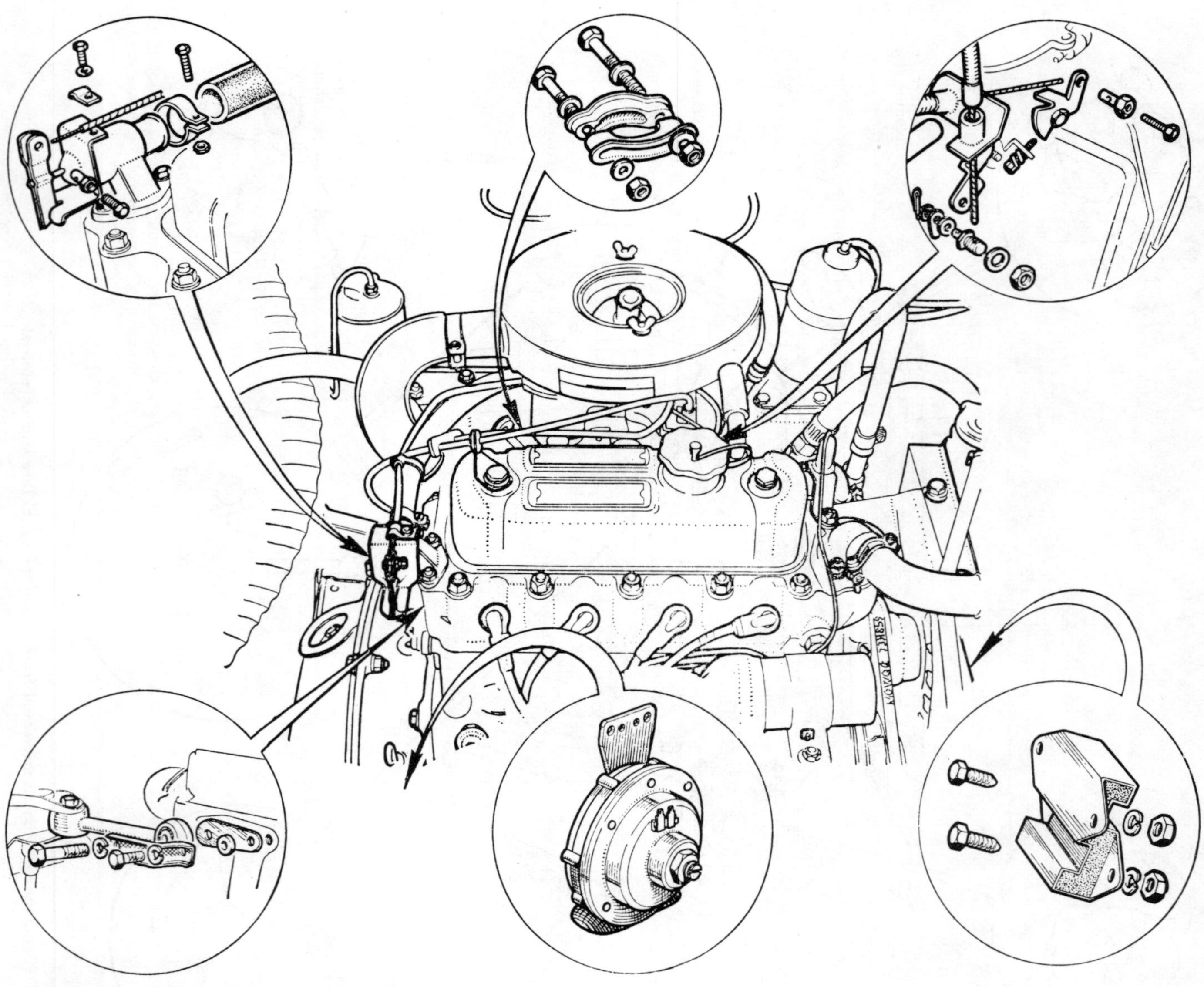

FIG 6a : 9 Components to be disconnected above the car before engine removal

Key to Fig 6a : 9

Heater hose and coolant control valve
Engine tie rod attachment
Exhaust pipe to manifold clamp
Horn
Carburetter controls
Front engine mounting (lefthand)

a slight readjustment to ensure that the movement required to engage or disengage gears is equal in each direction.

13 Check that all nuts and pins are secure, pack any rubber boots with grease before fitting and replace the bellcrank lever guard.

Modification:

In the event of slip being experienced in reverse gear on later types, a cure may be effected by filing a radius $\frac{1}{16}$ inch (1.6 mm) deep in the end of the gate beyond the R position, if this has not already been done.

Remove the handle from the selector lever and unscrew the four screws securing the indicator gate to the quadrant housing to remove the gate.

6a : 7 Transmission adjustments

The inhibitor switch located on the rear of the gear selector housing permits engine starting only when the gearchange lever is in the N position. Both leads to the terminals marked 2 and 4 on the switch are interchangeable and are used in the ignition/starter circuit. The terminals marked 1 and 3 are for the reversing light (when fitted) connections. The adjustment of the gearchange cable and selector rod must be checked for correctness before this adjustment is attempted.

To adjust the inhibitor switch proceed as follows:

1 Select N on the quadrant with the gearchange lever.
2 Disconnect the electrical leads from the inhibitor switch.
3 Slacken the switch securing locknut and screw in the switch as far as possible.
4 Connect a test lamp or voltmeter to the terminals marked 2 and 4 on the switch.
5 Unscrew the switch and then screw it forward into the housing until the circuit is closed and the light or meter registers. Mark the switch.
6 Continue screwing the switch into the housing, counting the number of turns until the circuit is broken and the light or meter fails to register.
7 Disconnect the test equipment and unscrew the switch half the number of turns counted.
8 Tighten the locknut and reconnect the electrical leads to the appropriate terminals.
9 Check that the starter only operates when the gearchange lever is in the N position, and that the reverse light (when fitted) only operates when R is selected.
10 If the switch cannot be adjusted to operate correctly it must be renewed. Later switches have only two terminals.

The governor control rod must only be adjusted after the adjustment of the gearchange cable and selector rod have been completed and the carburetter has been correctly tuned for slow running and set to give an idling speed of 650 rev/min. Proceed further as follows:

1 Run the engine up to normal running temperature and disconnect the governor control rod at the carburetter.
2 Proceed as in **Section 6a : 4**.

The stalling speed check provides useful data for the determination of several major faults and can be carried out by owners who have access to a suitable type of tachometer. The electrical impulse type of tachometer would be most convenient for this purpose providing it is known to be accurate or has a calibration table.

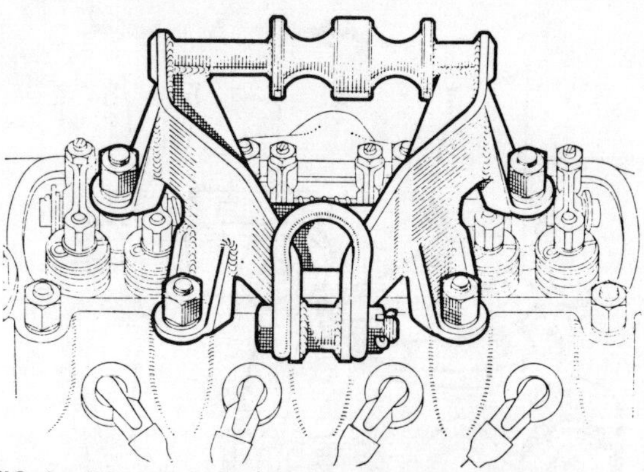

FIG 6a : 10 The special engine lifting attachment. The individual front lifting eye (nearest viewer) is used to provide an angled lift when removing and replacing the power unit

1 Start the engine and run it up to normal working temperature.
2 Check and if necessary rectify the oil level.
3 Connect the tachometer. Service Agents use a piece of special equipment designated Service Tool 18G.677 which contains a tachometer and an oil pressure gauge, for this and the following checks.
4 Apply the hand and foot brakes, which is most important to avoid any movement of the car.
5 Select any gear position on the quadrant except 1, N or R.
6 Apply maximum throttle for not more than 10 seconds and note the tachometer reading. Compare with the chart below.

Model	*Rev/min*	*Condition*	*Rectification*
845 cc	1300-1400	Satisfactory	—
998 cc	1400-1500	Satisfactory	—
Both	Under 1000	Stator freewheel slip	Change torque converter
Both	Over 1500	Transmission slip	Check transmission unit
Both	Under 1300	Engine down on power	Tune engine

The pressure check is carried out to determine the oil pressure in the automatic transmission system in all positions except R. With R selected the oil pressure should read approximately 120 lb/sq in. In all other positions, 80 lb/sq in. Service Agents use the Service Tool 18G.677, illustrated at **FIG 6a : 20** with the tachometer and oil pressure gauge, or a separate pressure gauge, Service Tool 18G.502A with pipe and adaptor 18G.502K. Any suitable oil pressure gauge of known accuracy and suitable reading range may be used.

1 The pressure gauge is connected to a pressure point on the top of the external fullflow oil filter by means of suitable unions.
2 Start the engine and run it up to full normal working temperature.
3 Check the oil level and top up if necessary.
4 Restart the engine and check the oil pressure readings in the R position and positions other than R. If these are not approximately correct, refer to Fault Diagnosis.
5 Remove the oil pressure gauge and insert and tighten the plug in the filter header.

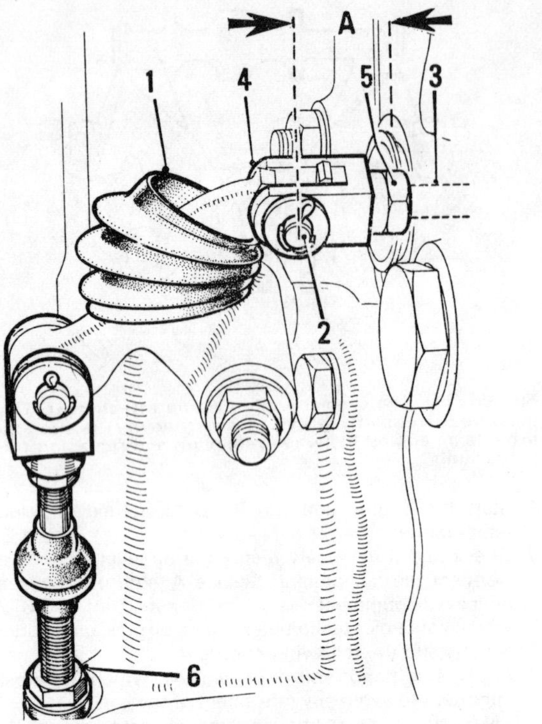

FIG 6a:11 Gearchange cable and selector rod adjustment

Key to Fig 6a:11 1 Rubber boot 2 Clevis pin 3 Selector rod 4 Selector rod yoke 5 Locknut 6 Cable adjusting nut **A**=20 mm ($\frac{25}{32}$ inch)

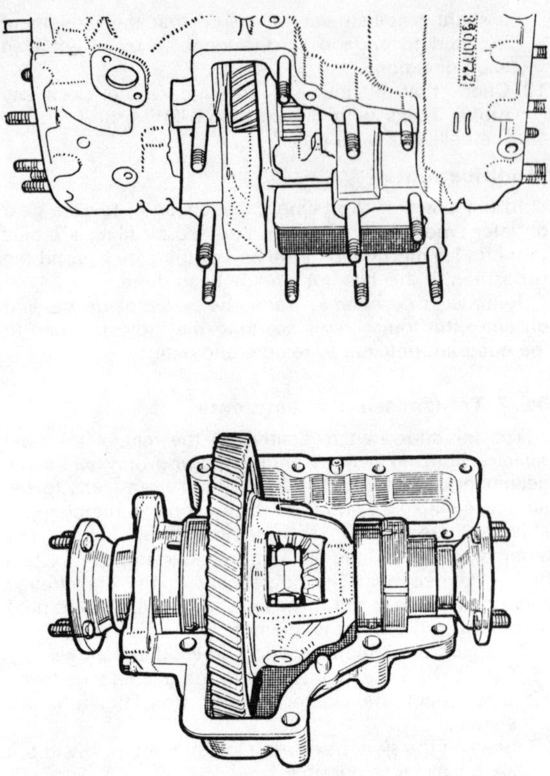

FIG 6a:12 The differential assembly removed from the transmission casing, showing the extended flange of the lefthand final drive shaft end cover

6a:8 Dismantling, overhaul and reassembly

It should be understood that complete dismantling, overhaul and reassembly of the automatic transmission will require an expensive range of special tools and also a considerable amount of skill and experience. There are however some assemblies which can be dealt with in the home workshop. These include the differential unit and the gearchange housing, lever and cable assemblies.

The differential unit is very similar to that used on cars having synchromesh transmission, the main difference being the drive shaft inboard universal coupling flanges, which are suited to all metal couplings as distinct from the rubber-bushed couplings found on the synchromesh transmissions. The flanges are secured to the final drive shafts in the differential unit by means of special set bolts, spring and plain washers, and split collets.

Note that before removing the differential unit from the transmission it is necessary to remove the securing screws and pull back the kick-down linkage assembly clear of the transmission casing.

The arrangement of the bearings and end covers in this differential unit also differs a little from the synchromesh type unit in that the righthand final drive shaft and bearing are housed in a stepped cylindrical spacer piece, which, when in position, is clamped between the differential housing and the transmission casing in a suitably machined annular space. The lefthand final drive shaft has a detachable cover not unlike the cover on the synchromesh model but as two of the securing set bolts screw into the transmission casing, the end cover and final drive must be removed before any attempt is made to remove the differential housing. Reference to **FIGS 6a:12** and **13** should clarify these design features. Further dismantling will then be generally in accordance with the instructions given in **Chapter 6** for the synchromesh differential unit. If any difficulty is experienced in removing the differential bearings, it may be possible to borrow from the Service Agent a special Service Tool 18G.2, illustrated in **Chapter 6**, for the purpose.

When reassembling the separated differential unit make sure that the differential gear thrust washers are assembled with the chamfered bores against the machined faces of the differential gears and when offering the differential unit to the transmission casing make sure the slot in the spacer indicated by the arrow in **FIG 6a:13** is in line with the dowel in the transmission casing. The new joint washer must be lightly coated with Hylomar jointing compound on both sides. Make sure the righthand oil seal is pressed well against the spacer as the differential unit housing is replaced on to the transmission casing and only lightly tighten the securing nuts at this stage.

Adjustment of preload on the differential bearings is carried out as follows:

1 Refit the (lefthand) end cover without a joint washer

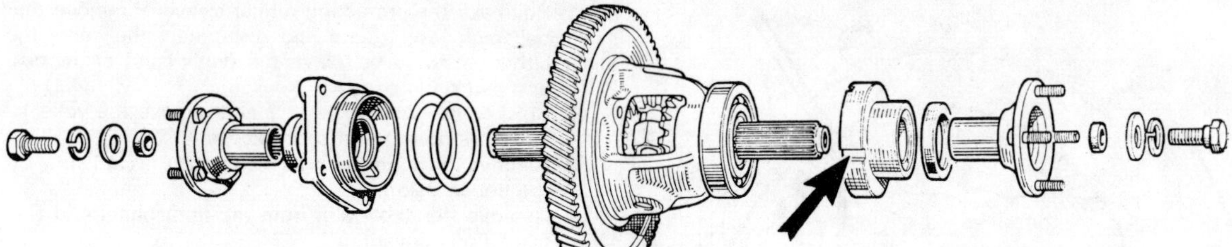

FIG 6a : 13 The components (less casing) of the differential and final drive shafts. The arrow indicates the alignment slot in the righthand final drive shaft bearing spacer

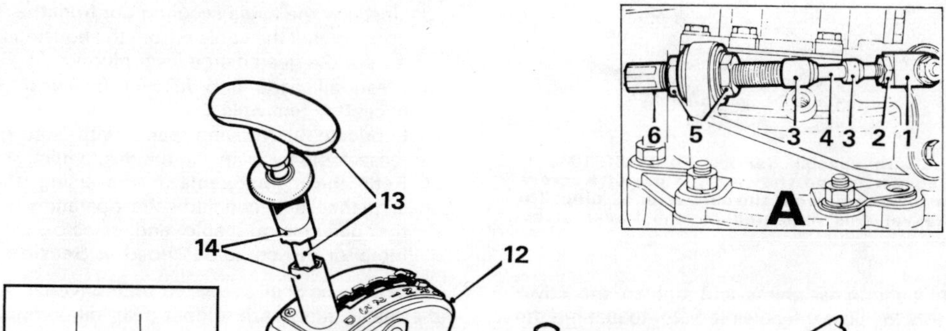

FIG 6a : 14 The components of the selector lever and cable mechanism. Inset A shows the later type cable assembly, B is the early type

Key to Fig 6a : 14 1 Yoke 2 Yoke locknut 3 Rubber ferrules 4 Cable sleeve 5 Adjusting nuts 6 Cable 7 Lever plunger 8 Housing 9 Switch locknut 10 Inhibitor switch 11 Reverse return spring 12 Quadrant 13 Selector lever 14 Spring loaded sleeve 15 Screws and washers

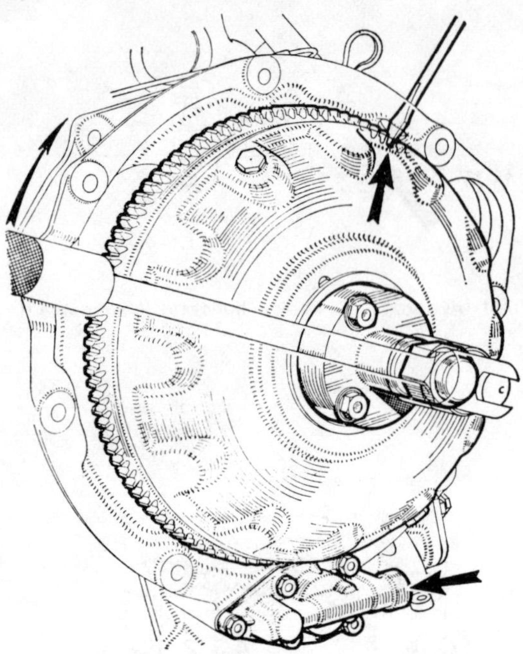

FIG 6a:15 Using special Service Tool 18G.1086 to remove the converter and showing the use of a screwdriver (top arrow) to prevent the converter turning. The low pressure valve is indicated by the lower arrow

but with the original shims and tighten the cover bolts evenly to allow the cover register to just nip the bearing outer race. Do not tighten beyond this point.

2 Adjust the cover bolts so that a feeler gauge measurement of the gap between the cover flange and the differential housing is the same all round.

3 The required preload is .002 inch and as the compressed thickness of the jointing material is .007 inch, the correct measured gap should be .009 inch. If the measured gap is not .009 inch, add or remove shims to give this figure.

4 Remove the end cover, fit the required shims, coat the new joint washer on both sides with Hylomar jointing compound, reassemble the cover with new locking plates and progressively tighten the securing set bolts and the differential housing nuts to 18 lb ft torque. Do not lock the nuts which will secure the exhaust pipe bracket when the engine is in the car.

5 Lubricate the driving flange oil seals and when refitting the flanges make certain the split collets are correctly fitted in the flanges on to the ends of the drive shafts. Fit new rubber sealing rings to the central bolts before fitting and tightening these. BMC Agents use the Service Tool 18G.1100 to hold the flanges and Service Tool 18G.372, a universal torque wrench for use with standard sockets to tighten the flange bolts to a torque of 40 to 45 lb ft.

6 Refit the governor control linkage with a new washer. Ensure that the lever is correctly positioned relative to the governor.

The gearchange cable can be serviced, lubricated or renewed as follows, referring to **FIG 6a:14**.

1 Pull back the protecting rubber sleeve or remove the bellcrank lever guard and disconnect the cable by either removing the clevis pin (early cars) or the nut and bolt on later cars.

2 Slacken the yoke locknut 2 and remove the yoke 1, rubber ferrules 3 and cable sleeve 4.

3 Remove the adjusting nuts 5 and pull the cable free of the transmission.

4 Remove the cable clip from the floor panel and the front floor covering.

5 Disconnect the electrical leads from the inhibitor switch 10.

6 Remove the screws securing the gearchange housing 8, carefully pull the cable through the rubber dust excluder and remove the housing and cable assembly complete.

7 Holding the housing in a vice, remove the four setscrews and spring washers securing the quadrant 12 to the housing. Release the reverse return spring 11 from the base of the housing and remove the quadrant and lever assembly.

8 Unscrew the cable securing nut from the front of the housing pull the cable 6 from the housing and release it from the gearchange lever plunger 7.

9 Clean all parts and inspect for wear. Make any necessary renewals.

10 Lubricate all moving parts with soft grease and reassemble by reversing the dismantling sequence.

11 Refit the components by reversing the removal sequence and conclude the operation by adjusting the gearchange cable and selector rod, and the inhibitor switch as described in **Section 6a:7.**

In order to gain access to the converter output gear, idler gear, transmission input gear, oil pump, crankshaft, main bearings connecting rods and piston assemblies, and camshaft, it is necessary to remove the torque converter and housing and the transmission unit with differential assembly. These operations are best carried out by the BMC Agent who has the necessary special service tools mentioned below. However, some owners will no doubt be interested to study the procedures, which are as follows:

1 Remove the radiator mounting bracket from the transmission case.

2 Take off the starter motor and converter cover.

3 Drain the converter by taking out one of the two drain plugs located near the converter starter gear teeth.

4 Unlock the converter centre securing bolt. Prevent the converter from turning by inserting a screwdriver through the hole in the top side of the converter casing and between two of the teeth on the starter ring gear. A special wrench, Service Tool 18G.587 is now useful to remove the converter centre bolt.

5 Unlock and remove three equally spaced setscrews from the converter centre, replace the screwdriver, and using the Service Tool 18G.587 and adaptor 18G.1086, draw off the converter as illustrated in **FIG 6a:15.** During this operation it is essential that the slot in the end of the crankshaft should be horizontal.

6 Take off five nuts and washers securing the low pressure valve to the casing below the converter as shown in **FIG 6a:15** and remove the valve.

7 Using the Service Tool 18G.1088 to hold the converter

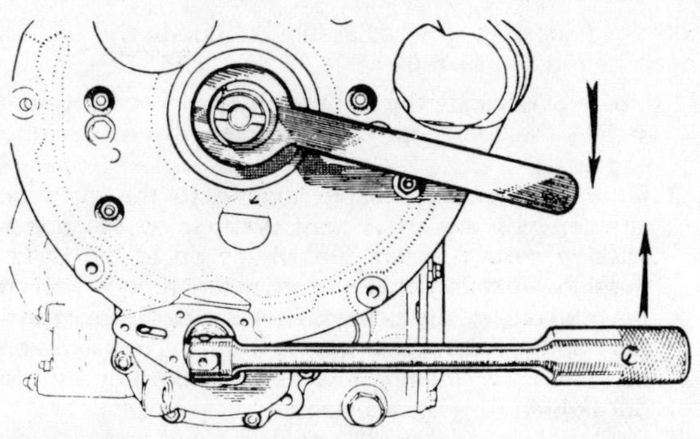

FIG 6a : 16 Using the special Service Tool 18G.1088 to hold the converter output gear with the slot horizontal when removing the input gear nut

output gear as shown in **FIG 6a : 16,** remove the transmission input gear self-locking nut under the low pressure valve housing position.

8 Remove the bellcrank lever clevis pin and nut, take off the bellcrank lever, then remove the lever pivot.

9 At this point the nylon protector sleeve 18G.1098 must be positioned over the converter output gear. The nuts and setscrews securing the converter housing to the transmission and crankcase can then be removed and the housing taken off.

10 The main oil feed pipe situated below and to the right of the distributor is next removed. It is secured with two set bolts and spring washers. Care should be exercised with the rubber seal and spring washer at the lower end.

11 Next remove the idler gear, thrust washers and converter output gear assembly, then the main oil filter and the engine oil feed pipe.

12 Now take the weight of the engine on suitable safe lifting tackle without lifting at this stage and remove all the nuts and setscrews securing the transmission unit. Lift the engine carefully away from the transmission.

13 It is important that all oil seals on pressure pipes should be in perfect condition and it is best to renew these on reassembly. The joint faces should be examined and cleaned and new washers obtained.

14 The idler gear bearings can be renewed if necessary by removing the old bearings from their housings using the Service Tool 18G.581. The rear input gear bearing is renewed by removing the circlip and pressing the bearing from the housing.

15 A special Service Tool 18G.1087 is also used to remove the main oil seal by hooking the tool into the oil seal groove and tapping outwards, working round the seal until it comes free.

16 To remove the stator carrier oil seal, remove the stator oil seal housing and carefully remove the seal. The new seal must be lubricated and pressed into the housing using the Service Tool 18G.134 and 18G.134CN as shown in **FIG 6a : 17.**

17 To replace the converter output gear oil seal the following sequence must be observed to ensure that the oil drain hole behind the seal remains unobstructed.

18 Take a depth measurement from any convenient point on the periphery of the housing bore, from the front face of the housing to the undercut face A, **FIG 6a : 18.** This measurement will be ⅜ inch or ⅜ inch plus or minus a small amount. If the measurement is exactly ⅜ inch or more, fit the new seal flush with the front face of the converter; if less than ⅜ inch, fit the seal proud of the face by that amount. Use the same point on the converter face for all measurements, as the face is not machined dead true. Screw the short threaded end of Service Tool 18G.1068A securely into the end of the crankshaft, lubricate the new oil seal, then assemble the seal with Tool 18G.1068 as shown in **FIG 6a : 18** and screw the wingnut forwards to push the seal to the required depth. Oil seals are always fitted with the knife edge lips towards the side on which the oil has to be retained.

Reassembly of the transmission and torque converter requires special care with a number of points as follows, noting that if the transmission is of the early type without an oil reservoir for additional lubrication for the

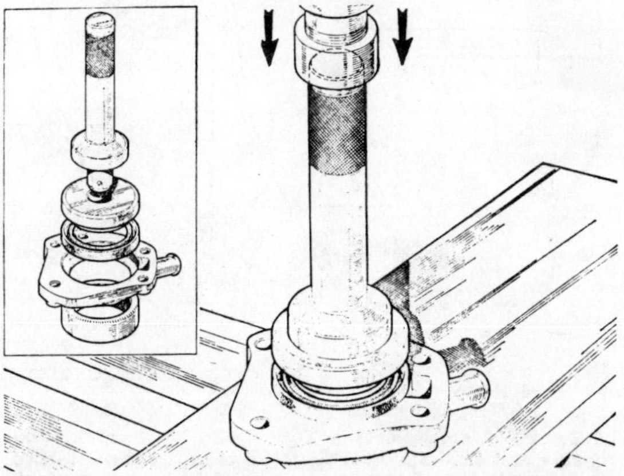

FIG 6a : 17 Using the special Service Tool 18G.134 and adaptor 18G.134.CN to press the stator housing oil seal into position. The inset shows an exploded view of the various parts in order of assembly for the operation

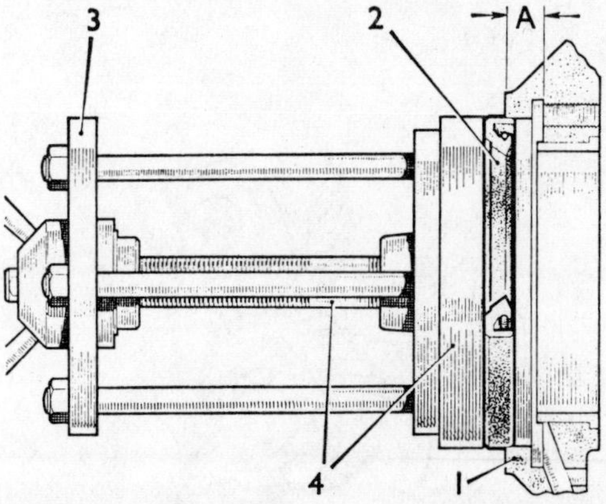

FIG 6a : 18 Part sectional view of the converter output gear oil seal and housing during the fitting operation. The depth measurement referred to in the text is shown at A

Key to Fig 6a : 18 1 Converter housing 2 Oil seal 3 Special Service Tool 18G.1068 4 Special Service Tool adaptor 18G.1068A

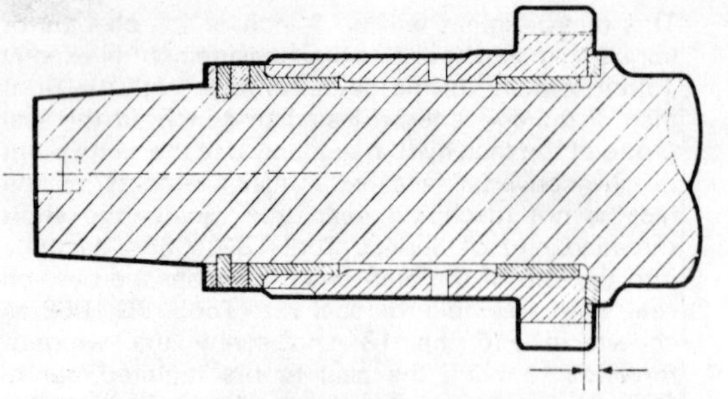

FIG 6a : 19 Section through the converter output gear. The gap indicated is the one to be measured for selection of the thrust washer to give correct running clearance

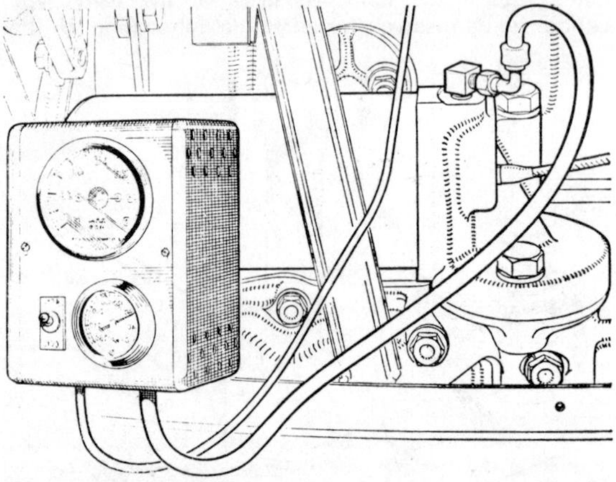

FIG 6a : 20 Using Service Tool 18G.677 to check oil pressure and stall speed. The green lead is connected to the ignition coil CB connection and the red and black leads to the battery positive and negative terminals respectively

FIG 6a : 21 Service Tool 18G.1089, comprising two sets of special washers, in use with wax washers, to assess the total thickness of thrust washers for the idler gear and input gear

idler gear bearing, it is advisable to modify the unit as described in **Section 6a : 2**.

1 Liberally lubricate the front main bearing cap oil seal and fit the seal with the lip facing the rear of the engine.

2 Fit a new rubber sealing ring on to the main oil strainer pipe and new joint washers to the transmission casing. Lower the engine on to the transmission, ensuring that the moulded rubber seal at the front is correctly located. **This is most important.** Tighten the screws and nuts securing the transmission as the engine is being lowered into position but do not tighten fully at this stage.

3 Refit the transmission-to-engine oil feed pipe, placing the spring under the seal. Refit the oil filter assembly, then refit the main oil pump-to-transmission oil pipe.

4 Trim off any protruding transmission jointing material visible at the rear end where the converter casing will be fitted and make sure the converter housing joint surfaces are clean. Fit a new joint washer.

5 Replace the converter output gear, checking the running clearance at .0035 to .0065 inch between the inner thrust washer and the gear as shown in **FIG 6a : 19.** If necessary select a new thrust washer from the range available to correct the running clearance and fit the new washer with the inner chamfered edge facing the crankshaft.

6 Assemble the idler gear to the transmission with a nominal washer, from the range fitted, on the transmission side of the idler gear. Assemble Service Tool 18G.1089, two sets of special washers, illustrated at **FIG 6a : 21** with a 'dental wax' washer interposed, on to the converter housing side of the gear. To cut holes in the wax strip place the larger washers of the tool, one on either side of the wax, opposite each other and press the two together.

7 Fit the input gear Service Tool 18G.1089 with a 'dental wax' washer interposed. Note that if considerable force would be required to mesh the input gear with the idler gear fully, it is likely that the third speed reaction gear thrust washer has become displaced. The gear train must then be removed, dismantled and reassembled to correct this.

8 Two pilot bars of the Service Tool 18G.1043 are now screwed into the two bottom tapped holes in the crankcase to assist refitting the converter housing. The nylon sleeve 18G.1098 is positioned over the converter output gear and the converter housing replaced temporarily, with the nuts tightened to the correct torque load of 18 lb ft. Do not fit the input shaft nut at this stage as the housing has to be removed to measure the thicknesses of the idler gear thrust washer plus the thickness of the Service Tool 18G.1089 together with its 'dental wax' washer.

9 From the total thickness of these subtract .004 to .007 inch and the balance will give the total thickness of thrust washers for the idler gear to ensure correct end float. Washers are available in thicknesses of .132 to .133 inch, .134 to .135 inch, .136 to .137 inch and .138 to .139 inch.

10 Now measure the total thickness of the input gear Service Tool 18G.1089 and its 'dental wax' washer. To the total add .001 to .003 inch and this will give the total thickness of thrust washers to provide

the required 'nip' on the input gear bearing. Input gear thrust washers are available in thicknesses of .128 to .130 inch, .132 to .134 inch, .140 to .142 inch, .148 to .150 inch and .152 to .154 inch.

11 Now divide the total thickness of idler gear thrust washers by two to arrive at the thickness of each washer to be fitted, one on each side of the gear.

12 Fit the two washers to make up the correct thickness for the input gear. Both washers are fitted to the outside of the gear with the chamfered inside edges of the washers towards the gear.

13 Refit and align the converter outlet pipe at exactly 90 deg. to the rear engine joint facing.

14 Using an entirely new joint washer, refit the converter housing, remove the pilot bars and progressively tighten the transmission and converter housing fixings so that the two are pulled gently on to the engine together before final tightening to the correct torque load.

15 Using special Tool 18G.1088 and 18G.592 refit the input gear shaft nut and tighten to the correct torque load of 70 lb ft.

16 Before refitting the converter remove each pair of bolts in turn, fit new locking plates and tighten the bolts to the correct torque load of 22 to 24 lb ft and lock.

17 Lubricate the converter oil seal and refit the converter, the washer with offset pegs and the centre bolt and new lockwasher. Tighten the centre bolt to the correct torque load of 110 to 115 lb ft, using Tools 18G.587 and 18G.592, and lock securely.

18 Refit the low pressure valve using a new joint washer and spring washers, the gear selector bellcrank lever and clevis pin using a new splitpin, and the rubber boot, converter cover, starter motor and rear engine mounting.

Special note

If it is desired to remove the camshaft without dismantling the transmission from the engine **take the most extreme care** not to allow the oil pump drive coupling to stick to it and fall into the transmission casing. Make sure the coupling is fully located on the oil pump splined driving spindle when replacing the camshaft

6a : 9 Fault diagnosis

Road testing must be carried out if any fault is suspected in the operation of the automatic transmission. The road test will indicate which components of the system are likely to be faulty or in need of adjustment. In any case of transmission slip or poor acceleration carry out a stalling speed test first as detailed in **Section 6a : 7.**

Next carry out operational checks throughout as follows:

1 Check that there is key start with the selector in the neutral position only.

2 Check that there is drive with no over-run engine braking with the selector in the 1 position.

3 Check that there is drive with over-run engine braking with the selector in the 2, 3 and 4 positions.

4 In accordance with the table below, check the road speeds at which all up and down changes are occurring, with the selector in the D position.

Throttle position	*Gearchange*	*Road speed, mile/hr*
Light	1 to 2	10 to 14
	2 to 3	15 to 19
	3 to 4	20 to 24
Kick-down	1 to 2	25 to 33
	2 to 3	37 to 45
	3 to 4	49 to 57
Kick-down	4 to 3	47 to 39
	3 to 2	39 to 31
	2 to 1	26 to 18
Closed	4 to 3	20 to 16
	3 to 2	14 to 10
	2 to 1	8 to 4

5 With the selector in the R position, check that there is drive with engine braking.

Slip in all gears indicates low oil pressure which can be checked by the method outlined in **Section 6a : 7.**

The following fault and rectification charts are used by [the] Service Agents as a preliminary to corrective action in relation to the automatic transmission. These will be of interest to owners but it will immediately be clear that some of the data will be of use only in respect of placing the owner in a better position to discuss his vehicle intelligently with the Service Agent when overhaul or rectification action becomes necessary. If, however, owners carry out those checks and adjustments which are within their ability, visits to and costs at the Service Agents will be kept to a reasonable minimum.

When the faults listed are noticed, the rectification action indicated by the numbers in the righthand column and outlined in the rectification chart numerically, should be instituted as soon as possible to prevent further development of the particular fault and possibly further more serious damage due to continued running with the automatic transmission in a faulty condition.

Fault:	*Carry out check or rectification listed in Rectification Chart*
Faulty gear selection, possibly with tie-up in D position on kick-down	1
Slip or no drive in forward gears	2, 3
Slip in reverse	4, 5, 6
Slip or no drive in all gears	7, 8, 13, 20, 23
Difficult or bumpy selection and shifts possibly with squawk on selection and with lubrication warning light on or low gauge pressure	7, 8, 9, 13, 20
Erratic automatic shifts	7, 10
Incorrect shift speeds	11
Excessive creep or engine stalls when selecting gear	12
Unable to tow-start	13, 14
Gear whine consistent with road speed but not in top gear	15
Continual whine consistent with engine speed	16
No drive in first gear automatic and manual	17, 18

Rectification chart:

1 Check gearchange cable and selector rod adjustment.
*2 Check the fitting of forward clutch feed pipe.
*3 Check the forward clutch and/or the shaft rings.
*4 Check the reverse gear band adjustment or remove the valve block and check the reverse servo feed pipe O-ring seals.
*5 Remove the valve block and clean; regulator valve or reverse booster piston faulty.
*6 Check the top and reverse clutch booster piston or shut-off valve.
7 Check engine/transmission oil level.
8 Carry out pressure check.
9 Check oil filter head O-ring seals.
*10 Remove and examine governor unit for sticking.
11 Check governor control rod adjustment.
12 Check carburetter adjustment—incorrect idle speed.
*13 Remove and clean valve block.
14 Check auxiliary pump, pipes, and seals.
*15 Check gear train adjustment.
*16 Check converter housing bush.
*17 Check freewheel support dowel bolt—sheared.
*18 Check the one-way clutch unit.
*19 Remove the valve block and check the servo feed pipe O-ring seals and check the second gear band adjustment.
*20 Check main oil pump and flow valve, the supply and feed pipe seals, and main oil strainer seals.
21 Carry out stall speed check.
*22 Change the torque converter unit.
*23 Check the low pressure valve.

*Checks marked * should be referred to the Service Agent.*

CHAPTER 7

DRIVE SHAFTS AND FRONT SUSPENSION

DRIVE SHAFTS

7:1 Description

Each front drive shaft assembly comprises a shaft splined at one end to fit the inner universal couplings at the transmission, and a constant speed universal coupling, at the outer end, the outer member of which has a short splined extension to carry the front wheel hub. Power transmission through the constant speed coupling is by means of six caged balls locating in six longitudinal slots machined in the exterior of the inner coupling member and the interior of the outer coupling member. All the slots are machined parallel to the shaft axis.

Maintenance of the drive shafts is minimal since they are now prepacked with grease on assembly. Early models were fitted with a grease lubricating nipple for the sliding joint only.

Throughout this chapter the constant velocity bell joints on the outer ends of the drive shafts are referred to simply as bell joints.

Later (1974) type offset sphere inboard joints:

The servicing procedures for this type of drive shaft and joint are described in **Sections 7:10** and **7:11**.

7:2 Removal

Removal of the shaft assemblies is described in **Section 7:8**. Removal of the constant velocity coupling is carried out for servicing but it should be noted that the replacement of individual parts is not permissible. A faulty rubber boot may cause loss of lubricant and should therefore, be renewed as early as possible. At the same time the coupling should be dismantled and inspected for damage due to unlubricated running.

7:3 Dismantling

1 Clean off all road dirt and grease and mount the shaft in a vice with soft jaws.

2 Prise off the boot and housing seal clips or cut the soft iron securing wire, turn back the housing seal and slide off the joint flange, then remove the housing seal and rubber boot. If worn or damaged order new parts for reassembly.

3 To remove the constant speed coupling, referred to as the bell joint, it is necessary to contract the round-section spring ring, locating it, in a groove at the end of the shaft. Hold the assembly as shown in **FIG 7:1** and tap the outer race sharply with a hide-faced hammer. This should contract the spring ring and enable the bell joint to be removed.

4 Before dismantling the bell joints mark the races and cage for correct mating on reassembly. With the shaft withdrawn, tilt the inner race, noting that the cage swivels only half this angle, until it is possible to remove one ball. Ease out the remaining balls in turn until all are removed. See **FIG 7:2**.

5 Now swivel the cage into line with the axis of the joint and turn it until two opposite elongated openings are opposite two lands of the outer member. One land will

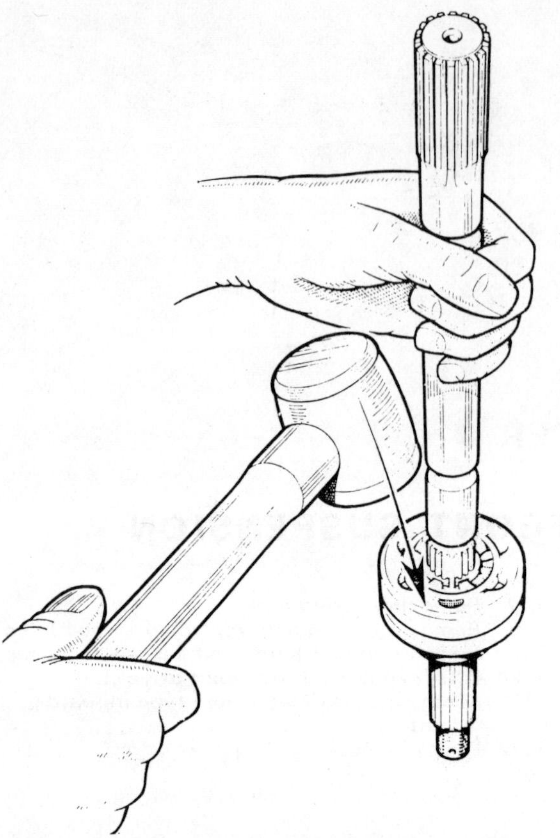

FIG 7:1 Removing the bell joint from the drive shaft. Use a mallet at the point indicated

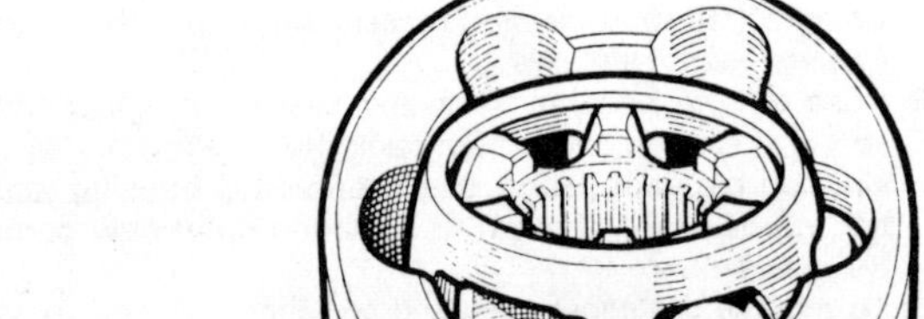

FIG 7:2 Tilting the bell joint inner race to remove or replace each of the balls in turn

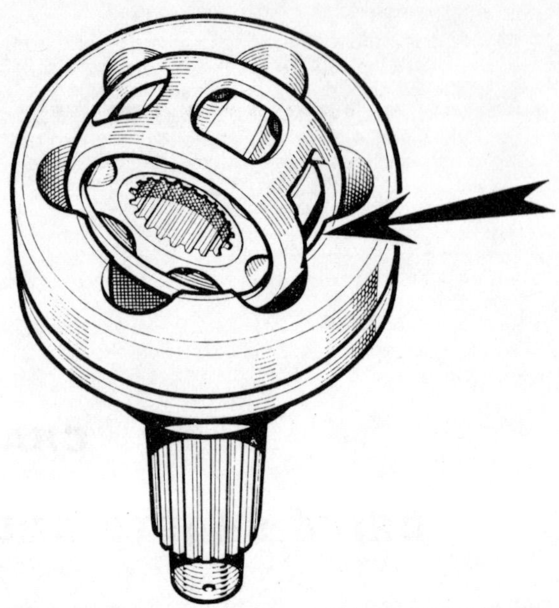

FIG 7:3 Removing the cage and inner race assembly from the bell joint

enter one of the openings and allow the cage and inner race to be removed. This operation is shown in **FIG 7:3**.

6 To remove the inner race, swivel it inside the cage so that the axes are at right angles and two lands are opposite openings in the cage, then lift it out.

7 Clean and degrease all parts and inspect as follows: Check the balls for corrosion, pitting, chipping or flats. Check the inner and outer tracks for evenness of wear, corrosion and chipping. Check the spherical surfaces of the cage and inner and outer races for 'picking up' and the outer edges of the cage openings for wear, which if severe may cause a knocking noise when operating at big angles. Examine the shaft and splines for wear, cracks and corrosion and check that the square-section outer circlip is firmly in its groove.

7:4 Refitting the ball cage

Any doubts about the condition of the bell joint or its component parts should be referred to the Service Agent. It should be noted that non-standard oversize cages were fitted to some shafts in original assembly and they are not interchangeable. The agent will be able to identify the non-standard assemblies (.004 and .010 inch oversize respectively) and will be able to advise on the need for renewal of the bell joint.

A service kit (BMC pack AKF.1457) is available, containing a suitable quantity of Duckham's MB grease, for reassembly purposes. To assemble the bell joint proceed by reversing the dismantling sequence, lubricating all components lightly with the MB grease. No excessive force should be required at any point and care should be taken to mate the parts correctly as marked during dismantling.

After assembly, make sure all parts move freely in each other and then pack the joint with the balance of the grease before inserting the shaft as follows:

7 : 5 Reassembling the bell joint and shaft

1 Always renew the round-section spring ring at the end of the shaft (see **FIG 7 : 4**), and if a new shaft is to be used, use also a new square-section circlip.

2 Hold the shaft in a vice, with the square-section spring ring and round-section ring positioned, and with the bell joint assembled with its internal chamfer centrally over the round-section ring. Give the joint a sharp tap with the hide-faced hammer to close the ring into the inner race bore. Tap the joint fully down into position against the square section ring and check that the ring has expanded fully into the internal groove in the inner race. Check that the round-section ring fits snugly into its groove against the inner race.

3 The rubber boot is fitted by sliding it over the shaft and bell joint until the radiused ribs locate in the grooves in the shaft and joint. Two methods of securing the boot are available. The first is to use soft iron locking wire turned twice round the boot, with the ends of the wire twisted to pull the wire tightly to give a grease-tight joint, and then bent down in the direction opposite to the normal direction of rotation of the shaft, as shown in **FIG 7 : 5** or secondly: to use the special clinching clips fitted as shown in **FIG 7 : 6**, using the Service Tool 18G.1099 or a suitable pair of pliers.

4 When fitting the yoke (inner) end of the shaft, lubricate the splines and the inside of the yoke housing seal and slide the seal over the shaft. Apply about $\frac{3}{4}$ oz. of MB grease into the cavity in the yoke and place the yoke on the shaft. Locate the seal into the grooves in the shaft and yoke and push the shaft right home so that the grease is driven out into the seal, holding the seal end open to allow air and surplus grease to escape.

5 Check that the diameter of the bellows does not exceed 1.75 inch, and if this is satisfactory, secure the seal with turns of soft iron wire or clinching clips as described for the bell joint seal. If wire is used, make sure the ends cannot damage the seal as it flexes.

6 Note that if a new drive shaft assembly having a rubber boot on the sliding joint is fitted as a replacement to older type cars, it will be necessary also to fit a new lefthand lower arm inner pivot pin of modified design to ensure sufficient clearance for the rubber boot. This is illustrated in **FIG 7 : 3a**. The dimension indicated by the arrows must be .312 inch.

FRONT SUSPENSION

7 : 6 Description

All models are fitted with independent front suspension either by rubber cones or by the Hydrolastic system described in **Chapter 8** where all necessary servicing instructions are given. Movement of the wheel is conveyed to the rubber cone by means of a strut fitted to the upper suspension support arm. Telescopic dampers are fitted between the upper suspension support arms and the wing valances. The wheels swivel in ball joints at the ends of the suspension support arms and the drive shafts are positioned between the two arms.

Manufacturing dimensions determine the geometry of the suspension which is not adjustable for other than mutual alignment of the front wheels. Maintenance is confined to cleaning externally and lubrication at the grease nipples provided for the steering knuckles, ball joints and suspension arms.

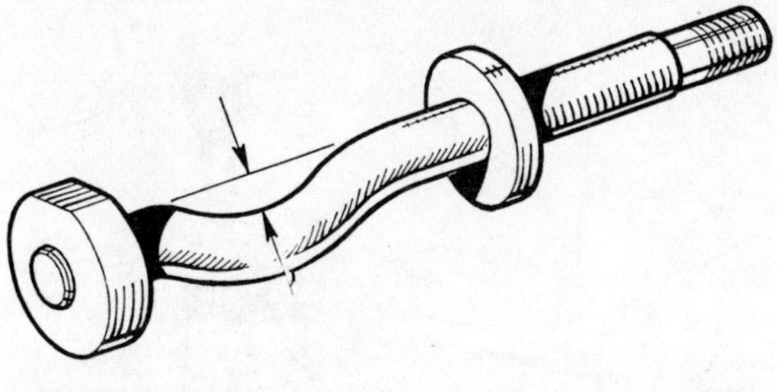

FIG 7 : 3a Lower arm pivot pin. Arrows indicate clearance of .312 inch to accommodate rubber boot of later-type drive shaft

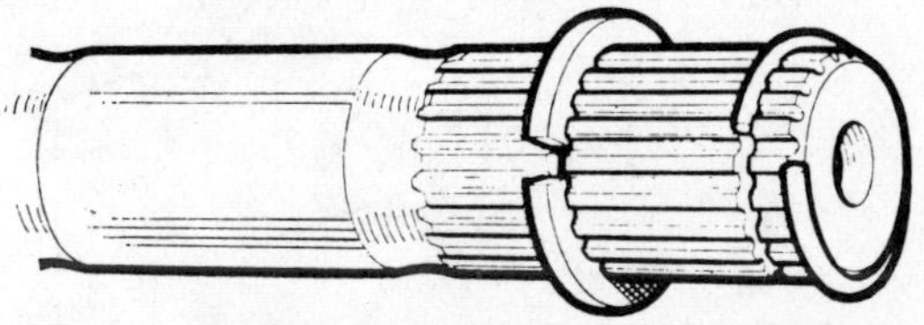

FIG 7 : 4 The round section spring ring and the square section circlip at the splined bell joint end of the drive shaft

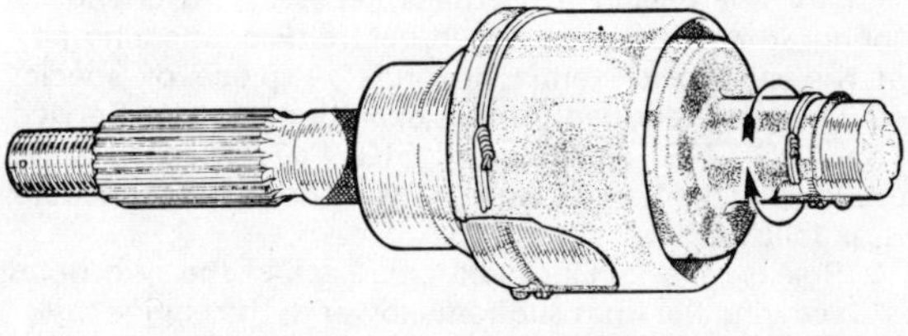

FIG 7 : 5 The method of securing the bell joint rubber boot using soft iron locking wire. Bend the twisted end away from the direction of rotation

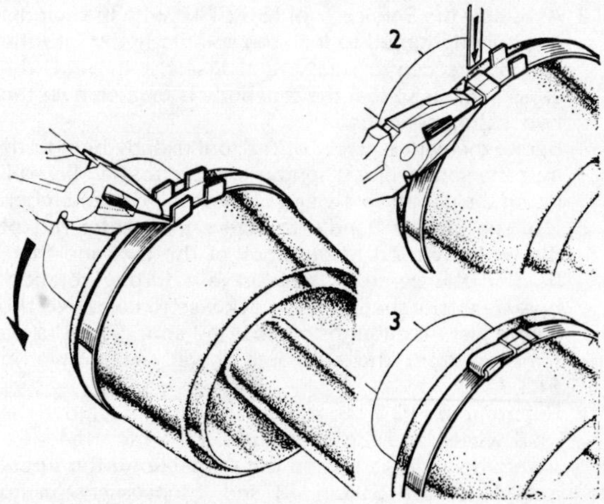

FIG 7 : 6 The method of securing the bell joint rubber boot using the clinching clips and the Service Tool 18G.1099

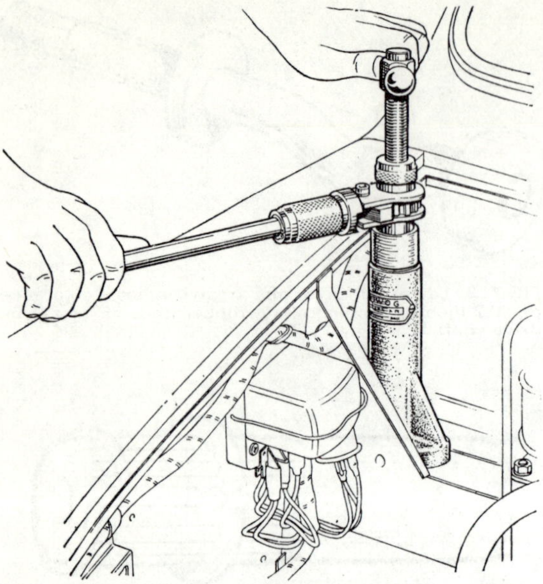

FIG 7 : 7 The method of applying the Service Tool 18G.574B to compress the spring unit

7 : 7 Removing spring unit

If for any reason it becomes necessary to change a spring, it must be compressed before disconnecting any of the suspension arms or struts. A piece of special equipment is required for this operation, namely Service Tool 18G.574B, illustrated in **FIG 7 : 7**, which will be available at the Service Agent's workshop. The procedure is as follows:

1 Release the locking tabs and slacken the two bolts securing the front subframe tower to the engine bulkhead crossmember.

2 Withdraw one bolt, move the washer plate to one side to expose the access hole in the crossmember, replace the bolt and tighten both.

3 Assemble the Service Tool 18G.574B with the spindle nut fully tightened to lock the spindle firmly into the end of the centre screw, and insert it through the crossmember so that the tool body is located over the two subframe bolts.

4 Screw the centre screw of the tool exactly nine turns into the spring unit, keeping the ratchet handle well up on the centre screw and clear of the crossmember.

5 Use the ratchet handle to screw the centre nut of the tool down on to the body of the tool and then, holding the centre nut to prevent further rotation, operate the ratchet handle clockwise to compress the spring just far enough to allow the spring strut to be removed from the subframe tower, as shown in **FIG 7 : 7.**

6 Referring to **FIG 7 : 8,** jack up the car and remove the road wheel, and the bump rubber 24 from the subframe tower. Take off the nut 44 securing the upper arm 40 to the ballpin 43 and if necessary, using Service Tool 18G.1063 (**FIG 7 : 11**), remove the arm from the ballpin.

7 Remove the spring strut 35 by levering.

8 Disconnect the hydraulic damper 29 at the lower end, remove the upper arm pivot 1 and remove the arm, as described in **Section 7 : 9.**

9 Holding the compression tool centre screw, operate the ratchet anticlockwise to release the pressure on the spring 39 and then extract the spring from within the subframe tower. Do not attempt to remove the centre screw from the spring unit without first slackening off the compressing nut.

10 Refitting is the exact reverse of the foregoing instructions.

11 On cars fitted with hydrolastic suspension, a displacer unit is fitted in place of the rubber spring. This is removed as follows:

12 Jack up the car and remove the road wheel, then depressurize and evacuate the hydrolastic system. See **Chapter 8** for this operation.

13 Release the displacer strut dust seal from the nylon seat and take out the strut.

14 Disconnect the displacer hose from the union on the engine bulkhead.

15 Remove the suspension top arm.

16 Push the displacer upwards and remove two screws from the displacer bracket to release it from inside the subframe tower, then turn the displacer anticlockwise and withdraw it from the subframe.

17 When refitting the displacer, rotate it clockwise to lock it into the registers on the locating plate. Lubricate the strut ball end and the nylon seat with Dextragrease Super GP lubricant and make sure the dust seal is fitted over the lip of the nylon cup. Evacuate and pressurize the system.

7 : 8 Removing, servicing and replacing the swivel hubs (see FIG 7 : 8)

Swivel hubs vary slightly in design according to model.

1 With the car jacked up and the road wheel removed, remove the steering ball joint nut and release the ball joint with Service Tool 18G.1063.

2 Mark the inner universal coupling members and disconnect the couplings by removing two nuts 66 from each of the outer U-bolts 65. On those models with a universal joint flange, remove the four retaining nuts.

3 Disconnect the brake hose from the backplate. On disc brake models remove the caliper and, if the hydraulic hose is not removed, tie it safely out of the way without straining the hose.

4 Remove the outer nuts 44 and 81 with their spring washers and detach the tie-rod 16 from the lower suspension arm 74, detach also the damper 29 from the upper arm.

5 Using Service Tool 18G 1063 release the ball pins from the suspension arms. Withdraw the hub and drive shaft assembly from the car.

6 Remove the brake drum (when applicable), then remove the splitpin, nut 78 and distance washer 79, or outer tapered collar on disc brake models, item 2 in **FIG 7 : 9**. Drift the drive shaft from the flange and hub or remove the shaft using Service Tool 18G 304, see **FIG 7 : 12**. Drift the driving flange 75 from the hub using Service Tool 18G 575 shown in **FIG 7 : 13**.
On disc brake models. Tap the end of the drive shaft with a hide mallet and pull off the driving flange and

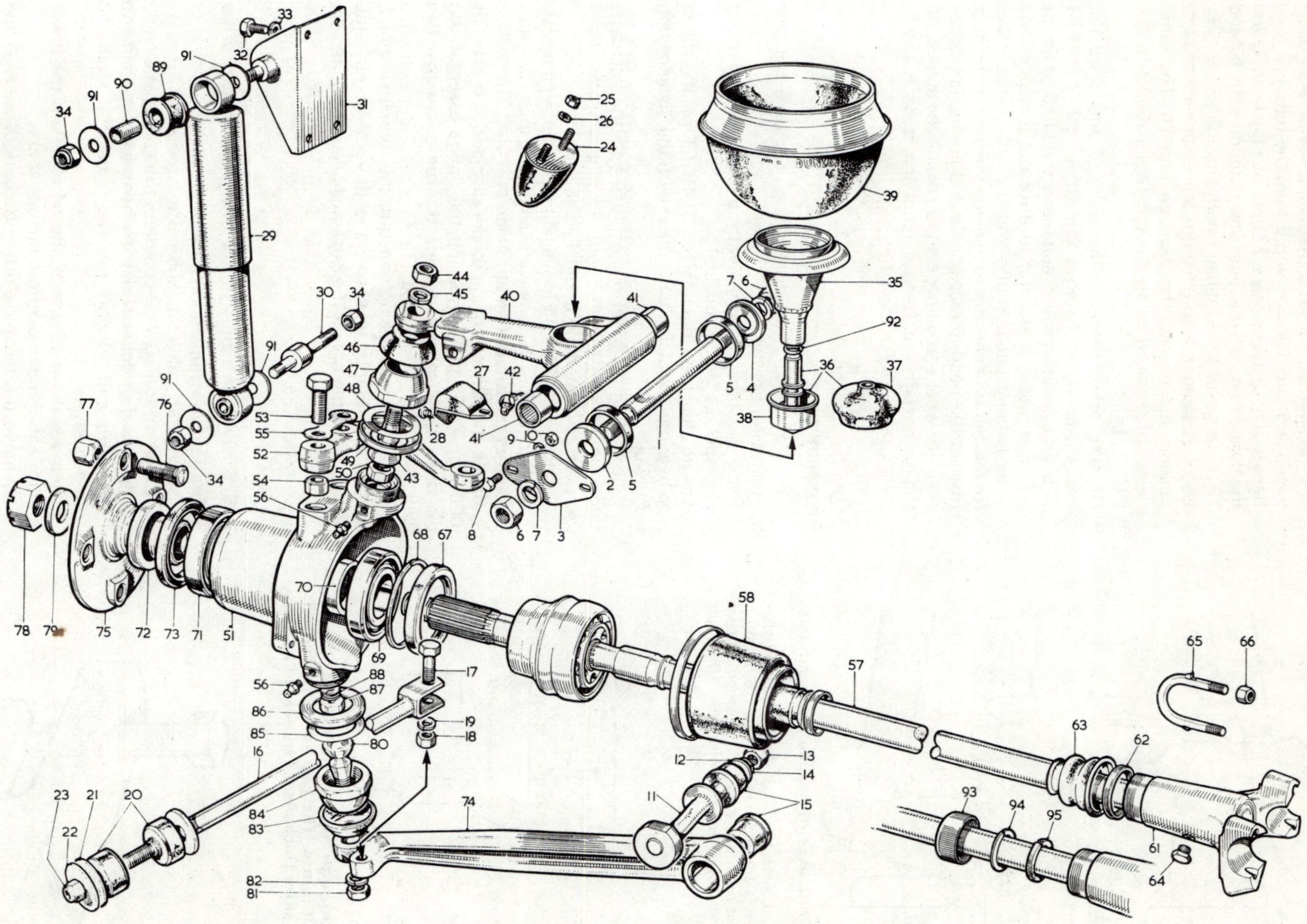

FIG 7:8 Component parts of front suspension

Key to Fig 7:8 (Parts referred to in text) 1 Upper support arm pivot shaft 2 Thrust collar 3 Retaining plate 4 Thrust washer 5 Sealing ring 6 Nut 7 Spring washer 13 Nut 14 Spring washer 16 Tie-rod 24 Bump rubber 29 Hydraulic damper 35 Spring strut assembly 39 Rubber cone spring 40 Upper support arm 41 Needle roller bearing assembly 43 Top ball pin 44 Nut for ball pin 45 Spring washer 46 Dust cover 47 Ball pin retainer 49 Locking washer for ball pin retainer 50 Ball seat 51 Swivel hub 56 Lubricator 57 Drive shaft assembly 67 Oil seal 68 Oil seal spacer 69 Inner bearing 70 Spacer 71 Outer bearing 72 Distance piece 73 Oil seal 74 Lower arm 75 Driving flange 78 Securing nut for driving flange 79 Plain washer 80 Lower ball pin 81 Ball pin nut 82 Spring washer

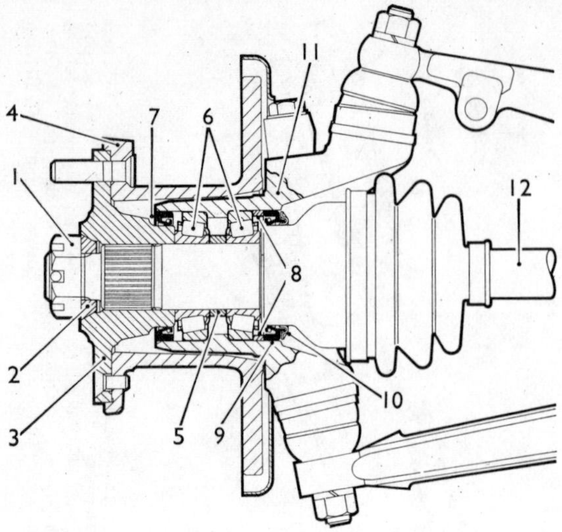

FIG 7:9 The swivel hub assembly, disc brake models

Key to Fig 7:9 1 Drive shaft nut 2 Outer tapered collar 3 Driving flange 4 Hub and disc assembly 5 Bearing distance ring 6 Taper roller bearings 7 Outer oil seal 8 Spacer (inner bearing to seal) 9 Inner oil seal 10 Water shield 11 Swivel hub 12 Drive shaft

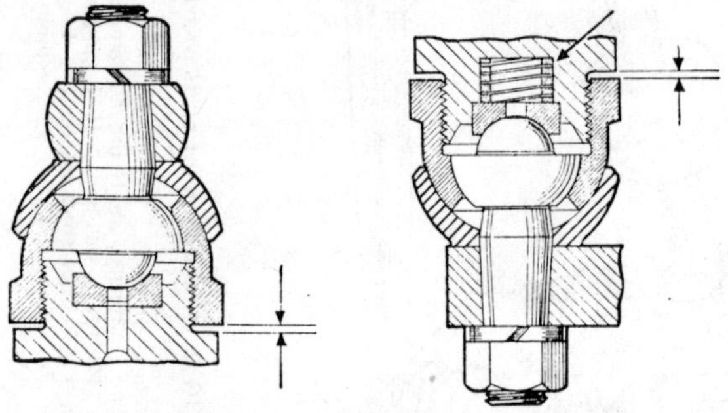

FIG 7:10 Section through upper (left) and lower (right) swivel hub ball joints. The gap to be measured for the calculation of shim thickness is indicated by the arrows

FIG 7:11 Service Tool 18G.1063 is used to release the taper joint on the swivel hub ball pins and the steering rack ball ends

disc assembly. Remove the shaft, inner and outer bearings 6 and distance ring 5 from the hub.

7 Remove the distance piece 72 between the bearing and the flange and also the inner and outer oil seals 67 and 73, with water shield when fitted, and the spacer 68.

8 Use a suitable drift to drive out the inner race of each bearing and remove the distance ring 70. The outer races are removed using Service Tool 18G 260H, see **FIG 7:14**.

9 On disc brake models. Operations 7 and 8 do not apply, substitute: Remove the outer seal, 7 in **FIG 7:9**, and the inner seal 9 and water shield 10 (if fitted) and then use a brass drift to drive out the inner and outer bearing cups, noting that the hub has recesses for this but take care not to damage the bore of the hub. Inspect the bearing races, balls and rollers, check the seals for wear and damage and examine the splines on the drive shafts and flanges, renewing as necessary.

Reassembly:

This is a reversal of the dismantling procedure, but note the following points:

Pack the bearings only with a high melting point grease such as Duckhams LB10.

Ensure that the sides marked THRUST on the thrust type bearings are facing each other with the distance ring in between.

When fitting the inner oil seal, use only the later type single lipped seal together with its plastic water shield irrespective of the type originally used.

Service Tool 18G 134 is available for refitting the seals to the hub. Ensure that the water shield is $\frac{1}{4}$ inch (6.4 mm) inboard of the drive shaft shoulder.

Check the run-out of the brake disc and if it exceeds .006 inch (.15 mm), reposition the flange assembly on the drive shaft splines to bring the run-out within this limit.

See that all nuts are tightened to the torque specified, use a new splitpin to secure the drive shaft nut and, finally, bleed the brakes if a hose has been disconnected.

7:9 Swivel hub ball joints and suspension arms

The following operations are required for removal of the swivel hub ball joints and suspension arms:

1 Referring to **FIG 7:8** compress the spring as already described or depressurize the hydrolastic system and jack up and support the car under the subframe sidemember.

2 Remove the road wheel, the tie rod from the lower arm and the damper from the upper arm.

3 Remove the retaining nut and spring washer at the ball joint for the upper suspension arm and release the arm from the ballpin, using Service Tool 18G.1063 as required.

4 Remove the ball housing dust seal 46 and lubricator 56, release the locking washer 49, and then unscrew the housing 47 to release the ballpin 43 and seat 50.

5 Remove the lower ball joint assembly in a similar manner.

6 To remove the upper suspension arm, first remove the nut 6 and washer 7 from each end of the suspension arm swivel shaft 1, then take off the front thrust collar retaining plate 3, the collar 2 and the seal 5.

7 Push the shaft forwards, remove the rear thrust washer 4 and seal 5 and then manoeuvre the arm from the frame. If required the needle roller bearings 41 can be removed from the suspension arm using a Service Tool 18G.581 as used for removing the transmission idler gear bearings.

8 To remove the lower suspension arm 74 first apply suitable supports under the brake drum or disc brake hub.

9 Release the lower arm by taking off the nut and spring washer securing it at the lower ball joint pin and using Service Tool 18G.1063 as necessary, disconnect the arm from the pin 80.

10 Remove the nut 13 and washer 14 from the inner support shaft 11 and withdraw the shaft. The lower suspension arm will now be free.

11 Clean and inspect all parts for wear, damage and corrosion. The upper and lower ball joints are illustrated in section in **FIG 7:10**.

12 For refitting the ball joints proceed as follows:

13 Fit and assemble the joints complete except for the packing shims, locking (tab) washer, and the seat spring in the lower ball joint. Screw down the ball housing until there is no free movement between the ball and its seating.

14 Measure the gap, indicated in **FIG 7:10** between the housing and the ball joint hub.

15 Dismantle the housing and ballpin and fit shims to the measured thickness less the thickness of the locking washer, which is .036 inch thick. Add one additional shim to ensure that the final assembly has .000 to .003 inch end float.

16 Pack the joint assembly with grease and reassemble it to the hub with the housing fully tightened, making sure the ballpin still swivels freely, if not, add a further shim. The Service Tool 18G.372 and adaptor 18G.587 are used to finally tighten the housing to the correct torque.

17 Lock the washer on three flats of the housing. Where disc brakes are fitted, one of these must be adjacent to the disc.

18 When refitting the upper suspension arm lubricate all parts with grease and fit the needle roller bearings with the marked ends outwards. It may be necessary to use a special Service Tool 18G.582 and adaptor 18G.582A to push the bearings into position.

19 Lubricate the spring unit strut nylon cup with a special lubricant, Dextragrease Super GP.

20 When refitting the lower arm, support the arm in the normal position when the shaft nut is locked up to avoid any pre-(torque) loading of the rubber bushes.

21 Refit the dust seals when reconnecting the arms to the ball joints and tighten the ballpin nuts to 35 to 40 lb ft torque, not forgetting to fit new spring washers at these points.

22 Reconnect the tie rod to the lower suspension arm and the damper to the top arm, release the spring or pressurize the hydrolastic system as required and refit the road wheel.

23 Where necessary, bleed the brake system.

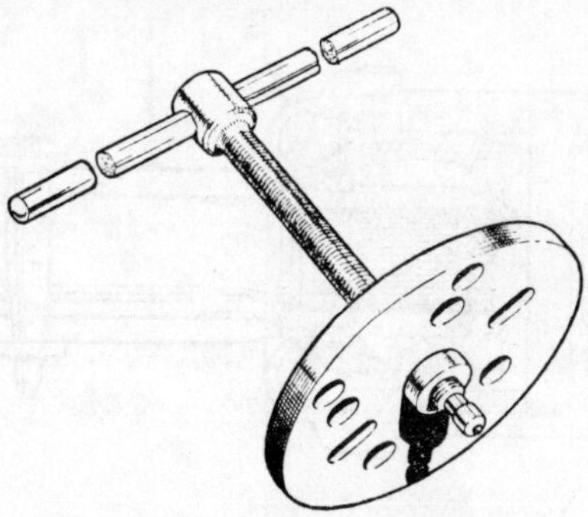

FIG 7:12 Service Tool 18G.304, front and rear hub remover and 18G.304F adaptor bolts (not shown) are used for removing the wheel hubs

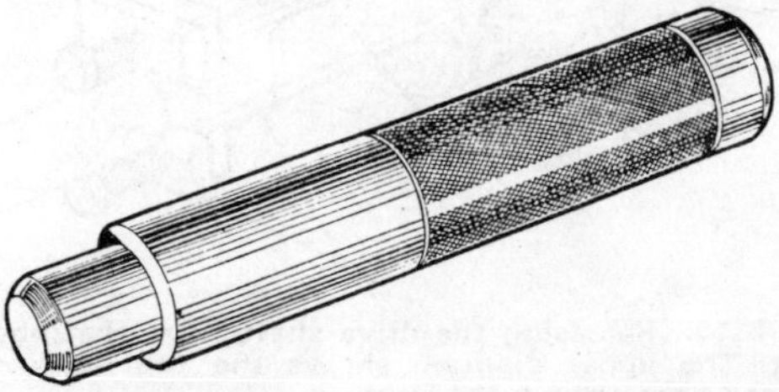

FIG 7:13 Service Tool 18G.575 is used for removing the front hub driving flanges

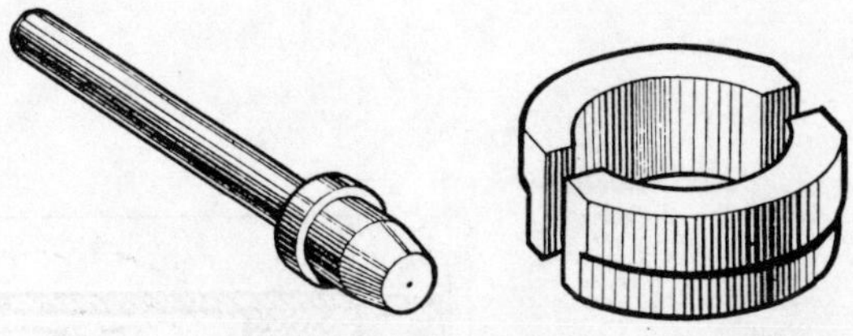

FIG 7:14 Service Tool 18G.260 (basic tool) and 18G.-260H (adaptor) are used together for removing the front hub drive flange bearing outer races

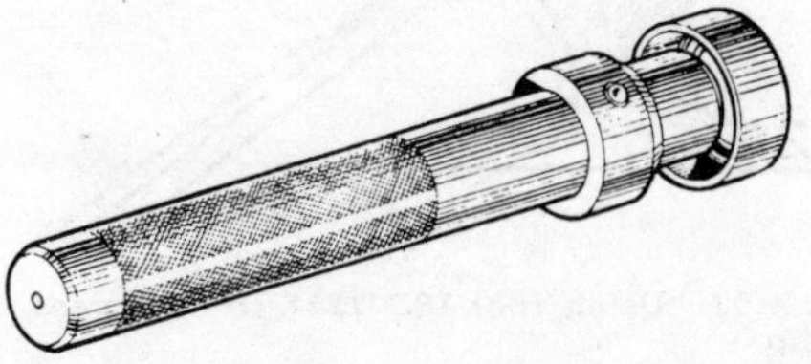

FIG 7:15 Service Tool 18G.582 is used for replacing the front suspension needle-roller bearings

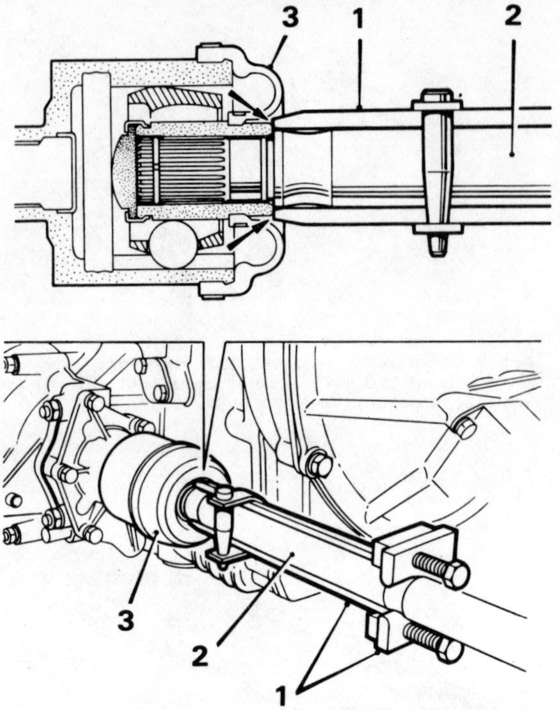

FIG 7:16 Releasing the drive shaft from the inboard joint. The upper diagram shows the tool (arrowed) pressed hard against the joint

Key to Fig 7:16 1 18G 1243 2 Drive shaft 3 Inboard joint

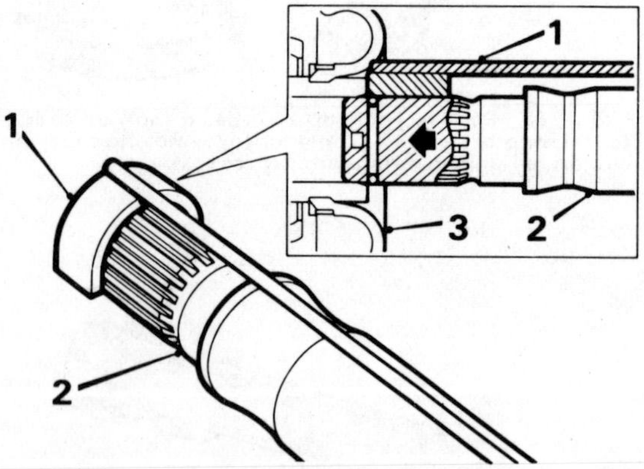

FIG 7:17 Using tool 18G 1241 to compress the joint circlip

Key to Fig 7:17 1 18G 1241 2 Drive shaft 3 Inboard joint

7:10 Offset sphere inboard joint drive shafts

Removal:

Take out the single cross-headed screw securing the rebound rubber for the upper suspension arm and replace the rubber block with a solid wedge of the same thickness.

Remove the wheel trim and slacken the wheel nuts. Remove the splitpin and slacken the drive shaft nut.

Raise the car onto suitable stands and remove the road wheel.

Remove the securing nut and release the tie-rod ball joint from the steering lever, using tool 18G 1063 or other suitable claw shaped tool.

Similarly release the upper swivel hub ballpin, but loosely refit the retaining nut.

Refer to **FIG 7:16** and fit the tool 18G 1243 as shown, with the tool hard against the inboard joint before inserting the tapered pin. Insert the U shaped part of the tool in the groove on the shaft and tighten the two bolts evenly until the drive shaft releases from the joint. Remove the tool.

Unscrew the nut and disconnect the swivel hub ballpin from the upper suspension arm, being careful not to strain the flexible brake hose.

Hold the inboard joint boot in place and pull the shaft out of the joint.

Push the shaft inwards and over the top of the final drive assembly. Remove the drive shaft retaining nut and tap the shaft out of the driving flange.

Pull the shaft out of the swivel hub and away from the car.

Refitting:

This is the reverse of the removal procedure, but note the following points:

When fitting the drive shaft into the inboard joint, tool 18G 1241 should be used to compress the joint circlip, this is shown in **FIG 7:17** and the shaft pushed hard into the joint to lock it in position.

The retaining nut on the swivel hub ballpin is tightened to a torque of 35 to 40 lb ft (4.8 to 5.5 kgm) and the drive shaft nut on standard models to 60 lb ft (8.3 kgm).

7:11 Removing an offset sphere type inboard joint

First drain the oil from the engine/transmission unit and then follow the appropriate instructions in **Section 7:10** to withdraw the drive shaft out of the inboard joint.

Refer to **FIG 7:18**. Insert tool 18G 1240 with its relieved side against the inboard joint and drive it between the joint and the final drive end cover until the block portion is over the end cover bolt as shown.

Smartly hit the tool on its flat face in the direction of the arrow. This will release the joint which may then be pulled off the splines of the final drive shaft.

Refitting:

Before commencing to refit a joint, check the condition of the nylon oil flinger and fit a new one if it is damaged at all.

Insert the joint into the final drive and press it in until the joint is firmly engaged over the retaining circlip on the splined shaft.

The joint circlip should be compressed with tool 18G 1241, as shown in **FIG 7:17**, when fitting the shaft into the joint. Push the joint smartly into the joint to lock it in position.

Complete the operation in the reverse order of removal.

7:12 Fault diagnosis

(a) Wheel wobble

1 Worn hub bearings or ball joints
2 Broken or weak front springs
3 Uneven tyre wear
4 Worn suspension linkage parts
5 Loose wheel fixings

(b) 'Bottoming' of suspension

1 Check 2 in (a)
2 Rebound rubbers worn or missing
3 Dampers ineffective

(c) Heavy steering

1 Neglected swivel hub ball joint lubrication
2 Incorrect suspension geometry due to strained or damaged part

(d) Excessive tyre wear

1 Check 4 in (a), 3 in (b) and 2 in (c)

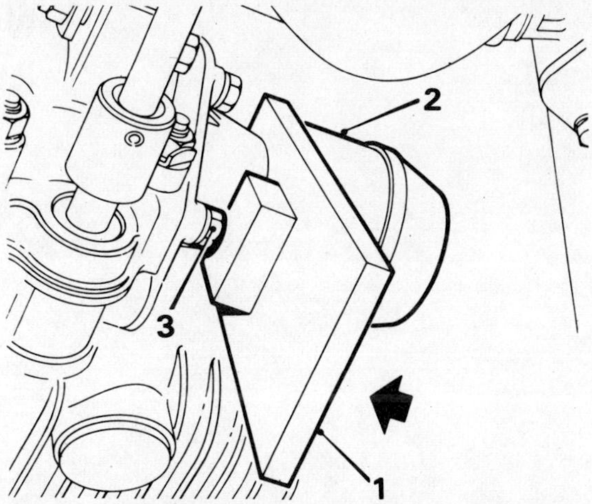

FIG 7:18 Removing an inboard joint. The arrow indicates where to hit the tool

Key to Fig 7:18 1 18G 1240 2 Inboard joint 3 Differential end cover bolt

(e) Rattles

1 Check 2 in (a)
2 Ball joint lubrication neglected, rubber bushes on lower arm or needle rollers on upper arm worn
3 Damper mountings loose
4 Radius arm mountings loose or worn
5 Tie-rod mountings loose or worn

(f) Excessive 'rolling'

1 Check 2 in (a) and 3 in (b)

NOTES

CHAPTER 8

THE REAR SUSPENSION

8 : 1 General description

All Mini vehicles have the rear suspension system built into a subframe which is, itself, completely detachable from the car body. The two rear road wheels are sprung entirely independently of each other.

Two systems of springing have been installed, the first employing rubber cone springs; the second type, described as the Hydrolastic system, employing two rubber displacer units in place of the rubber cone springs. Later cars reverted to the rubber cone suspension.

The rear road wheels and hubs are carried on the rear ends of trailing arms pivoted on pins fitted to the sidemembers of the rear subframes. The road wheels and trailing arms are able to swing in the vertical plane. The rubber cone spring units and the displacers of the Hydrolastic system are fitted horizontally inside the deep sidemembers of the rear subframe inboard of the rear road wheels. In both cases road wheel movement is conveyed to the spring unit by means of a suspension strut fitted between a boss offset below the trailing arm pivot pin axis and the spring unit. Upward movement of the wheel induces horizontal movement in the suspension strut which then compresses the spring unit. In the Hydrolastic system, compression of the spring or, as it will be termed from here on, the displacer, causes a flow of Hydrolastic fluid to the front displacer on the same side of the car, thus causing the front of the car to rise in unison with the rear. This action reduces pitching motion as the car negotiates bumps in the road surface and the system provides a smoother controlled ride and better handling of the car generally.

Models fitted with rubber cone springs are fitted with telescopic dampers operating in the vertical plane, with end fixings on the inboard ends of the stub axles and above them in the luggage compartment. The hydrolastic system has no separate dampers as provision for damping is embodied in the design of the displacer units.

FIG 8 : 1 illustrates in part-section the rear suspension incorporating the rubber cone spring. Details of the trailing arm, stub axle and the assembly of wheel and brake can be clearly seen. The rubber cone spring is shown in its correct relative position in the subframe member and the position of the suspension strut is indicated by means of broken lines between the boss on the trailing arm and the rubber cone spring. The general arrangement of this type of suspension is shown in **FIG 8 : 2** which illustrates the rear subframe complete with trailing arms and wheel hubs, the rubber cone springs inside the subframe sidemembers and the telescopic dampers.

A complementary view of the rear subframe equipped with Hydrolastic suspension is given in **FIG 8 : 3.** The two arrows indicate the Hydrolastic system pressure valves. Notice the 'helper spring' fitted between the wheel hub (inboard side) and the extended portion of the rear subframe front crossmember. The helper spring keeps

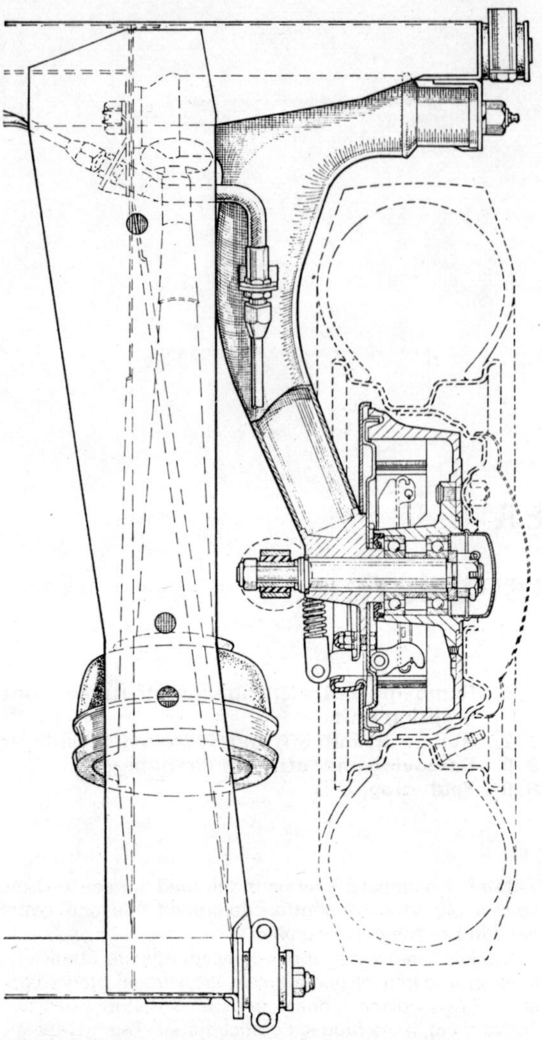

FIG 8 : 1 Part sectional plan view of the rear suspension showing the arrangement of the rubber cone spring, suspension strut, trailing arm and a section through the hub assembly

FIG 8 : 2 A view of the rear subframe and rear suspension units embodying the rubber cone springs

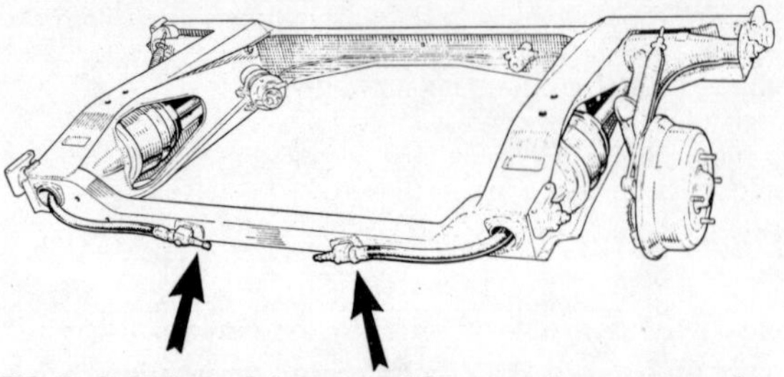

FIG 8 : 3 A view of the rear subframe and rear suspension units embodying Hydrolastic displacers. The two arrows indicate the Hydrolastic pressure valves on the subframe rear member

the Hydrolastic displacer lightly preloaded, maintains the suspension strut in its correct position when the Hydrolastic system has been evacuated and prevents the trailing arm and road wheel dropping too far and thus releasing the suspension strut from its correct position if the car is lifted off the rear wheels with the Hydrolastic system evacuated or suffering from loss of pressure following damage.

The stabilizing action of the Hydrolastic system is illustrated in **FIG 8 : 4** in which the top diagram shows how a rising front wheel causes the rear of the car to rise also. The bottom diagram shows the front of the car rising with a rising rear wheel. Note that in the actual equipment the rear displacer is nearly horizontal and not vertical as illustrated diagrammatically.

The stub axle is pressed into its boss at the end of the trailing arm.

The trailing arm pivots on a shaft located in brackets on the subframe. The shaft has a needle roller bearing at its inner end and a bronze bush at the outer end. Lubrication is by grease.

Flexible hydraulic pipes are connected between the ends of the steel pipes running through the car frame and the short steel pipes on the trailing arms.

The Hydrolastic displacer unit is shown in **FIG 8 : 5.** A road irregularity causing the road wheel to rise forces the piston 5 to push the diaphragm 8 up. Increased pressure in the chamber immediately above the diaphragm causes some of the Hydrolastic fluid in it to flow into the top chamber through the damper valve 6. At the same time, the rubber spring 2 forming the top portion of the unit is compressed and the rising fluid is forced along the interconnecting pipe 1 to the displacer unit at the other wheel on the same side of the car. This inflow of fluid causes the second displacer to extend resulting in a rise in this end of the car also.

The fluid used in the Hydrolastic system is a mixture of water and alcohol to which an anti-corrosive agent is added.

8 : 2 Routine maintenance

Routine maintenance of the rear suspension is kept to a minimum by the design of the units. Apart from general cleanliness, always a good policy, the removal of any surplus grease and accumulated grit, etc, greasing of the main pivot shafts of the trailing arms at 3000 mile intervals is all that is required.

The Hydrolastic system should be checked by a service agent after the first 12,000 miles running, when the pressure will be checked and corrected as necessary.

Under no circumstances must owners interfere with the Hydrolastic system or with the settings of the pressure valves located on the rear subframe.

If the owner should wish to carry out any operations which require the system to be de-pressurized first, he should have this done at the nearest service station and drive the car home carefully on the rubber bump stops.

8 : 3 Removing and refitting the rear subframe

If a major overhaul of the rear suspension is to be undertaken, it will be found most convenient to remove the complete rear subframe and rear suspension as a unit. The various assemblies will thereby become much more accessible. On models having Hydrolastic suspension, the system must be depressurized and evacuated first. To remove the rear subframe proceed as follows:

1 Drain the fuel from the fuel tank.

2 Disconnect the battery leads.

3 Disconnect the electrical leads and the flexible fuel pipes from the fuel pump, noting carefully how these were connected for correct reassembly. This operation is not required on the Moke model.

4 Unscrew the union nut to release the hydraulic feed pipe from the pressure regulating valve on the sub-frame member.

5 Remove the exhaust pipe manifold clamp and release the remaining exhaust system fixings other than the manifold. Remove the exhaust system as described in **Chapter 1**.

6 Remove the end finishers on the sill panels on models other than Moke.

7 Remove the fuel tank on models other than Moke as described in **Chapter 2, Section 2 : 12.**

8 On models with rear telescopic dampers, remove the top damper fixings to release the dampers for removal with the subframe and rear suspension. On the Moke this operation is performed inside the rear part of the car body.

9 On models with Hydrolastic suspension, disconnect the pipes from the Hydrolastic pressure valves on the rear subframe and remove both helper springs.

10 Refer to **Chapter 10.** Release the handbrake cable fairleads and disconnect the cables from the hand-brake lever trunnion. Pull the cables down through the floor.

11 Lift and support the body with padded hooks under the wings or luggage compartment top panel.

12 Release and withdraw the eight subframe mounting bolts, lift the car body a little further and withdraw the subframe complete.

The subframe mountings comprise a mounting bracket, rubber bushes and the mounting support pin. It is necessary to first remove the trailing arm before attempting to remove the front mountings. For the front mountings, unscrew and remove the nut securing the mounting support pin to the subframe, then pull off the support pin, rubbers and mounting block. This operation can be performed with the subframe in the car if desired. For both front and rear mountings it will also be found necessary to prise the body and subframe apart (after removing the subframe securing bolts) before the mountings can be removed from the subframe. The

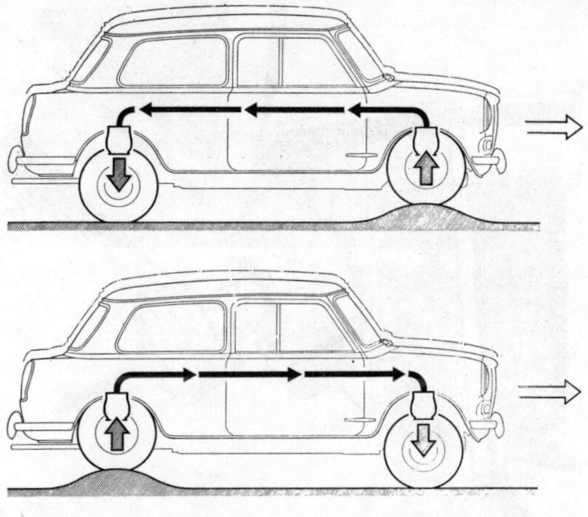

FIG 8 : 4 Diagrams illustrating the working principle of the Hydrolastic suspension. The illustration shows Elf and Hornet models. Other Mini models are similar

Top: The tail rises in response to upward motion of the front wheels
Bottom: The nose rises in response to upward motion of the rear wheels

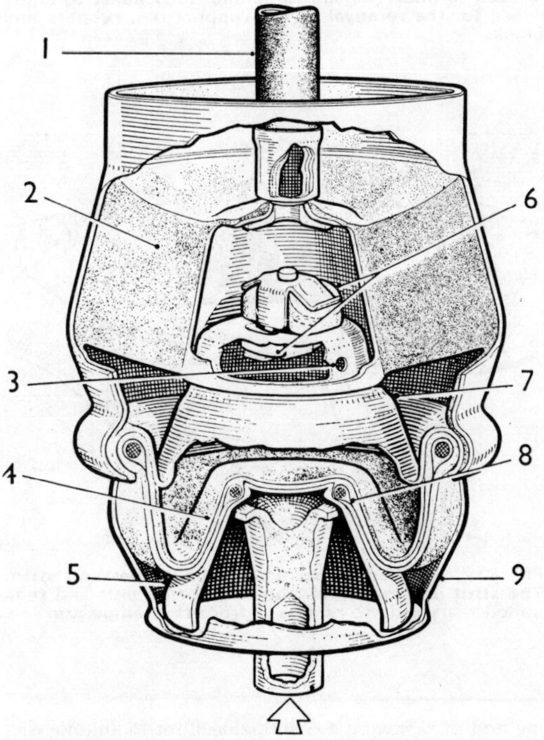

FIG 8 : 5 Sectional illustration of a Hydrolastic displacer unit

Key to Fig 8 : 5 1 Interconnecting pipe 2 Rubber spring 3 Damper bleed 4 Butyl liner 5 Tapered piston 6 Damper valve 7 Fluid separating member 8 Rubber diaphragm 9 Tapered cylinder

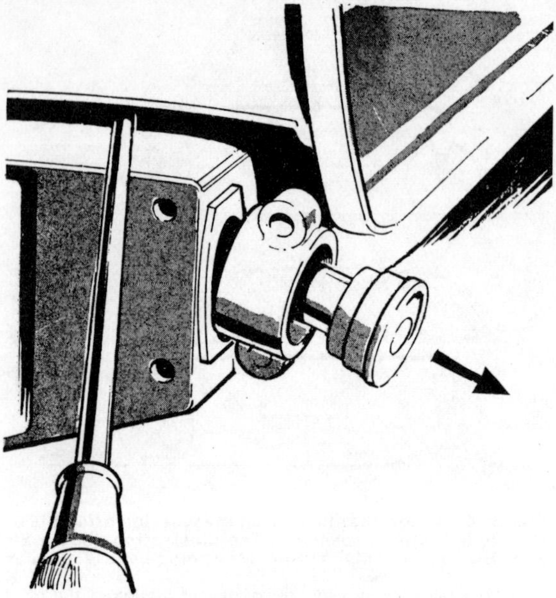

FIG 8:6 Method of removing the rear subframe front mounting support pin assembly. A screwdriver or lever is used to prise the subframe and body apart to allow space for the removal of the support pin, rubbers and blocks

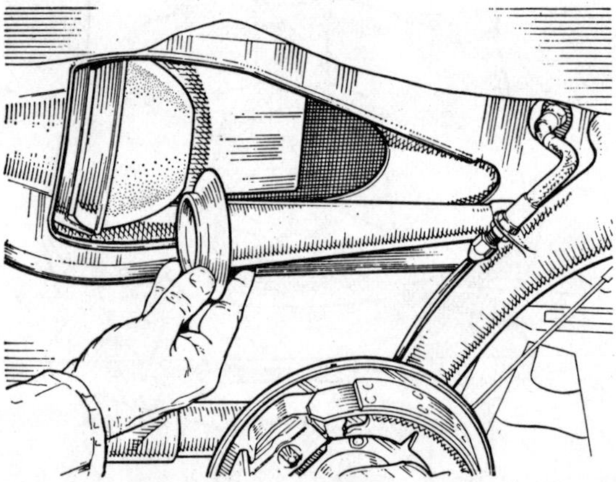

FIG 8:7 Method of extracting the suspension strut. The strut is disengaged from the spring unit and then pulled rearwards to release it from the radius arm

method of removing the subframe front mounting with the subframe still on the vehicle and the trailing arm removed, as illustrated in **FIG 8:6**.

Refitting of the subframe is generally the reverse of the removal procedure. When refitting the rear of the subframe it is advisable to insert the screws securing the mounting block to the car body before tightening up the support pin nut. This will provide for settlement of the subframe into its correct position. It will be found helpful if special care is given to lining up the mounting block holes with the tapped holes in the body when the subframe is positioned for refitting. Take care when refitting the exhaust system as outlined in **Chapter 1**. Remember to bleed the brakes.

After all work has been completed on cars with Hydrolastic suspension, drive the car to the Service Agent for the system to be pressurized. Owners should note that with the Hydrolastic system in the depressurized condition due to overhaul or damage, the suspension arm(s) will contact the bump rubbers at the front and rear of the car. The car can however be driven quite safely in this condition, with care, over metalled road surfaces at speeds not exceeding 30 mile/hr.

8:4 Removing and refitting trailing arms

To remove and refit the trailing arms adopt the following procedure:

1. On models with Hydrolastic suspension have the system depressurized.
2. On models with telescopic dampers, remove the fuel tank and release the top ends of the dampers from inside the luggage compartment. On Moke models the tanks do not require removal.
3. Raise the car, support it under the rear subframe side-member and chock the front road wheels to prevent any possible movement.
4. Remove the road wheel and disconnect the brake hydraulic hose from its bracket on the trailing arm.
5. On models with Hydrolastic suspension, release the helper spring from the trailing arm and disconnect the flexible Hydrolastic hose from its union on the rear face of the subframe.
6. With the trailing arm hanging at its lowest position to take the weight off the spring, prise out the suspension strut from the rubber spring unit or displacer and lift it out of the seating boss on the trailing arm, as illustrated at **FIG 8:7.** On models with rubber cone springs leave the Nylon cup in the boss of the trailing arm unless it appears to be damaged, in which case it can be prised out for renewal.
7. Disconnect the handbrake cable at the actuating lever, remove the nut from the cable sector pivot and remove the cable and sector from the trailing arm.
8. Remove the bump rubber from the subframe and the end finisher from the sill panel.
9. Release the trailing arm outer bracket shroud from the subframe.
10. Remove the nut and washers from the trailing arm pivot shaft and four screws to release the arm outer support bracket.
11. Lift the trailing arm assembly complete away from the car, taking care not to lose the thrust washers and rubber seal fitted between the arm and the subframe sidemember at the pivoting point.

The trailing arm pivot shaft can be withdrawn after removing the dust seal and thrust washers. A needle roller bearing is fitted to the inner end of the pivot shaft and a bronze bush on the outer end. Any serious wear of the bush or shaft, evident in the form of ridging, indicates the need for renewal of the bush or shaft. Service Agents use a Special Tool 18G.583, illustrated in **FIG 8:8** for removing the bush and another Service Tool 18G.584, illustrated in **FIG 8 : 9** to fit the new bush. It is necessary to ream the new bush to correct size and before doing so the needle roller bearing and grease tube must be removed. A reamer guide bush 18G.588A is placed in the needle roller bearing position and the reamer 18G.588, illustrated in **FIG 8 : 10** passed through it. After reaming, and removing the reamer and guide all swarf must be carefully removed. It will be found helpful to use the Service Tool 18G.583B for removal of the needle roller bearing outer race. This is illustrated in **FIG 8 : 11.** The new needle roller bearing outer race is fitted with Service Tool 18G.583 as used for the bronze bush.

When reassembling the trailing arm pivot assembly, lubricate all moving parts with Duckham's LB.10 or similar approved grease. Oil must not be used.

The rear hub stub shaft is pressed into the trailing arm boss and it is unlikely that this part will require renewal.

The assembly and refitting of the trailing arm are generally the reverse of dismantling according to model, giving special care to the following points:

1 Make sure the lubricator is clean and clear before refitting the pivot shaft to the trailing arm.
2 Lubricate the ball end of the suspension strut and the Nylon cup and dust seal with Dextragrease Super GP lubricant, available from the BMC agent in 1 lb tins (Part No. 97H.2276).
3 Refit the dust seal to the ball end of the suspension strut and lip the dust seal over the edge of the cup. **If the dust seal is fitted into the trailing arm and then followed by the strut ball end, the rubber seal cannot be lipped over the cup to make dust sealing effective.**
4 Refit the strut, make good all connections and finally bleed the brakes as described in **Chapter 10, Section 10 : 9.** Where Hydrolastic suspension is fitted take the car to the Service Agent for repressurizing.

8 : 5 Removing and refitting the dampers

Telescopic hydraulic dampers are fitted to all models having front and rear rubber cone springs. The rear dampers are rather longer than the front dampers. All dampers may be removed for inspection, renewal or priming.

Adopt the following procedure for removing the rear dampers:

1 Release the upper end of the damper as described in **Section 8 : 3.**
2 Jack up the car and remove the road wheel. Take off the lower mounting nut and washer, collapse the damper and remove it from the anchor pin on the trailing arm.
3 Maintain the damper in the upright position. Inspect the rubber bushes for serviceability and renew as necessary.
4 If it is suspected that air is present in a used damper, stand it in the vertical position for at least five hours.
5 For dampers of Armstrong manufacture, hold the damper vertically, extend it to its full length then compress it slowly. Continue to extend and compress it until no free travel is felt when changing the direction of stroke.

FIG 8 : 8 Service Tool 18G.583. The rear trailing arm bush remover

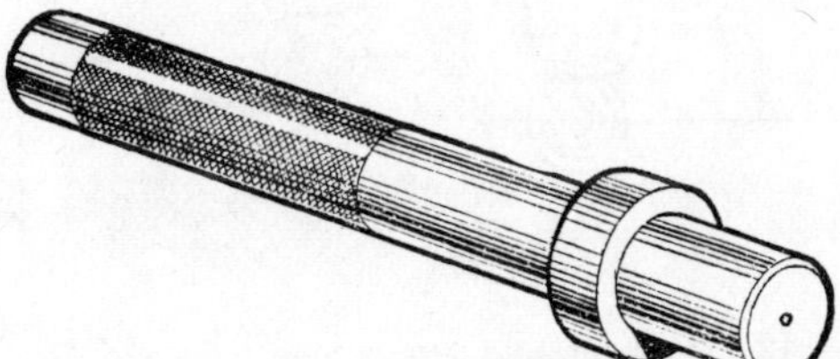

FIG 8 : 9 Service Tool 18G.584. The rear trailing arm bush replacer

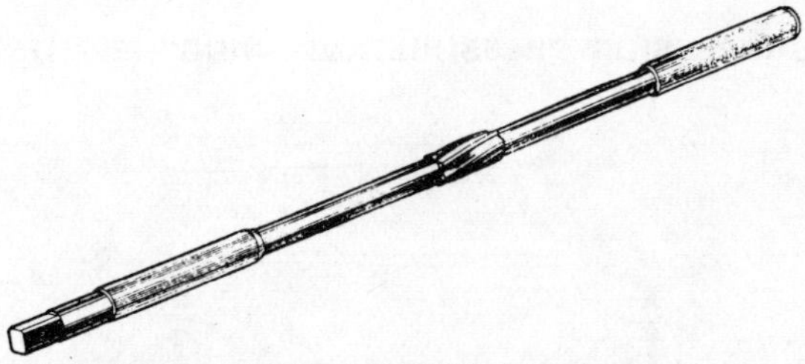

FIG 8 : 10 Service Tool 18G.588. The rear trailing arm bush reamer

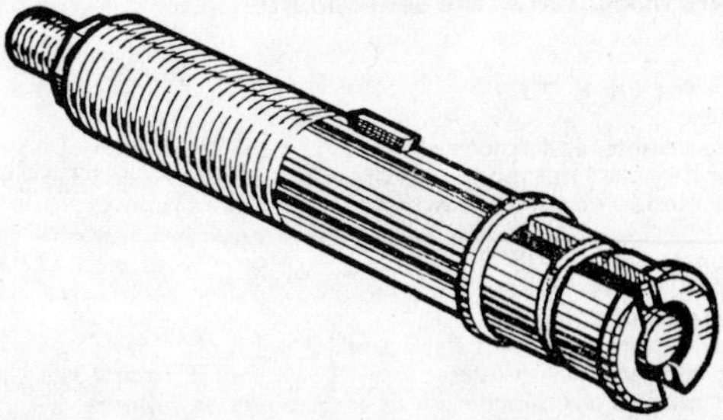

FIG 8 : 11 Service Tool 18G.583B. The rear trailing arm needle roller bearing remover adaptor used with Service Tool 18G.583

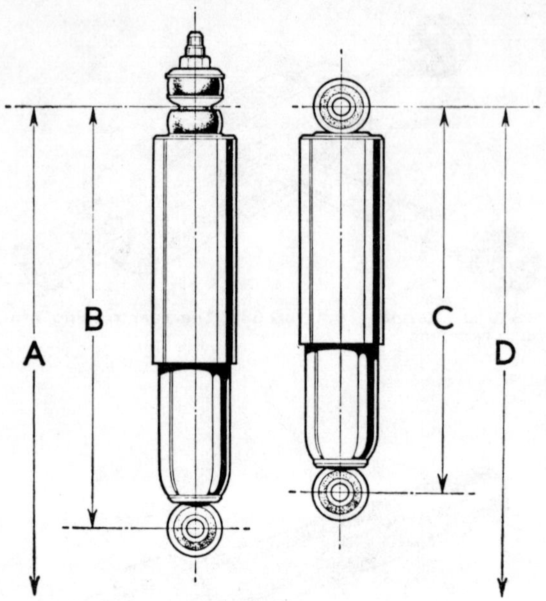

FIG 8 : 12 The hydraulic dampers

Left, the rear damper:
A Extended length $15\frac{3}{16}$ inch **B** Compressed length $9\frac{9}{16}$ inch
Right, the front damper:
C Compressed length $8\frac{1}{2}$ inch **D** Extended length $12\frac{3}{4}$ inch

SUSPENSION PRESSURE AND WING HEIGHTS

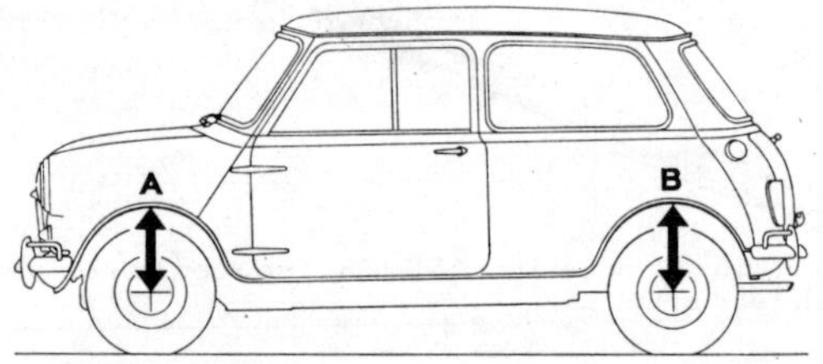

FIG 8 : 13 Checking measurements for suspension pressure and wing heights. Mini shown, but Hornet and Elf are measured at the same points

Data for Fig 8 : 13
Mini:
Wing heights, early models: Front $13 \pm \frac{1}{4}$ inch, Rear $13\frac{1}{2} \pm \frac{1}{4}$ inch
Wing heights, later models: Front $12\frac{5}{8} \pm \frac{1}{4}$ inch, Rear $13\frac{1}{8} \pm \frac{1}{4}$ inch
Later models commence with car numbers as follows:

Austin Mini 830899 Morris Mini 370004

Hornet and Elf:
Wing heights, early models: Front $13\frac{1}{2} \pm \frac{1}{4}$ inch, Rear $13\frac{1}{2} \pm \frac{1}{4}$ inch
Wing heights, later models: Front $13\frac{1}{8} \pm \frac{1}{4}$ inch, Rear $13\frac{1}{8} \pm \frac{1}{4}$ inch
Later models commence with car numbers as follows:
Wolseley Hornet 827058 Riley Elf 829535

Clubman: Front $13\frac{1}{2} \pm \frac{3}{8}$ inch, Rear $13\frac{1}{2} \pm \frac{3}{8}$ inch

6 For dampers of Girling manufacture, hold the damper with the dirt shield uppermost and at an angle of 15 to 20 deg. to the vertical, extend the damper approximately 3 inch very slowly, **but not the full length of its stroke,** and then compress it fully. Rotate the dust shield during the compressing operation and repeat the sequence until all free play has disappeared.
7 Store the dampers in the vertical position prior to refitting.
8 New dampers need only be held in the vertical position for a few minutes before priming.
9 Refer to **Chapter 7** in connection with these instructions for the treatment of front dampers.
10 When refitting a rear damper make certain that the rubber cone spring and suspension strut are correctly positioned on their individual spigots while raising the trailing arm to reconnect the upper end of the damper.
11 Individual checks of extended and compressed lengths of the dampers may be made according to the information accompanying **FIG 8 : 12.**

8 : 6 Removing and refitting separate rubber cone spring units

It is not necessary to remove the trailing arm assembly in order to remove the rubber cone spring. Carry out operations 1 to 6 in **Section 8 : 4** applicable to models with rubber cone springs and then remove the cone spring from inside the sidemember of the rear subframe.

Inspect the rubber for any signs of cracking or undue permanent distortion or other damage. Refit the spring and observe carefully the instruction for refitting the suspension strut given in **Section 8 : 4. Also observe carefully** the instruction in **Section 8 : 5,** item 10 when raising the trailing arm for refitting the top end of the hydraulic damper. Failure to observe the latter point may result in the vehicle appearing to be too highly trimmed at the rear and would probably damage the spring and the suspension strut beyond recovery.

8 : 7 Removing and refitting Hydrolastic displacer units

Before carrying out any work on the Hydrolastic displacer units it is essential to depressurize and evacuate the system. Although this is essentially a task for the Service Agent, a number of owners will no doubt wish to be familiar with the processes involved in this work. Special equipment is required, designated BMC Part No. 18G.682 (early type) or 18G.703 (later type). This equipment contains the necessary means of depressurizing, evacuating and repressurizing the system. A brief outline of the procedure is given as follows:

To depressurize before carrying out any overhaul work, connect the black connector of the unit to the pressure valve on the rear subframe of the car and open the depressurizing valve on the servicing unit, when the pressure in the system will fall to zero and the Hydrolastic fluid will flow out of it into the service unit pressure tank. The unit is then disconnected and the dust cover replaced on the pressure valve on the subframe. The procedure is then repeated for the second valve on the car subframe to depressurize the other side of the system.

When all work has been completed on the Hydrolastic system the system must be evacuated and repressurized by connecting the yellow connector of the service unit to one of the pressure valves on the subframe and closing the yellow valve on the unit.

The vacuum pump on the unit is then operated until the vacuum gauge shows a reading of 27 inch of mercury. Provision is made for adjustment of the figure if the operation is being performed at an appreciable altitude above sea level. The yellow valve on the service unit is opened and after one or two minutes during which the pressure in the car system and that in the service unit become equalized, the yellow connector is removed from the pressure valve on the car and the connector plug replaced.

To repressurize, the car must be standing freely on all four road wheels. The service unit black connector is fitted to the pressure valve on the car and the service unit valves operated in the prescribed manner so that the pressure in the system is raised to normal operating pressure. It is important to seal off the car pressure valves with dust caps after the operation has been completed for both sides of the system.

Apart from the technicalities of these procedures, it is essential for the work to be carried out by the Service Agent as different operating pressures apply to early and late type vehicles. The owner should note also that later models have modified displacer units, helper springs and rear suspension struts which are not interchangeable with those on earlier cars. The overall correctness of the Hydrolastic system can be checked by wing height measurements as indicated in **FIG 8 : 13** and accompanying data, which is applicable to cars filled with coolant, oil and four gallons of fuel.

To remove and refit the displacer unit proceed as follows:

1 Carry out the procedure outlined in **Section 8 : 4** to make the displacer units accessible.

2 After removing the suspension strut, turn the displacer anticlockwise and withdraw it from the subframe.

3 To refit the displacer unit, position it in the subframe and rotate it clockwise to lock it in position in the registers on the locking plate.

4 On completion of the reassembly of the rear suspension, return the car to the Service Agent for repressurizing.

8 : 8 Removing and refitting rear hubs

The rear wheel hubs can be removed and dismantled for inspection, cleaning and relubrication or renewal by the following procedure:

1 With the car jacked up safely at the rear end and the brake drum removed, prise off the grease retaining cap.

2 Extract the splitpin locking the slotted nut at the end of the stub shaft and discard it. Remove the slotted nut.

3 Using a suitable puller (BMC Service Tool 18G.304 and adaptor 18G.304F), illustrated in **FIG 8 : 14,** withdraw the hub assembly.

4 To dismantle the bearing it is necessary to drift the inner races from the hub first. Notice that there is a distance ring between the two inner races.

5 Remove the grease retaining seal by careful drifting.

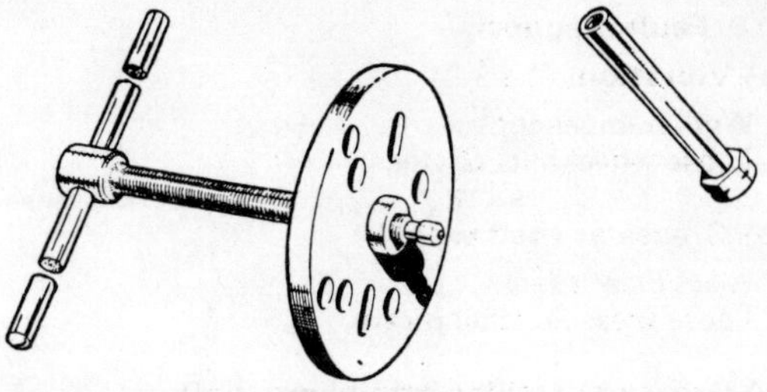

FIG 8 : 14 Service Tool 18G.304 (left). Front and rear hub remover, basic tool. Service Tool 18G.304F (right). Front and rear hub remover bolt adaptor

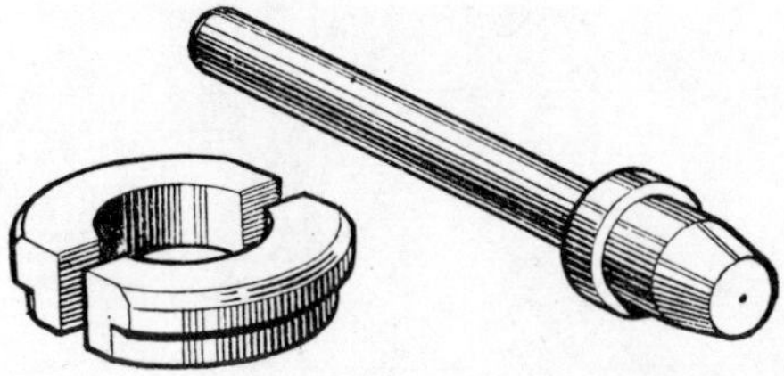

FIG 8 : 15 Service Tool 18G.260 (right) the hub bearing outer race remover, basic tool. Service Tool 18G.260C (left) the hub bearing outer race remover adaptor

6 Using a suitable extractor (BMC Service Tool 18G.260 and adaptor 18G.260C), illustrated in **FIG 8 : 15,** extract the outer races.

7 Inspect the inner and outer races for corrosion, chipping, uneven wear or other defects and the balls for corrosion, pitting and chipping of the surfaces. Check the cages for wear. In the absence of these visible defects, clean and assemble the bearings only, adding a few drops of engine oil and check for freedom and smoothness of movement without slackness. If the grease retaining seal shows any signs of cracking, distortion or wear following removal, renew it.

8 Reassembly is generally the reverse of dismantling with special attention directed to the following points:

9 Make sure the outer races are tight against the central register in the bore of the hub.

10 Refit the bearing distance ring between the inner races and pack the bearings with fresh grease of an approved type.

11 Make sure the grease retaining seal is fully and squarely home.

12 When refitting the hub to the stub shaft make sure the distance ring between the two inner races is over the shoulder on the stub shaft before applying any pressure to push the hub assembly on to the stub shaft.

13 The thrust washer must be fitted with the chamfered bore towards the bearings.

14 Use a new splitpin to lock the slotted nut after tightening it to 60 lb ft torque, if necessary tighten to line up the next slot.

15 Fill the grease retaining cap with fresh approved grease before pressing it back into position.

8:9 Fault diagnosis

(a) Vibration

1 Worn hub bearings
2 Loose wheel nuts or studs

(b) Grease at road wheel

1 Worn grease seal
2 Loose grease retaining cap

(c) Grease at trailing arm pivot shaft

1 Over-greasing or worn bush or needle roller bearing
2 Deteriorated or cracked rubber seal

(d) Noise at rear end of car

1 Damper rubbers worn
2 Dampers not tightly secured at end fixings
3 Worn bush or needle roller bearings at trailing arm pivot shaft
4 Loose rubber cone spring or Hydrolastic displacer
5 Wear of suspension strut seating cup in trailing arm boss

(e) Settling

1 Rubber cone spring or suspension strut damaged
2 Suspension strut incorrectly located at ends
3 Hydrolastic system requires attention for possible leakage or loss of pressure

CHAPTER 9

THE STEERING GEAR

9 : 1 Operating principle and construction

The steering gear on the BMC Mini cars is of the rack and pinion type, that is to say that the steering wheel is directly connected, at its lower end, to a small helical-toothed pinion which engages with the teeth machined on a straight member, the rack, set at right-angles to it. **FIG 9 : 1** shows how the rack slides laterally within an outer tubular member securely located on the engine bulkhead. Rotation of the steering wheel and pinion causes the rack to move to the right or left and this movement is conveyed to the steering arms by means of ball-jointed tie rods.

Provision is made for control of the end play of the pinion and backlash between the teeth of the pinion and the rack. The positions of the ball ends connecting the tie rods to the steering arms is adjustable on the tie rods, thus providing for alignment of the front road wheels. Following alignment, the ball ends are securely locked in position by means of locknuts. Lubrication of the rack and pinion mechanism is by Hypoid SAE.90.EP oil.

9 : 2 Routine maintenance and adjustment

On early models a grease nipple is situated on the steering tie rod end ball joint but none are provided on later models. Later ball ends at the steering arms have nylon seats and are 'life' lubricated. If the rubber caps on the ball ends become damaged, it is possible that road dirt will have caused excessive wear. Should this be the case the ball ends must be renewed. The rubber boot alone may be renewed if the ball end is otherwise satisfactory. The rubber gaiters at the ends of the rack and pinion assembly exclude road dirt and retain the lubricating oil. It is therefore important that these are always in first-class condition. A check of these points should be made at 6000 mile intervals. If inspection reveals oil around the rack housing or on the gaiters but the gaiters appear to be in good condition, the oil can be replenished by the following method:

1 Remove the retaining clip and release the gaiter from the righthand end of the rack housing.
2 Move the rack so that the road wheels are in the 'straight-ahead' position.
3 Using a suitable injector or syringe, inject not more than one third of a pint of Hypoid SAE.90.EP oil into the end of the rack housing.
4 Reconnect the rubber gaiter making sure that both ends are securely fixed and oiltight.
5 Move the rack **gently** from side to side to distribute the oil throughout the housing and mechanism.

If the vehicle is hoisted with the front wheels clear of the ground for this operation **care should be taken** to avoid any forceful movement of the wheels from lock to lock as this may cause damage within the steering mechanism.

No other adjustments will normally be called for during routine maintenance. There are however several points at which adjustment will be required when the steering gear is serviced and a careful note should be made of these items as outlined in the following sections of this Chapter.

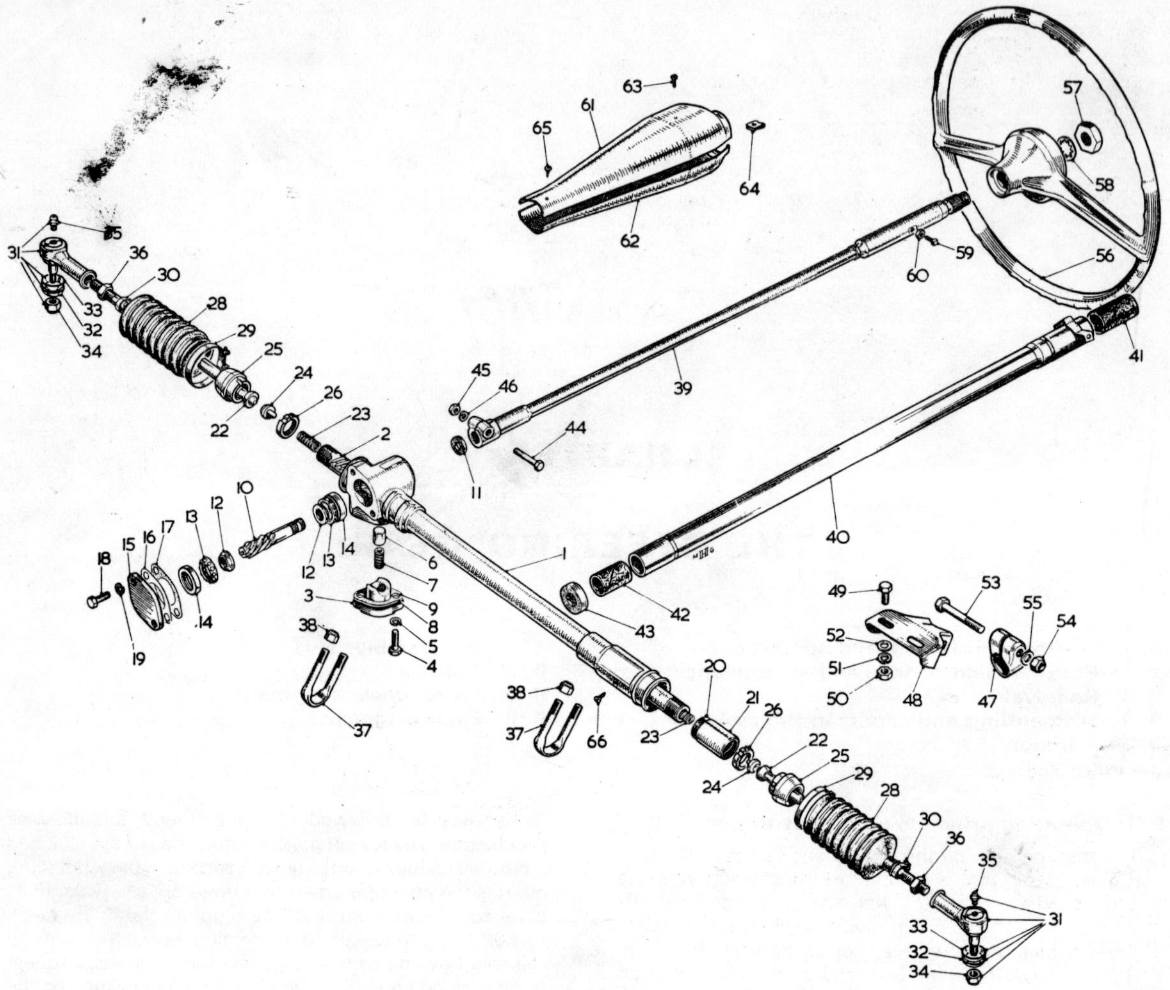

FIG 9 : 1 Component parts of steering system

Key to Fig 9 : 1 1 Rack housing 2 Rack 3 Yoke (damper housing) 4 Damper housing bolt 5 Spring washer 6 Damper pad 7 Damper spring 8 Shim 9 Joint washer 10 Pinion 11 Oil seal 12 Inner race (cone) 13 Ballbearing (and cage) 14 Outer race (cup) 15 End cover 16 Shim 17 Joint washer 18 End cover bolt 19 Spring washer 20 Felt or Vulkallon bush 21 Felt bush sleeve 22 Tie rod 23 Thrust spring 24 Ball seat 25 Ball housing 26 Locknut 27 Locking washer (not shown) 28 Gaiter or rack seal 29 Clip 30 Clip 31 Ball end assembly 32 Outer dust cover 33 Inner dust cover 34 Ball pin nut 35 Lubricator (not later models) 36 Locknut 37 U-bolt 38 U-bolt nut 39 Inner column 40 Outer column 41 Felt bearing 42 Lower felt bearing 43 Rubber floor sealing washer 44 Clamp bolt 45 Nut 46 Spring washer 47 Column clip for bracket 48 Bracket 49 Bolt 50 Nut 51 Spring washer 52 Plain washer 53 Clip bolt 54 Nut 55 Washer 56 Steering wheel 57 Steering wheel nut 58 Shakeproof washer 59 Flasher cancelling stud 60 Locknut 61 Cowl top half 62 Cowl bottom half 63 Fixing screw 64 Nut 65 Fixing screw 66 Bush housing retaining screw

9 : 3 Removal

To remove the steering wheel on early models, withdraw the grub screw in the wheel hub and lift up the horn switch. On Mk II Mini and 1968 Elf, Hornet and Clubman models, carefully prise up the centre cover of the hub. Disconnect the battery and horn leads at the snap connectors below the parcel shelf. Remove the horn switch and then unscrew the steering wheel retaining nut 57. A special service tool is available, if needed, to pull off the steering wheel (18G.310).

To remove the steering column, proceed as follows:

1. Disconnect the flasher unit at the connectors below the parcel shelf.
2. Mark the steering rack pinion shaft 10 spline in the split portion of the inner column clamp, at the lower end of the column 39, then remove the bolt 44 from the clamp.
3. Remove the column upper support clamp bolt 53 and slacken the bracket nuts 50.

4 Mark the fitted position of the outer column 40 at the upper support bracket 48.
5 Pull the column assembly upwards and out of the car.

To dismantle the steering column, proceed as follows:

1 Remove both halves of the column cowl.
2 Remove the flasher indicator switch and unscrew the cancelling stud 59 from the column.
3 Remove the horn slip-ring assembly on early models.
4 Withdraw the inner column through the lower end of the outer column tube.
5 Extract the upper 41 and lower 42 bushes from the outer column tube.

Inspection should include a check, and if necessary, rectification of the inner column alignment. When rotated the upper bearing face should not run-out more than $\frac{1}{8}$ inch radially. The upper and lower felt bushes should be examined and if necessary renewed. Cylindrical polythene bushes are now provided as replacements for the upper bush.

To remove the rack and pinion assembly proceed as follows:

1 Remove the air cleaner from the carburetter.
2 On all models with remote gearlever, disconnect the extension from the floor (see **FIG 1:3**).
3 Jack up and support the car under the front subframe and remove the front road wheels and dampers.
4 Remove the rack ball end retaining nuts 34 and, if necessary using Service Tool 18G.1063, release the ball ends 31 from the steering arms.
5 Remove the four nuts and bolts (or setscrews on Hornet and Elf models) securing the rear of the front subframe to the floor of the car body.
6 Lift the locking plate tabs and remove the four bolts securing the subframe towers to the bulkhead cross-member.
7 Disconnect the exhaust pipe from the manifold and gearchange extension.
8 Disconnect the engine tie rod at the cylinder block.
9 Slacken the front subframe mounting bolts.
10 Remove the four nuts 38 securing the two rack U-bolts 37.
11 Support the car body and lower the jacks supporting the subframe thus allowing the subframe to drop down and away from the car body and making space for removal of the U-bolts.
12 Withdraw the steering rack 1 from the driver's side of the car, if necessary using a lever to prise the subframe further down from the body to make sufficient space. The lever is inserted between the tops of the subframe towers and the wing valance.

Note that Mini Mk II and 1968 Elf, Hornet and Clubman rack is not interchangeable with racks on early vehicles, either as a unit or as individual parts. The new rack is associated with modified steering levers giving a smaller turning circle. **Correct wheel alignment is most important** (see **Section 9:7**).

9:4 Dismantling and servicing the rack and pinion

A start can now be made on dismantling and servicing the rack and pinion assembly. Careful attention to the following notes and procedures will result in safe and accurate steering so essential under modern motoring conditions. Proceed as follows:

1 Unlock the ball end retaining locknuts 36 at the ends of the tie rods and remove the ball ends.
2 Release the rubber gaiter clips 29/30 at the rack housing and on the tie rods, drain off the lubricating oil and remove the rubber gaiters 28.
3 Remove the two rack damper housing bolts 4 and take off the housing. Withdraw damper 6 and spring 7. Four types of damper have been fitted, as shown in **FIG 9:2 (a), (b), (c)** and **(d).**
(a) is an early type, **(b)** and **(c)** were fitted more recently, and **(d)** is the current type fitted to Mini Mk II models and to 1968 Elf, Hornet and Clubman.
4 Unscrew and remove the two bolts 18 securing the pinion shaft tail bearing retaining plate 15, remove the plate and shims 16/17. Remove the lower outer race 14, bearing 13 and inner race 12 and then withdraw the pinion 10. The top bearing outer race, bearing and inner race can then be extracted from behind the rack teeth.
5 Remove the pinion shaft oil seal 11 with a suitable extractor or by gentle drifting round the outer edge.
6 A special Service Tool is available (18G.707) for unlocking and removing the steering rack ball joints. The indentations in the locking ring must first be punched or prised up clear of the slots in the rack locknut 26 and ball housing 25. Then the Service Tool is applied to slacken back the locking ring and the housing unscrewed to release the tie rod 22, ball seat 24 and ball seat tension spring 23.
7 It is now possible to withdraw the rack from the pinion end of the rack housing. This is desirable in order to avoid damage to the felt or 'vulkollan' bush 20 at the opposite end of the rack housing.
8 Remove the bush securing screw 66 from the rack housing, then lever the felt bush at its joint and remove it with a pair of thin long-nosed pliers. If a 'vulkollan' bush is to be fitted in place of the felt bush the felt bush metal sleeve 21 must also be removed.
9 All parts should now be thoroughly cleaned and inspected for wear, corrosion and other deterioration. Avoid the use of powerful solvents on the non-metallic parts. Check carefully for any signs of cracks or fracturing. Pitting, hollows or roughness on the tooth surfaces of the pinion or rack are causes for renewal of these parts. The rubber gaiters, and caps on the ball ends should be free from gross distortion, cracks, age-hardening or decomposition. Tie rod ball housings and seats should be free from excessive wear and must be renewed if this is evident. The ball ends cannot be dismantled and if loose or worn must be renewed.

9:5 Reassembly

Reassemble the steering column as follows:

1 Thoroughly soak the lower felt bush with SAE.90/140 EP oil before refitting it.
2 Lubricate the (upper) polythene bush with a graphite-based grease before inserting it fully into the upper end of the outer column tube.
3 Insert the inner column into the lower end of the outer column rolling the felt bush round its fitted position on the inner column until the joint faces abut, then carefully insert the inner column fully home.
4 Make quite sure that the inner column turns freely

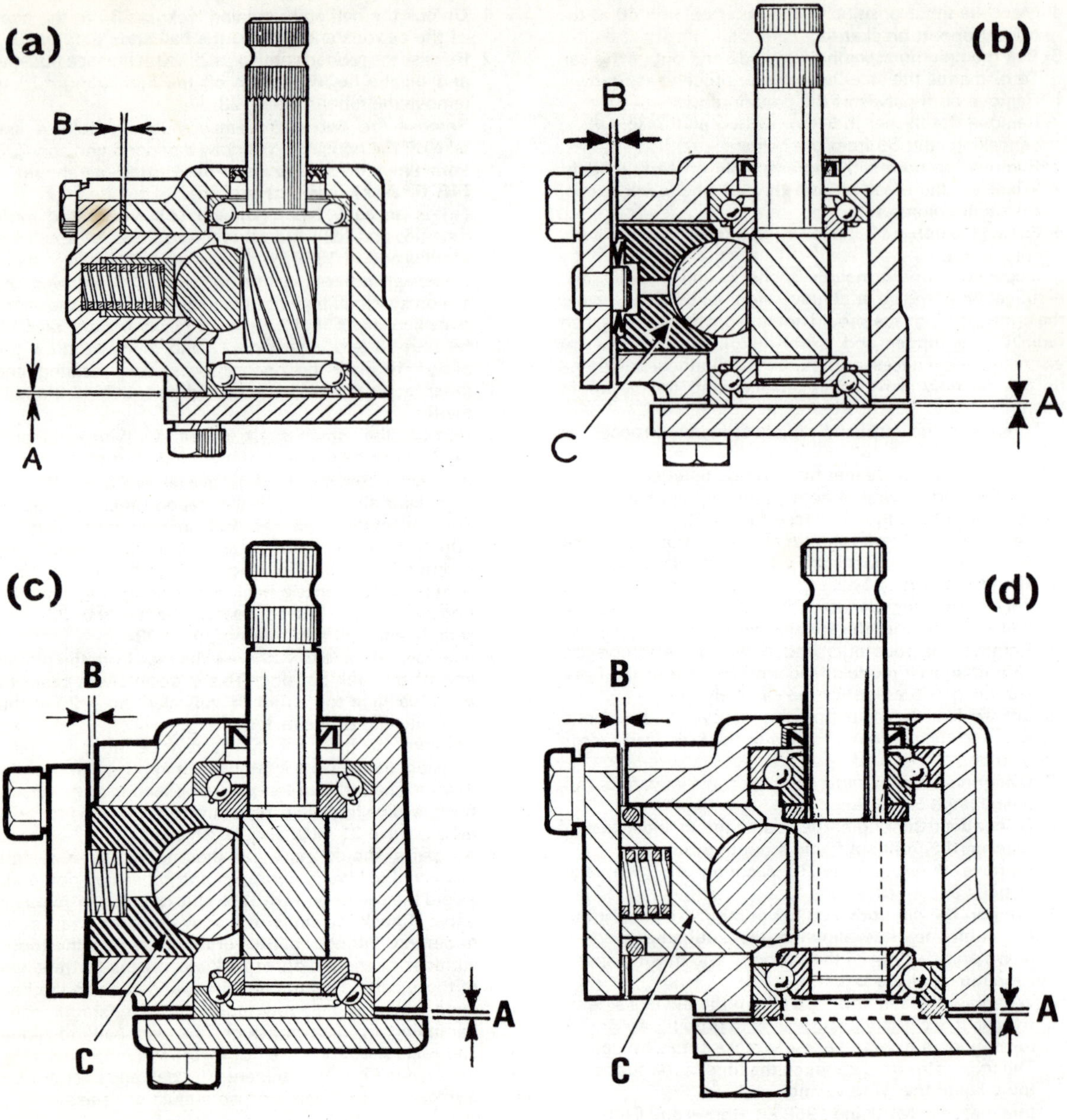

FIG 9:2 (a), (b), (c) and (d) The four types of steering pinion and rack damper in section. (a) is an early type, (b) and (c) are intermediate types, and (d) is the latest type as fitted to Mini Mk II and to 1968 Elf, Hornet and Clubman. C is the damper yoke

and reassemble the whole into the car by reversing the removal procedure described in **Section 9 : 3**.

5 Reassembly of the rack and pinion unit commences with the fitting of a new plastic 'vulkollan' bush into the rack housing. This bush is used with a steel sleeved bush and spacer. The spacer is first inserted, plain end first into the housing. Then the plastic bush is fitted into the steel sleeve and the whole inserted, plain end first, into the rack housing, with the flats on the plastic bush positioned offset to the retaining screw hole in the rack housing. When the spacer and bush are correctly positioned, drill through the retaining screw hole and the bush with a $\frac{7}{64}$ inch drill and clean off all drilling swarf. Coat the new retaining screw with jointing compound and screw it home to secure the bush and sleeve in position. Finally check that the screw does not project into the bore of the plastic bush.

6 Fit a new pinion oil seal (if required) and the top pinion bearing outer race, bearing and thrust washer; insert the rack into the rack housing and then refit the pinion. Refit the lower bearing complete, and the lower cover plate without shims. Do not overtighten. On Mini Mk II and Elf, Hornet and Clubman 1968 models, fit the cover plate with shims and spacer washer to give a clearance of approximately .010 inch between plate and housing as shown as A in **FIG 9:2(d)**. Again do not overtighten.

7 As at A in all the types in **FIG 9:2**, measure the gap with feelers.

8 Remove the cover plate and fit shims to the thickness of the feeler gauge reading less .002 inch to give the required preload. On Mini Mk II and 1968 Elf, Hornet and Clubman models, reduce the shimming by the clearance measured at A minus a further .002 to .005 inch to give the required preload. Smear the joint faces with shellac or thin jointing compound, replace the cover plate and fully tighten the securing screws.

9 Screw the ball housing locking rings on to the rack ends as far as possible and fit new locking washers. Some models are not fitted with a locking washer, in which case fit new locking rings. Refit the seat springs, seats, tie rods and ball housings, tightening up firmly until the tie rods are pinched (do not use excessive force). Screw the locking rings along the rack threads to meet the ball housings checking then that the tie rods are still pinched, slacken back the ball housings one-eighth of a turn to allow full articulation of the tie rods and relock the housings by tightening up the locking rings securely, making sure the ball housings do not rotate.

10 Where a locking washer is fitted punch the washer into the slots of the housing and the locking ring. If no locking washer is fitted, punch the lips of the locking ring into the slots of the ball housing and rack.

11 It is now necessary to adjust the rack damper shown in **FIG 9:2 (a)**, **(b)**, **(c)** or **(d)**. The agents use a bearing preload gauge for accuracy in this adjustment and owners may prefer to ask the Service Agent to carry out the work for them. The following method is used:

12 For type **(a)** damper, refit the plunger in the housing without the spring or shims at B. For type **(b)** damper, refit the yoke with spring but without shims at B. For type **(c)**, refit the yoke without spring or shims at B. For type **(d)**, refit yoke and cover plate without spring.

13 For all types of damper, fit the cover plate and securing bolts and tighten up the bolts with the rack in the straight-ahead position until it is just possible to rotate the pinion shaft with the bearing preload gauge, Service Tool 18G.207 and adaptor 18G.207A, set at 15 lb in. Measure the gap, using feeler gauges, at B, **FIG 9:2 (a)**, **(b)**, **(c)** or **(d)**, between the damper housing or cover plate and the rack housing.

14 For type **(a)** remove the damper housing, insert the spring and plunger and refit the assembly with packing shims to the thickness of the measured gap B plus .002 inch, coating the joint surfaces with shellac or thin jointing compound to prevent lubricant leaks when the securing bolts are fully tightened.

15 For type **(b)** damper, remove the cover plate and fit shims to the thickness of the measured gap B less .001 to .003 inch, coat the joint surfaces with shellac or thin jointing compound and refit the assembly with the securing bolts fully tightened. The torque load required to start movement of the pinion after assembly must not exceed 25 lb in.

16 For type **(c)** and **(d)** dampers, remove the cover plate, refit the yoke spring and shims to the thickness of gap B plus .002 to .005 inch. Fit the O-ring seal to the yoke on Mini Mk II and 1968 Hornet, Elf and Clubman. Coat the joint faces with shellac or thin jointing compound, refit the cover plate and tighten the securing bolts. The torque load required to start movement of the pinion after assembly must not exceed 35 lb in.

17 Refit the rubber gaiters to the rack housing and the tie rods but before securing the clip on the tie rod at the pinion end of the assembly, stand the assembly on end and pour in about one third of a pint of Hypoid SAE.90.EP oil through the end of the gaiter. Refit and tighten the gaiter clip.

18 Refit the ball ends and locking nuts.

19 Generally, the remainder of reassembly is the reverse of dismantling but special attention is required to the following:

20 Check that the tie rods are equal in length, with about seven or eight threads showing behind each locknut. On Mini Mk II and 1968 Elf, Hornet and Clubman models there should be eleven threads.

21 Centralize the rack in the housing. The full travel of the rack in both directions is 1.75 inch, which is equal to $2\frac{1}{3}$ complete turns of the pinion from stop to stop. This applies to early models only.

9:6 Refitting

Refitting of the rack and pinion assembly is, generally the reverse of the removal procedure, giving special attention to the following points:

1 Refit the rack and pinion assembly to the car, securing it in position with the U-bolts and nuts but with the nuts not fully tightened.

2 Check that the screws securing the steering column upper clamp bracket are slack and that the nut and bolt securing the column clip to the bracket allow movement of the column.

3 Check that the rack is still in the central position of its travel, push down the column assembly to engage the marked spline of the pinion shaft with the split portion of the inner column lower clamp, insert and tighten the clamp bolt so that its axis is below and parallel to the rack axis. For lefthand drive models the clamp bolt axis must be above the steering column at an angle of 16 deg. to the rack housing axis. On later Elf and Hornet models a line is stamped on the end of the pinion shaft. During assembly this stamped line must be vertical and below the horizontal centre-line of the column for a righthand drive vehicle, and above the horizontal centre-line for a lefthand drive vehicle. The tightening torque for the clamp bolt must be 8 to 9 lb ft. On Mini Mk II and 1968 Elf, Hornet and Clubman models refer to **FIG 9:3**. Pull out the plastic plug and insert a 2 inch length of $\frac{1}{4}$ inch diameter bar or a

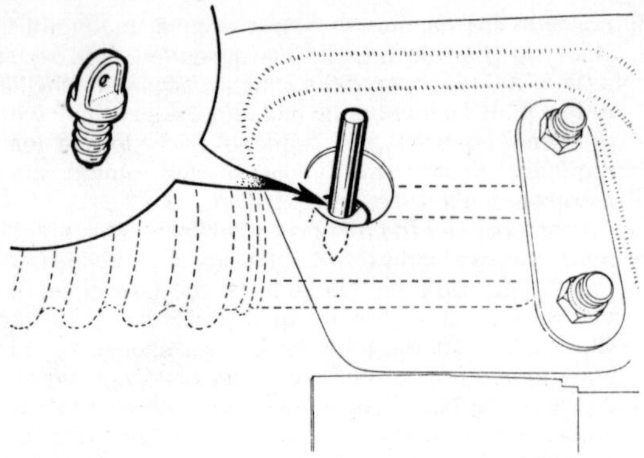

FIG 9:3 Using a locator pin to centralize the rack on Mini Mk II and 1968 Elf, Hornet and Clubman. Inset shows the plastic plug

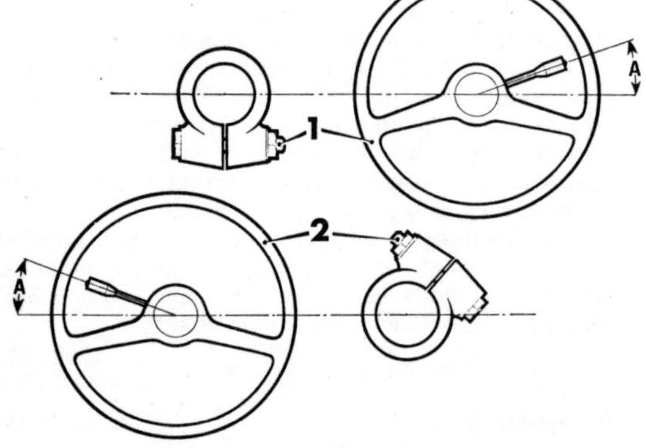

FIG 9:4 Position of steering column clamp bolt. 1 is for righthand drive cars, 2 is for lefthand drive cars. A is the angle of 20 deg. for the direction indicator lever

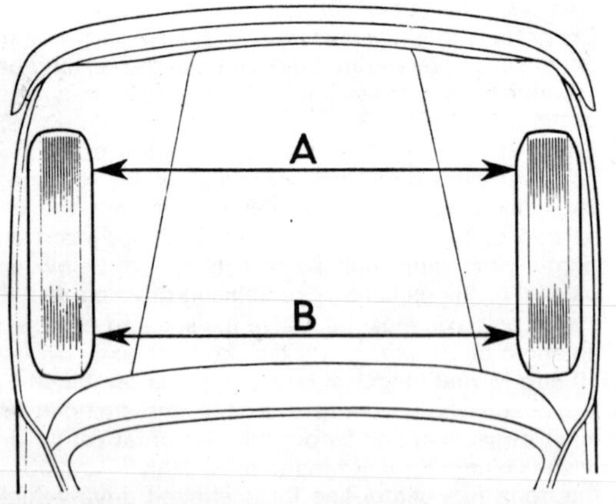

FIG 9:5 Diagram showing positions for checking front wheel alignment. The wheels must be straight-ahead and dimension A must be $\frac{1}{16}$ inch greater than B at 9.4 inches above ground level

suitable bolt into the hole in the rack housing. Move the rack so that the locator pin engages it and locks it in the central position. Refit the column to the pinion shaft with the bolt positioned as shown in **FIG 9:4**.

4 Lift the column and insert the clip into the bracket. **Move the bracket to the clip and not vice-versa to avoid loading the column.** Tighten the bracket-to-facia rail bolts. While observing the marked positions of the outer column clamp and the column shroud, complete the refitting of the steering column accessories and secure the steering column at the upper bracket. The cancelling stud of the direction indicator must be screwed in sufficiently to prevent it fouling the cancelling mechanisms and positioned midway between the two cancelling mechanisms. Check the switch operation on completion. Tighten each of the rack U-bolt nuts half a turn at a time in pairs. On Mini Mk II and 1968 Elf, Hornet and Clubman models, remove the locator pin and refit the plastic plug. **Never use the hole which takes this plastic plug for topping up the housing with lubricant.**

5 Complete the refitting of the front subframe, wheels, dampers, engine tie rod and exhaust system generally by reversing the removal sequences. Check the front wheel alignment.

9:7 Front wheel alignment

The alignment of the front wheels on Mini vehicles provides for a small degree of 'toe-out' that is to say that the distance between the front of the front wheels is slightly greater than the distance between the rear of the wheels. With the car unladen, all tyres at the specified pressures, and the steering in the straight-ahead position, each wheel should make an angle of 7 min 30 sec with the longitudinal axis of the car. In terms of distance between the wheels, this is $\frac{1}{16}$ inch greater at the front than at the rear of the wheels, measured on a $14\frac{1}{2}$ inch dia. circle on the side walls of the tyres and 9.4 inch above the ground surface.

In order to set this alignment accurately, it is essential to use suitable equipment capable of recording the correct measurements at the diameter and height specified, or preferably optical equipment capable of measuring the actual angle rather than distances.

Using the conventional base-bar type gauge, measurements in front of the wheel centres and behind them should be taken by marking the front position on the tyres when the first measurement is taken and then moving the car forward a distance equal to half of one road wheel revolution. The second measurement is then taken at the marked point now behind the wheel centre. If an optical gauge is available, two or three measurements should be taken at points represented by forward car movement equal to half of one road wheel revolution (180 deg.) or one third of a road wheel revolution (120 deg.). An average of the two or three measurements should be calculated to give the correct figure.

If the front wheel alignment is incorrect following this check, it may be adjusted by slackening the locknut of each tie rod ball end and the clips securing the rubber gaiters to the tie rods, ensuring that the tie rods rotate freely in the gaiters so that the gaiters are not twisted and damaged.

As both tie rods have righthand threads they must be turned in opposite directions to achieve an adjustment of front wheel alignment and to ensure maintenance of the steering geometry it is essential that they both be turned by exactly the same amount.

After adjusting the alignment correctly tighten the ball end locknuts by holding the ball end and the locknut in spanners to prevent undesirable loads being imposed on the ball sockets and causing damage to the nylon seatings. Finally tighten up the clips securing the gaiters to the tie rods.

Adjusting alignment on Mini Mk II and 1968 Elf, Hornet and Clubman models:

The latest steering rack gives a smaller turning circle and accurate adjustment is essential if incorrect wheel alignment is not to lead to trouble. This might be excessive articulation of the drive shaft joints, and fouling of the suspension tie rods by the road wheels when on full lock. The car must be checked when fully equipped but without passengers or luggage.

With the car standing on its wheels, turn the steering fully on both locks and check the clearance between the road wheels and suspension tie rods. Minimum clearance is $\frac{3}{4}$ inch, or with the suspension on full rebound, not less than $\frac{1}{4}$ inch. If the tie rods are correctly adjusted the clearance figures on each side should be approximately those given. Use an optical gauge to check wheel alignment as follows:

1 Slacken the tie rod locknuts and the gaiter clips. Disconnect the ball joints from the steering levers using Tool No. 18G.1063.
2 Lift the floor covering and remove the rubber grommet from the floor on the opposite side to the rack pinion. Pull out the plastic plug from the rack housing and insert a locator pin made from 2 inches of $\frac{1}{4}$ inch diameter steel bar or use a suitable bolt. Move the rack until the pin drops into place and locks the rack in the central position.
3 Use an optical gauge and align the front wheels to the straight-ahead position with a toe-out of $\frac{1}{16}$ inch, setting them in alignment with the centre line of the car.
4 Without disturbing the alignment, adjust the tie rods until each ball joint pin will correctly locate in its steering lever. Secure the ball joints in this position. Check this setting and adjust each tie rod if necessary by an equal amount and then tighten the locknuts.
5 See that the rubber gaiters are not under stress and tighten the securing clips. Remove the locator pin and refit the plastic plug. **Do not use this plug hole for topping-up with lubricant.**
6 Recheck the alignment as detailed in the paragraph preceding Operation 1. Refit the floor grommet and floor covering.

9:8 Fault diagnosis

(a) Wheel wobble

1 Unbalanced wheels and tyres
2 Slack steering connections
3 Incorrect steering geometry
4 Excessive play in steering gear parts
5 Damaged or distorted front spring or displacer
6 Worn hub bearings

(b) Wander

1 Check 2, 3 and 4 in (a)
2 Misalignment in front or rear suspension
3 Uneven tyre pressures
4 Uneven tyre wear
5 Weak dampers, springs or hydrolastic system out of order

(c) Heavy steering

1 Check 3 in (a)
2 Very low tyre pressures
3 Lack of lubrication
4 Wheels out of track
5 Steering gear incorrectly adjusted
6 Steering column bent or misaligned
7 Steering column bushes too tight or incorrectly fitted

(d) Lost motion

1 Excessive end play at pinion
2 Loose steering wheel, worn splines, looseness or wear at lower clamp connection splines
3 General wear in rack and pinion assembly
4 Worn ball ends or ball joints on rack
5 Worn suspension system and swivel connections

NOTES

CHAPTER 10

THE BRAKING SYSTEM

10 : 1 Description of layout

All variants of the BMC Mini car are equipped with Lockheed hydraulic brakes actuated by hydraulic pressure applied by the brake pedal through a combined master cylinder and reservoir. A pressure regulating valve is fitted in the fluid line to the rear wheels. This does not operate under normal running conditions but under emergency braking it limits the pressure at the rear wheel cylinders.

Early Minis and Mk I Elf and Hornet cars had one-leading-shoe front and rear brakes. Mk II Minis and Mk II and III Elf and Hornet and Clubman cars have two-leading-shoe front brakes.

The hydraulic fluid is carried in steel pipes and unions except at the positions adjacent to the wheels where flexible rubber pipes are fitted to allow for movement of the wheels.

The handbrake operates only on the shoes of the rear wheels by means of a cable. Handbrake adjustment is normally performed automatically when the hydraulic brake shoe adjustment is carried out but cable adjustment may sometimes be necessary.

The brakes are adjusted by means of the square adjusters visible on the backs of the brake backplates. Single adjusters are provided on brakes having one leading shoe and two on those having two leading shoes as shown in **FIGS 10 : 1** and **10 : 2.** Similarly, brakes having one leading shoe have one wheel cylinder and those having two leading shoes have two.

Bleed screws are provided on the brake backplates for use during the bleeding operation, to expel all air from the system.

At the end of 1969 a dual circuit braking system was introduced for cars designed for certain territories where such equipment is required by law. This ensures that in the event of a failure in one hydraulic circuit, full braking is still available on one pair of wheels. A description of the components used on these cars, where they differ from or are in addition to those used on the standard system, is given at the end of this chapter.

10 : 2 Routine maintenance, brake shoe adjustment

Every 3000 miles, or less if thought necessary.

1 Check and if necessary adjust the brakes.

2 Make a visual inspection of the brake pipes and hoses.

3 Check the level of the hydraulic fluid in the reservoir and if necessary top it up to within $\frac{1}{4}$ inch of the bottom of the filler neck, not higher.

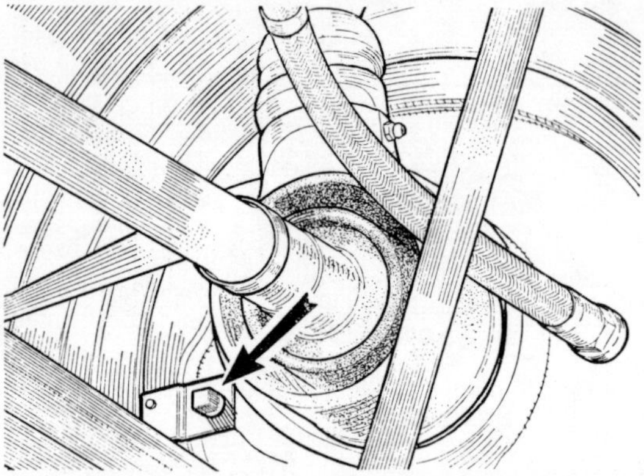

FIG 10 : 1 The single square-headed adjuster on one-leading-shoe brakes

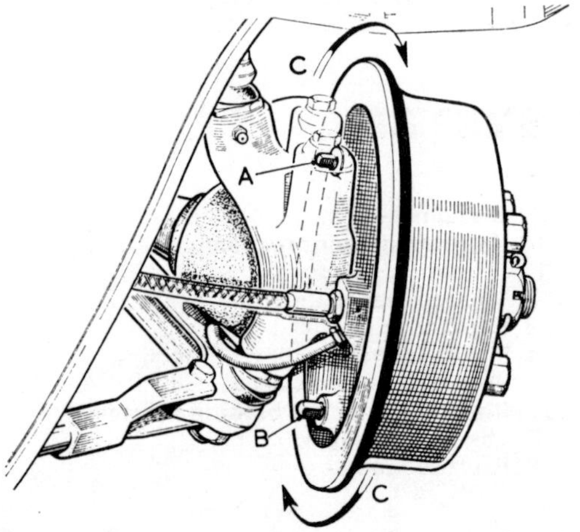

FIG 10 : 2 The two adjusters on the two-leading-shoe front brakes

Key to Fig 10 : 2 A Rear shoe adjuster **B** Front shoe adjuster **C** Direction of rotation of front wheel when car is moving forwards. Adjusters are turned in this direction to adjust the brakes

4 Every 12,000 miles remove the wheels and brake drums and blow away all dust and dirt from the brake components inside. Also inspect the parts visually to make sure they are all in good condition, especially the linings. Check that there is no hydraulic fluid leakage and that the return springs are not broken.

5 A complete change of hydraulic fluid should be made every 18 months or 24,000 miles, whichever is the sooner, and an examination and renewal of all fluid seals and flexible hoses every three years or 40,000 miles. At this stage the working surfaces of the pistons and bores of all hydraulic components should be examined and new parts fitted wherever necessary.

The need for brake adjustment is usually indicated by the foot pedal going down almost to the floorboard before solid resistance in the hydraulic system is felt.

If foot pedal travel has become excessive, the brake shoes must be adjusted to bring the linings into closer relationship with the brake drums. For brakes having one-leading-shoe, the car should be jacked up with the wheel clear of the ground and the single adjuster turned clockwise, viewed from the centre of the car, until the wheel is locked. The adjuster is then slackened until the wheel is just free to rotate without the drum rubbing the brake linings. The adjustment is then repeated for the other three wheels. The adjuster on the one-leading-shoe brakes is illustrated in **FIG 10 : 1.**

If the car is a model having two-leading-shoe front brakes, the two adjusters on the rear face of the brake backplate must receive attention. These are shown in **FIG 10 : 2.**

The following is the procedure for adjusting two-leading-shoe brakes:

1 Jack up the front of the car safely and deal with one adjuster at a time as follows:
2 Turn one adjuster in the direction of the forward rotation of the road wheel until the brake drum is locked.
3 Back off the adjuster just sufficiently to allow the brake drum to rotate freely.
4 Spin the brake drum and apply the foot brake firmly to centralize the shoe and recheck the adjustment.
5 Repeat the procedure for the other adjuster.
6 Repeat the process for the other front wheel.

10 : 3 Removing the master cylinder

The master cylinder is illustrated in **FIG 10 : 3** from which the arrangement of the internal components will be clear. **FIG 10 : 4** shows the installation of the brake (A) and the clutch (B) master cylinders and fluid reservoirs on the engine bulkhead.

The operation of the master cylinder is briefly as follows: Hydraulic fluid from the reservoir 4 flows into the annular space between the piston 11 and the cylinder 5 and is prevented from flowing out of the open end of the cylinder by the secondary cup 10. When the pushrod 1 is operated by the brake pedal, the piston 11, piston washer 12 and main cup 13 move upwards against the pressure of the return spring 15 causing the hydraulic fluid trapped in the upper end of the cylinder to be forced along the fluid lines to the wheel cylinders, thus operating the brakes. The supply of fluid in the upper portion of the master cylinder, fluid lines and wheel cylinders is maintained by a small orifice just above the main cup, connecting the interior of the master cylinder with the reservoir. This supply is cut off when the piston and main cup have been forced upwards by the brake pedal.

If for any reason a shortage of hydraulic fluid develops in the fluid lines or wheel cylinders this is made up without the entry of air into the system, as the piston returns to its 'at rest' position, by fluid flowing from the annular space round the piston, through holes in its upper end, past the piston washer and round the outer edges of the main cup. Some of this fluid will pass back into the reservoir during the initial movement of the piston on the next operating cycle. Thus it will be observed that the pressure system can never become short of fluid and the continual flow of fluid past the main cup keeps this lubricated and hydraulically sealed at all times. A small check valve 16 is fitted in the upper end of the cylinder. This prevents fluid pumped from the cylinder during the bleeding operation from returning to the cylinder as the piston moves back on its return stroke, thus preventing air entering the system through the bleed nipples on the brake backplates.

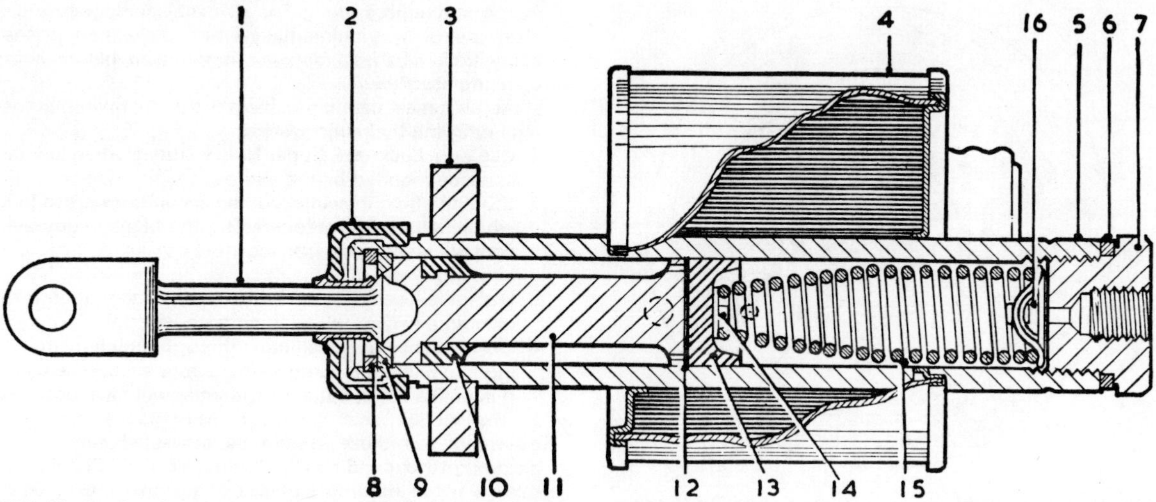

FIG 10 : 3 Sectional view of the brake master cylinder

Key to Fig 10 : 3 1 Pushrod 2 Rubber boot 3 Mounting flange 4 Supply tank 5 Body 6 Washer 7 End plug 8 Circlip 9 Stop washer 10 Secondary cup 11 Piston 12 Piston washer 13 Main cup 14 Spring retainer 15 Return spring 16 Non-return valve

To remove the brake master cylinder:

1 Disconnect the pressure pipe union at the top of the master cylinder.
2 Remove the splitpin and withdraw the clevis pin securing the master cylinder pushrod to the pedal lever.
3 Remove two bolts securing the master cylinder assembly to the bulkhead and withdraw the assembly complete.

10 : 4 Dismantling the brakes

During normal use a good deal of 'bedding' of the various brake components takes place and it is important therefore, when dismantling and reassembling the brakes, to take the necessary steps to ensure their return to their original positions and relationships.

To dismantle the one-leading-shoe brakes proceed as follows:

1 For front brakes, apply the handbrake, jack up the front of the car and remove the road wheel. For rear brakes, chock the front wheels to prevent the car moving and jack up the rear end.
2 Take out the two brake drum retaining screws, back off the adjusters and remove the brake drums.
3 Referring to **FIG 10 : 5**, note and mark the positions in which the pull-off springs are fitted, also mark the brake shoes for subsequent return to their correct positions. Release the springs from the webs of the shoes and remove the shoes from the back plate.

Do not operate the brake foot pedal with the shoes removed from the backplate, otherwise the pistons will be ejected from the wheel cylinder, fluid will be lost and air will enter the system.

A slightly different procedure is required for two-leading-shoe front brakes as follows:

1 With the adjusters backed off and the brake drums removed, withdraw the two spring loaded hooks

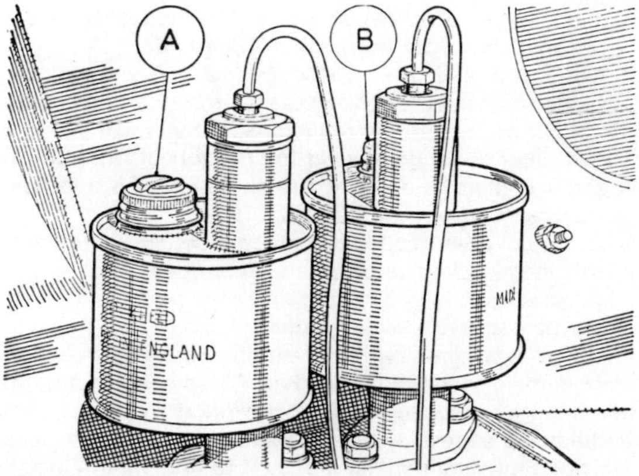

FIG 10 : 4 The brake (A) and clutch (B) master cylinders and hydraulic fluid reservoirs on the engine bulkhead

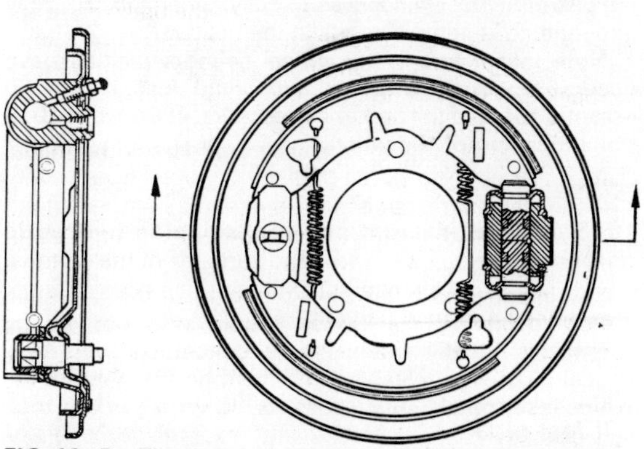

FIG 10 : 5 The righthand front, one-leading-shoe brake, showing the fitted positions of the leading and trailing brake shoes, with the pull-off springs anchored in the correct holes in the shoe webs.

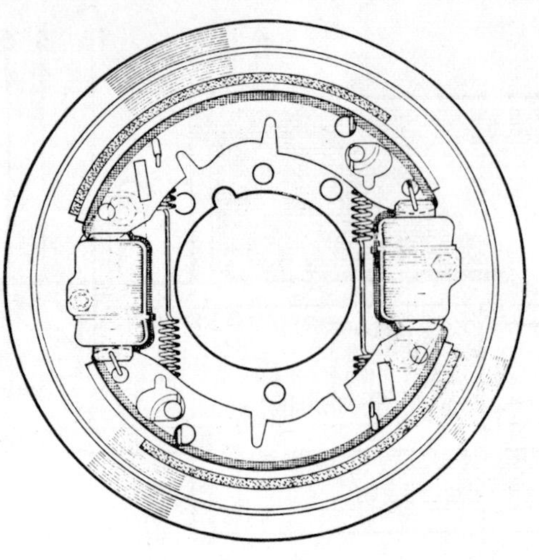

FIG 10 : 6 The lefthand two-leading-shoe front brake assembly, showing the fitted positions of the brake shoes, pull-off springs and hooks locating the shoes on the wheel cylinder pistons

anchoring the brake shoes to the wheel cylinder pistons. These can be seen in **FIG 10 : 6.**

2 Note, and if desired, mark the pull-off springs and shoes to ensure correct reassembly in due course.
3 Lift out one shoe from the recess in the wheel cylinder and pivot the shoe against the tension of the pull-off springs, then manoeuvre the assembly of shoes and springs over the front hub and away.
4 If it is not intended to dismantle the wheel cylinders at this stage, wire the pistons to the wheel cylinders to prevent them from being accidentally pushed out with the consequent loss of hydraulic fluid.

When reassembling and refitting the drum brakes reverse the dismantling procedure. Make sure the springs and shoes are returned to their original marked positions and apply a trace of grease to the mating metal surfaces. Do not allow any mineral lubricant to come into contact with the rubber dust covers or bores of the wheel cylinders. Do not forget to remove any wire used to hold the pistons in the cylinders and finally, when the assembly and refitting is complete, adjust the brakes.

Note that if any of the wheel cylinder pistons have become displaced and hydraulic fluid lost, it will be essential to bleed the brakes as described in **Section 10 : 9** on completion of the work.

10 : 5 General instructions for servicing hydraulic components

The importance of efficient servicing of the hydraulic system operating the brakes should not require any emphasis. Broadly, the work is concerned with very critical inspection, cleaning and the renewal of any parts which give the slightest cause for doubt regarding their serviceability.

Following dismantling, thoroughly clean all parts. For rubber components use only Lockheed Super Heavy Duty Brake Fluid and do not use the fluid subsequently in the hydraulic system. For all-metal components use clean petrol or trichlorethylene and make certain that every trace of these materials is removed before commencing assembly.

At all times carefully observe the following points regarding the hydraulic system:

1 Use only Lockheed Super Heavy Duty Hydraulic Fluid as recommended by the makers.
2 Store the fluid in sealed containers and never use fluid which has been kept for any length of time in unsealed containers, as it absorbs moisture quickly and this can be dangerous.
3 Do not re-use fluid drained from the system or used for bleeding, except for cleaning purposes only.
4 Observe absolute cleanliness throughout when attending to any matters to do with the hydraulic system.

It is unlikely that much severe wear will have occurred to the metal parts if regular maintenance has been observed, but these should be inspected carefully to ascertain their condition for further service. Consider in particular the rubbing surfaces of pistons, the bores of cylinders, the ends of the pistons where the brake shoes make contact, the length and overall shape of any springs and wear at pivoting points.

Inspect the rubber components if they are not all to be renewed as a matter of course every three years or 40,000 miles. Check for indications of wear, cracking, permanent distortion, age hardening or material deterioration. If desired, compare the flexibility of the rubber with that of a new component. If there is any noticeable difference, renew the part. Lubricate all moving parts with brake fluid on reassembly.

The hydraulic hoses should be inspected for any external damage and damage to the end connections. Abrasion marks on the external surfaces indicate that the hose has been rubbing on some part of the car when in use. Such marks should be regarded with the greatest suspicion and it would be generally advisable to renew the pipe.

10 : 6 Dismantling and servicing the master and wheel cylinders

Referring to **FIG 10 : 3,** the master cylinder is dismantled in the following manner:

1 Remove the filler cap and drain out the fluid.
2 Pull back the rubber dust cover 2, remove the circlip 8 which then becomes accessible, using a pair of long nosed pliers, and then take out the pushrod 1 complete with the dished washer 9.
3 Withdraw the piston 11 with the secondary cup 10, the piston washer 12, main cup 13, spring retainer 14, return spring 15 and non-return valve 16. To remove these parts it may be helpful first to remove the end plug 7 and washer 6 from the body 5, noticing carefully how the parts are assembled.
4 Clean and inspect all parts generally in accordance with the instructions in **Section 10 : 5.** If it is necessary to remove the secondary cup from the piston, do this only with the fingers and do not employ any sharp implements such as screwdrivers or pocket knives. When refitting it, turn it once or twice on the piston to ensure that it has settled properly over the raised portion.

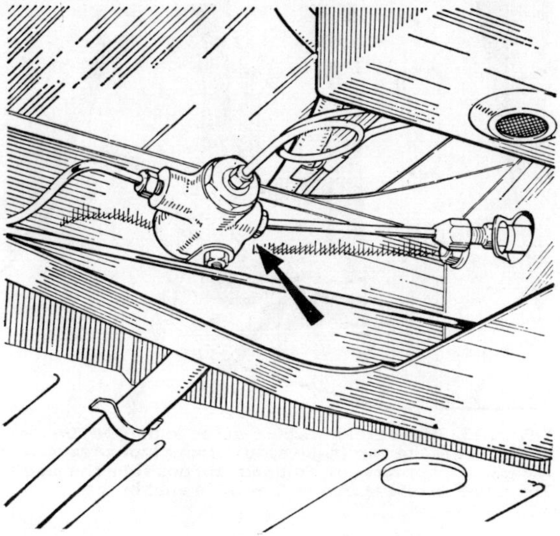

FIG 10:7 Hydraulic pressure regulating valve

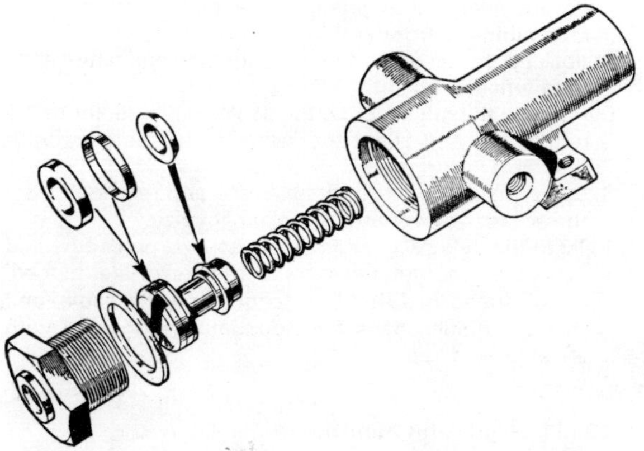

FIG 10:8 An exploded view of the hydraulic pressure regulating valve

When reassembling and refitting the master cylinder observe carefully the following points:

1 It will be found helpful to dip the internal parts in the hydraulic fluid prior to assembly. This will ease the work, especially on the rubber parts, and provide initial lubrication.
2 Assemble the valve cup and body 16 to the large end of the return spring 15 before entering the spring into the cylinder body 5. Make sure also that the spring retainer 14 is properly positioned at the small end of the spring before entering the piston main cup.
3 Insert the main cup 13, lip first, making sure the lip is not folded back or damaged during this operation, and press the cup well down on to the spring retainer.
4 The concave side of thin dished washer 12 should face the main cup.
5 Take care not to turn back or damage the lip of the secondary cup 10 when inserting the piston 11.
6 Make sure the circlip 8 is securely and correctly fitted before refitting the rubber dust cover 2.
7 Refit the master cylinder assembly to the bulkhead and after connecting the hydraulic pipe and reconnecting the yoke to the brake pedal, check brake shoe adjustment all round. Bleed the system and check for leaks with the brakes fully on.

For convenience of access the wheel cylinders may be removed from the brake backplates as follows:

1 With the car suitably jacked up and the road wheel, brake drum, brake shoes and springs removed, first clean the back plate.
2 Disconnect the fluid supply hose by unscrewing the metal pipe union nut from its connection on the hose, then hold the hexagon on the hose and remove the locknut securing the flexible hose union to its bracket. Unscrew the hose from the wheel cylinder.
3 For one-leading-shoe brakes unscrew and remove the bleed screw, remove the circlip and dished washer from the wheel cylinder boss protruding through the backplate and remove the cylinder.
4 Clean and examine the cylinder bores, pistons and seals as outlined in **Section 10 : 5,** using only the fingers to remove and refit the seals.
5 To remove the wheel cylinders on two-leading-shoe brakes, unscrew the two union nuts and detach the pipe bridging the two wheel cylinders, take out the two hexagon screws retaining each wheel cylinder to the backplate and remove the wheel cylinders.
6 Notice very carefully the way round the piston is assembled in the cylinder and that the bleed screw is fitted to the rearmost wheel cylinder before dismantling these components. Clean and service them in accordance with the instructions in **Section 10 : 5.**

The procedure for refitting the front and rear wheel cylinders is a reversal of the removal procedure. Note that on two-leading-shoe brakes, the piston of the wheel cylinder faces the same direction as the forward rotation of the brake drum. Brake adjustment and bleeding the hydraulic system must follow any operations in this group.

10:7 Servicing the pressure regulating valve

The pressure regulating valve is located on the rear subframe crossmember as shown in **FIG 10:7**. It has three hydraulic connections and its internal parts are illustrated in **FIG 10:8**. To remove the valve, disconnect the three hydraulic pipes on the valve body and remove the nut and washer securing it to the subframe crossmember.

To dismantle the valve, proceed as follows:

1 Clean the exterior.
2 Unscrew and remove the end plug and sealing washer.
3 Extract the valve assembly and return spring.
4 Servicing entails cleaning and examining the parts, giving special attention to the rubber seals and making any necessary renewals. Note carefully the method of assembly of the seals.
5 Make sure all parts are free from petrol or other cleaning agents and fit any new seals required. Lubricate all parts with Lockheed Super Heavy Duty Brake Fluid and reassemble, making certain that the tapered seal is fitted so that the small diameter enters the cylinder (body) first.

6 Refit the assembly to the subframe member, reconnect the hydraulic pipes securely and bleed the system as described in **Section 10 : 9.**

10 : 8 Brake linings

Although it is possible to obtain new linings for riveting to the brake shoes, this procedure is not recommended.

If it becomes necessary to renew the full set of brake linings due to excessive wear it is essential that the material used for relining is the same as originally specified, i.e. Don 202 or an approved alternative, otherwise the front-to-rear brake balance may be affected. All brakes must be lined with the same type of material and grease or oil contamination of the linings avoided.

It is strongly recommended that replacement shoes are obtained in axle sets from a BMC agent in order to maintain even braking conditions. The high spots will have been removed from these linings after fitting to the brake shoes. When the relined shoes have been fitted to the brake backplates, release the handbrake and turn the adjusters to the fully off position before refitting the brake drums.

10 : 9 Bleeding

The bleeding operation becomes necessary following any disconnection of the components of the hydraulic system or if the fluid in the reservoir has become so low as to allow air to enter the system.

First, fill the fluid reservoir to the correct level with Lockheed Super Heavy Duty Brake Fluid. As the bleeding operation will cause the level to fall, it is important to ensure that the reservoir is at least half full throughout the whole of the operation.

Operations are as follows:

1 Fit a suitable piece of rubber tube to the wheel cylinder bleeder screw and place the other end in a glass jar containing a few inches depth of hydraulic fluid.
2 Open the bleed screw one complete turn.
3 Operate the brake foot pedal slowly several times allowing it to return to the up position each time without assistance. Allow a short pause between each depression of the pedal and observe the fluid being pumped into the jar.
4 Continue pumping until there are no signs of air bubbles in the expelled fluid.
5 Hold the foot pedal fully down, tighten the bleed screw, remove the rubber pipe and top-up the reservoir fluid to the correct level.
6 On all models, the system must be bled at each wheel cylinder until all air has been expelled. Note that on two-leading-shoe brakes the bleed screw is fitted to the rearmost wheel cylinder only.
7 Apply the procedure outlined above to each brake in turn. Finally make sure all bleed screws are securely tightened and that the reservoir fluid is topped up to the correct level. Check the system for any leaks with the brake pedal applied.

10 : 10 Renewing handbrake cable

1 Chock the front road wheels and set the handbrake lever in the 'Off' position.
2 Remove the cable adjusting nuts and the cable fairlead located in the centre of the floor and to the rear of the front seat.
3 Draw the cable through the floor from underneath the car and release the cable from the guide channel on the rear subframe front crossmember.
4 Jack up the car under the rear subframe and remove the road wheel.
5 Remove the nut securing the cable swivel sector to the radius arm and allow the sector to be removed with the cable.
6 Draw the cable through the frame and release it from the actuating lever on the brake backplate.
7 To fit the new cable reverse the removal procedure and make sure the outer corners of the sector are 'nipped' as illustrated in **FIG 10 : 9** to position the cable, and that the guide channel is adequately lubricated with an approved grease.

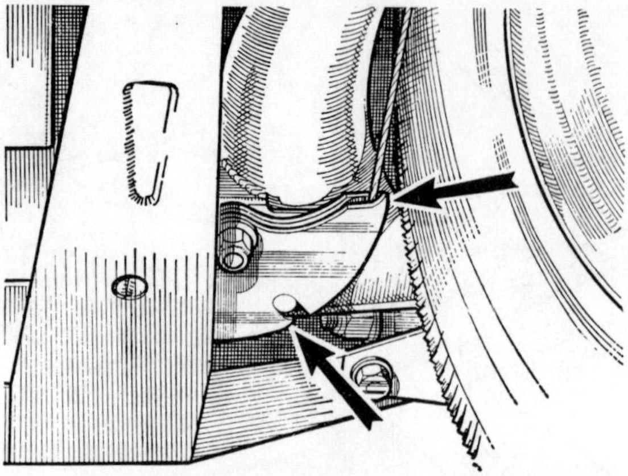

FIG 10 : 9 Handbrake cable sector mounted on rear radius arm. The top (righthand) arrow indicates where the sector corners are 'nipped' to position the cable. The lower arrow indicates the cable anchorage.

10 : 11 Adjusting handbrake

If the travel of the handbrake lever becomes excessive, it will be necessary to adjust the rear brake shoes into closer relationship with the brake drums, and some adjustment of the handbrake cable nuts at the lever trunnion may be necessary.

1 Chock the front wheels and jack up the rear of the car until both rear wheels are free to rotate.
2 With the handbrake in the fully 'Off' position adjust the brake shoes as described in **Section 10 : 2.**
3 Apply the handbrake to the third notch on the ratchet.
4 Turn the cable adjusting nuts at the handbrake lever until the rear road wheels can just be turned by heavy hand pressure.
5 When both wheels offer the same resistance to turning, return the handbrake lever to the fully 'Off' position and check that both wheels turn quite freely. Any binding calls for investigation of the brake components at the wheel, also check the cable sector pivots for stiffness and lubricate them with a few drops of engine lubricating oil.
6 If any faults are found and rectification action carried out it is essential to readjust the brakes completely.

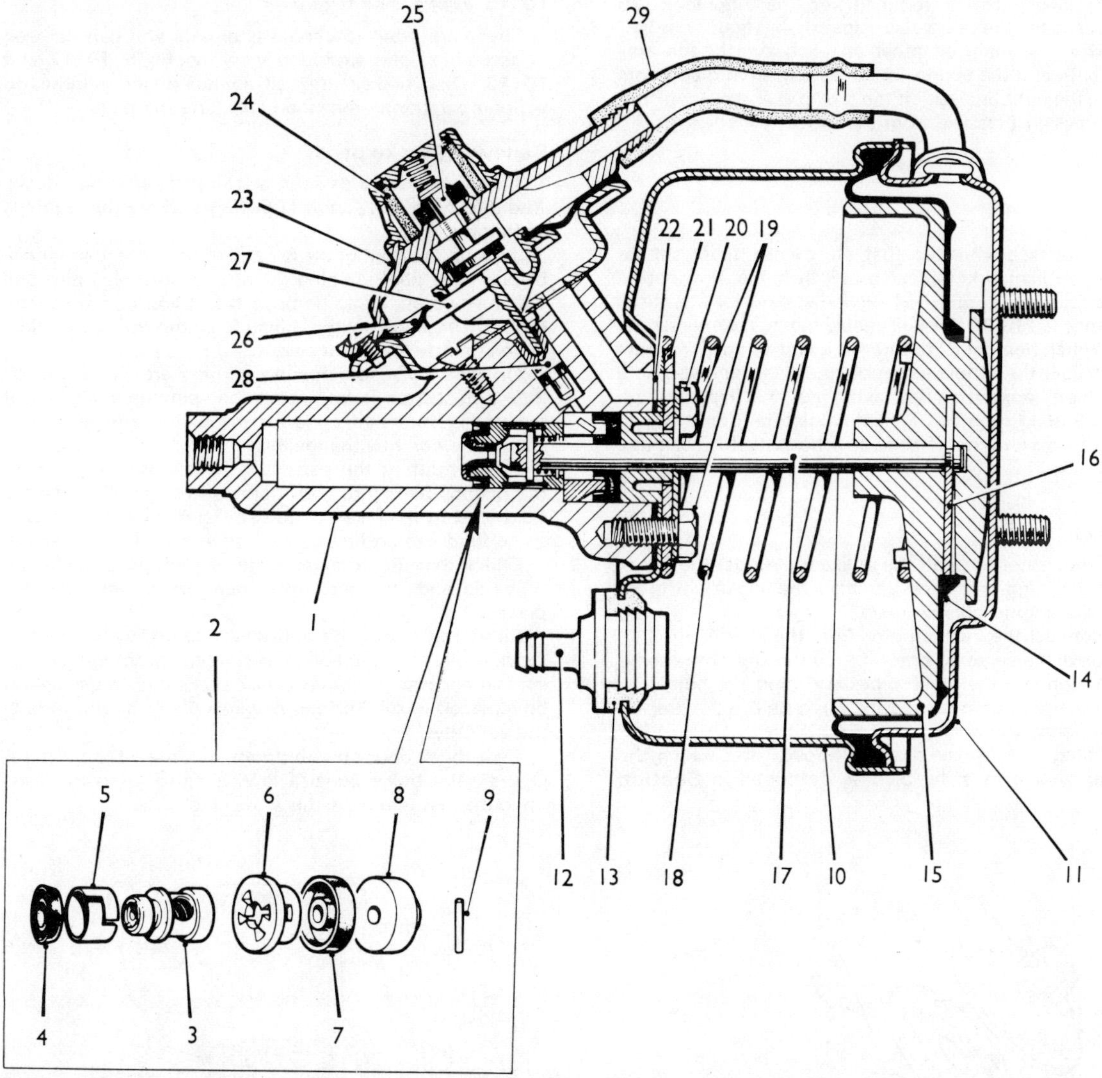

FIG 10:10 Lockheed vacuum servo unit

Key to Fig 10:10 1 Slave cylinder 2 Slave piston components 3 Slave piston* 4 Piston seal* 5 Retaining clip* 6 Spacer* 7 Cup* 8 Bearing* 9 Connecting pin* 10 Servo shell 11 End cover 12 Non-return valve 13 Rubber mounting 14 Main servo diaphragm 15 Diaphragm support 16 Retaining key 17 Pushrod 18 Main return spring 19 Servo shell retaining bolts 20 Locking plate 21 Abutment plate 22 Joint washer 23 Air valve cover 24 Air filter 25 Air valve 26 Air valve diaphragm 27 Diaphragm support 28 Air valve piston 29 Rubber pipe **Shown inset*

10:12 Vacuum servo unit

In order still further to improve the braking on the high performance models Mini 1275 GT a Lockheed vacuum servo unit has been incorporated in the braking system. This is shown in section in **FIG 10:10**, from which will be seen that there are three main components, the vacuum cylinder 10, the air valve assembly 23 and the slave cylinder 1, which is connected in the hydraulic circuit between the master cylinder and the wheel cylinders.

Under light braking the fluid passes directly to the wheel cylinders through the hollow centre of the slave piston 3 and no assistance is obtained.

With heavier pressure the air valve piston 28 is moved upwards, thus opening the air valve 25 and allowing air to enter and pass into the chamber behind the main diaphragm 14 destroying the vacuum. The pushrod 17 is thus moved to the left, sealing the hollow centre of the slave piston and pushing it down the bore and so increasing the fluid pressure at the wheel cylinders.

When the brake pedal is released the pressure under

the air valve piston is reduced and the diaphragm 26 re-opens and the air valve closes. A vacuum is re-created in the main chamber on each side of the diaphragm 14 and the spring 18 forces the servo diaphragm back to the right and with it the pushrod and slave piston thus releasing pressure from the wheel cylinders.

Servicing:

It is not recommended that the owner driver should attempt to dismantle the servo unit at home, but that he should take it to a qualified service station for attention. Reference to **FIG 10:11** will enable him to clean or renew the air filter element 2, but in the event of suspected air valve failure the whole assembly must be renewed as a unit. This is removed after taking out the five securing screws 3 and lifting off. This must also be done to gain access to the interior of the valve housing for cleaning.

Removal:

Pull the heater hose off the intake unit under the right-hand front wing and then withdraw the intake unit from inside the engine compartment.

Disconnect the vacuum pipe from the servo unit.

Remove the securing bracket from the end of the servo unit, disconnect the brake pipes and plug the holes.

Remove the nuts securing the servo unit to the bracket and withdraw the unit.

Refitting is the reverse of the above, after which the braking system must be bled as described in **Section 10:9.**

10:13 Front disc brakes

These are fitted to certain later cars and can be seen in assembled and exploded views in **FIGS 10:12** and **10:13**. Disc brakes are self-adjusting and require no periodic attention other than checking the pads.

Renewing brake pads:

This is necessary as soon as the pads are worn down to a thickness of $\frac{1}{16}$ inch (1.6 mm) and the procedure is as follows:

Jack up the front of the car and remove the road wheel. Depress the pad retaining spring (when fitted) and pull out the two splitpins. Remove the spring and withdraw the pads from the caliper. Clean the exposed face of each piston and the caliper recesses.

On later cars no retaining springs are fitted and all that is necessary is to remove the splitpins and pull out the pads. Note that pads for the earlier and later type caliper are *not* interchangeable.

When refitting the pads it is necessary first to press the pistons back into their bores and this will cause the fluid level in the reservoir to rise. To prevent an overspill some fluid should first be syphoned out of the reservoir.

Check that the cutaway edge of each piston is facing upwards and that the anti-squeak shims are correctly placed.

Insert the new pads and check that they are free to move easily in the caliper, carefully filing down any high spots if necessary. Note that disc brake pads must always be replaced in sets of four, never singly or on one side of the car only.

Refit the spring, press it down and insert the splitpins. Operate the brake pedal a few times to bring the pads up to the disc and then check the fluid level.

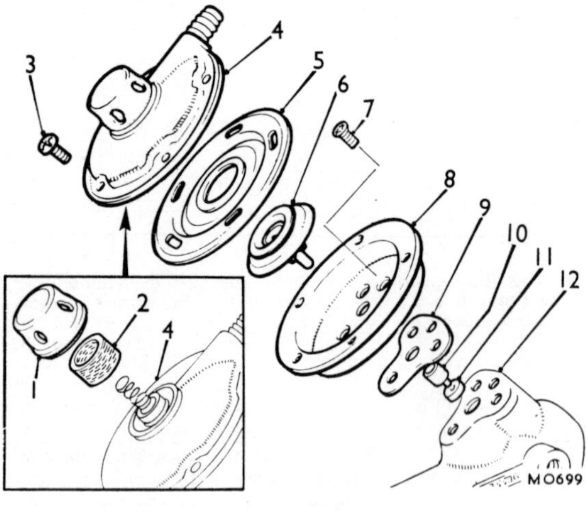

FIG 10:11 **Components of air valve**

Key to Fig 10:11 1 Domed cover for filter 2 Air filter 3 Air valve cover securing screws 4 Air valve cover 5 Diaphragm 6 Diaphragm support 7 Valve housing securing screws 8 Valve housing 9 Joint washer 10 Piston 11 Piston cup 12 Slave cylinder

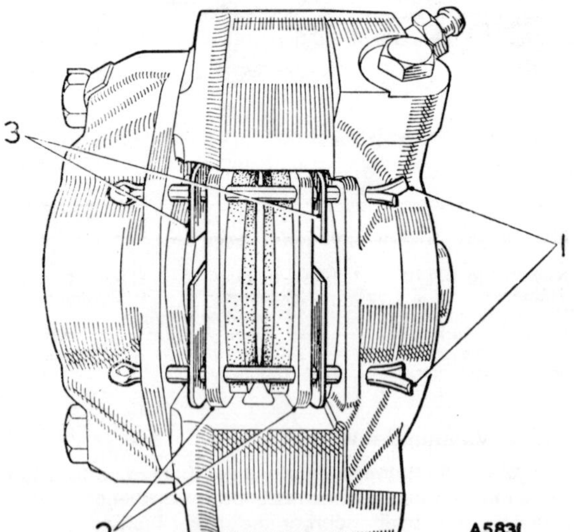

FIG 10:12 **Front brake caliper assembly**

Key to Fig 10:12 1 Splitpins 2 Pads 3 Anti-squeak shims

Removing and dismantling a caliper

Disconnect the tie-rod from the steering arm and remove the locking plate from the dust cover.

Unscrew the two bolts holding the caliper to the hub, detach both parts of the dust cover and remove the caliper. It is not necessary to disconnect the brake pipe unless this is required for later operations.

Withdraw the pads, clean the caliper and clamp one piston while applying (pedal) pressure to remove the other. Remove the fluid seal and the dust seal.

Reassembling:

Dip a new fluid seal in clean brake fluid and fit it into its groove.

Slacken off the bleed screw one complete turn.

Dip the piston in fluid and insert it into the bore with the cutaway face upwards until about $\frac{5}{16}$ inch (8 mm) remains protruding.

Dip a new dust seal, fit it to the retainer and position them on the protruding part of the piston with the seal innermost. Press in the piston and seal and then tighten the bleed screw.

Clamp the piston in the caliper and then repeat the whole procedure for the removal and replacement of the other piston.

Refit the caliper and the two parts of the dust cover to the hub. Refit the hosepipe and the dust cover locking plate.

Reconnect the tie rod and tighten the caliper mounting bolts.

Fit the brake pads and bleed the system.

Note: Never attempt to separate the two halves of a caliper as reassembly without specialized equipment is not possible.

10:14 The tandem master cylinder

The components of the tandem master cylinder used in dual line braking systems are shown in the exploded view of **FIG 10:14**. The operation of the master cylinder is different from the single type in that two pistons are used to pressurise the hydraulic pipe lines to the brakes, one piston acting only on the front brake circuit and the other on the rear brake circuit. A separate supply of fluid is provided for each section by means of a partitioned reservoir.

Removal:

Disconnect the two pipes from the master cylinder and plug the open ends to prevent fluid loss and the entry of any dirt.

Unscrew the two nuts securing the unit to the bulkhead and lift it off, leaving the pushrod attached to the brake pedal. Drain off any fluid remaining in the reservoir and replace the cap.

Dismantling:

Thoroughly clean the exterior of the master cylinder and mount it between soft jaws in a vice with the cylinder bore uppermost.

Remove the rubber boot 2, then press in on the spring and remove the Spirolox ring from its groove in the primary piston, being careful not to distort the coils of the ring or scratch the cylinder bore.

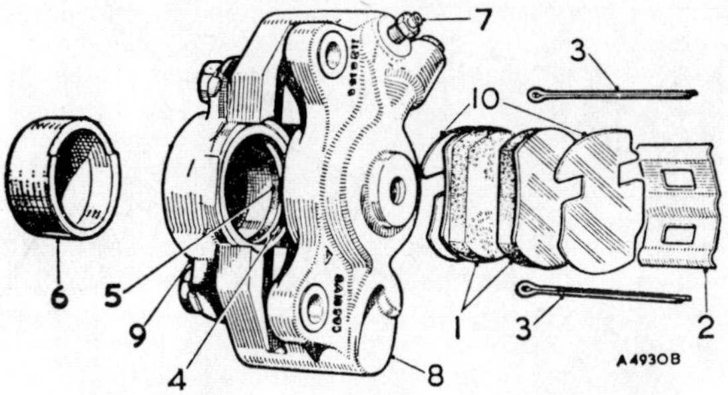

FIG 10:13 Components of a caliper

Key to Fig 10:13 1 Friction pads 2 Pad retaining spring 3 Splitpins 4 Dust seal 5 Fluid seal 6 Piston showing cutaway at top 7 Bleed screw 8 Mounting half caliper 9 Rim half caliper 10 Anti-squeak shim

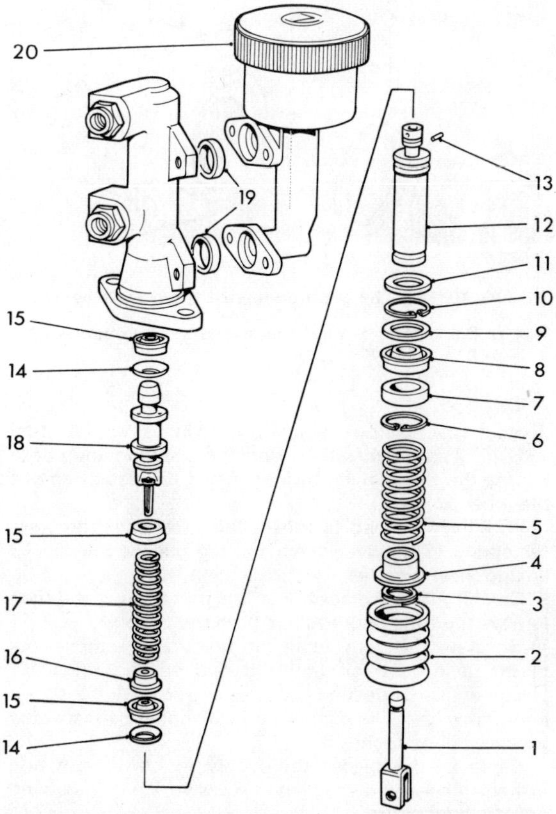

FIG 10:14 The components of the tandem master cylinder

Key to Fig 10:14 1 Pushrod 2 Rubber boot 3 Spirolox ring 4 Spring retainer 5 Spring 6 Circlip 7 Nylon guide bearing 8 Secondary cup 9 Washer 10 Circlip 11 Stop washer 12 Primary piston 13 Roll-pin 14 Piston washer 15 Main cup 16 Pin retainer 17 Spring 18 Secondary piston 19 Reservoir seals 20 Fluid reservoir

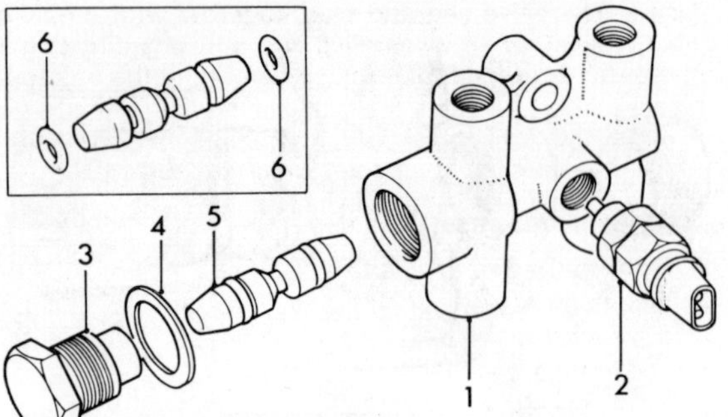

FIG 10:15 The components of the pressure failure switch

Key to Fig 10:15 1 Body 2 Nylon switch 3 End plug 4 Copper washer 5 Shuttle valve piston 6 Rubber seals

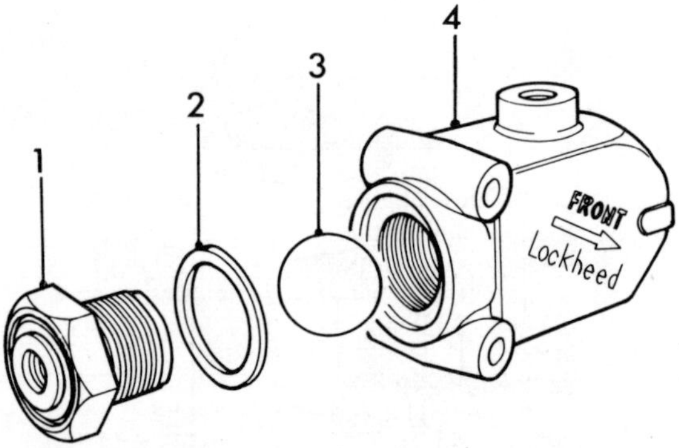

FIG 10:16 The components of the inertia valve

Key to Fig 10:16 1 Valve sub-assembly 2 Copper washer 3 Steel ball 4 Body

Extract the piston retaining circlip 6, using tool 18G 1112 if available, then work the piston in and out to release the nylon guide bearing 7 and cap seal. Remove the inner circlip 10.

Withdraw the two pistons as an assembly, compress the spring 17 between them and tap out the roll-pin 13 linking them together.

Carefully note the position of the rubber cups and then remove the cups and washers from the pistons.

Unscrew the four retaining bolts and remove the plastic fluid reservoir and the two sealing rings 19. Unscrew the connection adaptors and remove the spring and trap valves. The copper gaskets should be discarded in favour of new ones.

Clean all the pieces thoroughly in brake fluid and inspect them for damage or excessive wear, renewing any doubtful parts.

Reassembly:

This is carried out in reverse to dismantling but a few points may need special mention.

Always use a complete set of new rubber seals and wet all parts in clean brake fluid before assembly.

Note that the piston washer 14 is fitted over the head of the secondary piston with the concave surface as shown and then the main cup 15 fitted with its flat surface against the washer.

Using new copper gaskets on the connection adaptors, tighten the connections to a torque of just 5 lb ft (.7 kgm).

Refit the master cylinder, guiding the pushrod 1 carefully through the rubber boot and securing the two retaining nuts. Connect the two outlet pipes and refill the reservoir with Unipart 550 brake fluid or any other proprietary brand conforming to specification SAE 1703c. Bleed the brake system as described in **Section 10:16**.

10:15 Pressure failure switch

This component, which in tandem circuits replaces the three way connector on the righthand side of the engine bulkhead crossmember, is coupled in the hydraulic circuits to the two sets of brakes and is designed to give a visual warning in the event of a pressure failure in either circuit.

The main item in the construction of the device is the shuttle valve piston 5 which moves in the bore connecting the front and the rear brake hydraulic circuits. With full or equal pressure in each circuit, the piston takes a central position in its bore, but if pressure drops in either circuit, the piston is moved in that direction and operates the electrical switch 2 which causes a warning light on the instrument panel to glow. No repairs or adjustment are possible, so a new unit must be fitted in the event of a switch assembly being faulty.

Removal:

Pull off the electrical connector from the switch and carefully clean the outside of the whole unit before disconnecting the four hydraulic pipes, plugging the open ends to prevent fluid loss or the entry of foreign matter.

Unscrew the single securing bolt and lift off.

Dismantling:

The components of the pressure failure switch, sometimes referred to as a differential warning switch, are shown in **FIG 10:15**.

Unscrew the end plug 3, discarding the copper washer, and also the nylon switch 2.

Shake out the shuttle valve piston assembly 5, remove and discard the two rubber seals 6.

Clean all the parts in brake fluid or methylated spirit and renew the complete unit if any faulty parts are discovered. The operation of the switch may be tested at this time by connecting the wiring plug and pressing in the switch plunger by hand.

Reassemble the switch in reverse order, using new rubber and copper seals. Tighten the switch body to a torque of 12 to 15 lb ft (1.6 to 2.1 kgm) and the end plug to 20 to 33 lb ft (2.8 to 4.5 kgm).

Fill up the brake reservoir with the recommended fluid and bleed the braking system.

10:16 Bleeding the dual braking system

The procedure for bleeding the dual system differs from that described for the single system in **Section 10:9** in the following details.

Do not allow the fluid level in the reservoir to fall more than ½ inch (13 mm) during the operation.

First bleed the front and rear brakes on the driver's side of the car, opening and closing the two bleed screws together. The manufacturers advise that the bleed screws should be closed between each stroke of the brake pedal and that it should be pumped at least four more times after clean, air-free, fluid is pumped into the glass jar.

When the two brakes on the driver's side are bled, transfer the bleed tubes to those on the passenger's side and treat them in the same manner. It is advised that the brake fluid expelled from the bleed points should be discarded and not re-used in the system.

10:17 The inertia valve

This is fitted in the hydraulic circuit to the rear brakes on tandem systems in place of the pressure regulating valve described in **Section 10:7**. The angle at which the unit is mounted on the rear subframe crossmember allows the steel ball inside the body, see **FIG 10:16**, to hold the valve in the open position so that the fluid path to the rear brakes is unobstructed.

When the car is braked heavily, the transfer of weight to the front tilts the inertia valve and the ball moves away from the valve, which is then closed by means of a light spring. In this way no further pressure is applied to the rear brakes and all extra effort on the brake pedal is applied to the front wheels and so reduces the likelihood of rear wheel locking.

Removal of the inertia valve is a simple matter of unscrewing the hydraulic pipes and the two mounting bolts.

Remove the end plug and extract the steel ball, clean the parts in methylated spirit and examine most carefully for wear or damage. Only those parts in perfect condition should be re-used.

Use a new valve and end plug, together with a new copper washer when assembling and note the direction of the arrow pointing to the front when fitting the unit to the car.

Fill up the brake reservoir and bleed the system, testing for leaks both at rest and under pressure.

10:18 Fault diagnosis

(a) Spongy pedal

1 Leak in the system
2 Worn master cylinder
3 Leaking wheel cylinders
4 Air in system
5 Gaps between shoes and underside of lining

(b) Excessive pedal movement

1 Check 1 and 4 in (a)
2 Excessive lining wear
3 Brakes need adjusting
4 Very low fluid level in supply reservoir
5 Too much free movement of pedal

(c) Brakes grab or pull to one side

1 Brake backplate loose
2 Scored, cracked or distorted drum or disc
3 High spots on drum
4 Unbalanced shoe adjustment
5 Wet or oily linings or pads
6 Worn or loose rear spring fixings
7 Front suspension or rear axle anchorages loose
8 Worn steering connections
9 Mixed linings of different grades
10 Uneven tyre pressures
11 Broken shoe return springs
12 Seized handbrake cable

(d) Excessive braking at rear wheels

1 Faulty pressure regulating valve or inertia valve

NOTES

CHAPTER 11

THE ELECTRICAL SYSTEM

11 : 1 General description

The main components of the 12 volt electrical system with which Mini vehicles are equipped, are:

1 The lead-acid battery, located in the well of the luggage compartment.
2 The generator, mounted on the righthand side of the engine and driven by a V-belt from the crankshaft pulley at the front of the engine. The mounting is adjustable for correct belt tension.
3 The starter motor, mounted on the flywheel housing on the righthand side of the engine and incorporating a conventional worm and pinion drive.
4 A voltage control and cut-out unit which is normally sealed and should not require attention.
5 The lighting system comprising headlamps, sidelamps, stop lights, flasher indicators and internal lights, panel lights and electrical instruments in various arrangements according to car model.

The wiring diagrams appropriate to the different models are illustrated in the Appendix.

Whilst servicing of the main components is within the ability of owners who have a reasonable understanding of electrical equipment, those less experienced may find it more convenient and economical to consult a BMC agent with a view to exchanging the faulty unit for a new or reconditioned one. If servicing is to be undertaken, the owner should have available an accurate amp/volt/ohm meter.

Coincident with the introduction of NEGATIVE earth electrical systems a number of changes have been made in the electrical equipment fitted to these cars and for convenience they are grouped together in the latter part of this chapter.

These changes include the provision of an alternator in place of the direct current generator, a Lucas M35J starter motor, a permanent magnet two-speed windshield wiper and a printed circuit instrument panel which eliminates an amount of intricate wiring.

11 : 2 Battery maintenance and testing

At all times keep the battery clean and dry. Keep the surrounding parts of the car clean, dry and free from liquid spilled from the battery cells. Remove any signs of corrosion from the battery connections, strap and tray using a little diluted ammonia and if possible painting the vehicle parts with some anti-sulphuric-acid paint to protect them from any further attack. Smear the terminal posts and clamps with some petroleum jelly after cleaning them and prior to their reconnection. Make sure the terminal bolts are tight.

The specific gravity of the electrolyte is a good indication of the electrical condition of the battery, but it should not be overlooked that a battery can suffer from physical damage such as cracks in the casing exterior or between the cells.

To test the electrolyte a hydrometer is used to draw out a small quantity of the liquid from each cell in turn. The level of the float in the instrument enables the specific gravity of the electrolyte to be read. The following figures indicate the state of charge of the cell being tested:

At 16°C (60°F)
Cell fully charged—Specific gravity 1.270 to 1.290
Cell about half charged—Specific gravity 1.190 to 1.210
Cell completely discharged—Specific gravity 1.110 to 1.130

Add .002 to each hydrometer reading for every 3°C above 16°C or subtract .002 from each reading for every 3°C below 16°C.

If the electrolyte level of one or more cells is very low or gives a reading very different from the remaining cells it may be that some leakage or internal fault has developed, in which event the case should be inspected for signs of cracks and if necessary taken to a specialist for advice. If the cells all give readings indicating a low state of charge, due, for example, to a long period of limited use of the car, the battery should be recharged by taking the car for a long day-time run, or by means of external charging equipment. Charging from an external source should be at the rate of 3 amps until all cells are gassing freely. At no time should the electrolyte temperature during charging exceed 38°C (100°F). If this temperature is reached the charge should be discontinued until the temperature has fallen by at least 6°C (10°F), otherwise damage to the battery may result.

11 : 3 Generator maintenance, electrical tests in situ

The maintenance requirements of the generator are limited to checking and if necessary, adjusting the drive belt tension every 6000 miles as described in **Chapter 4.** At the same interval apply two or three drops of engine lubricating oil into the centre of the end bearing housing indicated in **FIG 11 : 1.**

Before carrying out any tests in situ, make sure the trouble, in all probability loss of charge, is not due to drive belt slip.

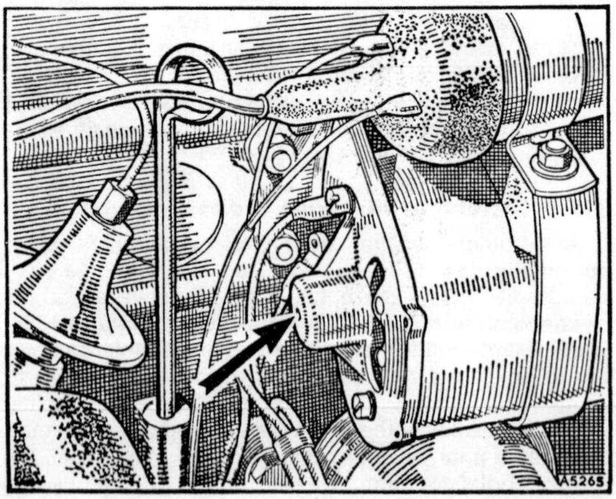

FIG 11 : 1 Oil hole for lubricating the generator end bearing

For the first test, switch off all lights and accessories and disconnect the two cables on the generator marked D and F. Connect the two terminals with a short length of copper wire or cable and start the engine, allowing it to run at normal idling speed. Connect the negative lead of an accurate moving-coil voltmeter, having a 0-20 volt range, to the generator terminals and the other lead to earth. Speed up the engine to about 1000 rev/min when the voltmeter reading should rise rapidly without fluctuation. Do not allow the voltmeter reading to reach 20 volts, and do not race the engine in order to obtain an increased reading.

If there is no reading, check the brush gear. If the reading is only about 1 volt, the field winding may be faulty. If the reading is about 5 volts, the armature windings may be faulty.

If the readings appear to be in order, leave the link in position between the terminals and restore the original leads to their correct D and F terminals from the generator to the control box. Remove the lead from the D terminal on the control box and connect the voltmeter between this lead and a good earth. On speeding up the engine, the reading should be the same as that registered direct on the generator. No reading indicates a break in the cable. Carry out the same test on the F lead.

Finally, remove the connecting link on the generator. If the reading is still correct, test the control box.

11 : 4 Removing and dismantling the generator

To remove the generator:

1 Disconnect the two leads from the generator terminals.
2 Slacken the four attachment bolts, move the generator bodily towards the cylinder block and lift the drive belt out of the generator pulley groove. Remove the two upper and one lower bolts, nuts and washers and lift out the generator.

Referring to **FIG 11 : 2,** the generator is dismantled as follows:

1 Remove the pulley securing nut 12 and washer and pull off the drive pulley. Remove the Woodruff key 11 and spacer 24.
2 Unscrew and remove the two through-bolts 17 and take off the commutator end bracket 1.
3 Lift out from the yoke 7 the driving end bracket 23 complete with the armature 19 and its ballbearing 21.
4 If required, the ball bearing can be removed by first taking off the bearing retaining plate 20 and then pressing the armature complete from the end bracket by means of a hand press. Do not lose the corrugated washer 22 and the felt washer 10.

11 : 5 Brushes and commutator, field coil testing

Servicing of the generator should follow broadly the pattern outlined below:

1 If the brushes appear to be sticking in their holders, remove them and clean them with petrol. If necessary lightly file the sides using a smooth file only. Always replace the brushes in their original positions.
2 If the brushes have worn to less than $\frac{9}{32}$ inch long new brushes must be fitted and bedded to the commutator by winding a strip of abrasive cloth round the commutator, fitting the brushes and rotating the commutator to rub a concave surface on the end of

the brushes. Clean thoroughly.

3 Using a light spring balance or suitable weights, test the tension of the brush springs. This should register between 18 and 24 oz. Fit new springs if the tension is inadequate.

4 The commutator segments should be clean and free from pitting and burning. If desired, clean the surfaces with fuel or rotate the commutator inside a strip of fine glasspaper. A badly worn surface can be rectified by mounting the complete armature in a lathe and taking off a very light cut with a sharp tool, polishing afterwards with a strip of very fine glasspaper. The mica insulation between the segments should be undercut to a depth of $\frac{1}{32}$ inch using a hacksaw blade ground down to the thickness of the mica.

5 Using an accurate ohmmeter, check the resistance of the field coils. The reading should be between 6.0 and 6.3 ohms. A 12 volt DC supply connected in series with the field coils and an ammeter will give a current reading of 2 amps if the field coils are in good order. No reading indicates an open-circuit. To test for earthed field coils, unsolder the end of the field winding from the earth terminal on the generator yoke and apply a suitable current supply and test lamp to the field terminal and earth. If the lamp lights the field coils are earthed and must be renewed.

6 To renew the field coils first drill out the rivet securing the field coil terminal assembly to the yoke and unsolder the field coil connections. Remove the insulation piece which prevents the junction of the field coils from making contact with the yoke.

7 Mark the yoke and polepieces for refitting in their original positions. Unscrew the pole-shoe retaining screws using a wheel-operated screwdriver and draw the pole-shoes and coils out of the yoke. Lift off the coils.

8 Place the new coils and pole-shoes inside the yoke taking care not to trap the insulation between the shoes and the yoke. Insert and lightly tighten the fixing screws and use a pole-shoe expander to correctly locate the shoes, tighten up the screws as far as possible, finally securing them with the wheel-operated screwdriver and caulking to lock. Replace the insulation piece, resolder the connections at the field coil terminal tags and re-rivet the terminal assembly to the yoke.

9 Armature testing is not possible without special equipment. If desired, test by substitution. Never attempt to machine the armature core or straighten a distorted shaft.

If the generator bearings are worn sufficiently to allow some perceptible side movement of the shaft, they must be renewed as follows, referring to **FIG 11 : 2**.

1 Screw a $\frac{5}{8}$ inch tap into the commutator end porous bronze bearing 4 and pull it out of the end bracket 1. Immerse the new bearing in SAE 30 grade engine lubricating oil at room temperature for 24 hours or at 100°C for two hours and then press it into the end bracket using a shouldered mandrel having the same diameter as the armature shaft. This operation is illustrated in **FIG 11 : 3.**

2 To remove the ballbearing first remove the rivets securing the bearing retaining plate to the end bracket and remove the plate. Press the bearing out of the end bracket and remove the corrugated and felt washers.

3 Clean the new bearing and pack it with high-melting-point grease, fit the felt and corrugated washers in the bearing housing, locate the bearing in the housing and,

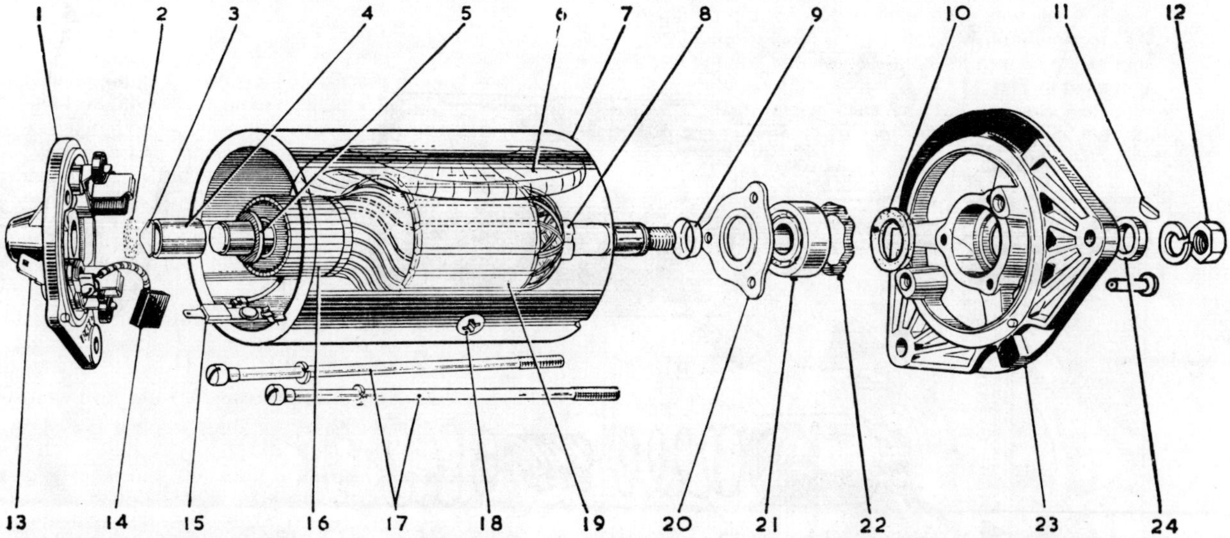

FIG 11 : 2 An exploded view of the generator, type C40/1

Key to Fig 11 : 2 1 Commutator end bracket 2 Felt ring 3 Felt ring retainer 4 Bronze bush 5 Thrust washer 6 Field coils 7 Yoke 8 Shaft collar 9 Shaft collar retaining cup 10 Felt ring 11 Shaft key 12 Shaft nut 13 Output terminal 'D' 14 Brushes 15 Field terminal 'F' 16 Commutator 17 Through-bolts 18 Pole-shoe securing screws 19 Armature 20 Bearing retaining plate 21 Ballbearing 22 Corrugated washer 23 Driving end bracket 24 Pulley spacer using a hand press, press it firmly home. Insert new rivets to secure the retaining plate from the outside of the end bracket and open them by means of a punch to secure the plate tightly in position. Press the drive end bracket on to the armature shaft **using the inner race of the bearing to take the pressure of the press.** A suitable sized piece of tube should be used between the press and the inner race.

11 : 6 Reassembly and refitting

Reassembly of the generator is substantially the reverse of dismantling, taking care with the brushes when assembling the commutator end bracket. Hold the brushes clear of the commutator by partially withdrawing them from their housings so that they are trapped in position by the side pressure of the brush springs. When the end bracket has been assembled to within about ½ inch of the yoke release the brushes on to the commutator by manipulating a screwdriver between the end bracket and the yoke. Make sure the springs are bearing correctly on the ends of the brushes before finally closing the gap between the end bracket and the yoke.

Add two or three drops of engine lubricating oil through the hole in the armature end cover, mount the generator on the engine, adjust its position for correct drive belt tension and connect the cables correctly. Make sure a flat washer is fitted beneath the head of each upper fixing bolt.

11 : 7 Testing starter motor in situ

With the battery in a satisfactory state of charge, sluggish action of the starter is most likely to be caused by a poor connection in the starter wiring, which will produce high resistance in the starter circuit. Check the connections at the starter switch, starter and battery. If

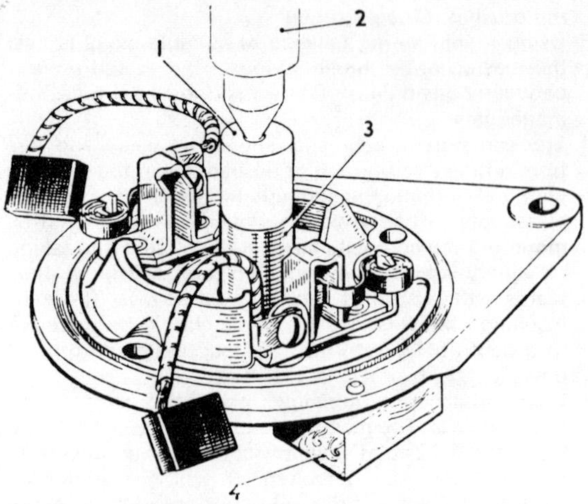

FIG 11 : 3 Method of using a press to refit the commutator end bracket bush

Key to Fig 11 : 3 1 Shouldered mandrel 2 Hand-press 3 Bearing bush 4 Support block

these are in order and there is no sign of broken wiring between them, check the starter switch for correct operation. Check engine earth strap.

The brightness of the headlamps will be affected if the normal current is flowing in the starter motor. If full brilliance is maintained with the headlamps switched on and the starter switch operated, current in the motor is less than normal and, provided the switch and all connections are in good order, there is probably an internal fault in the motor which must then be removed from the car for investigation.

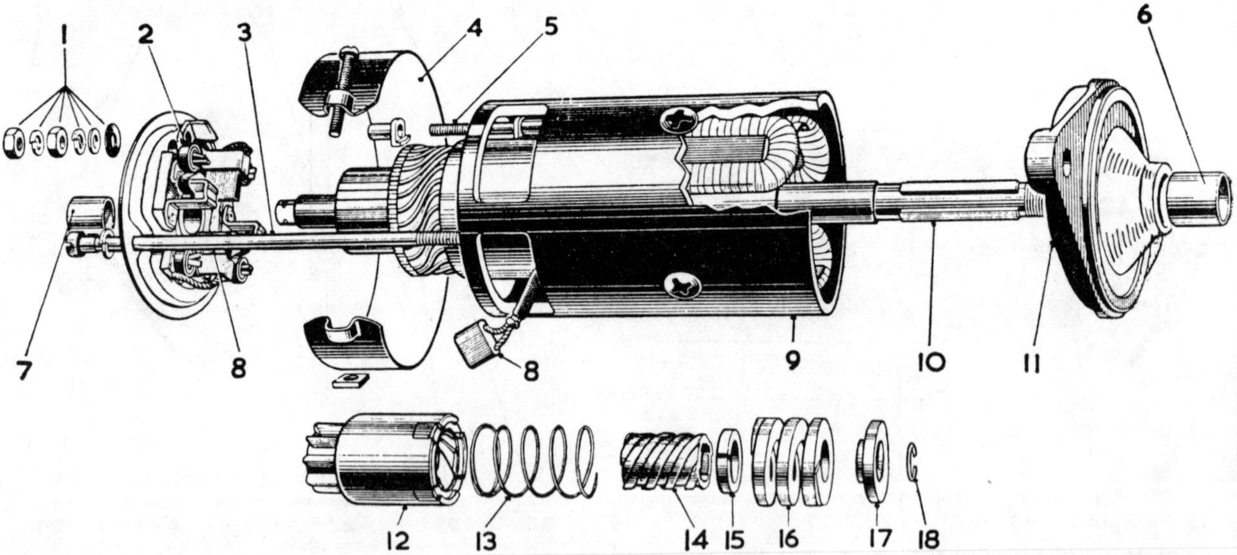

FIG 11 : 4 An exploded view of the starter motor and drive

Key to Fig 11 : 4 1 Terminal nuts and washers 2 Brush spring 3 Through-bolt 4 Band cover 5 Terminal post 6 Bearing bush 7 Bearing 8 Brushes 9 Yoke 10 Armature shaft 11 Driving end bracket 12 Pinion assembly 13 Restraining spring 14 Sleeve 15 Impact washer 16 Main spring 17 Locating washer 18 Circlip

Operation of the starter with the headlamps switched on normally causes the lamps to lose brightness but if this occurs without the accompanying sound of the starter pinion meshing in the flywheel teeth, it is possible that the starter pinion teeth have become permanently meshed with the flywheel. This may have been caused by the starter being operated with the engine running, and the starter must be removed for examination.

Should the starter be heard to operate but not turn the engine the starter drive unit is probably out of order.

The starter motor and drive are shown in the exploded view at **FIG 11 : 4**.

11 : 8 Removing, testing and dismantling the starter

To remove the starter, refer to **FIG 11 : 4** and release the starter cable from the terminal by taking off the nut and spring washer at 1. Remove the two starter securing bolts, manoeuvre the starter towards the radiator and lift it clear of the power unit. Further operations are as follows:

1 Examination of the brushes 8 and commutator becomes possible after removal of the cover band 4. Hold back each of the brush springs and pull gently on the brush flexible connectors. If there are signs of the brushes being tight in their holders, remove and clean them, if necessary polishing the sides lightly with a smooth file.

2 If the brushes are defective or worn to the degree that the flexible connectors show on the running faces, renew them.

3 If the commutator surface is only dirty and discoloured but otherwise satisfactory, clean it by holding a fuel-moistened cloth against it while rotating the armature.

4 Test for correct running of the starter by holding it in a vice and connecting the starter terminal and body to a 12 volt battery by means of heavy gauge cable. With no applied load, the starter should run at very high speed. If it does not, dismantle it as follows for further inspection:

1 Remove the brushes from their holders.

2 Remove the armature complete with drive from the commutator end bracket and yoke. Two through-bolts 3 secure the starter assembly as a unit.

3 Remove the terminal nut and washers 1 from the terminal post 5 and withdraw the two through-bolts.

4 Lift off the commutator end bracket and the attachment bracket from opposite ends of the yoke.

5 Use a light spring balance to test the brush spring tension which should be in the range 15 to 25 oz. If the tension is incorrect renew the springs.

6 For renewal purposes, the flexible leads have to be unsoldered, two from terminal eyelets on the brush holders on the commutator end bracket, and two from the field coil tappings. When the new brushes have been secured by resoldering, they may be put to immediate service without bedding as the working faces are preformed.

7 To dismantle the drive unit, compress the spring 16 and remove the circlip 18, then remove the main spring and locating washer 17. Pull the complete drive assembly from the splined armature shaft and unscrew the sleeve 14 from the barrel and pinion assembly 12. Any stiffness of the pinion on the sleeve

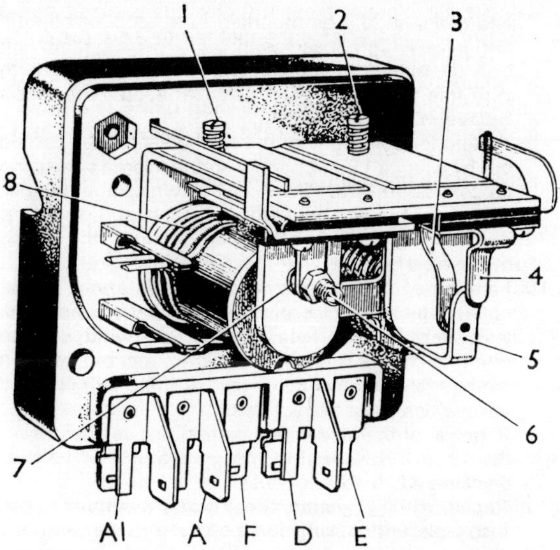

FIG 11 : 5 The control box with the cover removed

Key to Fig 11 : 5 1 Regulator adjusting screw 2 Cut-out adjusting screw 3 Fixed contact blade 4 Stop arm 5 Armature tongue and moving contact 6 Regulator fixed contact screw 7 Regulator moving contact 8 Regulator series windings

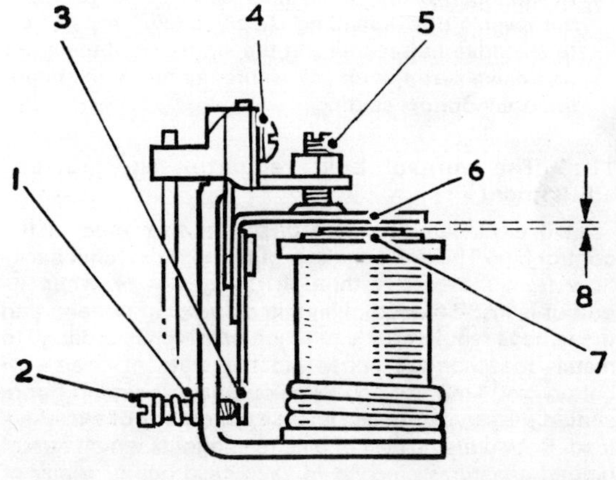

FIG 11 : 6 The mechanical setting of the voltage regulator

Key to Fig 11 : 6 1 Locknut 2 Voltage adjusting screw 3 Armature tension spring 4 Armature securing screws 5 Fixed contact adjustment screw 6 Armature 7 Core face and shim 8 .021 inch (.533 mm)

can be eased by cleaning and lubrication. If the screwed sleeve is damaged, renew the complete assembly of sleeve, barrel and pinion. **Do not renew these items individually.**

8 Clean the commutator with a cloth moistened with petrol. More effective cleaning of the commutator can be achieved by wrapping a piece of fine glass-paper round it while rotating the armature. If this is not successful the armature, less attachment bracket

and drive, should be mounted in a lathe and lightly cut at very high speed with a sharp tool, removing only the minimum of metal and finally polishing with very fine glasspaper. **Do not undercut the mica between the segments.**

9 Testing for continuity of the field coils can be carried out by using a 12 volt battery and test lamp across the tapping point of the field coils to which the brushes are connected and the field terminal post. If the lamp does not light, there is an open circuit in the wiring of the field coils.

10 Earthing of the field coils to the pole-shoes or the yoke is tested by connecting the battery and test lamp between the field terminal post and a clean point on the yoke. If the lamp lights there is an earth connection between some part of the field coils and yoke which must be rectified.

11 Renewal of the field coil is carried out in the manner described for renewal of the generator field coils in **Section 11 : 5** (6).

12 Repair of the armature/commutator assembly is not a suitable undertaking for the home owner and any damage observed during inspection calls for renewal of the assembly.

13 The bearings are of the porous bronze type. They can be renewed if they show any signs of slackness when the starter is assembled with the armature in position. Soak new bushes in engine lubricating oil for 24 hours before pressing them into the end brackets of the starter.

14 Reassembly of the starter after overhaul is generally the reverse of dismantling. Apply a few drops of oil to the drive before refitting the starter on the engine and make sure the unit is secure, as heavy loads are imposed during starting.

11 : 9 The control box, regulator and cut-out adjustments

Two electrically separate units are embodied in the control box. These are the cut-out which prevents back-flow from the battery through the generator when its output is insufficient to maintain a charging current, and the voltage regulator, the function of which is broadly, to match the charging current to the state of charge of battery and limit the generator output to its rated figure should the services in use impose conditions of excessive load. Both units consist of electro-magnets which attract hinged armatures carrying in each case one of a pair of contact points. Temperature control is provided by the inclusion of a bi-metallic armature spring which varies the resistance of the armature to attraction by the electro-magnet. This is necessary in order more accurately to match the generator characteristics to those of the battery under all climatic conditions.

Regulator adjustments should not normally be necessary but if the battery does not charge or the charging rate falls off as the battery becomes charged, it may be advisable to check the setting. First make sure the battery is in good order.

A high-resistance (ohms per volt) voltmeter is essential for these operations, having a 0-20 volt scale. Referring to **FIG 11 : 5,** proceed as follows:

1 Disconnect the cables at the control box terminals A and A1 and connect the cables together. Connect the voltmeter negative lead to control box terminal D and the positive lead to terminal E.

2 Start the engine and increase speed until the voltmeter needle flicks and steadies. At this point the voltmeter reading should be 15.8 to 16.7 volts according to ambient temperature. Readings outside this range call for regulator adjustment.

3 Switch off the engine and remove the control box cover. Referring to **FIG 11 : 5,** turn the voltage adjusting screw 1 a fraction of a turn clockwise to raise the setting, or anticlockwise to decrease it. Start up the engine and check and if still incorrect, repeat the operation as necessary. Each resetting should be completed within 30 seconds otherwise heating effects in the shunt winding may affect accuracy. Always increase engine speed very gradually.

It is unlikely that mechanical adjustment will be required unless the armature has been removed for any reason. If necessary proceed as follows:

1 Unscrew the locknut and contact screw 5 **(FIG 11 : 6)** far enough to clear the armature contact, and unscrew the voltage adjusting screw until it clears the armature tension spring 3. Slacken the two securing screws 4. Insert a .021 inch thick feeler gauge between the armature 6 and the core face and shim 7 taking care not to damage the edge of the shim. Press the armature down **squarely** against the feeler gauge and retighten the securing screws. With the gauge still in position, screw down the adjustable contact until it just touches the armature contact and retighten the locknut. Carry out the electrical setting as described.

2 The voltage regulator contact points may be cleaned, if desired, using a fine carborundum stone or fine emery cloth. Clean off all dust or foreign matter afterwards, using methylated spirits.

To check the voltage at which the cut-out operates:

1 Connect the voltmeter (0-20 volt range) to the control box terminals D and E. Start the engine and slowly increase speed until the cut-out contacts close. The voltage reading at which this occurs should be 12.7 to 13.3 volts. If this is incorrect, the cut-out may be adjusted as follows:

2 Referring to **FIG 11 : 5,** turn the adjusting screw 2 clockwise to raise the cut-in voltage or anticlockwise to reduce the setting. The screw should be turned only a fraction of a turn at a time. Note the voltage reading at the instant of contact closure at each adjustment. Make each adjustment as quickly as possible to avoid temperature effects. Non-operation of the cut-out means that there may be an open circuit in the wiring of the control box unit and further examination, rectification or renewal is necessary.

The mechanical setting is rather different from that required for the voltage regulator and is as follows:

1 Unscrew the cut-out adjusting screw until it is well clear of armature spring 2 **(FIG 11 : 7).** Slacken the two armature securing screws 6, then press the armature squarely down on the copper-sprayed core face and retighten the securing screws. Using thin nosed pliers or other suitable tool, adjust the gap 8 between the armature stop arm 4 and the armature tongue 5 by bending the stop arm slightly. When the armature is pressed squarely down on the core, this gap must be .030 inch.

2 The gap 9 between the contacts, when the armature is in the free position should be .010 to .020 inch. To adjust this gap, bend the fixed contact blade 7 so that when the armature is pressed squarely down against the core face, there is a 'follow-through' of blade deflection of .010 to .020 inch. Notice that the total of gap 9 and blade deflection, as indicated at 3, **FIG 11 : 7** will be between .020 and .040 inch.
3 For cleaning dirty, rough or burnt contacts, place a thin strip of fine glasspaper between the contacts, close them gently by hand and draw the glasspaper through, with the abrasive side of the glasspaper towards each contact in turn. Remove any dust or foreign matter with a non-fluffy cloth moistened in methylated spirits.

11 : 10 Fuses

FIG 11 : 8 illustrates the fuse-block mounted separately from the control box, on the righthand wing valance. Two 35 amp fuses are incorporated to protect the equipment. A blown fuse is indicated by the non-operation of all the units protected by that fuse.

For confirmation, inspect the fuse after removing it from its spring clips. The broken fuse wire inside the glass tube should be visible. Before renewing the fuse investigate the cause in the wiring and units protected by the fuse and rectify the defect, otherwise it is probable that the fault will recur. Reference to the wiring diagrams in the Appendix of this manual will assist in fault-finding.

11 : 11 Headlamp dismantling and beam setting

The headlamps have double filaments dipped by a foot switch. Early lamps may be non-sealed with separate bulbs which are prefocussed. Later headlamps will be of the sealed-beam type.

To renew a sealed-beam unit which has failed:

1 Remove the bottom screw and lift off the rim and dust excluder. Referring to **FIG 11 : 9,** remove the three cross-head screws and lift off the retaining plate, supporting the light unit meanwhile.
2 Pull unit forward and detach three-pin plug from the rear.
3 When refitting the unit ensure that the lugs on the rear outer edge engage slots in back shell. Fit retaining plate and dust excluder with flange facing forward.

Dismantle non-sealed-beam headlamps as follows:

1 Remove bottom screw and lift off rim. Press light unit inwards and turn anticlockwise to release it from the three spring-loaded screws.
2 Release bayonet cap behind reflector to reach bulb.
3 When replacing bulb, register slot in flange with key inside bulb housing.

Adjustment of the headlamp beams should preferably be carried out by a service station using special optical equipment so that the legal requirements may be satisfied. In an emergency the two screws arrowed in **FIG 11 : 9** can be used for aiming the lamps, the screw at the top being used for vertical adjustment and the screw at the side for lateral adjustment.

On most cars it is necessary to remove the circular rim shown to gain access to the adjusting screws. On Clubman and 1275 GT models the front grille extensions (four screws each) must be removed.

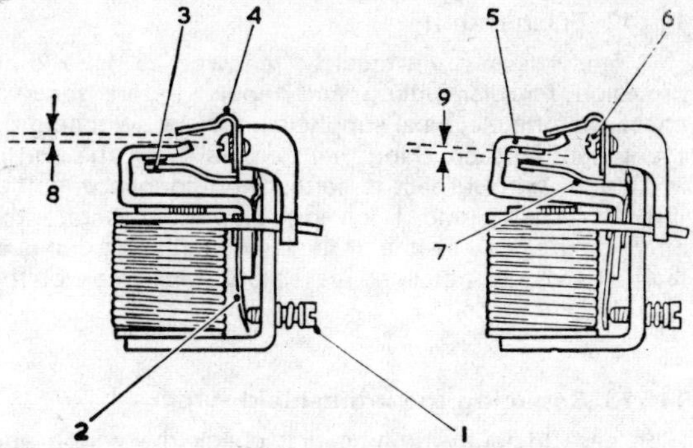

FIG 11 : 7 Mechanical setting of the cut-out

Key to Fig 11 : 7 1 Cut-out adjusting screw 2 Armature tension spring 3 'Follow through'—.010 to .020 inch (.25 to .50 mm) 4 Stop arm 5 Armature tongue and moving contact 6 Armature securing screws 7 Fixed contact blade 8 .030 inch (.76 mm) 9 .010 to .020 inch (.25 to .50 mm)

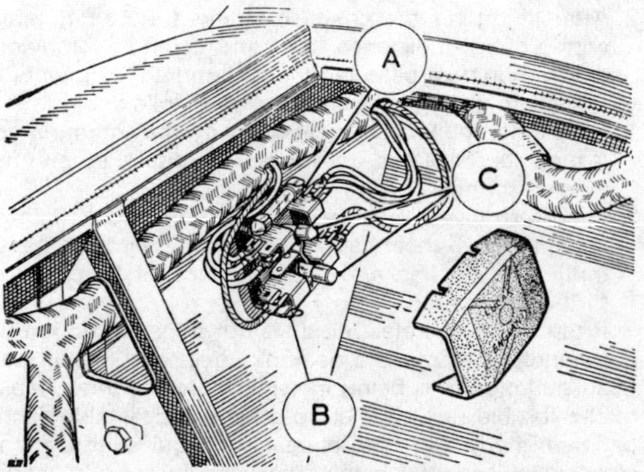

FIG 11 : 8 Fuse block mounted on the righthand valance

Key to Fig 11 : 8 A 35 amp fuse B 35 amp fuse C Spare fuses

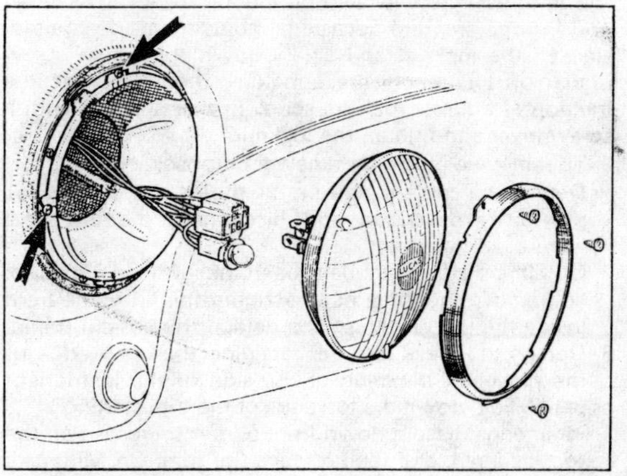

FIG 11 : 9 The sealed-beam type headlamp unit. The arrows indicate the beam setting adjusting screws

11 : 12 Flasher unit

A faulty flasher unit must be renewed as there is no provision for dismantling and repair. Before renewal check that the electrical supply is intact by switching on the ignition and checking that terminal B on the unit is at 12 volts with respect to earth. Then connect together the terminals B and L on the unit and operate the direction indicator switch. If the lamps light, the unit is at fault. If they do not light make a further check of the circuitry and switch.

11 : 13 Servicing the windshield wiper

In case of faulty running first check the wiring and electrical supply.

To detach the cable rack from the motor and gearbox, first unscrew the pipe union nut, then remove the gearbox cover and also the retaining washer from the crankpin and final gearwheel. Lift off the connecting link.

A dirty commutator can be cleaned by:

1 Removing the connecting leads to the terminals and withdrawing the three screws securing the cover at the commutator end of the unit.
2 After lifting off the cover, cleaning the commutator with a petrol-moistened cloth and carefully removing any carbon dust between the commutator segments.

The brush gear should be serviced as follows:

1 Check that the brushes bear freely on the commutator. If they are loose and do not make contact, renew the tension springs.
2 The brush levers must be free on their pivots. If they are stiff, move them backwards and forwards by hand until they are free and apply a trace of thin oil for further lubrication.

If the motor operates but does not transmit motion to the spindles, remove the gearbox cover and check that push-pull motion is being transmitted to the inner cable of the flexible rack. If the cross-head moves sluggishly between the guides, and appears to require lubrication, smear a small quantity of medium grade engine lubricating oil in the groove formed in the die-cast housing. Gear lubrication is by lightly packing the gearbox with grease approved by the manufacturers for the purpose of grease lubrication on these vehicles.

The thrust screw located on the top of the cross-head housing may require occasional adjustment. If required, slacken the locknut and screw down the thrust screw until it just contacts the armature, then unscrew it a fraction of a turn. Hold the screw in this position with a screwdriver and tighten the locknut.

To remove a motor for renewal purposes:

1 Detach the cable rack from the motor and gearbox as previously described and disconnect the electrical leads.
2 On Elf and Hornet models, open the lefthand glovebox lid, remove the three nuts retaining the lid frame from inside the the glovebox and detach the lid and frame.
3 Detach the press fastener retaining the inner edge of the glovebox trimming at the side of the instrument panel. Fold down the top edge of the trim starting at its inner edge, ease it down from under the recess on the top facia rail, and then remove the trim. On Mini cars turn back the body trim on the lefthand side of the scuttle panel above the parcel tray to remove the trim.
4 The three windshield wiper motor retaining nuts then become accessible and can be removed in order to detach the motor from under the bonnet.

To remove the windshield wiper from the Moke model:

1 Referring to **FIG 11 : 10,** slacken the hexagon screw 1 securing the wiper arm to the spindle. Remove the arm and blade.
2 Remove the nuts, locknuts, washers and seals securing the motor to the scuttle.
3 Disconnect the leads from inside the vehicle and take out the motor.
4 Note that a rubber flange with steel inserts is fitted between the wiper motor and the scuttle to prevent the insulating flange from being over-compressed.

11 : 14 Fuel and temperature gauges

It is necessary to ensure a constant electrical supply at predetermined voltage to the fuel and temperature gauges. For this purpose a voltage stabilizer 5 in

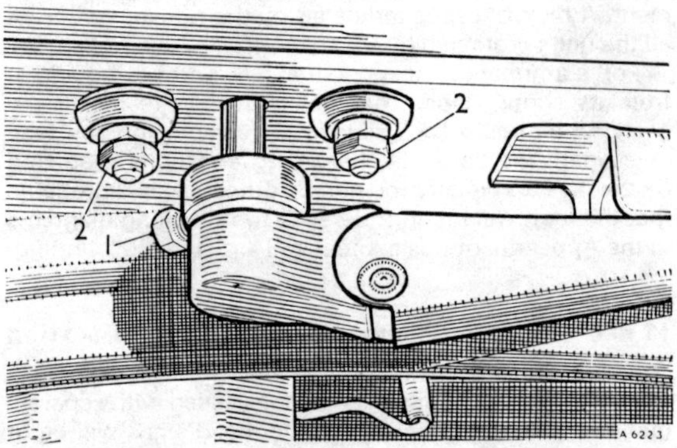

FIG 11 : 10 Attachment of the Moke windshield wiper motor and arm

Key to Fig 11 : 10 1 Arm locating screw 2 Motor mountings

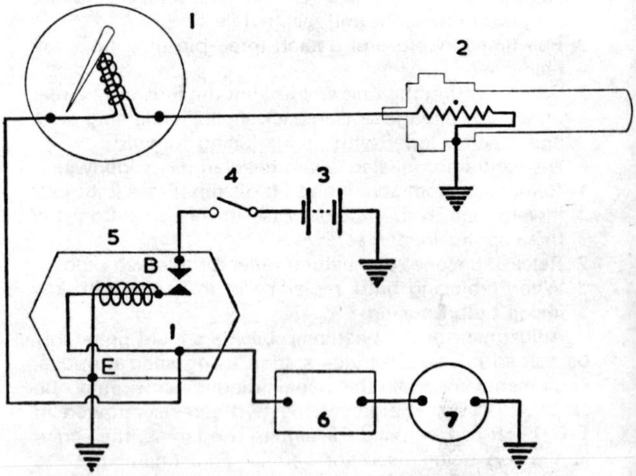

FIG 11 : 11 Wiring diagram for the bi-metallic fuel and temperature gauges

Key to Fig 11 : 11 1 Temperature gauge 2 Temperature gauge transmitter 3 Battery 4 Ignition switch 5 Voltage stabilizer 6 Fuel gauge 7 Fuel gauge transmitter

FIG 11:11 is provided which operates through the bi-metallic resistance circuit shown in **FIG 11:11.** In each case an indicator head, operated by thermal bi-metallic action, and a transmitter unit of resistance type, 2 and 7 are connected to the common voltage stabilizer 5.

Check that the correct operation of these components is as follows:

To check the operation of the voltage stabilizer, connect a voltmeter (0-20 volt range) to the stabilizer output terminal 1 and earth. If the reading is not 10 volts, the unit requires renewal.

Check for continuity in the gauges by first disconnecting the wiring. The gauges must not be checked by short-circuiting to earth.

Check for continuity in the transmitter between the terminal and the case with the lead disconnected.

In both cases lack of continuity means that renewal of the unit is necessary.

If the voltage stabilizer is removed, it is essential when refitting it that B and E in **FIG 11:11** are uppermost and not more than 20 deg. from vertical.

11:15 The alternator

The alternator fitted to these cars may be either a Lucas 11AC, which has an external voltage regulating unit, or a 16 ACR which has an integral voltage regulator.

The following precautions must be observed when servicing vehicles fitted with an alternator.

Make sure that the correct polarity is observed on both alternator and battery.

If a high rate charger is used to charge the battery in position on the car, or for starting the engine, detach the connectors from the regulator (when fitted). Reconnect the regulator after the charger has been disconnected and the engine running at idling speed (if applicable).

Do not run the engine with any connections in the alternator circuit broken, and do not disconnect the battery.

Do not earth the alternator terminal or the cable end if removed from the terminal. Disconnect the alternator when welding on the vehicle.

Note that the field connector block which is marked 'B+' and 'IND' has an offset moulded stop and must be removed before the main output connector block which has two blades and is marked '+' and '—'. Since the B+ connector blade, although shrouded is always live the battery earth must be disconnected before removing the field connector block.

Testing:

Check first that the belt tension is correct and that all connections are clean and tight. Check that the battery is fully charged. Run the engine until the full operating temperature is reached. Stop the engine.

Disconnect both connector blocks from the alternator. Switch on the ignition and connect a voltmeter with the negative lead to earth and positive lead to each cable connector blade of the two blocks in turn. If battery voltage is not available at any cable, locate and rectify the fault.

Remove the alternator end cover (7 in **FIG 11:12**) and bridge the regulator field connector (3 in **FIG 11:13**) to a suitable earth such as the earth-lead tag.

Refit the three-way connector block and instead of fitting the two-way block connect an ammeter between its positive blade and the main positive output terminal of the alternator. Leave the inner (negative) main terminal free.

Start the engine and run it at 2800 rev/min. The ammeter should show 34 amps and if this output is not obtained the alternator must be renewed.

Remove the earthing bridge wire just mentioned and connect the voltmeter across the battery terminals.

Run the engine at 2800 rev/min and observe the ammeter reading. If this is zero renew the regulator.

Adjust the engine speed until the ammeter reading falls below 10 amps. The voltmeter should show between 14.0 and 14.4 volts. If it does not, either the regulator is faulty or there is a high resistance in the charging circuit. Restore the original connections and make the following check.

Connect a voltmeter between the positive terminal of the alternator and the battery positive terminal. Start the engine, switch on the headlamps, and run the engine at 2800 rev/min and note the reading. Transfer the voltmeter connection to the negative terminal of the alternator and the battery negative and repeat the test. If the readings

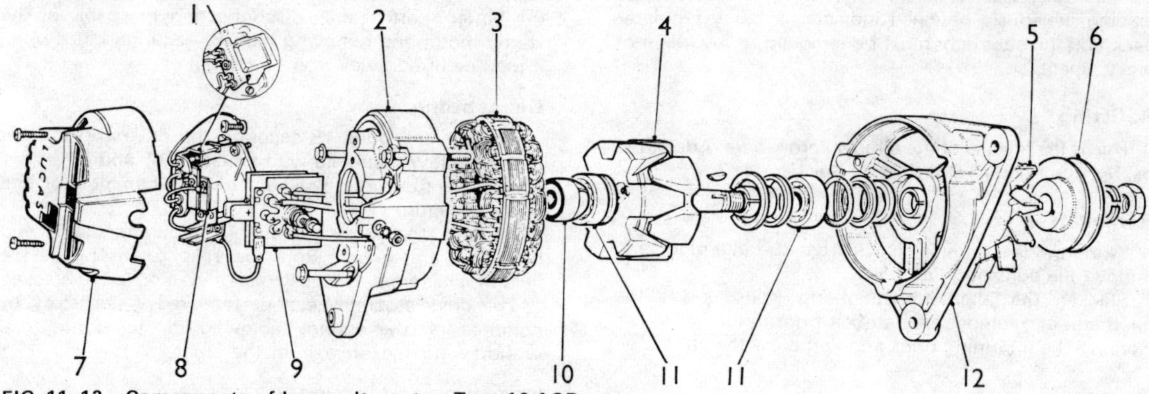

FIG 11:12 Components of Lucas alternator. Type 16.ACR

Key to Fig 11:12 1 Regulator pack 2 Slip ring end bracket 3 Stator 4 Rotor 5 Fan 6 Pulley 7 End cover 8 Brush box moulding 9 Rectifier pack 10 Slip rings 11 Rotor bearings 12 Drive end bracket

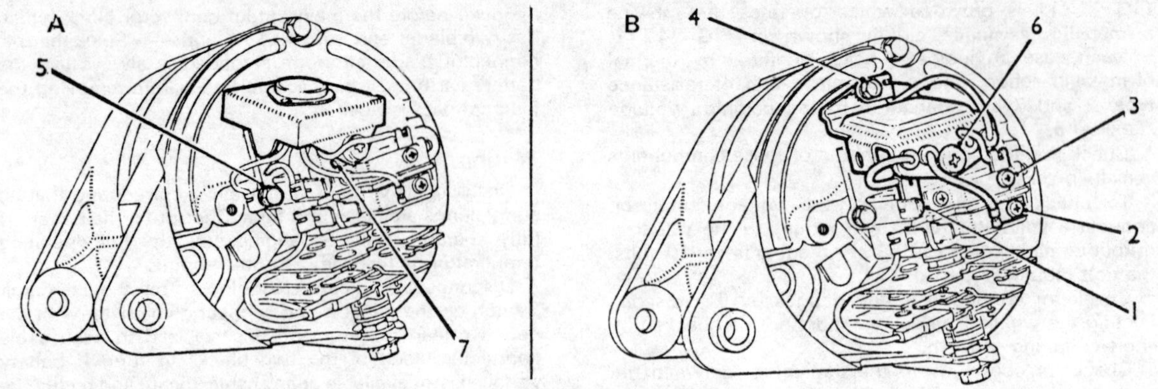

FIG 11:13 Built-in regulator connection. A Type 11TR. B Type 8TR

Key to Fig 11:13 1 B+ 2 Positive (+) 3 Field (F) 4 Earth (—) 5 Earth (—) 6 Mounting screw 7 Long mounting screw and spacer

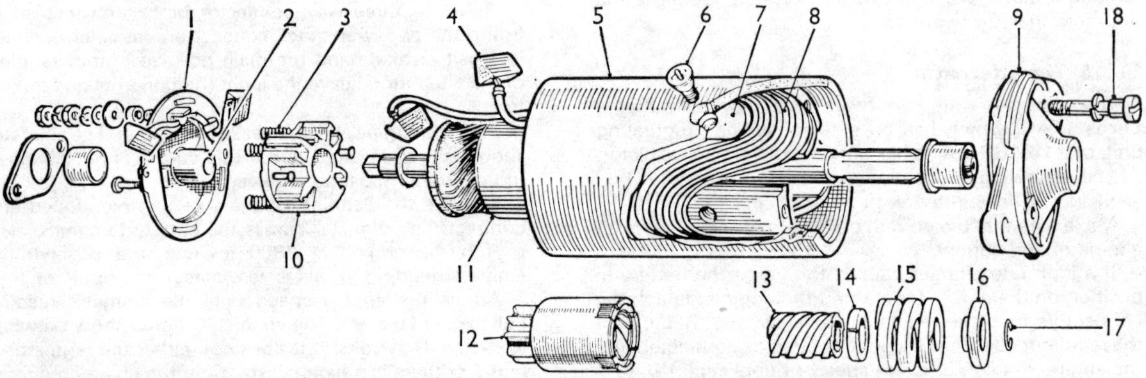

FIG 11:14 Components of starter motor. Lucas Type M35J

Key to Fig 11:14 1 Commutator end bracket 2 Bush housing 3 Brush springs 4 Brushes 5 Yoke 6 Pole screw 7 Pole shoe 8 Field coils 9 Drive end bracket 10 Brush box mouldings 11 Armature 12 Pinion and barrel 13 Screwed sleeve 14 Buffer washer 15 Main spring 16 Spring cup 17 Circlip 18 Drive end bracket bolt

exceed .5 and .25 volts respectively there is a high resistance in the charging circuit which must be rectified.

If this last test is satisfactory, the incorrect voltage reading previously obtained indicates a faulty regulator pack and the alternator must be removed for overhaul or replacement.

Refitting:

This is the reverse of the removal procedure. Adjust the belt as described in **Chapter 4, Section 4:2.**

Removal:

Withdraw the terminal block from the alternator and remove the adjusting link bolt.

Slacken the alternator mounting bolts, lower the alternator and remove the fan belt from the pulley. Remove the mounting bolts and withdraw the alternator.

11:16 Lucas M35J starter motor

A Lucas type M35J starter is fitted to later cars and has several points of difference from the earlier type as will be seen from the exploded diagram shown in **FIG 11:14.**

The motor is removed from the engine by disconnecting the battery earth cable, disconnecting the cable at the starter motor and removing the two securing bolts when it may be lifted away from the engine.

Dismantling:

Remove the bolts 18 securing the drive end bracket and withdraw complete with armature 11 and drive.

Remove the thrust washer from the commutator end of the armature.

Remove the screws securing the commutator end bracket 1 and detach from the yoke 5. Disengage the field brushes from the brush gear and remove the bracket.

The drive assembly can be removed if necessary by compressing the spring, removing the jump ring and withdrawing the drive from the shaft.

Inspecting and testing:

Brush gear:

To check brush spring tension, fit a new brush in each

holder in turn and press in with a push-type spring gauge until the brush protrudes about $\frac{1}{16}$ inch (1.5 mm) from the holder. The gauge should read approximately 28 oz (794 gm) and the commutator end bracket should be renewed if the tension is incorrect.

Renew any brushes worn down to $\frac{3}{8}$ inch (9.5 mm).

To renew the end bracket brushes, cut the brush leads from the terminal post, slot the head of the post to accommodate the new leads and solder in position.

To renew field winding brushes, cut the brush leads approximately $\frac{1}{2}$ inch (6.4 mm) from the field winding junction and solder on the new brush leads ensuring that the insulation sleeves are adequate (see **FIG 11:15**).

Commutator:

After cleaning with a petrol moistened cloth examine the surfaces for burning and pitting. If necessary it may be polished with very fine sandpaper or in very severe cases skimmed down on a lathe, removing the minimum amount of metal necessary to restore the surface.

DO NOT undercut the insulation between the segments.

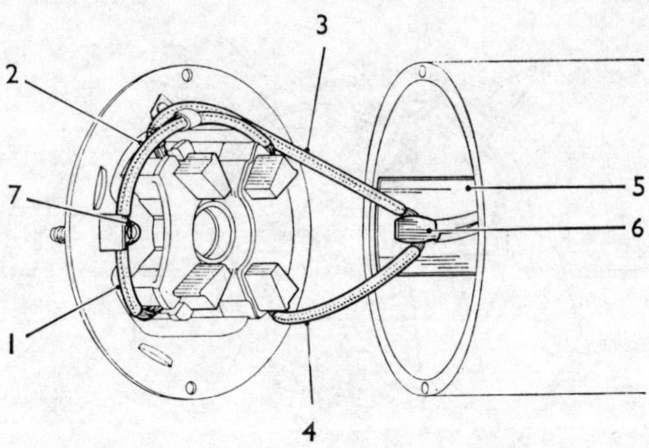

Key to Fig 11:15 Commutator end bracket assembly

Key to Fig 11:15 1 Short brush—flexible, commutator end bracket 2 Long brush—flexible, commutator end bracket 3 Long brush—flexible, field winding 4 Short brush—flexible, field winding 5 Yoke insulation piece 6 Field winding junction 7 Terminal post

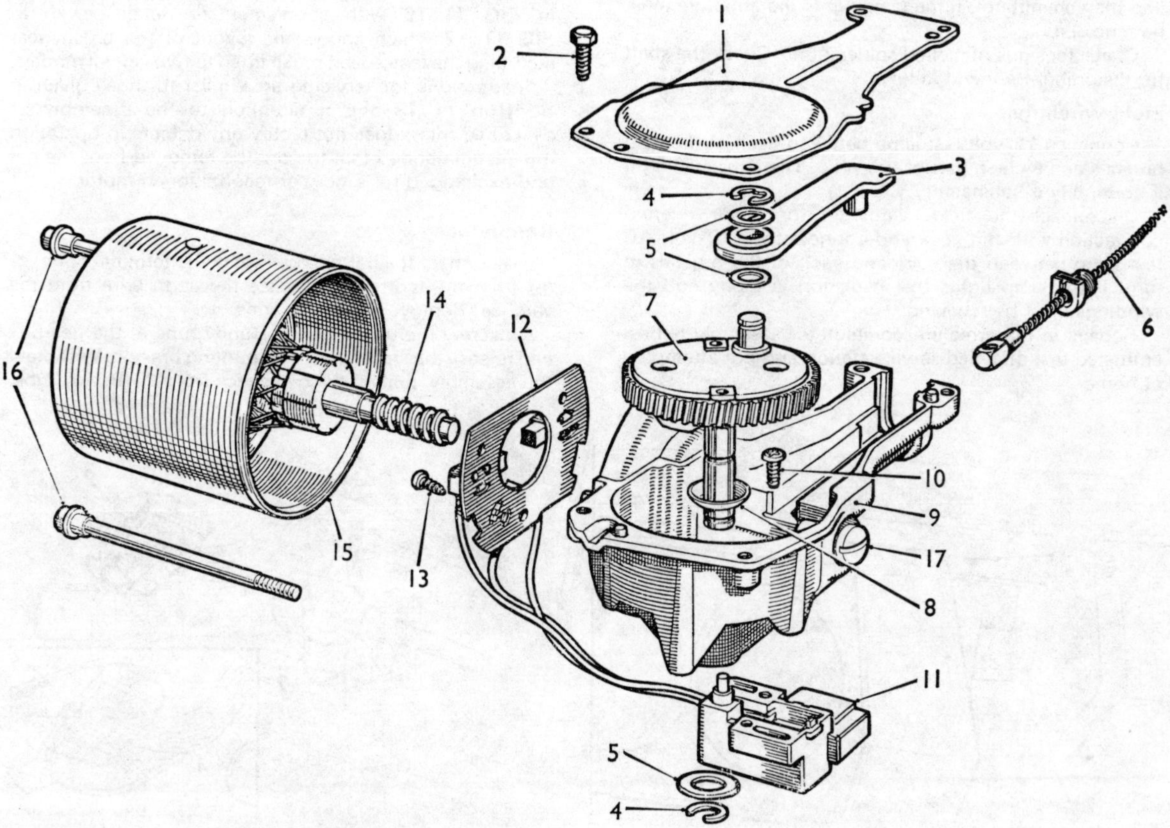

FIG 11:16 Components of two-speed wiper motor

Key to Fig 11:16 1 Gearbox cover 2 Screw for cover 3 Connecting rod 4 Circlip 5 Plain washers 6 Cross-head and rack 7 Shaft and gear 8 Dished washer 9 Gearbox 10 Screw for limit switch 11 Limit switch assembly 12 Brush gear 13 Screw for brush gear 14 Armature 15 Yoke assembly 16 Yoke bolts 17 Armature thrust screw

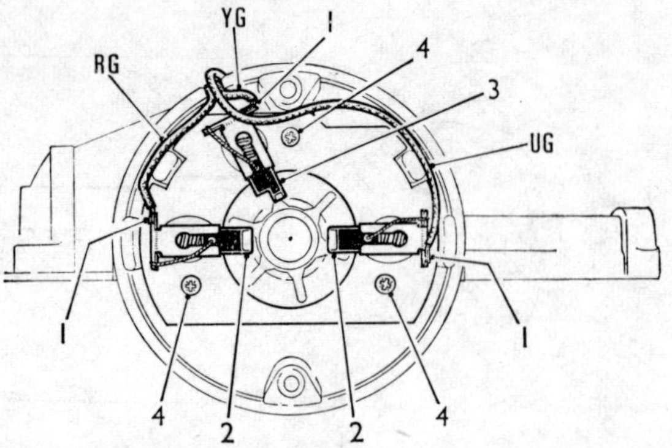

FIG 11:17 Brush gear assembly

Key to Fig 11:17 1 Soldered brush box connections 2 Main brushes 3 Fast-speed brush (where fitted) 4 Brush gear assembly securing screws **RG** Red with green **YG** Yellow with green **UG** Blue with green

Armature:

Test the insulation by connecting a 110 volt AC supply and a 15 watt lamp in series between the armature shaft and the commutator. If the lamp lights the armature must be renewed.

Check for signs of melted solder joints. Check the shaft for distortion. Renew if faulty.

Field windings:

Connect a 12-volt test lamp between each of the field brushes and a clean part of the yoke. The lamp will light if continuity is satisfactory.

Disconnect the field windings from their rivetted connection with the yoke and connect the 110-volt AC test lamp between the yoke and each of the brushes in turn. If the lamp lights the insulation is faulty and the windings must be renewed.

Repairs to the armature/commutator assembly is best entrusted to a qualified service station and not attempted at home.

Bearings:

If a bearing is worn sufficiently to allow side play of the armature shaft, the bearing bush must be renewed as follows:

Commutator end bracket:

Drill out the rivets securing the brush box moulding and remove the moulding, bearing seal retaining plate and felt washer seal.

Screw in a $\frac{1}{2}$ inch tap and extract the bush.

Drive end bracket:

Support the bracket and press out the bush.

In both cases the new bush is pressed into its bracket using a polished shouldered mandrel, the same diameter as the shaft bearing journal.

New bushes must be immersed in engine oil for 24 hours before fitting, or for 2 hours if the oil is heated to 100°C (212°F). Note that no reaming is permissible after installation.

11:17 Windshield wiper. Lucas type 14W—Permanent magnet

The components of this type of motor are clearly shown in **FIG 11:16** with supplementary details given in **FIG 11:17** which shows the layout of the brush gear including the fast-speed brush fitted to two-speed models.

Instructions for servicing are similar to those given in **Section 11:13** and if attention to the assembly as described there does not rectify any defects in operation it is recommended that the unit be removed from the car and exchanged for a new or reconditioned motor.

Removing:

Disconnect the battery, withdraw the terminal connector from the motor and release the earth wire from the valance. Remove the wiper arms.

Unscrew the union on the Bundy tube at the gearbox and release the strap from the mounting bracket. Withdraw the assembly, pulling the cable rack from the Bundy tube.

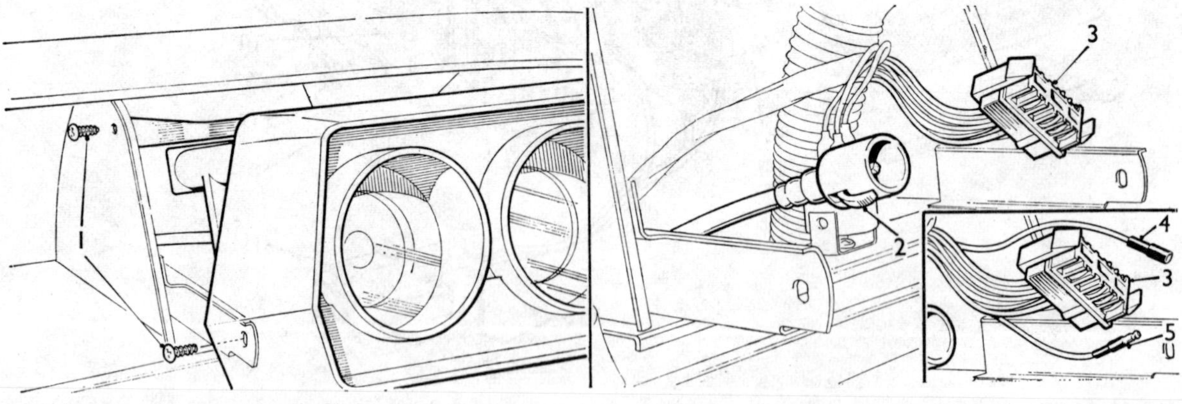

FIG 11:18 Removing the instrument panel. Clubman and 1275 GT

Key to Fig 11:18 1 Panel securing screws 2 Speedometer cable release lever 3 Multi-plug wiring connector 4 Tachometer connection—1275 GT 5 Tachometer connection—1275 GT

Armature end float:

This may cause the motor to be noisy in operation if neglected and is adjusted by means of the thrust screw (17 in **FIG 11:16**). This should be tightened until the end float is just eliminated, then turned back one quarter turn which will give an end float of between .002 and .008 inch (.05 to .2 mm). Measure the gap under the head of the thrust screw with a feeler gauge, fit a suitable shim and fully tighten the screw.

Refitting:

This is the reverse of the removal procedure but leave the wheel box covers slack until the cable rack has been located and the motor secured. Check the action of the wheel boxes before refitting the wiper blades.

11:18 Printed circuit instrument panel

On the Clubman and 1275 GT models an instrument panel incorporating a printed circuit for the necessary wiring is used and is fully illustrated in **FIGS 11:18, 11:19** and **11:20.**

Removing the instrument panel:

Disconnect the battery earth cable (NEGATIVE).

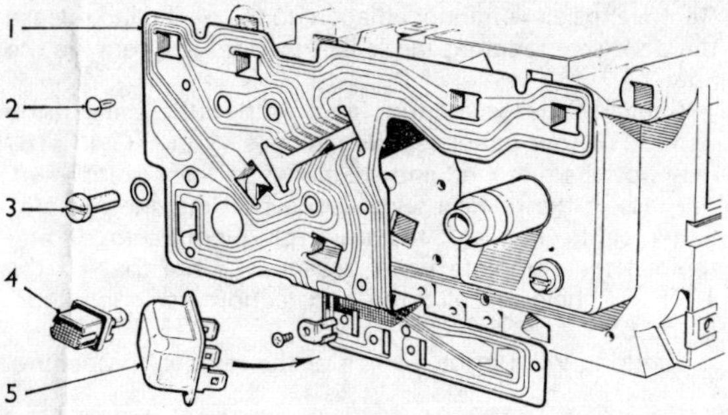

FIG 11:19 Removing the printed circuit

Key to Fig 11:19 1 Printed circuit 2 Printed circuit securing stud 3 Fuel and temperature gauge securing screws 4 Panel and warning lamp bulb holders 5 Voltage stabilizer

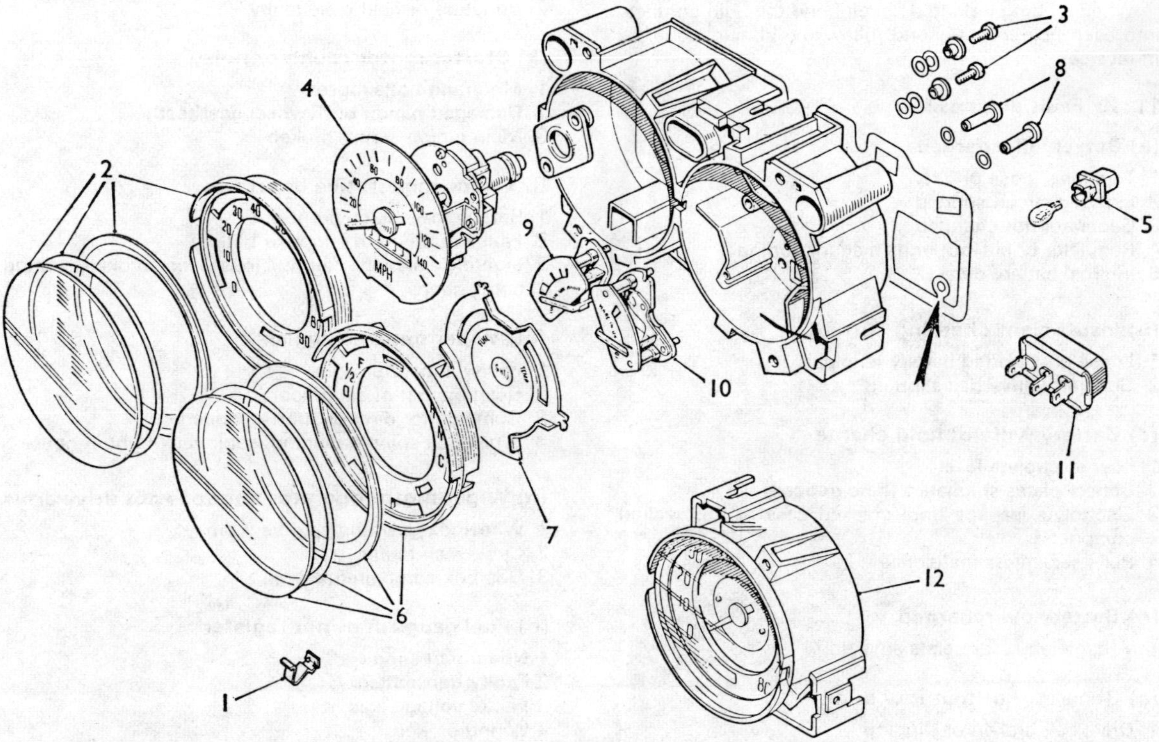

FIG 11:20 Exploded view of the instrument assembly. Clubman and 1275 GT

Key to Fig 11:20 1 Instrument lens securing clips 2 Speedometer dial and lens assembly 3 Speedometer securing screws 4 Speedometer unit 5 Panel lamp bulb and holder 6 Fuel/temperature gauge dial and lens assembly 7 Fuel/temperature gauge sub-dial 8 Fuel/temperature gauge securing screws 9 Fuel gauge 10 Temperature gauge 11 Voltage stabilizer 12 Tachometer assembly *Arrow shows earth connection*

Remove the air ventilator adjacent to the panel and release the door seal securing the facia trim liner and remove the liner.

Similarly release the trim liner on the other side of the panel. The four panel securing screws (1 in **FIG 11:18**) may now be removed and the panel partially withdrawn.

Press in the release lever 2 and pull out the speedometer cable. Pull out the multi-plug connector 3 and remove the complete panel assembly. Note that on the 1275 GT there are also the two tachometer connectors 4 and 5.

Refitting will be the reverse of the removal procedure.

Instruments:

These may be taken out after the instrument panel has been removed and reference to **FIG 11:20** should make the procedure clear without any further instructions.

Printed circuit:

(See **FIG 11:19**). Remove the instrument panel as already described then take out all panel and warning light bulb holders 4 and pull off the voltage stabilizer 5. Remove the three voltage stabilizer terminals.

To avoid damage the fuel and temperature gauges should be removed. On the 1275 GT the tachometer connections must be released and the extra bulb holder removed. Pull out the pins 2 and remove the printed circuit.

When refitting a printed circuit bend the bulb contacts into each holder recess and follow the above sequence in reverse.

11:19 Fault diagnosis

(a) Battery discharged

1 Terminals loose or dirty
2 Lighting circuit shorted
3 Generator not charging
4 Regulator or cut-out units malfunctioning
5 Internal battery defect

(b) Insufficient charging current

1 Loose or corroded battery terminals
2 Generator drive belt slipping

(c) Battery will not hold charge

1 Low electrolyte level
2 Battery plates sulphated (hard deposit)
3 Electrolyte leakage from cracked case or top sealing compound
4 Plate separators ineffective

(d) Battery overcharged

1 Voltage regulator needs adjusting

(e) Generator output low or nil

1 Drive belt broken or slipping
2 Regulator unit out of adjustment
3 Worn bearings or loose polepieces
4 Commutator worn, burnt or shorted
5 Armature shaft bent or worn
6 Insulation proud between commutator segments
7 Brushes sticking or brush springs weak or broken
8 Field coil wires shorted, broken or burnt

(f) Starter motor lacks power or will not operate

1 Battery discharged or loose cable connections
2 Starter pinion jammed in mesh with flywheel gear
3 Starter switch faulty
4 Brushes worn or sticking, leads detached or shorting
5 Commutator dirty or worn
6 Starter shaft bent
7 Engine abnormally stiff

(g) Starter motor runs but does not turn engine

1 Pinion sticking on screwed sleeve
2 Broken teeth on pinion or flywheel gears

(h) Noisy starter pinion when engine is running

1 Restraining spring weak or broken

(j) Starter motor inoperative

1 Check 1 and 4 in (f)
2 Armature or field coils faulty

(k) Starter motor rough or noisy

1 Mounting bolts loose
2 Damaged pinion or flywheel gear teeth
3 Main pinion spring broken

(l) Lamps inoperative or erratic

1 Battery low, bulbs burnt out
2 Faulty earthing of lamps or battery
3 Lighting switch faulty, loose or broken wiring connections

(m) Wiper motor sluggish

1 Faulty armature
2 Bearings out of alignment
3 Commutator dirty or short-circuited
4 Wheelbox spindle binding, cable rack tight in housing

(n) Wiper motor operates but does not drive arms

1 Wheelbox gear and spindle worn
2 Cable rack faulty
3 Gearbox components worn

(o) Fuel gauge does not register

1 No current supply
2 Faulty transmitter
3 Faulty voltage stabilizer
4 Wiring broken

CHAPTER 12

THE BODY

12 : 1 Servicing the door locks, remote control gear

To remove the door locks on early models without the remote control device remove the screw, or three screws for Mk I and II Hornet and Elf models, securing the lock to the inner door panel and the retaining screw from the end of the locking handle spindle. In order to remove the outer door handle release the inner operating handle by slackening the screw clamping the inner handle to the spindle Both the outer handle and the escutcheon can then be withdrawn.

Inspect the moving parts for wear and make any renewals necessary, lubricate lightly with a smear of grease and reassemble by reversing the removal procedure. Do not interfere with the setting of the striker plate unless the striker itself has been renewed. If adjustment is necessary, this is carried out by a process of trial and error involving observation of the position of the door when closed and its actual closing action. When refitting the lock make sure that the inner operating handle is fitted correctly with the control cable lever upright to ensure correct operation from inside the car when the handle is pushed downwards. Make sure the inner handle clamping screw is tight.

Mk III Hornet and Elf and later Mini models have locks with remote control. These are illustrated in **FIG 12 : 1** and are removed as follows:

1 Remove the interior door handle, window regulator handle, door pocket and trim panel. Pull back the adhesive sealing strip adjacent to the lock.
2 Remove the screws 1 (see **FIG 12 : 1**), securing the remote control, the screws 2 securing the lock and the two screws, indicated by bold arrows, securing the external handle.
3 Disconnect the locking link 3 (see **FIG 12 : 2**), from the operating rod visible in **FIG 12 : 1** by sliding the spring clip 2 in **FIG 12 : 2** upwards.
4 Ease the lock and remote control outwards and turn the assembly sideways as shown at 3 in **FIG 12 : 1**, to withdraw the lock from the door panel.
5 Remove the circlip securing the remote control to the lock assembly and remove both units from the door frame.
6 Inspect and make any necessary renewals, lubricate the moving parts lightly with grease or viscous oil and refit by reversing the removal procedure and giving special attention to the following:
7 Ensure that the spring clip is properly repositioned to

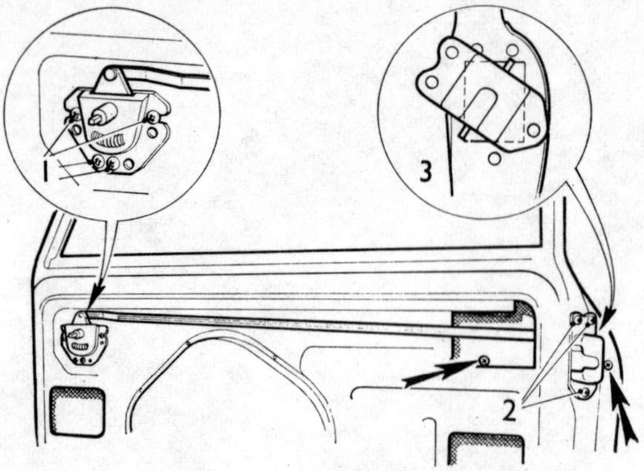

FIG 12:1 Remote control door lock on later cars

Key to Fig 12:1 1 The remote control securing screws 2 The door lock screws 3 The lock turned over at a suitable angle for removal. The external handle securing screws are indicated by the two bold arrows on the righthand side

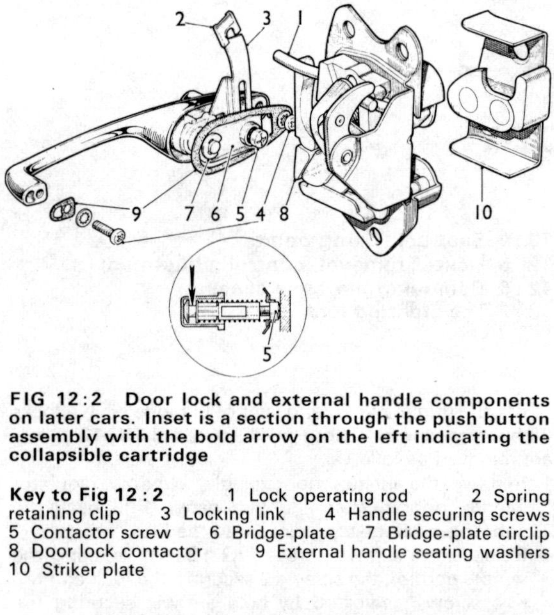

FIG 12:2 Door lock and external handle components on later cars. Inset is a section through the push button assembly with the bold arrow on the left indicating the collapsible cartridge

Key to Fig 12:2 1 Lock operating rod 2 Spring retaining clip 3 Locking link 4 Handle securing screws 5 Contactor screw 6 Bridge-plate 7 Bridge-plate circlip 8 Door lock contactor 9 External handle seating washers 10 Striker plate

secure the lock operating rod with the locking link of the external pushbutton handle.

8 Refit or if necessary fit a new adhesive sealing patch to the door panel.

9 Check the operation of the door lock before refitting the trim panel, door pocket, window regulator handle and internal door operating handle.

The external door handles on the Mk III Hornet and Elf models have a collapsible plastic cartridge inside the pushbutton. The pushbutton cannot be pushed in when the door is locked and if extreme force is used, the cartridge will collapse and prevent the lock mechanism operating. The cartridge is, however, sufficiently robust to withstand severe treatment such as that required if the button is frozen in the unlocked condition in severe weather.

To remove the external door handle, carry out the above procedure as far as operation 4, make sure the window is fully closed, remove the two door handle screws indicated by the bold arrows in **FIG 12:1** and manoeuvre the handle away from the door.

The pushbutton cartridge is renewed as follows:

1 Remove the bridge plate circlip 7 (see **FIG 12:2**), carefully file off the top of the projection and remove the bridge plate 6.

2 Detach the pushbutton from the handle, unscrew and retain the contactor screw 5 and take off the pushbutton return spring and its seating washer.

3 Remove and discard the broken pieces of plastic from the pushbutton.

4 Insert a new cartridge and press it firmly into the button. Refit the contactor screw so that when the handle is reassembled and refitted to the door, a clearance of $\frac{1}{32}$ to $\frac{1}{16}$ inch is maintained between the screw head and the lock contactor mechanism 8.

5 Note that to assist pushbutton adjustment it is recommended that the projection is riveted over again before refitting the handle to the door.

To refit the handle reverse the removal sequence giving special attention to the following:

1 Make sure that the two seating washers 9 are fitted between the external handle and the door panel.

2 The spring clip 2 is positioned to secure the lock operating rod with the locking link of the handle.

3 Check the lock operation and fit a new adhesive sealing patch before refitting the trim panel.

Later Mini models have locks with remote control which differ from those fitted to the Hornet and Elf models by the addition of an interior locking lever.

To remove these locks proceed as follows:

1 Remove the interior door handle, window regulator handle and the door trim panel. Pull back the adhesive sealing strip adjacent to the lock.

2 Remove the screws securing the lock, the remote control and the interior locking control.

3 Refer to **FIG 12:3** and disconnect the locking rod 4 from the key operated lock link 3.

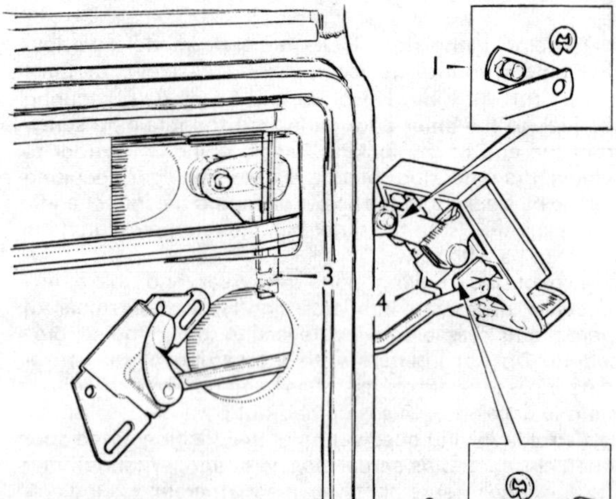

FIG 12:3 Removing the lock from later Mini models

4 Separate the remote control link and the interior locking control link from the lock by removing the circlips shown and withdraw the parts.

Refit the components by reversing the removal procedure.

Remove the exterior door handle and adjust the plunger screw if required. With the plunger correctly adjusted there should be a clearance of $\frac{1}{32}$ to $\frac{1}{16}$ inch (1 to 1.5 mm) between the head of the screw and the lock contact as shown at A in **FIG 12:4**. The plastic bush under the head of the plunger screw should not be screwed in fully against the plastic push button stem as this will stop the lock from operating.

12:2 Renewing window glasses, servicing the window winders

On early cars sliding windows are fitted to the front doors of most models and these glasses are removed by taking out the self-tapping screws securing the bottom channel to the top of the door panel. The sliding glasses and the bottom channel can then be lifted away from the door. For Countryman and Traveller models, first remove the trim panel from above the sliding window glasses, remove the upper channels, support the insides of the glasses and push them inwards from the outside.

To refit the window glasses reverse the removal sequences.

On those models with winding windows with raising and lowering regulators in the door panels the mechanisms are removed as follows:

1 Remove the interior door handle, window regulator handle, door pocket and trim panel. Pull back the adhesive sealing strips where necessary.
2 Remove the inner waist rail finisher.
3 Remove the external upper surround finisher and external waist rail finisher.

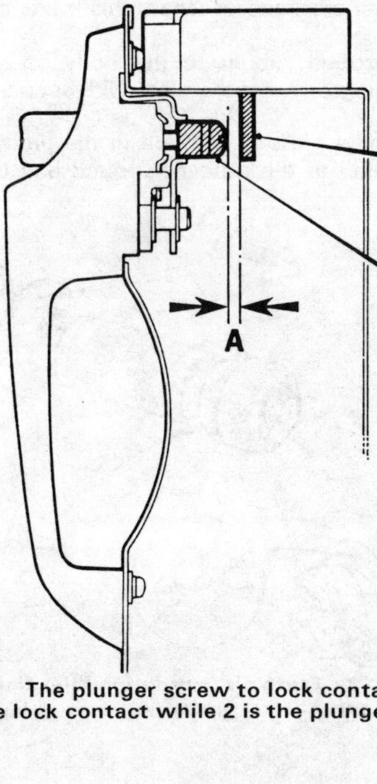

FIG 12:4 The plunger screw to lock contact clearance A. 1 is the lock contact while 2 is the plunger screw

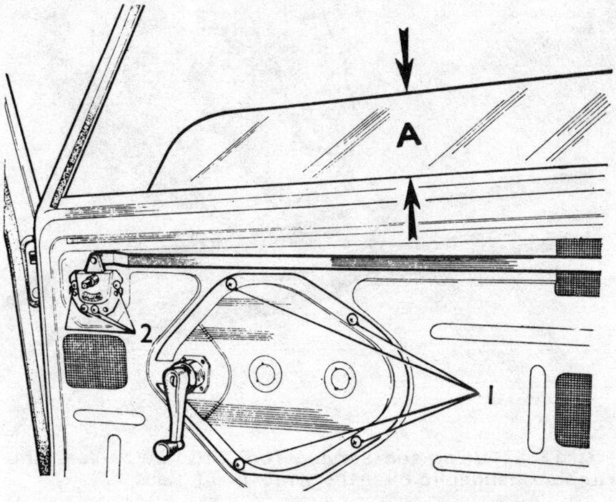

FIG 12:5 Removing a door glass and regulating mechanism. A shows window raised approximately one-third

Key to Fig 12:5 1 Regulator assembly securing screws 2 Door lock remote control securing screws

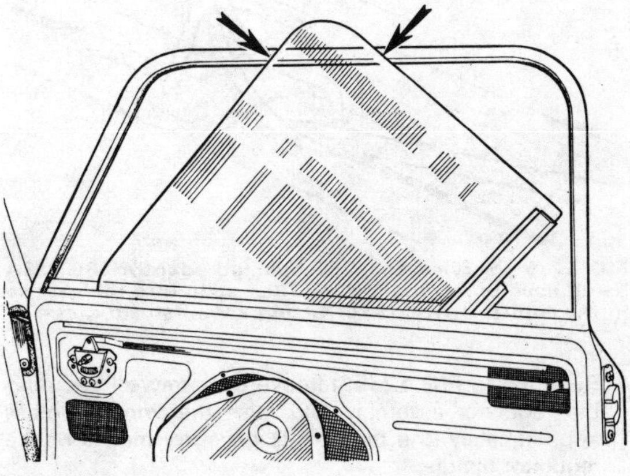

FIG 12:6 Removing the door glass

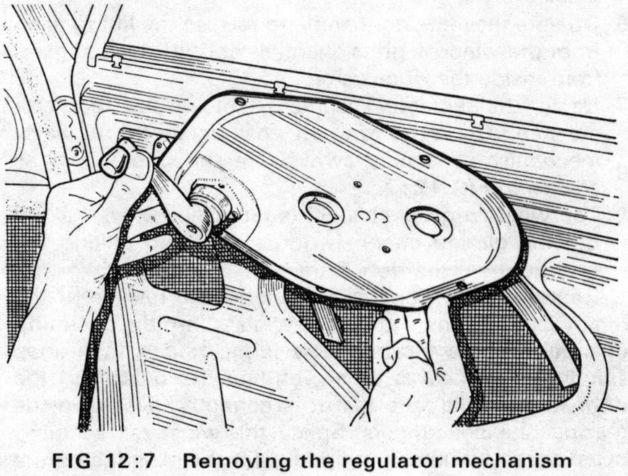

FIG 12:7 Removing the regulator mechanism

FIG 12:8 Using the Service Tool 18G.468 to ease the rubber channel lip over the windshield glass

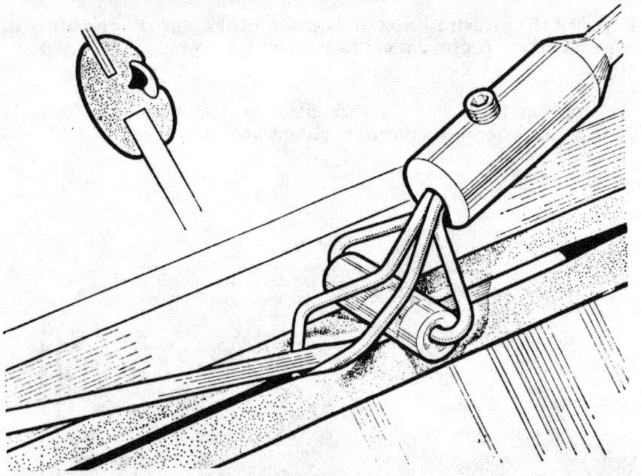

FIG 12:9 Service Tool 18G.468 and adaptor 18G.468A being used to roll the locking filler strip into the groove in the rubber surround for fitting a windshield glass

4 Referring to **FIG 12:5,** remove the screws 1 securing the regulator assembly and raise the window glass approximately one third of its travel by means of the regulator handle.
5 Lever the regulator assembly slightly away from the door panel and lift the window glass so that the upper corner is inside the door frame as shown in **FIG 12:6,** black arrows.
6 Operate the regulator handle to release the lifting arms from the window glass channels and lift out the glass from inside the door frame.
7 Using the regulator handle to move the regulator mechanism into the 'lowered' position, lift the regulator mechanism assembly away from the door panel as shown in **FIG 12:7.**
8 The window glass channel is removed by first taking out the glazing channel rubber strip and pulling the channel from the door frame.

Refitting these parts is, in general, the reverse of the removal operations. Fitting a new glass into the operating channel may be facilitated by lubricating with a soap solution or glycerine. When refitting the glass into the door frame make sure that it is correctly located in the glazing channel runners. Space the waist rail securing clips equally when refitting the finishers and butt the forward end of the inner waist rail finisher firmly against the glazing channel rubber seal before fitting the remainder. Fit new adhesive patches as necessary.

To remove the fixed quarter light glasses on Mini models, support the outside of the glass and strike it firmly with the palm of the hand at the inside top portion, then remove the glass and rubber. When refitting the glass or fitting a new glass, fit the surround rubber to the glass, pass a length of strong thin cord round the outer channel in the surround rubber leaving the ends hanging down on the inside of the glass. Lubricate the body edge with a soapy water solution, press the glass lightly into position on the outside of the window frame and draw out the cord from inside the car to lift the lip of the rubber over the edge of the frame.

To remove the hinged type quarter light proceed as follows:

1 Unscrew the cross-head screws fixing the quarter light catch to the body and swing the quarter light wide open to expose the hinge.
2 Ease back the rubber seal on the body and remove the cross-head screws securing the hinge to the body.
3 Lift out the window assembly.
4 Take out the cross-head screws fixing the quarter light frame to the hinge top and bottom, and ease the frame away from the glass.

The quarter light window is reassembled and refitted by reversing the removal procedures.

The windshield and back light glasses may be removed and renewed as follows:

1 Lift the windshield wiper arms and blades clear of the glass.
2 Very carefully prise up the ends of the locking filler and pull it out of the channel in the glass surround rubber.
3 Press the glass from inside the car, starting at one corner, and ease the glass and surround rubber from the edge of the body aperture.

Before fitting the new glass remove all glass particles from the rubber surround or renew this if it is damaged, then:

1 Fit the surround rubber to the body aperture and lubricate the groove for the glass with soap and water solution.
2 Place the new glass in position in the groove in the lower channel of the rubber surround and using the

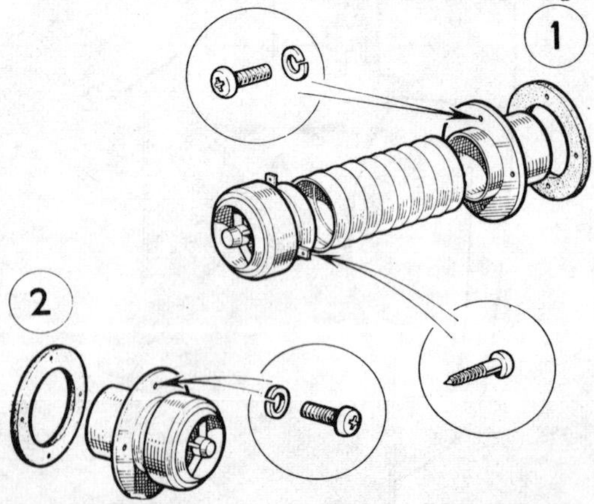

FIG 12:10 Fresh air ventilation inlet fixings
Key to Fig 12:10 1 Elf Mk III 2 Hornet Mk III

Service Tool 18G.468, starting at a lower corner, lift the lip of the rubber over the outside of the glass as shown in **FIG 12:8**.

3 Lubricate the locking filler groove in the rubber channel strip with soap and water.

4 Assemble Service Tool 18G.468 with the adaptor 18G.468A and thread the end of the locking filler strip through the eye of the adaptor and under the roller as shown in **FIG 12:9**. Position the end of the filler strip over the groove in the rubber and push the eye of the tool into the groove. Then holding the filler strip in line with the groove, push the tool along the groove so that the strip is rolled down into position. A slight side to side action will be helpful at the corners.

5 Cut off any surplus strip at the centre line of the windshield to form a neat butt joint.

Note that if the windshield glass has been broken, particles of glass will be present in the demister ducts and tubes. It is therefore essential to disconnect the demister ducts and tubing from the heater box and blow them out to ensure that any glass particles present are not discharged into the driver's and passenger's faces when the demister is first operated after removal of the glass.

On the Moke model an entirely different type of windshield is fitted. This is removed as follows:

1 Remove the windshield wiper arm and blade.

2 Remove four nuts and screws.

3 Slacken the bottom retaining screws and lift the frame and glass from the car.

4 Remove the two screws securing the bottom channel and remove the glass from the frame.

To refit the windshield, reverse these removal instructions.

12:3 Removing and refitting fresh air ventilation fittings

Not all cars covered by this manual are equipped with these fittings and in the space available only a limited selection of types can be described, but the owner should not have any difficulty in servicing these components.

The fresh air vents on Mini models are easily removed. The vents are housed in plastic mouldings which are secured by retaining rings screwed on their ends. After removing the retaining ring the moulding and vent can be removed.

To remove the facia mounted fittings on Hornet and Elf models proceed as follows:

1 Remove the facia instrument nacelle on the Hornet model.

2 Remove the facia ashtray and bend up the retaining tab.

3 Release the portion of the door seal covering the facia trim liner and carefully lift this portion of the liner, which is fixed by adhesive solution to the body.

4 Ease the trim liner from under the top facia rail, towards the centre of the dash, and withdraw it.

5 From under the wing, release the clip securing the intake hose to the inlet, remove the inlet securing screws and the assembly complete with its rubber seal.

6 On Elf models, bend back the portion of the glovebox liner adjacent to the fresh air inlet.

7 Remove the two wing nuts adjacent to the instrument panel and the one located near the inlet.

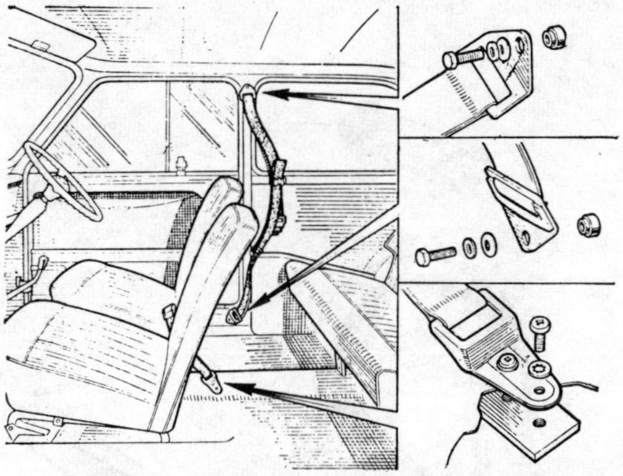

FIG 12:11 Seat belt fittings and locations

8 Withdraw the glovebox panel assembly complete with the inlet and hose.

9 Remove the securing screws and the inlet assembly from behind the facia board.

Refer to **FIG 12:10** for details of the Mk III Hornet and Elf fresh air ventilation inlet fixings.

To refit the Hornet inlet:

1 Refit the inlet assembly and sealing rubber with the small bracket on the inlet assembly positioned at the bottom and tighten the securing screws.

2 Make sure the inlet hose is correctly positioned on the inlet and tighten the securing clip.

3 Refit the other components by reversing the order of removal.

4 For Elf models reverse the removal procedure, items 6, 7, 8 and 9, making sure that the short connecting hose is correctly located on the intake connection when refitting the glovebox panel and refit the dash liner after tightening the wing nuts.

12:4 Seat belt fixing points

Since 1965 front seat belts have been a compulsory fitment on all new cars registered in the UK. The belts on some of these earlier models should be checked for deterioration and wear, particularly where they are threaded through the metal fixings and adjusting buckles. The mounting points should also be checked for security.

'Park' the belts in the hooks provided on the side pillars when not in use, otherwise they will sustain damage by passengers entering and leaving the car or by trapping them in the doors or the seats.

Seat belt fixing points are provided on early models at the top of the centre door pillars, the rear of the door sills and on the sides of the central floor tunnel. Where belts are not fitted as initial equipment, the fitting points will be found to be sealed with rubber plugs. The official seat belt design is such that all three fixing points are employed.

To fit seat belts proceed as follows:

1 Refer to **FIG 12:11** for details of position and fixings.

2 Remove the plug from the tapped attachment point at the top of the door pillar and assemble the screw, plain washer, anti-rattle washer and distance piece to

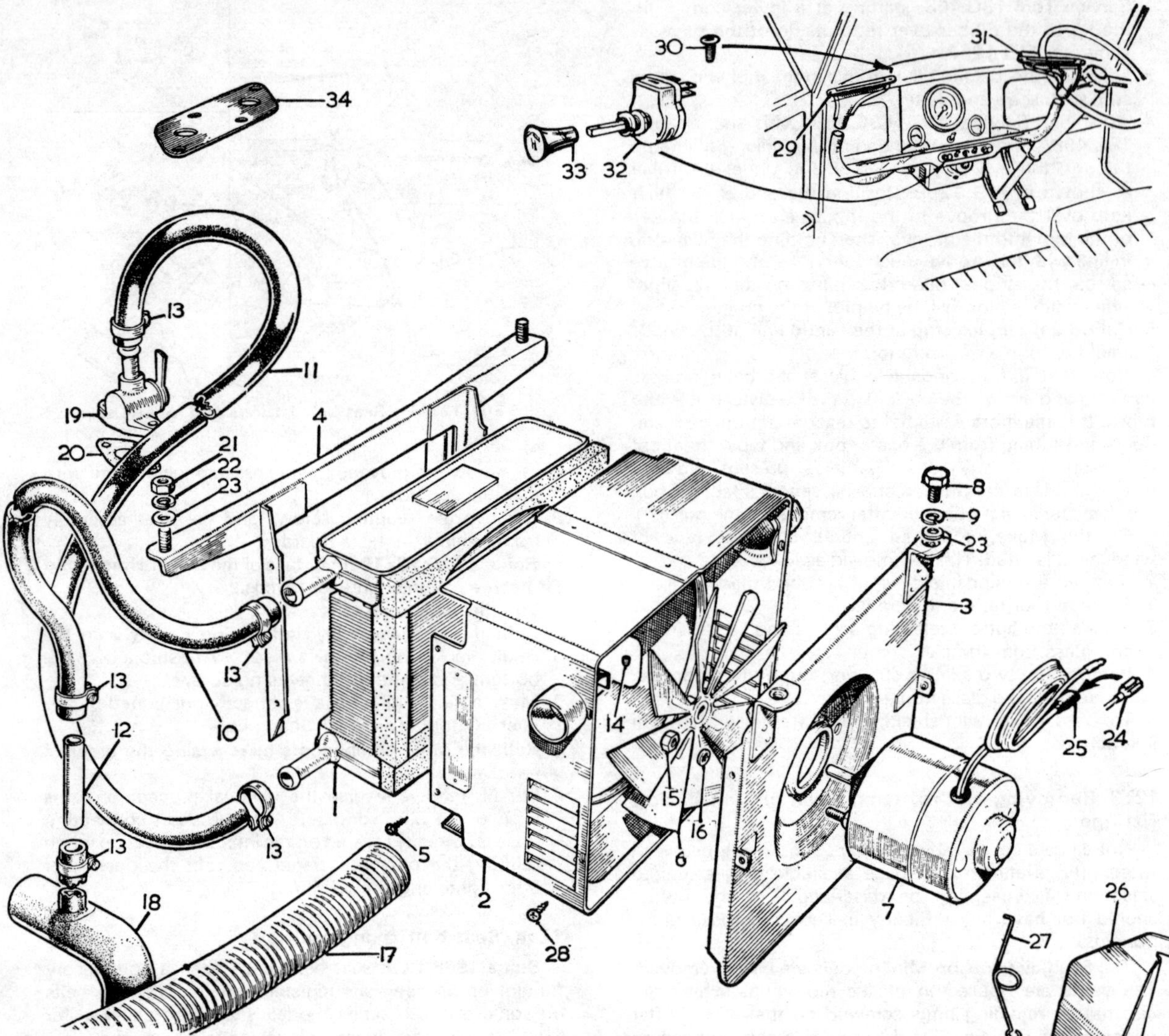

FIG 12:12 An exploded view of the recirculatory heater

Key to Fig 12:12 1 Radiator matrix, frame and padding strips 2 Cowling 3 Cover and motor mounting plate 4 Mounting bracket assembly 5 Securing screw, cowling to bracket 6 Fan assembly 7 Fan motor 8 Heater fixing screw 9 Spring washer 10 Outlet hose 11 Inlet hose 12 Outlet hose connection 13 Hose clips 14 Fan retaining screw 15 Motor fixing nut 16 Shakeproof washer 17 Demister hose 18 Engine radiator hose to coolant pump 19 Heater tap 20 Heater tap gasket 21/22/23 Mounting bracket fixing 24/25 Lucar connector and sleeve 26 Demister flap 27 Flap springs 28 Cover plate securing screws 29 Lefthand demister duct 30 Demister duct screw 31 Righthand demister duct 32 Heater switch 33 Heater switch control knob 34 Sealing plate for hoses

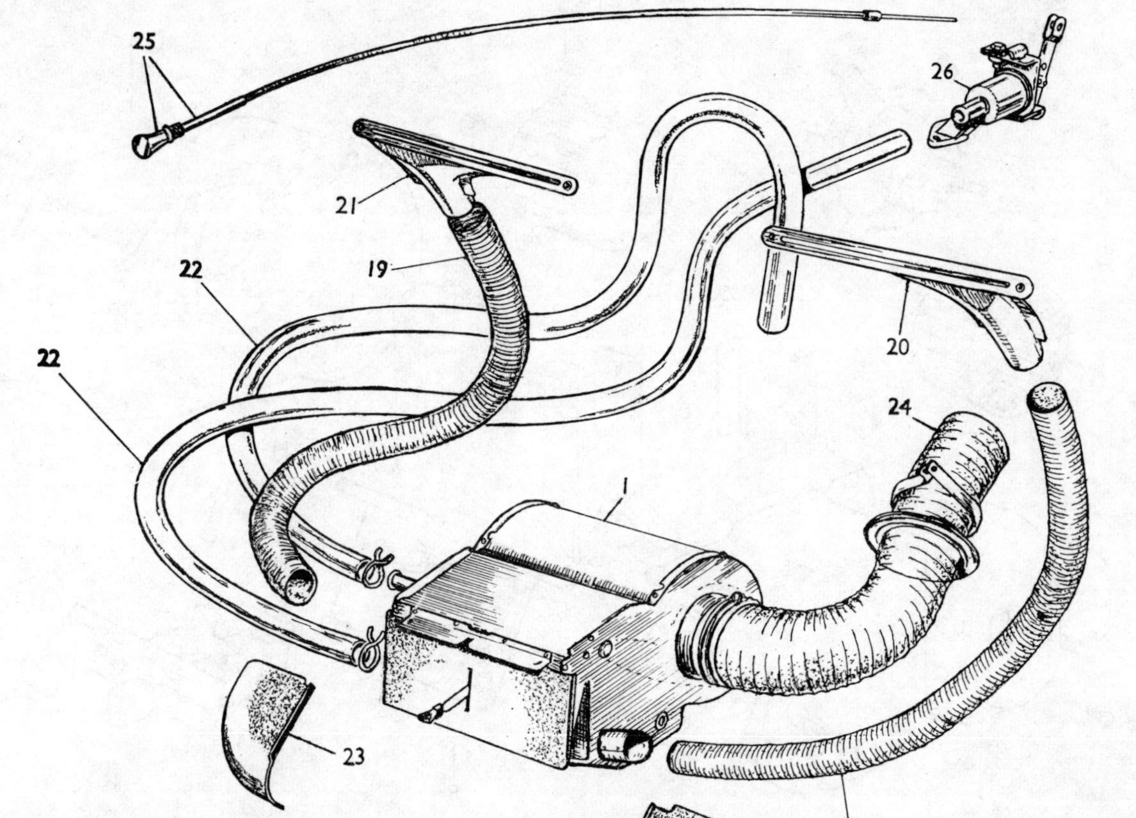

FIG 12:13 An exploded view of the fresh air heater. Early type

Key to Fig 12:13 1 Heater unit 2 Air intake side cover 3 Motor side cover 4 Control panel 5 Radiator matrix, frame and padding pieces 6 Motor 7 Sealing ring 8 Fan rotor 9 Fan rotor securing ring 10 Blower switch 11 Flap valve 12 Control knob 13 Side cover securing screws 14 Control panel securing screws 15 Heater assembly upper securing screws 16 Heater assembly securing nut (not shown) 17/18 Plain and spring washers (not shown) 19 Demister tubes 20 Righthand demister duct 21 Lefthand demister duct 22 Coolant hoses 23 Demister tube covers 24 Air intake hose 25 Heat control cable 26 Water control valve

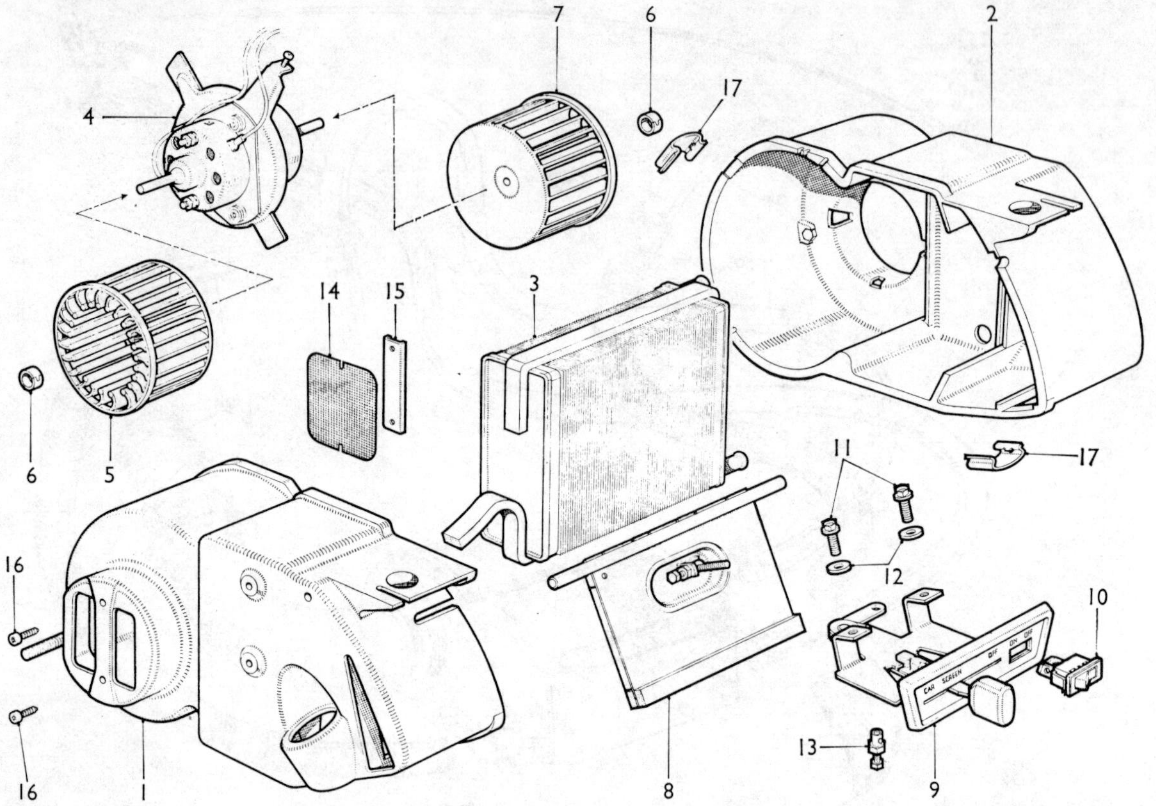

FIG 12:14 An exploded view of the fresh air heater. Later type

Key to Fig 12:14 1 Heater casing 2 Heater casing 3 Matrix 4 Blower motor 5 Rotor (recirculatory) 6 Rotor securing clips 7 Rotor (air intake) 8 Air distribution flap 9 Heater control panel 10 Blower switch 11 Securing screws—control panel to casing 12 Washers for item (11) 13 Trunnion and screw—control lever to flap 14 One-way valve 15 Valve securing plate 16 Valve securing screws 17 Heater casing joining clips

the upper bracket of the long belt as indicated in the top inset of **FIG 12:11**. Fit the assembly to the tapped attachment point and tighten the screw fully.

3 Assemble the screw, plain washer, anti-rattle washer and distance piece to the lower belt bracket, remove the rubber plug from the sill attachment point, fit the bracket assembly as indicated in the middle inset of **FIG 12:11** and tighten the screw fully.

4 Note carefully that the angle of the belt brackets in both cases must face away from the body and the large diameter of the distance pieces should be against the body of the car.

5 After lifting the floor covering, remove the rubber plugs from the sides of the floor tunnel, then cut two holes in the floor covering to correspond with the holes in the tunnel.

6 The short belt from the righthand seat must cross over the tunnel to its lefthand side and that from the lefthand seat must cross over the tunnel to the righthand side. Fit the tapping plates from the underside of the tunnel, place the brackets of the short belts on the floor covering, insert the two screws in each, complete with locking washers, through the tunnel walls and tighten them fully into the tapping plates. **Take great care not to damage the wiring harness,** running through the righthand side of the tunnel close to the tapping plate, when performing these operations.

7 To secure the stowage clips mark a vertical line on the waist rail $6\frac{1}{4}$ inch from the front face of the door pillar and using the stowage clip as a template mark off and drill two holes .120 inch dia. on the marked line. Screw the stowage clip, open end facing forward, to the waist rail using the two self-tapping screws provided with the clip.

12:5 Heater removal, control adjustment

Two different types of heaters have been fitted to these cars. The first is described as the recirculatory type and is illustrated in **FIG 12:12**. This type can be used to circulate warm air, heated by hot water from the engine cooling system or, if this is turned off at the tap 19 on the engine the air in the car at normal temperature. Some of the air can be directed to the demister ducts 29 and 31.

The second type of heater is illustrated in **FIGS 12 : 13** and **12 : 14**. This type draws air from outside the car and passes it through the matrix, which is kept filled with water from the cars cooling system, into the interior of the car, either for general heating or for demisting or defrosting the windscreen, or both. To assist the natural ram effect an electric blower fan is incorporated to increase the air flow when required.

Both types of unit may be removed and dismantled for inspection or overhaul. The recirculatory type heater is removed as follows:

1 Disconnect the battery.
2 Drain the water from the coolant system and store for reuse if it contains antifreeze.
3 On Mini models disconnect the heater motor leads. On Hornet and Elf models disconnect the snap connector on the heater motor lead located under the parcel shelf and disconnect the lead from the Lucar connector at the back of the heater switch.
4 Cover the floor covering and upholstery to prevent splashing by residual coolant in the heater unit.
5 Slacken the demister pipe and water hose clips and pull these off the heater.
6 On Minis, withdraw the screws securing the unit to the parcel shelf and remove it. On Hornet and Elf models, remove the glovebox lids and frames, lift up the trimming on the bottom of the glovebox at its inner edge to expose the heater box fixing screws. Slacken and remove the two hexagon screws, one at each rear corner; and the two at the front edge and lift away the heater unit.
7 If desired the demister hose can be pulled out after the hose clips have been slackened.

The heater may be dismantled by referring to **FIG 12 : 12** in which all the component parts are numbered for reference purposes. The motor may require removal. It is taken off with the heater front cover plate 3. After removal take out the fan retaining screw 14 and detach the fan, remove the nut 15 and spring washer 16 and then lift off the motor.

The matrix is removed by taking out the four screws 5 and lifting the mounting bracket 4 from the cowling 2.

Reassembly and refitting are carried out by reversing the above operations. After making good all connections, fill the coolant system, open the heater tap at the rear of the engine, start the engine and run it at a fast-idle speed. If the return hose does not heat up within a few minutes, it is probable that there is an air lock in the heater coolant system. If this is suspected, switch off the engine and disconnect the return hose at the radiator bottom hose. Extend the return hose by enough to return the coolant to the radiator filler direct. Plug return connection on bottom hose and start the engine again to observe the coolant flowing into the radiator. When the flow is smooth and free from bubbles, stop the engine, remove the added hose and reconnect the return hose at the radiator bottom hose, tightening up the clip as quickly as possible.

The second type of heater shown in **FIG 12 : 13** may be removed by the following procedure:

1 Disconnect the battery and drain the coolant system.
2 Remove or cover the front floor covering to prevent damage from coolant.
3 Disconnect the two snap connectors below the parcel shelf and the blower switch connection from the ignition switch.

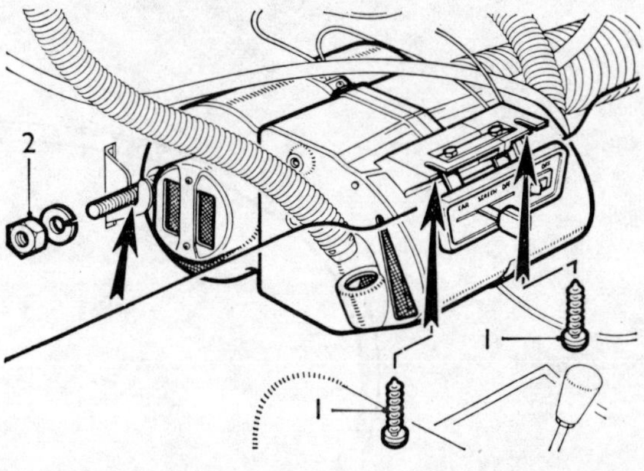

FIG 12 : 15 The two screws securing the front of the fresh air heater and the nut securing the rear of the unit to the slotted bracket

4 Remove the demister tube covers 23 (see **FIG 12 : 13**), pull off the demister tubes 19 and release the air intake hose 24.
5 Release the heater coolant hose clips and pull off the hoses 22.
6 Slacken the nut securing the rear of the unit and remove the two screws under the parcel shelf securing the front of the heater.
7 Lift the unit from the slotted rear bracket, retaining the coolant by placing the fingers over the hose connections. Take the heater out of the car and drain the coolant from the unit.

The heater matrix can be removed for renewal by slackening the control panel securing screws 14, removing the end cover securing screws 13, lifting off the end cover and motor, and lifting out the matrix.

If the heater motor requires renewal, drill out the three pop rivets securing the motor to the end cover and remove the motor.

To remove the blower switch, first remove the control panel and the switch securing nut, then pull the flap valve outwards, withdraw the switch and pull off the wiring connections.

Reassembly and refitting operations are the reverse of the removal and reassembly procedures. When refitting the blower motor fit the motor to the end cover with the wiring positioned to the top of the heater box when assembled, then rivet the motor into position. When refitting the end cover, make sure that the flap valve is correctly located on the end cover pivot and operates correctly before refitting the heater to the car.

To remove the heater shown in **FIG 12 : 14**, which was introduced coincident with the adoption of a NEGATIVE earth electrical system, proceed as follows:

Drain the cooling system. Remove the front floor covering and pull out the demister and air intake tubes from the heater unit.

Refer to **FIG 12 : 15**. Remove the two securing screws 1 and slacken the nut 2 at the rear of the unit.

Disconnect the electrical connections from the blower motor and switch.

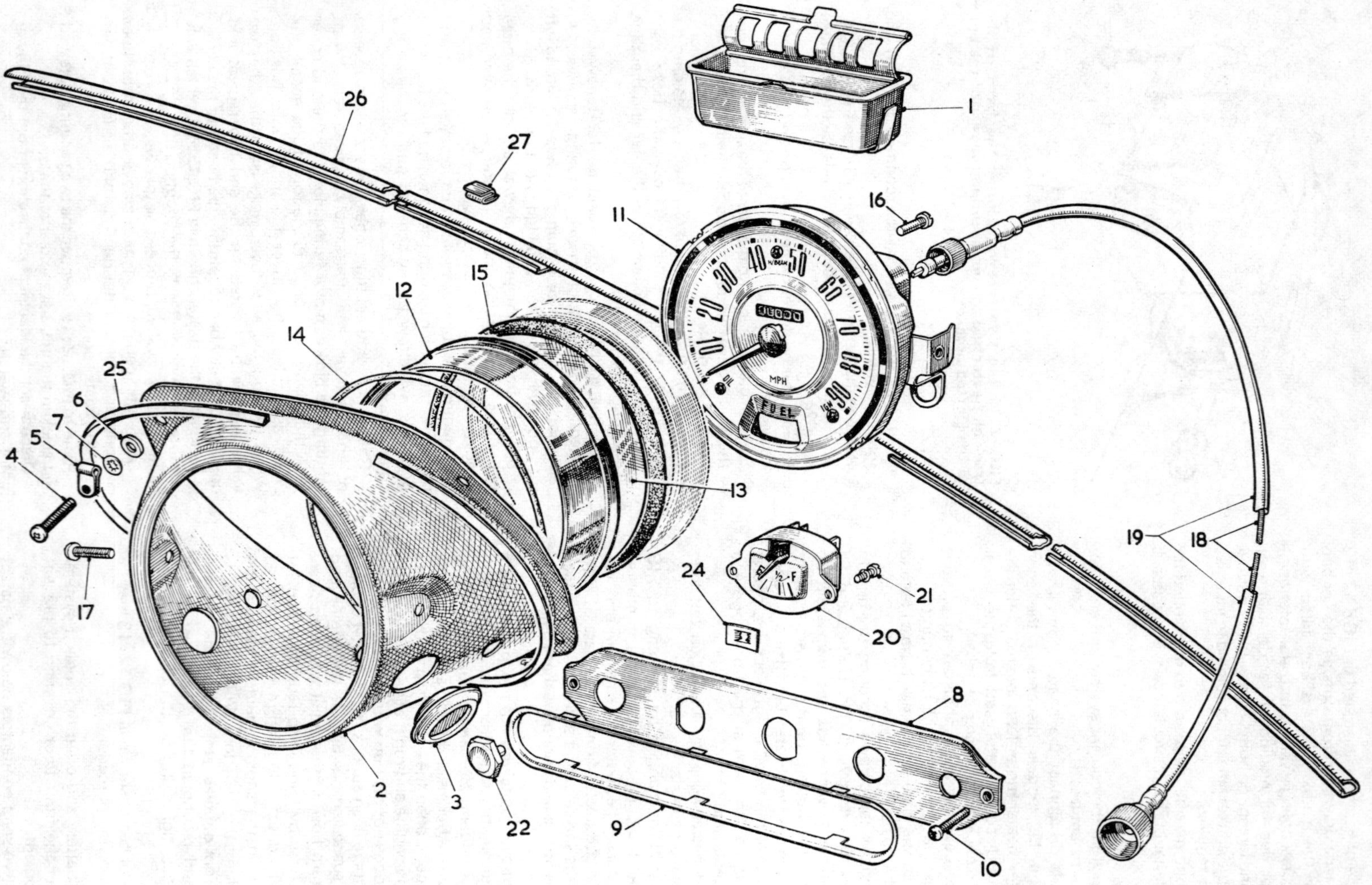

FIG 12:16 An exploded view of the instrument assembly provided on the Morris and Austin Saloon, Van and Pickup models

Key to Fig 12:16 1 Facia ashtray 2 Instrument panel cover 3 Instrument cover plug 4 Panel retaining screw 5 Windshield washer pipe clip 6/7 Plain and locking washers 8 Switch carrier assembly 9 Switch panel bezel 10 Switch carrier fixing screw 11 Speedometer 12 Bezel 13 Glass 14/15 Rubber rings 16 Rear cover retaining screw 17 Speedometer to front cover fixing screw 18/19 Speedometer inner and outer cable 20 Fuel gauge 21 Fuel gauge retaining screw 22 Heater switch alloy plug 23/24 Switch carrier plug nut 25 Instrument housing edge moulding 26 Front parcel shelf finisher 27 Clip

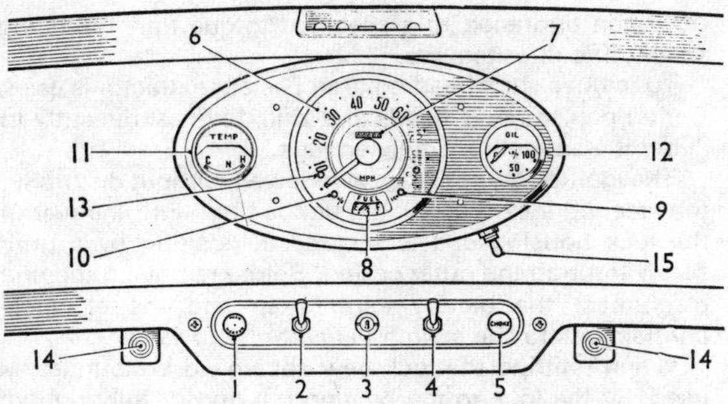

FIG 12:17 The type of instrument panel of the Morris and Austin Mini Super-de-Luxe, Traveller, Countryman and Wolseley Hornet models

Key to Fig 12:17 1 Heater control 2 Wiper switch 3 Ignition and starter switch 4 Lighting switch 5 Choke control 6 Speedometer 7 Distance recorder 8 Fuel contents gauge 9 Ignition warning light 10 Headlamp main beam warning light 11 Coolant temperature gauge 12 Oil pressure gauge 13 Lubrication warning light 14 Windshield washer control 15 Instrument panel light switch

(Controls 1 and 5 may be reversed on later models)

Disconnect the heater water hoses, hold the fingers over the matrix pipes and lift out the heater from the car.

Further dismantling will be simplified by reference to the illustrations. Refit the heater by reversing the removal procedure.

12:6 Removing the facia panel

Several different arrangements of the instruments exist for the various Mini models. **FIG 12:16** illustrates the arrangement used for the Morris and Austin Saloon, Van and Pickup models in which the instruments and indicators are all embodied in the speedometer dial.

Morris and Austin Super-de-Luxe, Traveller and Countryman, and the Wolseley Hornet are fitted with instrument arrangements similar to that shown in **FIG 12:17**. The Riley Elf arrangement is illustrated in **FIG 12:18**.

For the first type shown in **FIG 12:16**, removal of the instruments and panel lights is effected by taking out the screws 4 securing the cover 2 to the dash and releasing the instrument unit 11 by removing the two screws 17. The fuel gauge 20 is detached by removing two screws 21 and disconnecting the electrical lead. The oil pressure warning and panel illumination light lead connections become accessible when the instrument unit is moved back into the car.

Referring to **FIG 12:17**, the panel fitted to Super-de-Luxe, Traveller, Countryman and Hornet models is removed as follows:

1 Remove four cross-head screws seen on the front of the instrument panel shroud and withdraw the shroud.
2 Disconnect the panel light switch leads.
3 Disconnect the pipe union to the oil pressure gauge.
4 Disconnect the electrical leads from the temperature and oil pressure gauges.
5 Remove four countersunk cross-head screws from the front of the instrument panel and remove the panel and instruments from the dash.
6 Release the two knurled nuts and remove the oil pressure and coolant temperature gauges.
7 Take out two screws retaining the instrument panel brackets and speedometer to the speedometer cowling.
8 From under the bonnet, unscrew the knurled nut fixing the speedometer cable to the speedometer and detach the cable.
9 Pull the four bulb holders from the speedometer and disconnect the electrical lead from the fuel gauge.
10 Withdraw the speedometer and fuel gauge forwards into the engine compartment.

The instrument panel fitted to the Elf models shown in **FIG 12:18** requires rather different treatment due to the modified design. Remove the panel and speedometer as follows:

1 Disconnect the battery.
2 From inside each glovebox remove the three nuts, shakeproof washers and plain washers securing the glovebox lids and frames to their brackets.
3 Withdraw the glovebox lid and frame assemblies.
4 Remove the screws retaining the speedometer housing to either side of the instrument panel brackets.
5 Take out the two screws securing the instrument panel to each support bracket, pull the panel rearwards and disconnect the electrical leads and bulb holders from the back of the instruments and from the panel light switch.
6 Disconnect the oil pressure gauge pipe.
7 Withdraw the panel complete with gauges.

On Mk 2 models the instrument nacelle is removed as follows:

Take out the ashtray from the facia panel and bend up the retaining tab.

Release the section of the door seal covering the facia trim liner and carefully lift away the liner. This is attached to the body with glue. Lift the liner up sufficiently from the panel to gain access to the screws securing the instrument nacelle.

Remove these securing screws and lift off the nacelle complete with instruments, after disconnecting the speedometer cable, oil gauge pipe and the electrical connections.

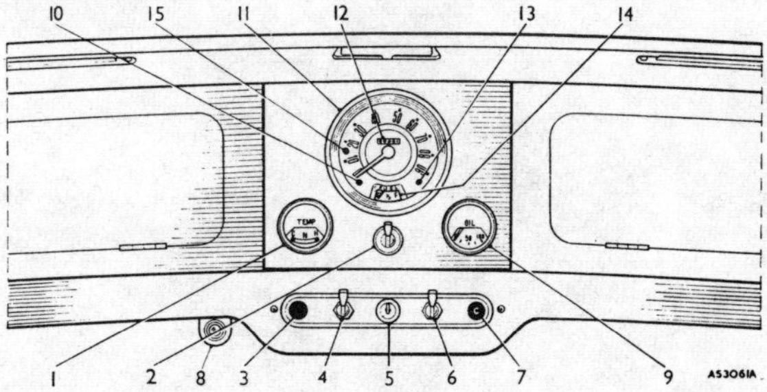

FIG 12:18 The instrument panel of the Riley Elf

Key to Fig 12:18 1 Coolant temperature gauge 2 Instrument panel light switch 3 Heater switch 4 Windshield wiper switch 5 Ignition and starter switch 6 Lighting switch 7 Choke control 8 Windshield washer control 9 Oil pressure gauge 10 Headlight beam warning light 11 Speedometer 12 Distance recorder 13 Ignition warning light 14 Fuel contents gauge 15 Lubrication warning light

The instrument nacelle is refitted by reversing the removal procedure.

It is not necessary to remove the nacelle in order to service the instruments, access to these is from under the bonnet after removing the carburetter air cleaner and the sound insulating material from the speedometer aperture.

Reassembly and refitting of these items for all models is a direct reversal of the removal instructions.

12:7 The steering lock

A steering lock is fitted to later models and is incorporated with the ignition switch on the steering column. The lock is secured to the column by shearhead bolts. These are bolts designed such that their heads will shear off when tightened to a specified torque thus rendering them difficult to remove.

To remove shearhead bolts an Easiout extractor is used. Centre pop the bolt heads and drill down sufficiently to allow the extractor to fully engage.

The ignition switch may be renewed without disturbing the steering lock. The switch unit is fitted into the rear of the lock housing and is secured in position by a grub screw through the outer casing. Before removing the unit disconnect the battery earth strap and the electrical connections to the switch beneath the facia.

When refitting the lock new shearhead bolts must be used. Fit the lock to the column but do not fully tighten the bolts until the operation of the lock has been checked. Then tighten the bolts until their heads shear off. This should occur at a torque of about 18 lb ft.

APPENDIX

METRIC CONVERSION TABLE

TECHNICAL DATA

Engine details
Fuel system
Ignition system
Cooling system
Clutch
Gearbox
Automatic transmission
Front and rear suspension
Steering
Brakes
Electrical equipment
Tightening torques

WIRING DIAGRAMS

HINTS ON MAINTENANCE AND OVERHAUL

GLOSSARY OF TERMS

Inches	Decimals	Millimetres	Inches to Millimetres: Inches	Inches to Millimetres: mm	Millimetres to Inches: mm	Millimetres to Inches: Inches
1/64	.015625	.3969	.001	.0254	.01	.00039
1/32	.03125	.7937	.002	.0508	.02	.00079
3/64	.046875	1.1906	.003	.0762	.03	.00118
1/16	.0625	1.5875	.004	.1016	.04	.00157
5/64	.078125	1.9844	.005	.1270	.05	.00197
3/32	.09375	2.3812	.006	.1524	.06	.00236
7/64	.109375	2.7781	.007	.1778	.07	.00276
1/8	.125	3.1750	.008	.2032	.08	.00315
9/64	.140625	3.5719	.009	.2286	.09	.00354
5/32	.15625	3.9687	.01	.254	.1	.00394
11/64	.171875	4.3656	.02	.508	.2	.00787
3/16	.1875	4.7625	.03	.762	.3	.01181
13/64	.203125	5·1594	.04	1.016	.4	.01575
7/32	.21875	5.5562	.05	1.270	.5	.01969
15/64	.234375	5.9531	.06	1.524	.6	.02362
1/4	.25	6.3500	.07	1.778	.7	.02756
17/64	.265625	6.7469	.08	2.032	.8	.03150
9/32	.28125	7.1437	.09	2.286	.9	.03543
19/64	.296875	7.5406	.1	2.54	1	.03937
5/16	.3125	7.9375	.2	5.08	2	.07874
21/64	.328125	8.3344	.3	7.62	3	.11811
11/32	.34375	8.7312	.4	10.16	4	.15748
23/64	.359375	9.1281	.5	12.70	5	.19685
3/8	.375	9.5250	.6	15.24	6	.23622
25/64	.390625	9.9219	.7	17.78	7	.27559
13/32	.40625	10.3187	.8	20.32	8	.31496
27/64	.421875	10.7156	.9	22.86	9	.35433
7/16	.4375	11.1125	1	25.4	10	.39370
29/64	.453125	11.5094	2	50.8	11	.43307
15/32	.46875	11.9062	3	76.2	12	.47244
31/64	.484375	12.3031	4	101.6	13	.51181
1/2	.5	12.7000	5	127.0	14	.55118
33/64	.515625	13.0969	6	152.4	15	.59055
17/32	.53125	13.4937	7	177.8	16	.62992
35/64	.546875	13.8906	8	203.2	17	.66929
9/16	.5625	14.2875	9	228.6	18	.70866
37/64	.578125	14.6844	10	254.0	19	.74803
19/32	.59375	15.0812	11	279.4	20	.78740
39/64	.609375	15.4781	12	304.8	21	.82677
5/8	.625	15.8750	13	330.2	22	.86614
41/64	.640625	16.2719	14	355.6	23	.90551
21/32	.65625	16.6687	15	381.0	24	.94488
43/64	.671875	17.0656	16	406.4	25	.98425
11/16	.6875	17.4625	17	431.8	26	1.02362
45/64	.703125	17.8594	18	457.2	27	1.06299
23/32	.71875	18.2562	19	482.6	28	1.10236
47/64	.734375	18.6531	20	508.0	29	1.14173
3/4	.75	19.0500	21	533.4	30	1.18110
49/64	.765625	19.4469	22	558.8	31	1.22047
25/32	.78125	19.8437	23	584.2	32	1.25984
51/64	.796875	20.2406	24	609.6	33	1.29921
13/16	.8125	20.6375	25	635.0	34	1.33858
53/64	.828125	21.0344	26	660.4	35	1.37795
27/32	.84375	21.4312	27	685.8	36	1.41732
55/64	.859375	21.8281	28	711.2	37	1.4567
7/8	.875	22.2250	29	736.6	38	1.4961
57/64	.890625	22.6219	30	762.0	39	1.5354
29/32	.90625	23.0187	31	787.4	40	1.5748
59/64	.921875	23.4156	32	812.8	41	1.6142
15/16	.9375	23.8125	33	838.2	42	1.6535
61/64	.953125	24.2094	34	863.6	43	1.6929
31/32	.96875	24.6062	35	889.0	44	1.7323
63/64	.984375	25.0031	36	914.4	45	1.7717

UNITS	Pints to Litres	Gallons to Litres	Litres to Pints	Litres to Gallons	Miles to Kilometres	Kilometres to Miles	Lbs. per sq. In. to Kg. per sq. Cm.	Kg. per sq. Cm. to Lbs. per sq. In.
1	.57	4.55	1.76	.22	1.61	.62	.07	14.22
2	1.14	9.09	3.52	.44	3.22	1.24	.14	28.50
3	1.70	13.64	5.28	.66	4.83	1.86	.21	42.67
4	2.27	18.18	7.04	.88	6.44	2.49	.28	56.89
5	2.84	22.73	8.80	1.10	8.05	3.11	.35	71.12
6	3.41	27.28	10.56	1.32	9.66	3.73	.42	85.34
7	3.98	31.82	12.32	1.54	11.27	4.35	.49	99.56
8	4.55	36.37	14.08	1.76	12.88	4.97	.56	113.79
9		40.91	15.84	1.98	14.48	5.59	.63	128.00
10		45.46	17.60	2.20	16.09	6.21	.70	142.23
20				4.40	32.19	12.43	1.41	284.47
30				6.60	48.28	18.64	2.11	426.70
40				8.80	64.37	24.85		
50					80.47	31.07		
60					96.56	37.28		
70					112.65	43.50		
80					128.75	49.71		
90					144.84	55.92		
100					160.93	62.14		

UNITS	Lb ft to kgm	Kgm to lb ft	UNITS	Lb ft to kgm	Kgm to lb ft
1	.138	7.233	7	.967	50.631
2	.276	14.466	8	1.106	57.864
3	.414	21.699	9	1.244	65.097
4	.553	28.932	10	1.382	72.330
5	.691	36.165	20	2.765	144.660
6	.829	43.398	30	4.147	216.990

TECHNICAL DATA

Dimensions are in inches unless otherwise stated

ENGINE DETAILS

Type	4 cylinder in-line, ohv, transversely mounted
Bore and stroke:	
848 cc Mini, Elf and Hornet Mk I	2.478 x 2.687
998 cc Mini Mk II, Elf and Hornet Mk II and III, Clubman	2.543 x 3.000
1098 cc Clubman (1976)	2.543 × 3.296 (64.58 × 83.72 mm)
1275 GT	2.78 x 3.2 (70.61 x 81.28 mm)
Firing order	1–3–4–2
Compression ratio:	
848 cc Mini, Elf and Hornet Mk I	8.3:1
848 cc Mini automatic	8.9:1
998 cc Mini Mk II, Elf and Hornet Mk II and III	8.3:1
998 cc Mini Mk II automatic, Elf and Hornet Mk III automatic	8.9:1 or 9:1
998 cc Mini with exhaust emission control	8.9:1
998 cc Clubman	8.3:1 or 7.6:1
1098 cc Clubman (1976)	8.5:1
1275 cc GT	8.8:1 or 8.0:1
Camshaft:	
Type of bearings:	
Mini, Elf and Hornet Mk I:	
Front	Steel-backed whitemetal lined
Centre and rear	Plain (running in block)
Mini Mk II, Elf and Hornet Mk II and III, 1275 GT	Steel-backed whitemetal lined
Number of bearings	3
Journal diameter:	
Front	1.6655 to 1.6660
Centre	1.62275 to 1.62325
Rear	1.3725 to 1.3735
Inside bearing diameter, reamed in position:	
Mini, Elf and Hornet Mk I:	
Front	1.6670 to 1.6675
Mini Mk II, Elf, Hornet Mk II and III and Clubman:	
Front	1.6670 to 1.6675
Centre	1.6245 to 1.6255
Rear	1.3748 to 1.3755
Bearing clearance:	
Mini, Elf and Hornet Mk I:	
Front	.00100 to .00200
Centre and rear	.00125 to .00275
Mini Mk II, Elf, Hornet Mk II and III, Clubman and 1275 GT:	
Front, centre and rear	.00100 to .00200
End float	.003 to .007
Connecting rods:	
Length between centres:	
All models	5.75

Big-end bearing diametrical clearance:	
All models	.0010 to .0025
Crankshaft:	
Main bearing types:	
Mini, Elf and Hornet Mk I	Steel-backed whitemetal lined
Mini Mk II, Elf and Hornet Mk II and III	Steel-backed copper/lead, thinwall
Main bearing journal diameters:	
Mini, Elf, Hornet and Clubman	1.7505 to 1.7510
1275 GT	2.0005 to 2.0010 (50.81 to 50.82 mm)
Running clearances:	
Mini, Elf and Hornet Mk I	.0005 to .0020
Mini Mk II, Elf, Hornet Mk II and III and Clubman	.0010 to .0027
Main journal minimum regrind diameter:	
Mini, Elf, Hornet and Clubman	1.7105
Crankpin diameter:	
All models	1.6254 to 1.6259
1275 GT	1.7504 to 1.7509 (44.45 to 44.47 mm)
Crankpin minimum regrind diameter:	
All models	1.5854
End clearance:	
All models	.002 to .003
End thrust	Taken on centre main bearing
Engine lubrication:	
Oil filter	Fullflow type. Capacity 1 pint
Sump capacities:	
Synchromesh transmission	$8\frac{1}{2}$ pints, including filter
Automatic transmission	13 pints
Refill capacity	9 pints (approx)
Oil pump:	
Type	Eccentric rotor
Relief valve spring free length:	
Mini, Elf, Hornet and Clubman	$2\frac{55}{64}$
Relief pressure:	
Mini, Elf and Hornet, Elf, Hornet Mk III automatic and Clubman	60 lb/sq in
Mini Mk I and II automatic, 1275 GT	50 lb/sq in
Pistons:	
Type:	
Mini, Elf and Hornet Mk I	Split skirt
Mini Mk II, Elf, Hornet Mk II and III and Clubman	Solid skirt
Piston rings:	
Top ring	Plain
Second and third rings	Tapered
Oil control ring	Slotted scraper
Gap in position:	
Mini, Elf, Hornet and Clubman	.007 to .012
1275 GT:	
Top	.011 to .016 (.28 to .40 mm)
Second and Third	.008 to .013 (.20 to .33 mm)
Ring to groove clearance:	
All models	.0015 to .0035
Compression rings width:	
Mini, Elf and Hornet Mk 1	.0690 to .0700
Mini Mk II, Elf, Hornet Mk II and III and Clubman	.0620 to .0625

Oil control rings width:		
Mini, Elf and Hornet	.1240 to .1250	
Piston clearance:	*Top of skirt*	*Bottom of skirt*
Mini, Elf and Hornet Mk I	.0026 to .0032	.0006 to .0012
Mini, Mk II, Elf and Hornet Mk II and III	—	.0005 to .0011
Clubman 1098	.0021 to .0033	.0005 to .0015
1275 GT:		
Top of skirt	.0029 to .0037 (.07 to .09 mm)	
Bottom of skirt	.0015 to .0021 (.04 to .05 mm)	
Piston oversizes available, machined to provide for running clearances. Stamped markings allow for bore of +.0001 or —.0002:		
Mini, Elf and Hornet Mk I	+.010, +.020, +.030, +.040	
Mini Mk II, Elf and Hornet Mk II and III	+.010, +.020	
Clubman 1098	+.020	
Gudgeon pin:		
Type:		
Mini, Elf and Hornet Mk I	Clamped in little-end	
Mini Mk II, Elf, Hornet Mk II and III and Clubman	Fully floating with circlip location	
1275 GT	Pressed in connecting rod	
Fit in piston:		
All models	Hand push-fit	
Valves, spring and tappets:		
Valve head diameters:	*Inlet*	*Exhaust*
Mini, Elf and Hornet	1.093 to 1.098	1.000 to 1.005
1275 GT	1.307 to 1.312	1.1515 to 1.1565
Valve stem diameters:		
All models	.2793 to .2798	.2788 to .2793
Angle of seat, inlet and exhaust	45 deg.	
Valve springs free length:		
Mini, Elf and Hornet	1.625	
Clubman 1098	1.750	
1275 GT	1.95	
Valve guide bore:		
All models	.2813 to .2818	
Tappets:		
All models	.812 dia., 1.500 long	
Valve clearance (cold)	.012	
Valve rocker bush bore (reamed)	.5630 to .5635	
Timing marks	Dimples on timing wheels, marks on flywheel	

Valve timing (rocker clearance .019 for timing only): 1275 GT (rocker clearance .021 for timing only)	*Inlet valve* Opens BTDC	Closes ABDC	*Exhaust valve* Opens BBDC	Closes ATDC
Mini, Elf and Hornet	5 deg.	45 deg.	40 deg.	10 deg.
1275 GT and 1098	5 deg.	45 deg.	51 deg.	21 deg.

Exhaust emission control:	
Exhaust gas analyser reading at engine idling speed	4.5 per cent CO maximum
Air pump test speed	1200 rev/min (engine)

FUEL SYSTEM

Carburetters:	
Type, early cars with manual transmission	SU HS2
early cars with automatic transmission ...	SU HS4
later cars	SU HS4

Needles:	Standard	Rich	Weak
Mini 848 cc, 1959 to 72	EB	M	GG
Mini 848 cc, 1972 to 74	AAV	—	—
Mini 848 cc, 1974 on	ABS	—	—
Mini 998 cc, 1967 to 72	GX	M	GG
Mini 998 cc, 1972 to 74	AAV	—	—
Mini 998 cc, 1974 on	ABX	—	—
Mini 848 cc, automatic 1965 to 69	AN	H6	EB
Mini 998 cc, automatic 1967 to 74	AC	M1	HA
Clubman 998 cc, 1969 to 72	GX	M	GG
Clubman 1098 cc	ABP	—	—
1275 GT, 1969 to 72	AC	BQ	HA
1275 GT, 1972 on	ABB	—	—
Mini 1000 (Canada) 1970 to 73	AAG	—	—
Mini 1000 (Canada) 1973 on	ABJ	—	—

Idle speeds:	
All models up to 1972	500 rev/min (M); 650 rev/min (A)
848 cc, 1972 on	800 rev/min (M and A)
998 cc, 1972 to 74	800 rev/min (M and A)
998 cc, 1974 on	750 rev/min (M and A)
1275 GT, 1969 to 72	650 rev/min
1275 GT, 1972 on	750 rev/min
1000 (Canada) to 1973	800 rev/min
1000 (Canada) 1973 on	850 rev/min
1098 cc	750 rev/min
Fuel pump:	
Make	SU electric
Type	PD, SP or AUF
1275 GT and Clubman	SU Mechanical AUF 700 or 800

IGNITION SYSTEM

Sparking plugs:		
Type:		
All models	Champion N5 or N9Y	
1275 GT	Champion N9Y	
Gap	.025 (.625 mm)	
Distributor:		
Contact breaker points gap	.014 to .016	
Rotor arm rotation	Anticlockwise	
Capacitor capacity	.18 to .24 microfarad	
Ignition timing:		
Mini Mk I and II, 848 cc, and variants, to 1972:		
Static	TDC	
Stroboscopic at 600 rev/min	3 deg. BTDC	
Mini Mk II, 998 cc and variants, 1000, to 1972:		*Van*
Static	5 deg. BTDC	7 deg. BTDC
Stroboscopic at 600 rev/min	8 deg. BTDC	10 deg. BTDC
Mini Mk I and II, 848 cc, Automatic, to 1969:		
Static	3 deg. BTDC	
Stroboscopic at 600 rev/min	6 deg. BTDC	
Mini Mk II, 1000, Clubman, 998 cc Automatic, to 1974:		
Static	4 deg. BTDC	
Stroboscopic at 600 rev/min	6 deg. BTDC	
Mini Clubman, 1969-72:		
Static	5 deg. BTDC	
Stroboscopic at 600 rev/min	8 deg. BTDC	

Mini Clubman, 1000 and variants, 1972-74:		
Static ...	5 deg. BTDC	*10 deg. BTDC
Stroboscopic at 1000 rev/min ...	11 deg. BTDC	*13 deg. BTDC
Mini 848 cc and variants, 1972-74:		
Static ...	TDC	*9 deg. BTDC
Stroboscopic at 1000 rev/min ...	19 deg. BTDC	*14 deg. BTDC
Mini 848 cc and variants, 1974 on:		
Static ...	6 deg. BTDC	
Stroboscopic at 1000 rev/min ...	11 deg. BTDC	
*1974 on: Some manual transmission models		
Mini 1275 GT, 1969-72:		
Static ...	8 deg. BTDC	
Stroboscopic at 600 rev/min ...	10 deg. BTDC	
at 1000 rev/min ...	13 deg BTDC (1972 on)	
Mini 1000 (Canada):		
Static ...	1 deg. BTDC (to 1972) 2 deg. BTDC (1972) 6 deg. BTDC (1973 on)	
Stroboscopic at 1000 rev/min ...	9 deg. BTDC	
at 1500 rev/min ...	8 deg. BTDC (1973 on)	

Ignition timing, emission control (ECE 15) models:	
Mini, 848 cc, 1972-73:	
Static ...	TDC
Stroboscopic at 1000 rev/min ...	19 deg. BTDC
Mini 848 cc, variants, 1974 on:	
Static ...	6 deg. BTDC
Stroboscopic at 1000 rev/min ...	11 deg. BTDC
Mini Clubman, 1000, 998 cc, 1972-74:	
Static ...	5 deg. BTDC
Stroboscopic at 1000 rev/min ...	11 deg. BTDC
Mini Clubman, 1000, 998 cc, 1974 on:	
Static ...	4 deg. BTDC
Stroboscopic at 1000 rev/min ...	7 deg. BTDC
Mini Clubman, 1098 cc, 1974 on:	
Static ...	9 deg. BTDC
Stroboscopic at 1000 rev/min ...	12 deg. BTDC
Mini 1275 GT, 1972 on:	
Static ...	8 deg. BTDC
Stroboscopic at 1000 rev/min ...	13 deg. BTDC

Note: Stroboscopic timing is set with the vacuum pipe disconnected

COOLING SYSTEM

Capacity including heater ...	$6\frac{1}{4}$ pints
Heater capacity ...	1 pint
Thermostat setting ...	82°C (180°F)
Pressure cap ...	13 lb/sq inch

CLUTCH

Type:	
Synchromesh transmission ...	Single dry plate, coil or diaphragm springs, hydraulic operation
Coil spring colour code:	
Mini, Elf and Hornet Mk I ...	Red spot
Mini Mk II, Elf and Hornet Mk II and III ...	Black with white spot
Diaphragm spring colour code:	
Mini, Elf and Hornet Mk 1 ...	Brown
Mini Mk II, Elf, Hornet Mk II and III, Clubman ...	Light green
1275 GT ...	Green/Blue

GEARBOX

Ratios:	*First*	*Second*	*Third*	*Top*	*Reverse*
Mini, Elf and Hornet ...	3.627:1	2.172:1	1.412:1	1.000:1	3.627:1
Clubman and later 850, 1000	3.52:1	2.21:1	1.43:1	1.00:1	3.54:1
1275 GT	3.33:1	2.09:1	1.35:1	1.00:1	3.35:1

Oil capacity	See ENGINE DETAILS
Differential ratios, synchromesh transmission:	
Mini 848 cc, Elf and Hornet Mk I, II and III ...	3.765:1
Differential ratios, automatic transmission:	
Mini 848 cc and Mk II, Elf and Hornet Mk III ...	3.27:1 or 3.76:1
Clubman	3.44:1
1275 GT	3.65:1 or 3.44:1

AUTOMATIC TRANSMISSION

	First	*Second*	*Third*	*Top*	*Reverse*
Ratios	2.690:1	1.845:1	1.460:1	1.000:1	2.690:1

Torque converter:	
Type	3 element
Ratio	2:1 maximum
Converter output gear ratio	1.15:1
End float	.0035 to .0065

FRONT AND REAR SUSPENSION

Type—Independent rubber-cone spring units or hydraulic interconnected Hydrolastic system

Dampers—Hydraulic tubular telescopic in association with rubber-cone spring units, front and rear. Hydrolastic units incorporate own damping arrangements

Hydrolastic system:

Fluid capacity	4 pints
Fluid pressure, unladen	263 lb/sq in (early models)
Fluid pressure, unladen	282 lb/sq in., from car numbers:

	RHD	LHD		RHD	LHD
Austin Mini	830899	832055	Morris Mini	370004	370197
Riley Elf	829535	829540	Wolseley Hornet	827058	827060

Fluid pressure, Clubman and 1275 GT	292 lb/sq in

STEERING

Type:	Rack and pinion
Wheel alignment, unladen:	
Camber angle	1 to 3 deg. positive
Castor angle	3 deg.
Kingpin (swivel pin) inclination	9 deg. 30 min.
Toe-out	$\frac{1}{16}$
Lock angle, outer wheel at 20 deg.	Inner wheel 23 deg.

BRAKES

Type:	
All cars	Hydraulically operated drum type
Drum diameter...	7
Brake fluid	Lockheed Super Heavy Duty or fluid to Specification SAE.70.R3

1275 GT:

Type	Lockheed hydraulic. Disc front. Drum rear
Servo unit	Lockheed Type 6
Fluid	Lockheed Series 329
Disc diameter	7.5 or 8.4 (later)
Pad material	Mintex M78 Red/green/red/green/red
Minimum thickness	$\frac{1}{16}$
Drum diameter	7.0
Lining material	Don 202

ELECTRICAL EQUIPMENT

Battery	12 volt earth return, positive earth
Normal capacity:	
All cars	34 amp/hr or 30 amp/hr. GT 40 amp/hr
Generator:	
Type	Lucas C.40
Maximum output	22 amp at 2250 rev/min
Regulator:	
Cut-out: cut-in voltage	12.7 to 13.3
Drop-off voltage	8.5 to 11.0
Reverse current	5 amp maximum
Open circuit setting at 3000 rev/min generator speed	
20°C (68°F)	16.0 to 16.6 volt
Temperature correction	Subtract or add .1 volt for every 10°C above or below 20°C respectively
Alternator:	
Type	Lucas 11AC
Output	43 amps
Minimum brush length	$\frac{1}{6}$ inch (4 mm)
Type	Lucas 16 ACR
Output	34 amps at 2800 (engine) rev/min
Brush spring tension	7 to 10 oz
Control unit	Lucas 4 TR (11 AC only)
Windscreen wiper	Lucas 14W
Starter motor	Lucas M35G or M35J

TIGHTENING TORQUES

lb ft except where otherwise stated

Cylinder head stud nuts	40
Connecting rod big-end bolts	35
Main bearing setscrews	60
Flywheel centre bolt	110 to 115
Gudgeon pin clamp screws	25
Rocker shaft bracket nuts	25
Transmission case to crankcase	6
Transmission drain plug	40 to 50
Cylinder side cover	2
Second type—deep pressed cover	5
Timing cover—$\frac{1}{4}$ inch UNF bolts	6
Timing cover—$\frac{5}{16}$ inch UNF bolts	14
Water pump	17
Water outlet elbow	8
Oil filter	16
Oil pump	9
Manifold to cylinder head	15
Rocker cover	4
Crankshaft pulley nut	70
Transmission case studs—$\frac{3}{8}$ inch dia. UNC	8
Transmission case studs—$\frac{5}{16}$ inch dia. UNC	6
Transmission case stud nuts—$\frac{3}{8}$ inch UNF	25
Transmission case stud nuts—$\frac{5}{16}$ inch UNF	18
Bottom cover setscrews—$\frac{1}{4}$ inch dia. UNC (changespeed tower)	6
First motion shaft nut	150
Third motion shaft nut	150
Flywheel housing bolts and stud nuts	18
Setscrew, driving strap to flywheel	16
Setscrew, clutch spring housing to pressure plate	16
Distributor clamp bolt—Fixed nut type	50 lb in
Fixed bolt type	30 lb in
Final drive:	
Driven gear to differential cage	60
Nut, driving flange to differential	70 (align to next splitpin hole)
End cover bolts (differential housing)	18
Suspension and steering	
Steering column/rack pinion clamp bolt	8 to 9
Steering lever to hub bolts	35
Steering lever ball joint nut	20 to 24
Steering knuckle ball pin bottom nut	35 to 40
Steering knuckle ball pin top nut	35 to 40
Steering knuckle ball pin retainer	70
Front hub nut (drive shaft)	60
Rear suspension stub axle nut	60 (align to next slot)
Front suspension upper arm pivot pin nut	26 to 28
Steering wheel nut	32 to 37
Road wheel nuts	38 to 43
MINI AUTOMATIC:	
Governor to auxiliary pump housing bolts	10 to 15
Converter centre bolt	110 to 115
Converter (six central bolts)	22 to 24
Converter drain plugs	18 to 20
Converter housing bolts	18
Differential driving flange securing bolts	40 to 45
Gear train bearing caps	12

Gear train carrier strap	12
Input shaft nut	70
Servo unit securing bolts	17
Top and reverse clutch hub nut	150
Transmission to engine securing nut	12
Valve block securing bolts	10
Valve block bolts (securing three sections)	7
$\frac{5}{16}$ inch UNF bolts	18 to 20
$\frac{3}{8}$ inch UNF bolts	30
Oil filter bowl	10 to 15
Alternator shaft nut	25 to 30
1275 GT:	
Cylinder head nuts	50
Caliper retaining bolts	35 to 40
Drive shaft nut	150
Steering lever ball joint	25 to 30

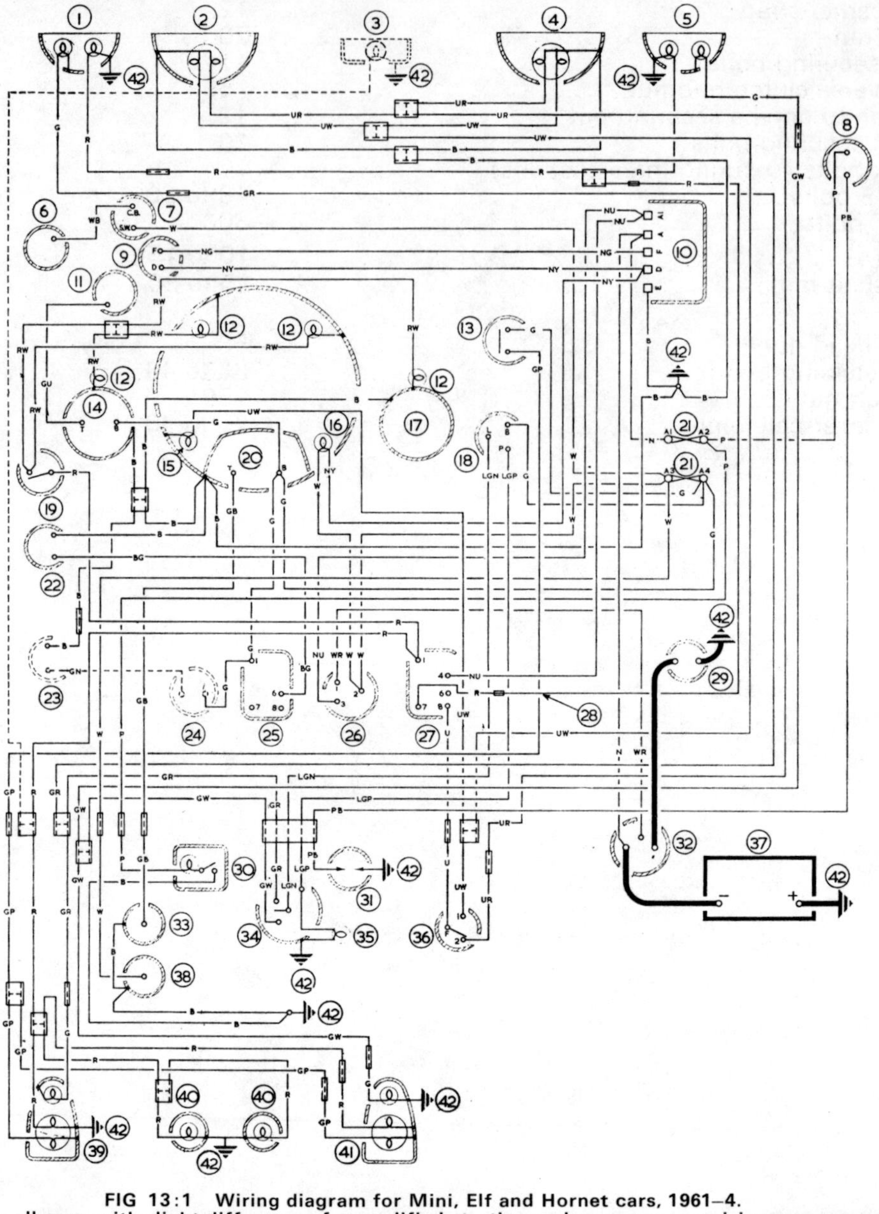

FIG 13:1 Wiring diagram for Mini, Elf and Hornet cars, 1961–4.
(Similar for all cars, with slight differences for modified starting and accessory provisions on some models)

Key to Fig 13:1 1 Lefthand pilot and flashing indicator lamp 2 Lefthand headlamp 3 Bonnet badge lamp (Hornet only) 4 Righthand headlamp 5 Righthand pilot and flashing indicator lamp 6 Distributor 7 Ignition coil 8 Horn 9 Generator 10 Voltage regulator and cut-out 11 Thermal element 12 Panel illumination lights 13 Stop lamp switch 14 Temperature gauge 15 Main beam warning light 16 Ignition warning light 17 Oil pressure gauge 18 Flasher unit 19 Panel lights switch 20 Fuel gauge 21 Fuse (35 amp) 22 Windscreen wiper motor 23 Heater motor 24 Heater motor switch 25 Windscreen wiper switch 26 Ignition/starter switch 27 Headlamp and pilot lamp switch 28 Connect to terminal No. 8 for U.S.A. 29 Starter motor 30 Interior lamp 31 Horn push 32 Starter solenoid switch 33 Fuel gauge tank unit 34 Flashing indicator switch 35 Flashing indicator warning light 36 Headlamp dipswitch 37 Battery (12 volt) 38 Fuel pump 39 Lefthand stop, tail, and flashing indicator lamp 40 Number plate illumination lamp 41 Righthand stop, tail, and flashing indicator lamp 42 Earth connection

Cable colour code: **B** Black **U** Blue **N** Brown **G** Green **P** Purple **R** Red **S** Slate **W** White **Y** Yellow **L** Light **D** Dark **M** Medium

When a cable has two colour code letters, the first denotes the main colour and the second denotes the tracer colour

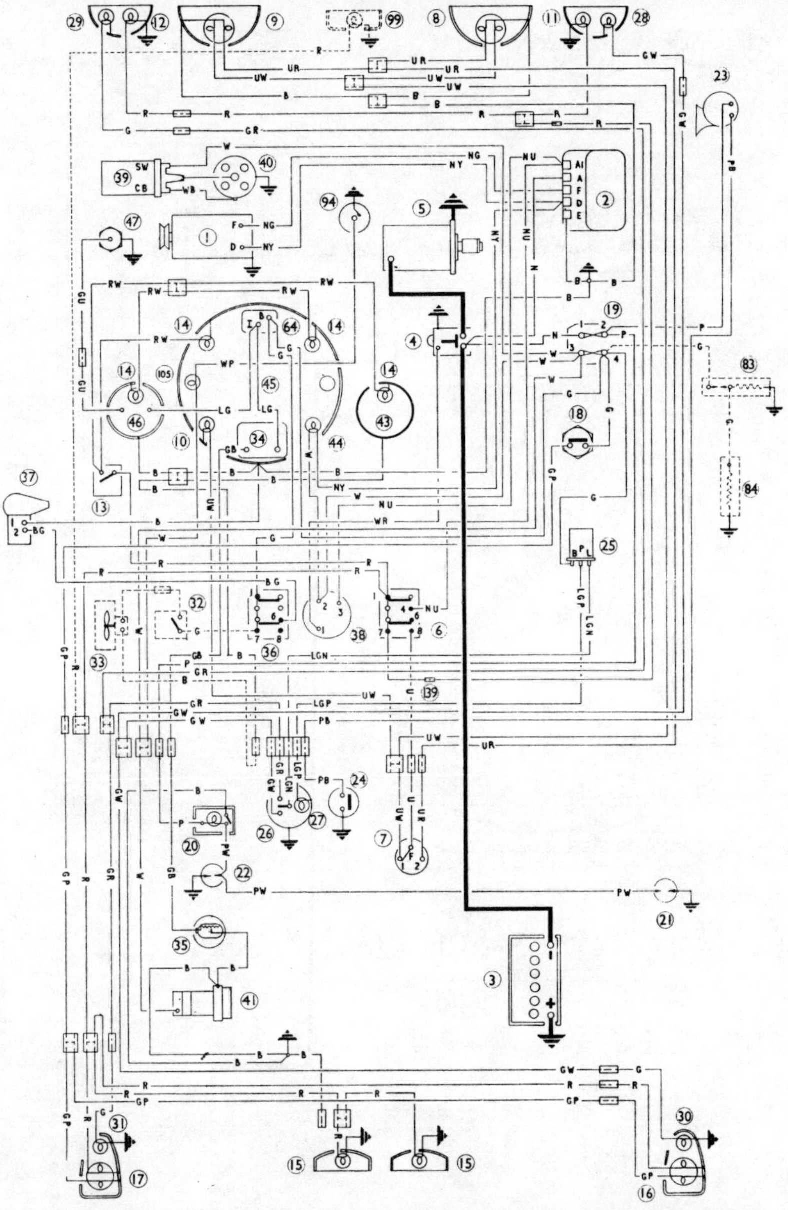

FIG 13:2 Wiring diagram for Mini, Elf and Hornet cars, 1964 onwards

Key to Fig 13:2 1 Generator 2 Control box 3 Battery (12 volt) 4 Starter solenoid 5 Starter motor 6 Lighting switch 7 Headlamp dipswitch 8 Righthand headlamp 9 Lefthand headlamp 10 Main beam warning lamp 11 Righthand sidelamp 12 Lefthand sidelamp 13 Panel lamps switch 14 Panel lamps 15 Number plate illumination lamps 16 Righthand stop and tail lamp 17 Lefthand stop and tail lamp 18 Stop lamp switch 19 Fuse unit (35 amp 1–2, 35 amp 3–4) 20 Interior light 21 Righthand door switch 22 Lefthand door switch 23 Horn 24 Horn push 25 Flasher unit 26 Direction indicator switch 27 Direction indicator warning lamp 28 Righthand front flasher lamp 29 Lefthand front flasher lamp 30 Righthand rear flasher lamp 31 Lefthand rear flasher lamp 32 Heater switch (when fitted) 33 Heater motor (when fitted) 34 Fuel gauge 35 Fuel gauge tank unit 36 Windscreen wiper switch 37 Windscreen wiper motor 38 Ignition/starter switch 39 Ignition coil 40 Distributor 41 Fuel pump 43 Oil pressure gauge 44 Ignition warning lamp 45 Speedometer 46 Water temperature gauge 47 Water temperature transmitter 64 Bi-metal instrument voltage stabilizer 83 Induction heater and thermostat (when fitted) 84 Suction chamber heater (when fitted) 94 Oil filter switch 99 Radiator badge illumination lamp 105 Oil filter warning lamp 139 Connect to No. 6 for U.S.A.

Cable colour code: **N** Brown **U** Blue **R** Red **P** Purple **G** Green **LG** Light Green **W** White **Y** Yellow **B** Black

When a cable has two colour code letters, the first denotes the main colour and the second denotes the tracer colour

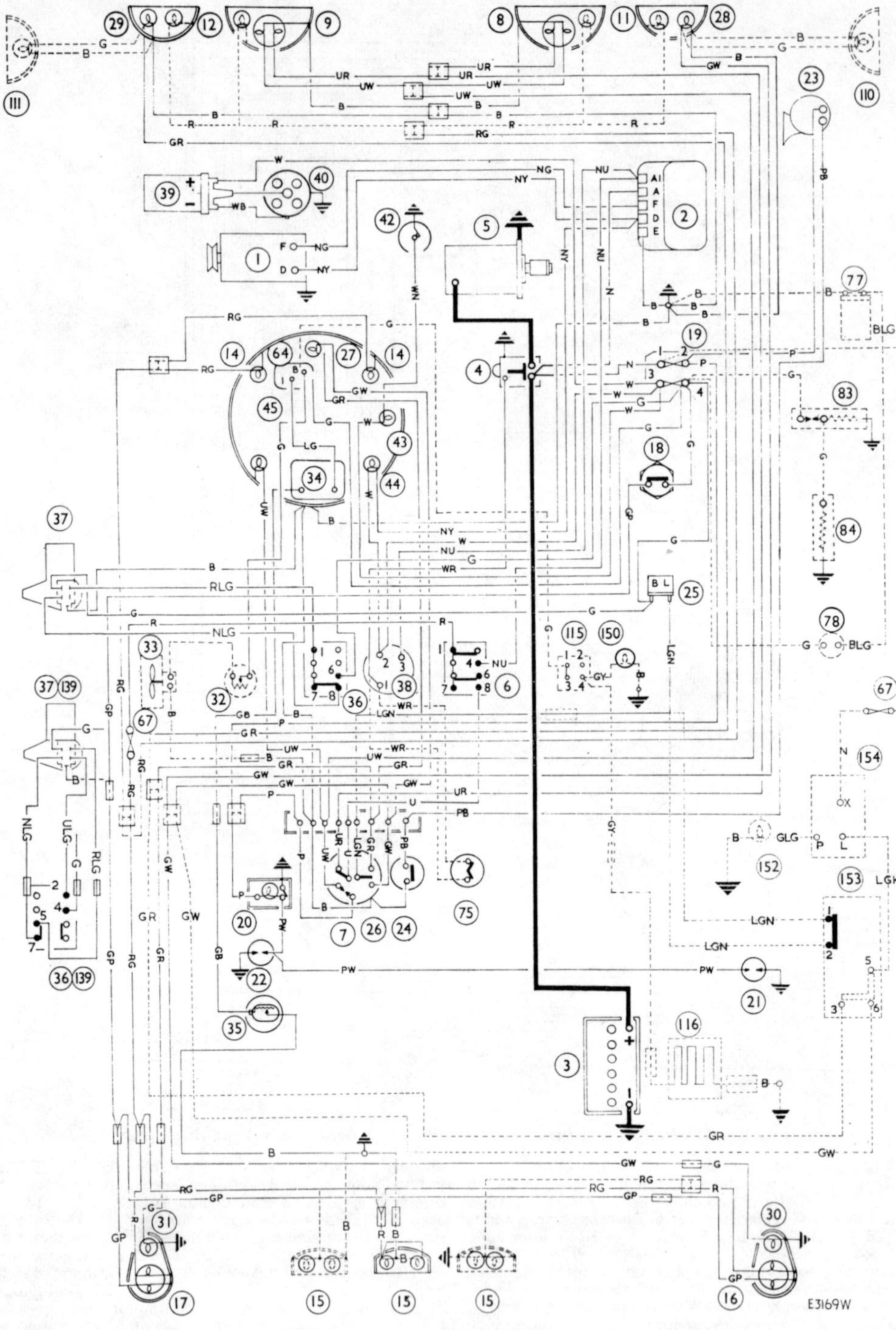

FIG 13:3 Wiring diagram for Mini 850 De-luxe Saloon, Van and Pick-up

Some of the components listed in the key may not be fitted to individual models

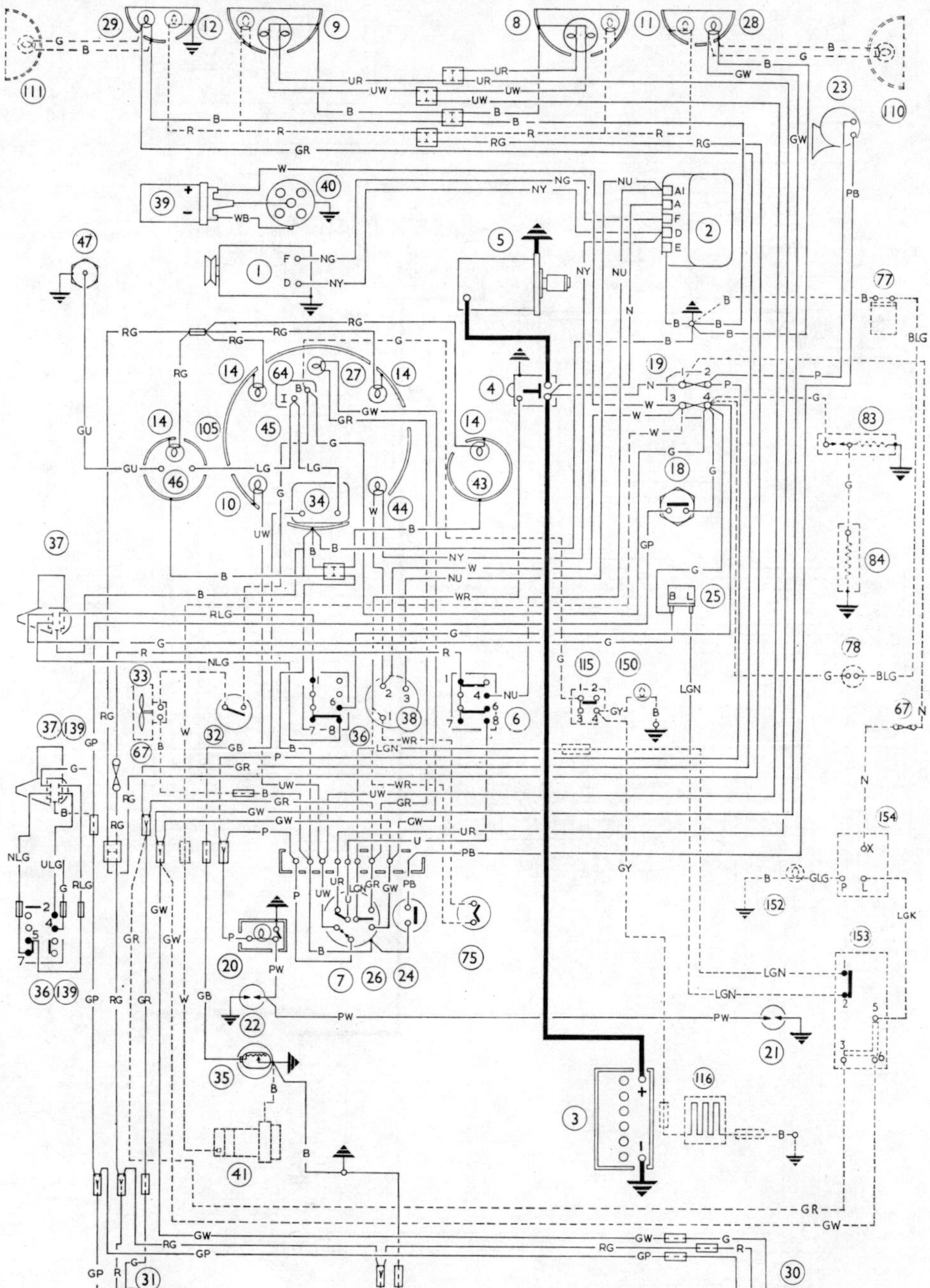

FIG 13:4 Wiring diagram for Mini 1000 Special De-luxe Saloon

Some of the components listed in the key may not be fitted to individual models

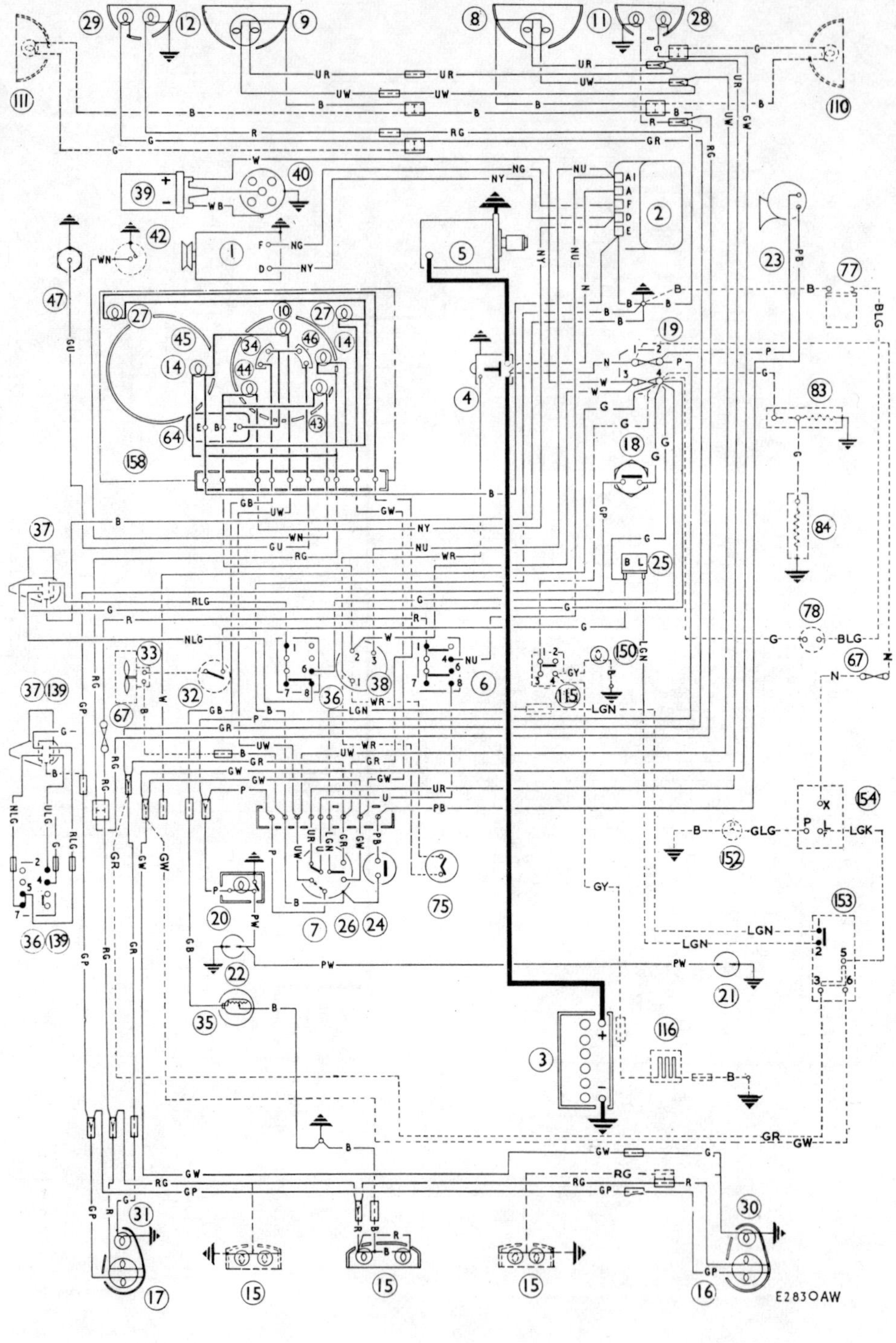

FIG 13:5 Wiring diagram for Mini Clubman Saloon and Estate

Some of the components listed in the key may not be fitted to individual models

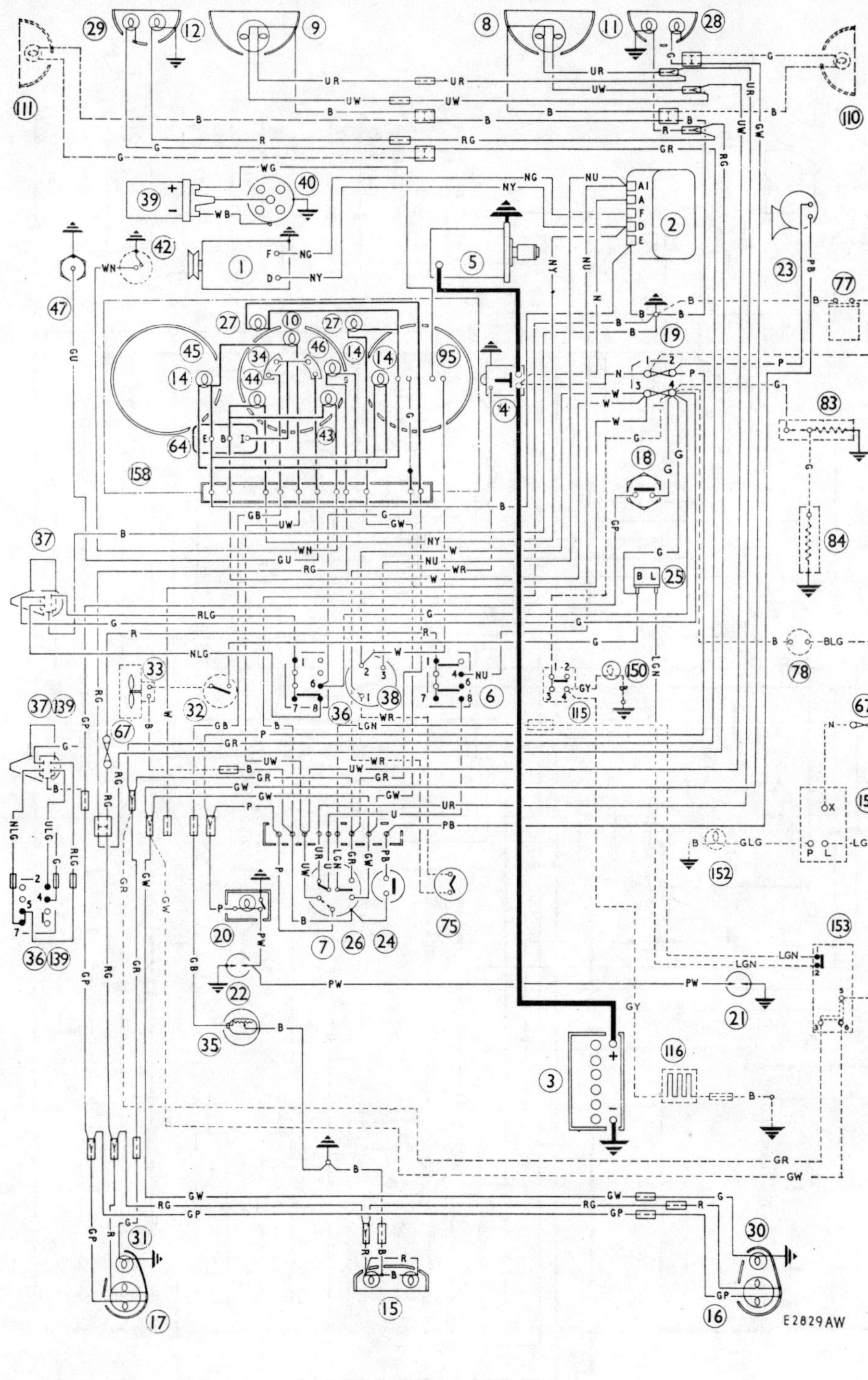

FIG 13:6 Wiring diagram for Mini 1275 GT

Some of the components listed in the key may not be fitted to individual models

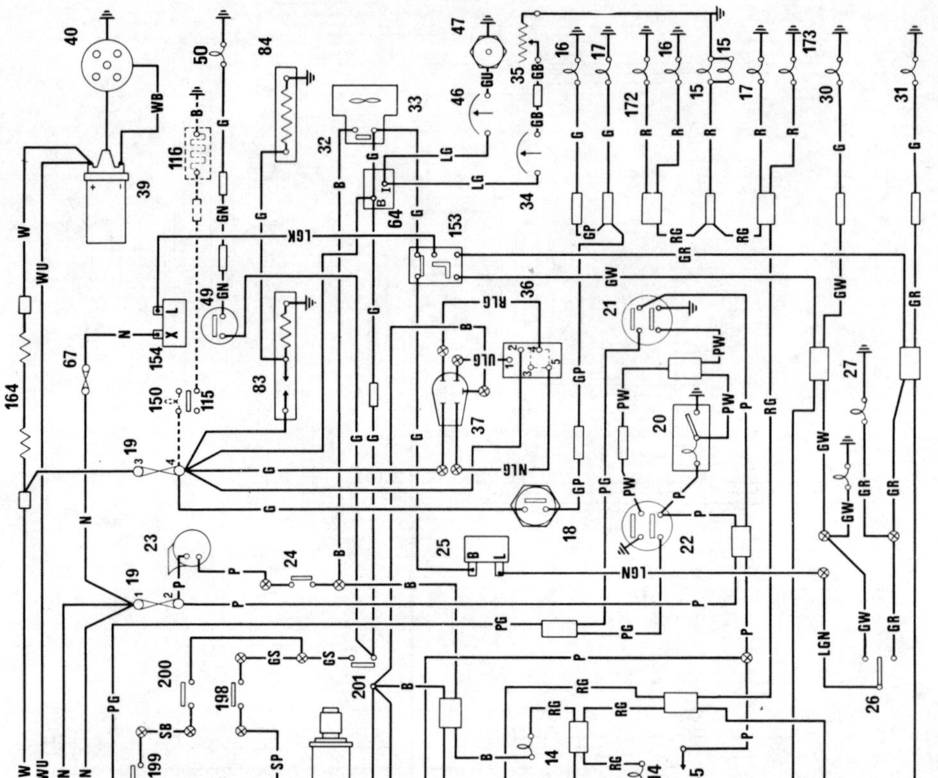

FIG 13:7 Wiring diagram for Mini 1000 Saloon (Canada)

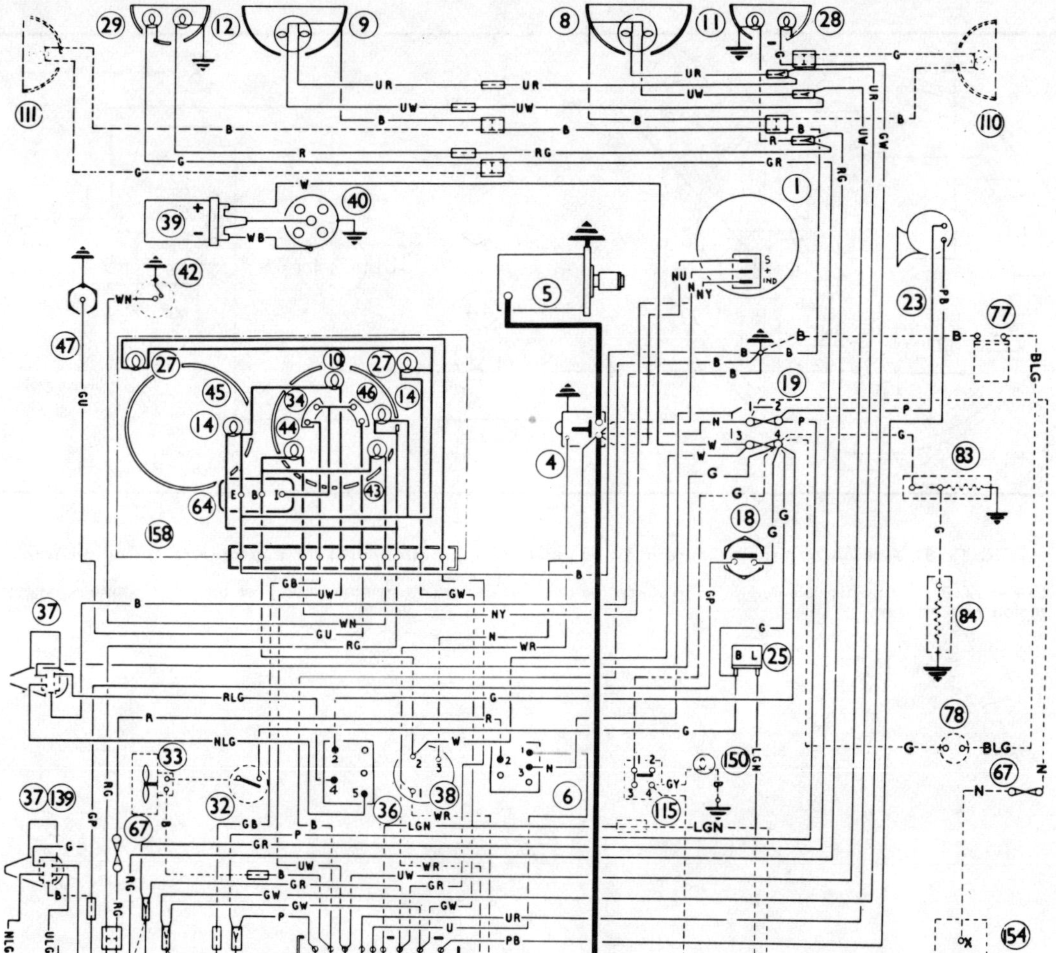

FIG 13:8 Wiring diagram for Mini Clubman Saloon and Estate (with alternator)

Some of the components listed in the key may not be fitted to individual models

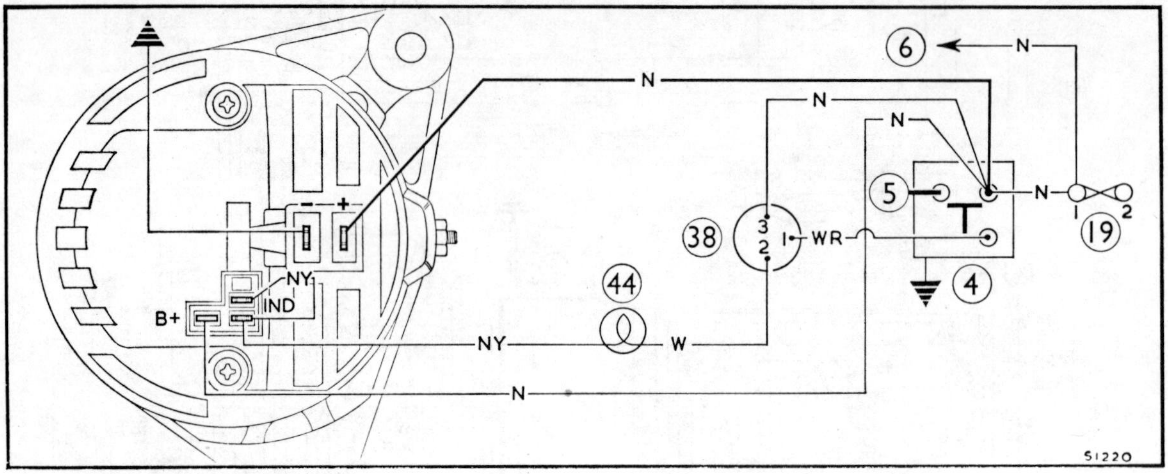

FIG 13:9 Alternator circuit diagram. To be used in conjunction with the appropriate wiring diagram

Key to Fig 13:9 4 Starter solenoid 5 To starter motor 6 To lighting switch 19 Fuse unit 38 Ignition/starter switch 44 Ignition warning lamp

MASTER KEY TO WIRING DIAGRAMS

Several of the components listed in this key may not be fitted to individual models. Some are a special fitment to vehicles exported to certain countries or territories to conform to the mandatory requirements or legislation of those countries

Key to Figs 13:3, 13:4, 13:5, 13:6, 13:7 and 13:8 1 Alternator or dynamo 2 Control box 3 Battery (12-volt) 4 Starter solenoid 5 Starter motor 6 Lighting switch 7 Headlamp dip switch 8 Righthand headlamp 9 Lefthand headlamp 10 Main beam warning lamp 11 Righthand sidelamp/parking lamp 12 Lefthand sidelamp/parking lamp 14 Panel lamps 15 Number plate lamp(s) 16 Righthand stop and tail lamps 17 Lefthand stop and tail lamps 18 Stop lamp switch 19 Fuse block 20 Interior light 21 Righthand door switch (and buzzer) (when fitted) 22 Lefthand door switch (and buzzer) (when fitted) 23 Horn(s) 24 Horn-push 25 Flasher unit 26 Direction indicator, headlamp flasher and dip switch 27 Direction indicator warning lamp(s) 28 Righthand front direction indicator lamp 29 Lefthand front direction indicator lamp 30 Righthand rear direction indicator lamp 31 Lefthand rear direction indicator lamp 32 Heater or fresh air blower switch 33 Heater or fresh air blower 34 Fuel gauge 35 Fuel gauge tank unit 36 Windscreen wiper switch 37 Windscreen wiper motor 38 Ignition/starter switch 39 Ignition coil 40 Distributor 41 Fuel pump 42 Oil pressure switch 43 Oil pressure gauge or warning lamp 44 Ignition warning lamp 45 Headlamp flasher switch (Mini 1000 Canada) 46 Coolant temperature gauge 47 Coolant temperature transmitter 49 Reverse lamp switch 50 Reverse lamp 64 Bi-metal instrument voltage stabilizer 67 Line fuse 75 Automatic transmission safety switch (when fitted) 83 Induction heater and thermostat 84 Suction chamber heater 95 Tachometer 110 Righthand direction indicator repeater lamp (when fitted) 111 Lefthand direction indicator repeater lamp (when fitted) 115 Rear window demister switch 116 Rear window demister unit 139 Alternative connection for two-speed wiper motor and switch 150 Rear window demist warning lamp 153 Hazard warning switch 154 Hazard warning flasher unit 158 Printed circuit instrument panel 159 Brake pressure warning lamp and lamp test switch 160 Brake pressure differential switch 164 Ballast resistor 168 Ignition key audible warning buzzer 170 Righthand front side marker lamp 171 Lefthand front side marker lamp 172 Righthand rear side marker lamp 173 Lefthand rear side marker lamp 198 Driver's seat belt switch 199 Passenger's seat belt switch 200 Passenger's seat switch 201 Seat belt warning gearbox switch 202 Seat belt warning lamp 203 Seat belt warning diode

Cable colour code: **B** Black **G** Green **K** Pink **LG** Light green **N** Brown **O** Orange **P** Purple **R** Red **U** Blue **W** White **Y** Yellow

When a cable has two colour code letters the first denotes the main colour and the second denotes the tracer colour

HINTS ON MAINTENANCE AND OVERHAUL

There are few things more rewarding than the restoration of a vehicle's original peak of efficiency and smooth performance.

The following notes are intended to help the owner to reach that state of perfection. Providing that he possesses the basic manual skills he should have no difficulty in performing most of the operations detailed in this manual. It must be stressed, however, that where recommended in the manual, highly-skilled operations ought to be entrusted to experts, who have the necessary equipment, to carry out the work satisfactorily.

Quality of workmanship:

The hazardous driving conditions on the roads to-day demand that vehicles should be as nearly perfect, mechanically, as possible. It is therefore most important that amateur work be carried out with care, bearing in mind the often inadequate working conditions, and also the inferior tools which may have to be used. It is easy to counsel perfection in all things, and we recognize that it may be setting an impossibly high standard. We do, however, suggest that every care should be taken to ensure that a vehicle is as safe to take on the road as it is humanly possible to make it.

Safe working conditions:

Even though a vehicle may be stationary, it is still potentially dangerous if certain sensible precautions are not taken when working on it while it is supported on jacks or blocks. It is indeed preferable not to use jacks alone, but to supplement them with carefully placed blocks, so that there will be plenty of support if the car rolls off the jacks during a strenuous manoeuvre. Axle stands are an excellent way of providing a rigid base which is not readily disturbed. Piles of bricks are a dangerous substitute. Be careful not to get under heavy loads on lifting tackle, the load could fall. It is preferable not to work alone when lifting an engine, or when working underneath a vehicle which is supported well off the ground. To be trapped, particularly under the vehicle, may have unpleasant results if help is not quickly forthcoming. Make some provision, however humble, to deal with fires. Always disconnect a battery if there is a likelihood of electrical shorts. These may start a fire if there is leaking fuel about. This applies particularly to leads which can carry a heavy current, like those in the starter circuit. While on the subject of electricity, we must also stress the danger of using equipment which is run off the mains and which has no earth or has faulty wiring or connections. So many workshops have damp floors, and electrical shocks are of such a nature that it is sometimes impossible to let go of a live lead or piece of equipment due to the muscular spasms which take place.

Work demanding special care:

This involves the servicing of braking, steering and suspension systems. On the road, failure of the braking system may be disastrous. Make quite sure that there can be no possibility of failure through the bursting of rusty brake pipes or rotten hoses, nor to a sudden loss of pressure due to defective seals or valves.

Problems:

The chief problems which may face an operator are:

1 External dirt.
2 Difficulty in undoing tight fixings
3 Dismantling unfamiliar mechanisms.
4 Deciding in what respect parts are defective.
5 Confusion about the correct order for reassembly.
6 Adjusting running clearances.
7 Road testing.
8 Final tuning.

Practical suggestion to solve the problems:

1 Preliminary cleaning of large parts—engines, transmissions, steering, suspensions, etc.,—should be carried out before removal from the car. Where road dirt and mud alone are present, wash clean with a high-pressure water jet, brushing to remove stubborn adhesions, and allow to drain and dry. Where oil or grease is also present, wash down with a proprietary compound (Gunk, Teepol etc.,) applying with a stiff brush—an old paint brush is suitable—into all crevices. Cover the distributor and ignition coils with a polythene bag and then apply a strong water jet to clear the loosened deposits. Allow to drain and dry. The assemblies will then be sufficiently clean to remove and transfer to the bench for the next stage.

On the bench, further cleaning can be carried out, first wiping the parts as free as possible from grease with old newspaper. Avoid using rag or cotton waste which can leave clogging fibres behind. Any remaining grease can be removed with a brush dipped in paraffin. If necessary, traces of paraffin can be removed by carbon tetrachloride. Avoid using paraffin or petrol in large quantities for cleaning in enclosed areas, such as garages, on account of the high fire risk.

When all exteriors have been cleaned, and not before, dismantling can be commenced. This ensures that dirt will not enter into interiors and orifices revealed by dismantling. In the next phases, where components have to be cleaned, use carbon tetrachloride in preference to petrol and keep the containers covered except when in use. After the components have been cleaned, plug small holes with tapered hard wood plugs cut to size and blank off larger orifices with grease-proof paper and masking tape. Do not use soft wood plugs or matchsticks as they may break.

2 It is not advisable to hammer on the end of a screw thread, but if it must be done, first screw on a nut to protect the thread, and use a lead hammer. This applies particularly to the removal of tapered cotters. Nuts and bolts seem to 'grow' together, especially in exhaust systems. If penetrating oil does not work, try the judicious application of heat, but be careful of starting a fire. Asbestos sheet or cloth is useful to isolate heat.

Tight bushes or pieces of tail-pipe rusted into a silencer can be removed by splitting them with an open-ended hacksaw. Tight screws can sometimes be started by a tap from a hammer on the end of a suitable screwdriver. Many tight fittings will yield to the judicious use of a hammer, but it must be a soft-faced hammer if damage is to be avoided, use a heavy block on the opposite side to absorb shock. Any parts of the steering system which have been damaged should be renewed, as attempts to repair them may lead to cracking and subsequent failure, and steering ball joints should be disconnected using a recommended tool to prevent damage.

3 If often happens that an owner is baffled when trying to dismantle an unfamiliar piece of equipment. So many modern devices are pressed together or assembled by spinning-over flanges, that they must be sawn apart. The intention is that the whole assembly must be renewed. However, parts which appear to be in one piece to the naked eye, may reveal close-fitting joint lines when inspected with a magnifying glass, and, this may provide the necessary clue to dismantling. Left-handed screw threads are used where rotational forces would tend to unscrew a righthanded screw thread.

Be very careful when dismantling mechanisms which may come apart suddenly. Work in an enclosed space where the parts will be contained, and drape a piece of cloth over the device if springs are likely to fly in all directions. Mark everything which might be reassembled in the wrong position, scratched symbols may be used on unstressed parts, or a sequence of tiny dots from a centre punch can be useful. Stressed parts should never be scratched or centre-popped as this may lead to cracking under working conditions. Store parts which look alike in the correct order for reassembly. Never rely upon memory to assist in the assembly of complicated mechanisms, especially when they will be dismantled for a long time, but make notes, and drawings to supplement the diagrams in the manual, and put labels on detached wires. Rust stains may indicate unlubricated wear. This can sometimes be seen round the outside edge of a bearing cup in a universal joint. Look for bright rubbing marks on parts which normally should not make heavy contact. These might prove that something is bent or running out of truth. For example, there might be bright marks on one side of a piston, at the top near the ring grooves, and others at the bottom of the skirt on the other side. This could well be the clue to a bent connecting rod. Suspected cracks can be proved by heating the component in a light oil to approximately 100°C, removing, drying off, and dusting with french chalk, if a crack is present the oil retained in the crack will stain the french chalk.

4 In determining wear, and the degree, against the permissible limits set in the manual, accurate measurement can only be achieved by the use of a micrometer. In many cases, the wear is given to the fourth place of decimals; that is in ten-thousandths of an inch. This can be read by the vernier scale on the barrel of a good micrometer. Bore diameters are more difficult to determine. If, however, the matching shaft is accurately measured, the degree of play in the bore can be felt as a guide to its suitability. In other cases, the shank of a twist drill of known diameter is a handy check.

Many methods have been devised for determining the clearance between bearing surfaces. To-day the best and simplest is by the use of Plastigage, obtainable from most garages. A thin plastic thread is laid between the two surfaces and the bearing is tightened, flattening the thread. On removal, the width of the thread is compared with a scale supplied with the thread and the clearance is read off directly. Sometimes joint faces leak persistently, even after gasket renewal. The fault will then be traceable to distortion, dirt or burrs. Studs which are screwed into soft metal frequently raise burrs at the point of entry. A quick cure for this is to chamfer the edge of the hole in the part which fits over the stud.

5 **Always check a replacement part with the original one before it is fitted.**

If parts are not marked, and the order for reassembly is not known, a little detective work will help. Look for marks which are due to wear to see if they can be mated. Joint faces may not be identical due to manufacturing errors, and parts which overlap may be stained, giving a clue to the correct position. Most fixings leave identifying marks especially if they were painted over on assembly. It is then easier to decide whether a nut, for instance, has a plain, a spring, or a shakeproof washer under it. All running surfaces become 'bedded' together after long spells of work and tiny imperfections on one part will be found to have left corresponding marks on the other. This is particularly true of shafts and bearings and even a score on a cylinder wall will show on the piston.

6 Checking end float or rocker clearances by feeler gauge may not always give accurate results because of wear. For instance, the rocker tip which bears on a valve stem may be deeply pitted, in which case the feeler will simply be bridging a depression. Thrust washers may also wear depressions in opposing faces to make accurate measurement difficult. End float is then easier to check by using a dial gauge. It is common practice to adjust end play in bearing assemblies, like front hubs with taper rollers, by doing up the axle nut until the hub becomes stiff to turn and then backing it off a little. Do not use this method with ballbearing hubs as the assembly is often preloaded by tightening the axle nut to its fullest extent. If the splitpin hole will not line up, file the base of the nut a little.

Steering assemblies often wear in the straight-ahead position. If any part is adjusted, make sure that it remains free when moved from lock to lock. Do not be surprised if an assembly like a steering gearbox, which is known to be carefully adjusted outside the car, becomes stiff when it is bolted in place. This will be due to distortion of the case by the pull of the mounting bolts, particularly if the mounting points are not all touching together. This problem may be met in other equipment and is cured by careful attention to the alignment of mounting points.

When a spanner is stamped with a size and A/F it means that the dimension is the width between the jaws and has no connection with ANF, which is the designation for the American National Fine thread. Coarse threads like Whitworth are rarely used on cars to-day except for studs which screw into soft aluminium or cast iron. For this reason it might be found that the top end of a cylinder head stud has a fine thread and the lower end a coarse thread to screw into the cylinder block. If the car has mainly UNF threads then it is likely that any coarse threads will be UNC, which are not the same as Whitworth. Small sizes have the same number of threads in Whitworth and UNC, but in the $\frac{1}{2}$ inch size for example, there are twelve threads to the inch in the former and thirteen in the latter.

7 After a major overhaul, particularly if a great deal of work has been done on the braking, steering and suspension systems, it is advisable to approach the problem of testing with care. If the braking system has been overhauled, apply heavy pressure to the brake pedal and get a second operator to check every possible source of leakage. The brakes may work extremely well, but a leak could cause complete failure after a few miles.

Do not fit the hub caps until every wheel nut has been checked for tightness, and make sure the tyre pressures are correct. Check the levels of coolant, lubricants and hydraulic fluids. Being satisfied that all is well, take the car on the road and test the brakes at once. Check the steering and the action of the handbrake. Do all this at moderate speeds on quiet roads, and make sure there is no other vehicle behind you when you try a rapid stop.

Finally, remember that many parts settle down after a time, so check for tightness of all fixings after the car has been on the road for a hundred miles or so.

8 It is useless to tune an engine which has not reached its normal running temperature. In the same way, the tune of an engine which is stiff after a rebore will be different when the engine is again running free. Remember too, that rocker clearances on pushrod operated valve gear will change when the cylinder head nuts are tightened after an initial period of running with a new head gasket.

Trouble may not always be due to what seems the obvious cause. Ignition, carburation and mechanical condition are interdependent and spitting back through the carburetter, which might be attributed to a weak mixture, can be caused by a sticking inlet valve.

For one final hint on tuning, never adjust more than one thing at a time or it will be impossible to tell which adjustment produced the desired result.

NOTES

GLOSSARY OF TERMS

Allen key Cranked wrench of hexagonal section for use with socket head screws.

Alternator Electrical generator producing alternating current. Rectified to direct current for battery charging.

Ambient temperature Surrounding atmospheric temperature.

Annulus Used in engineering to indicate the outer ring gear of an epicyclic gear train.

Armature The shaft carrying the windings, which rotates in the magnetic field of a generator or starter motor. That part of a solenoid or relay which is activated by the magnetic field.

Axial In line with, or pertaining to, an axis.

Backlash Play in meshing gears.

Balance lever A bar where force applied at the centre is equally divided between connections at the ends.

Banjo axle Axle casing with large diameter housing for the crownwheel and differential.

Bendix pinion A self-engaging and self-disengaging drive on a starter motor shaft.

Bevel pinion A conical shaped gearwheel, designed to mesh with a similar gear with an axis usually at 90 deg. to its own.

bhp Brake horse power, measured on a dynamometer.

bmep Brake mean effective pressure. Average pressure on a piston during the working stroke.

Brake cylinder Cylinder with hydraulically operated piston(s) acting on brake shoes or pad(s).

Brake regulator Control valve fitted in hydraulic braking system which limits brake pressure to rear brakes during heavy braking to prevent rear wheel locking.

Camber Angle at which a wheel is tilted from the vertical.

Capacitor Modern term for an electrical condenser. Part of distributor assembly, connected across contact breaker points, acts as an interference suppressor.

Castellated Top face of a nut, slotted across the flats, to take a locking splitpin.

Castor Angle at which the kingpin or swivel pin is tilted when viewed from the side.

cc Cubic centimetres. Engine capacity is arrived at by multiplying the area of the bore in sq cm by the stroke in cm by the number of cylinders.

Clevis U-shaped forked connector used with a clevis pin, usually at handbrake connections.

Collet A type of collar, usually split and located in a groove in a shaft, and held in place by a retainer. The arrangement used to retain the spring(s) on a valve stem in most cases.

Commutator Rotating segmented current distributor between armature windings and brushes in generator or motor.

Compression ratio The ratio, or quantitative relation, of the total volume (piston at bottom of stroke) to the unswept volume (piston at top of stroke) in an engine cylinder.

Condenser See capacitor.

Core plug Plug for blanking off a manufacturing hole in a casting.

Crownwheel Large bevel gear in rear axle, driven by a bevel pinion attached to the propeller shaft. Sometimes called a 'ring gear'.

'C'-spanner Like a 'C' with a handle. For use on screwed collars without flats, but with slots or holes.

Damper Modern term for shock-absorber, used in vehicle suspension systems to damp out spring oscillations.

Depression The lowering of atmospheric pressure as in the inlet manifold and carburetter.

Dowel Close tolerance pin, peg, tube, or bolt, which accurately locates mating parts.

Drag link Rod connecting steering box drop arm (pitman arm) to nearest front wheel steering arm in certain types of steering systems.

Dry liner Thinwall tube pressed into cylinder bore

Dry sump Lubrication system where all oil is scavenged from the sump, and returned to a separate tank.

Dynamo See Generator.

Electrode Terminal, part of an electrical component, such as the points or 'Electrodes' of a sparking plug.

Electrolyte In lead-acid car batteries a solution of sulphuric acid and distilled water.

End float The axial movement between associated parts, end play.

EP Extreme pressure. In lubricants, special grades for heavily loaded bearing surfaces, such as gear teeth in a gearbox, or crownwheel and pinion in a rear axle.

Fade	Of brakes. Reduced efficiency due to overheating.
Field coils	Windings on the polepieces of motors and generators.
Fillets	Narrow finishing strips usually applied to interior bodywork.
First motion shaft	Input shaft from clutch to gear-box.
Fullflow filter	Filters in which all the oil is pumped to the engine. If the element becomes clogged, a bypass valve operates to pass unfiltered oil to the engine.
FWD	Front wheel drive.
Gear pump	Two meshing gears in a close fitting casing. Oil is carried from the inlet round the outside of both gears in the spaces between the gear teeth and casing to the outlet, the meshing gear teeth prevent oil passing back to the inlet, and the oil is forced through the outlet port.
Generator	Modern term for 'Dynamo'. When rotated produces electrical current.
Grommet	A ring of protective or sealing material. Can be used to protect pipes or leads passing through bulkheads.
Grubscrew	Fully threaded headless screw with screwdriver slot. Used for locking, or alignment purposes.
Gudgeon pin	Shaft which connects a piston to its connecting rod. Sometimes called 'wrist pin', or 'piston pin'.
Halfshaft	One of a pair transmitting drive from the differential.
Helical	In spiral form. The teeth of helical gears are cut at a spiral angle to the side faces of the gearwheel.
Hot spot	Hot area that assists vapourisation of fuel on its way to cylinders. Often provided by close contact between inlet and exhaust manifolds.
HT	High Tension. Applied to electrical current produced by the ignition coil for the sparking plugs.
Hydrometer	A device for checking specific gravity of liquids. Used to check specific gravity of electrolyte.
Hypoid bevel gears	A form of bevel gear used in the rear axle drive gears. The bevel pinion meshes below the centre line of the crownwheel, giving a lower propeller shaft line.
Idler	A device for passing on movement. A free running gear between driving and driven gears. A lever transmitting track rod movement to a side rod in steering gear.
Impeller	A centrifugal pumping element. Used in water pumps to stimulate flow.
Journals	Those parts of a shaft that are in contact with the bearings.
Kingpin	The main vertical pin which carries the front wheel spindle, and permits steering movement. May be called 'steering pin' or 'swivel pin'.
Layshaft	The shaft which carries the laygear in the gearbox. The laygear is driven by the first motion shaft and drives the third motion shaft according to the gear selected. Sometimes called the 'countershaft' or 'second motion shaft.'
lb ft	A measure of twist or torque. A pull of 10 lb at a radius of 1 ft is a torque of 10 lb ft.
lb/sq in	Pounds per square inch.
Little-end	The small, or piston end of a connecting rod. Sometimes called the 'small-end'.
LT	Low Tension. The current output from the battery.
Mandrel	Accurately manufactured bar or rod used for test or centring purposes.
Manifold	A pipe, duct, or chamber, with several branches.
Needle rollers	Bearing rollers with a length many times their diameter.
Oil bath	Reservoir which lubricates parts by immersion. In air filters, a separate oil supply for wetting a wire mesh element to hold the dust.
Oil wetted	In air filters, a wire mesh element lightly oiled to trap and hold airborne dust.
Overlap	Period during which inlet and exhaust valves are open together.
Panhard rod	Bar connected between fixed point on chassis and another on axle to control sideways movement.
Pawl	Pivoted catch which engages in the teeth of a ratchet to permit movement in one direction only.
Peg spanner	Tool with pegs, or pins, to engage in holes or slots in the part to be turned.
Pendant pedals	Pedals with levers that are pivoted at the top end.
Phillips screwdriver	A cross-point screwdriver for use with the cross-slotted heads of Phillips screws.
Pinion	A small gear, usually in relation to another gear.
Piston-type damper	Shock absorber in which damping is controlled by a piston working in a closed oil-filled cylinder.
Preloading	Preset static pressure on ball or roller bearings not due to working loads.
Radial	Radiating from a centre, like the spokes of a wheel.

Radius rod	Pivoted arm confining movement of a part to an arc of fixed radius.
Ratchet	Toothed wheel or rack which can move in one direction only, movement in the other being prevented by a pawl.
Ring gear	A gear tooth ring attached to outer periphery of flywheel. Starter pinion engages with it during starting.
Runout	Amount by which rotating part is out of true.
Semi-floating axle	Outer end of rear axle halfshaft is carried on bearing inside axle casing. Wheel hub is secured to end of shaft.
Servo	A hydraulic or pneumatic system for assisting, or, augmenting a physical effort. See 'Vacuum Servo'.
Setscrew	One which is threaded for the full length of the shank.
Shackle	A coupling link, used in the form of two parallel pins connected by side plates to secure the end of the master suspension spring and absorb the effects of deflection.
Shell bearing	Thinwalled steel shell lined with antifriction metal. Usually semi-circular and used in pairs for main and big-end bearings.
Shock absorber	See 'Damper'.
Silentbloc	Rubber bush bonded to inner and outer metal sleeves.
Socket-head screw	Screw with hexagonal socket for an Allen key.
Solenoid	A coil of wire creating a magnetic field when electric current passes through it. Used with a soft iron core to operate contacts or a mechanical device.
Spur gear	A gear with teeth cut axially across the periphery.
Stub axle	Short axle fixed at one end only.
Tachometer	An instrument for accurate measurement of rotating speed. Usually indicates in revolutions per minute.
TDC	Top Dead Centre. The highest point reached by a piston in a cylinder, with the crank and connecting rod in line.
Thermostat	Automatic device for regulating temperature. Used in vehicle coolant systems to open a valve which restricts circulation at low temperature.
Third motion shaft	Output shaft of gearbox.
Threequarter floating axle	Outer end of rear axle halfshaft flanged and bolted to wheel hub, which runs on bearing mounted on outside of axle casing. Vehicle weight is not carried by the axle shaft.
Thrust bearing or washer	Used to reduce friction in rotating parts subject to axial loads.
Torque	Turning or twisting effort. See 'lb ft'.
Track rod	The bar(s) across the vehicle which connect the steering arms and maintain the front wheels in their correct alignment.
UJ	Universal joint. A coupling between shafts which permits angular movement.
UNF	Unified National Fine screw thread.
Vacuum servo	Device used in brake system, using difference between atmospheric pressure and inlet manifold depression to operate a piston which acts to augment brake pressure as required. See 'Servo'.
Venturi	A restriction or 'choke' in a tube, as in a carburetter, used to increase velocity to obtain a reduction in pressure.
Vernier	A sliding scale for obtaining fractional readings of the graduations of an adjacent scale.
Welch plug	A domed thin metal disc which is partially flattened to lock in a recess. Used to plug core holes in castings.
Wet liner	Removable cylinder barrel, sealed against coolant leakage, where the coolant is in direct contact with the outer surface.
Wet sump	A reservoir attached to the crankcase to hold the lubricating oil.

NOTES

INDEX

D

E

F

G

T

U

V

W

Alfa Romeo Giulia 1600, 1750, 2000 1962 on
Aston Martin 1921-58
Auto Union Audi 70, 80, Super 90, 1966-72
Audi 100 1969 on
Austin, Morris etc. 1100 Mk. 1 1962-67
Austin, Morris etc. 1100 Mk. 2, 3, 1300 Mk. 1, 2, 3 America 1968 on
Austin A30, A35, A40 Farina 1951-67
Austin A55 Mk. 2, A60 1958-69
Austin A99, A110 1959-68
Austin J4 1960 on
Austin Allegro 1973 on
Austin Maxi 1969 on
Austin, Morris 1800 1964 on
Austin, Morris 2200 1972 on
Austin Kimberley, Tasman 1970 on
Austin, Morris 1300, 1500 Nomad 1969 on
BMC 3 (Austin A50, A55 Mk. 1, Morris Oxford 2, 3 1954-59)
Austin Healey 100/6, 3000 1956-68
Austin Healey, MG Sprite, Midget 1958 on
Bedford CA Mk. 2 1964-69
Bedford CF Vans 1969 on
Bedford Beagle HA Vans 1964 on
BMW 1600 1966 on
BMW 1800 1964-71
BMW 2000, 2002 1966 on
Chevrolet Corvair 1960-69
Chevrolet Corvette V8 1957-65
Chevrolet Corvette V8 1965 on
Chevrolet Vega 2300 1970 on
Chrysler Valiant V8 1965 on
Chrysler Valiant Straight Six 1963 on
Citroen DS 19, ID 19 1955-66
Citroen ID 19, DS 19, 20, 21 1966 on
Citroen Dyane Ami 1964 on
Daf 31, 32, 33, 44, 55 1961 on
Datsun Bluebird 610 series 1972 on
Datsun Cherry 100A, 120A 1971 on
Datsun 1000, 1200 1968 on
Datsun 1300, 1400, 1600 1968 on
Datsun 240C 1971 on
Datsun 240Z Sport 1970 on
Fiat 124 1966 on
Fiat 124 Sport 1966 on
Fiat 125 1967-72
Fiat 127 1971 on
Fiat 128 1969 on
Fiat 500 1957 on
Fiat 600, 600D 1955-69
Fiat 850 1964 on
Fiat 1100 1957-69
Fiat 1300, 1500 1961-67
Ford Anglia Prefect 100E 1953-62
Ford Anglia 105E, Prefect 107E 1959-67
Ford Capri 1300, 1600 OHV 1968 on
Ford Capri 1300, 1600, 2000 OHC 1972 on
Ford Capri 2000 V4, 3000 V6 1969 on
Ford Classic, Capri 1961-64
Ford Consul, Zephyr, Zodiac, 1, 2 1950-62
Ford Corsair Straight Four 1963-65
Ford Corsair V4 1965-68
Ford Corsair V4 2000 1969-70
Ford Cortina 1962-66
Ford Cortina 1967-68
Ford Cortina 1969-70
Ford Cortina Mk. 3 1970 on
Ford Escort 1967 on
Ford Falcon 6 1964-70
Ford Falcon XK, XL 1960-63
Ford Falcon 6 XR/XA 1966 on
Ford Falcon V8 (U.S.A.) 1965-71
Ford Falcon V8 (Aust.) 1966 on
Ford Pinto 1970 on
Ford Maverick 6 1969 on
Ford Maverick V8 1970 on
Ford Mustang 6 1965 on
Ford Mustang V8 1965 on
Ford Thames 10, 12, 15 cwt 1957-65
Ford Transit V4 1965 on
Ford Zephyr Zodiac Mk. 3 1962-66
Ford Zephyr Zodiac V4, V6, Mk. 4 1966-72
Ford Consul, Granada 1972 on
Hillman Avenger 1970 on
Hillman Hunter 1966 on
Hillman Imp 1963-68
Hillman Imp 1969 on
Hillman Minx 1 to 5 1956-65
Hillman Minx 1965-67
Hillman Minx 1966-70
Hillman Super Minx 1961-65
Jaguar XK120, 140, 150, Mk. 7, 8, 9 1948-61
Jaguar 2.4, 3.4, 3.8 Mk. 1, 2 1955-69
Jaguar 'E' Type 1961-72
Jaguar 'S' Type 420 1963-68
Jaguar XJ6 1968 on
Jowett Javelin Jupiter 1947-53
Landrover 1, 2 1948-61
Landrover 2, 2a, 3 1959 on
Mazda 616 1970 on
Mazda 808, 818 1972 on
Mazda 1200, 1300 1969 on
Mazda 1500, 1800 1967 on
Mazda RX-2 1971 on
Mazda R100, RX-3 1970 on
Mercedes-Benz 190b, 190c, 200 1959-68
Mercedes-Benz 220 1959-65
Mercedes-Benz 220/8 1968 on
Mercedes-Benz 230 1963-68
Mercedes-Benz 250 1965-67
Mercedes-Benz 250 1968 on
Mercedes-Benz 280 1968 on
MG TA to TF 1936-55
MGA MGB 1955-68
MGB 1969 on
Mini 1959 on
Mini Cooper 1961-72
Morgan Four 1936-72
Morris Marina 1971 on
Morris (Aust) Marina 1972 on
Morris Minor 2, 1000 1952-71
Morris Oxford 5, 6 1959-71
NSU 1000 1963-72
NSU Prinz 1 to 4 1957-72
Opel Ascona, Manta 1970 on
Opel GT 1900 1968 on
Opel Kadett, Olympia 993 cc 1078 cc 1962 on
Opel Kadett, Olympia 1492, 1698, 1897 cc 1967 on
Opel Rekord C 1966-72
Peugeot 204 1965 on
Peugeot 304 1970 on
Peugeot 404 1960 on
Peugeot 504 1968 on
Porsche 356A, B, C 1957-65
Porsche 911 1964 on
Porsche 912 1965-69
Porsche 914 S 1969 on
Reliant Regal 1952-73
Renault R4, R4L, 4 1961 on
Renault 5 1972 on
Renault 6 1968 on
Renault 8, 10, 1100 1962-71
Renault 12, 1969 on
Renault 15, 17 1971 on
Renault R16 1965 on
Renault Dauphine Floride 1957-67
Renault Caravelle 1962-68
Rover 60 to 110 1953-64
Rover 2000 1963-73
Rover 3 Litre 1958-67
Rover 3500, 3500S 1968 on
Saab 95, 96, Sport 1960-68
Saab 99 1969 on
Saab V4 1966 on
Simca 1000 1961 on
Simca 1100 1967 on
Simca 1300, 1301, 1500, 1501 1963 on
Skoda One (440, 445, 450) 1955-70
Sunbeam Rapier Alpine 1955-65
Toyota Carina, Celica 1971 on
Toyota Corolla 1100, 1200 1967 on
Toyota Corona 1500 Mk. 1 1965-70
Toyota Corona Mk. 2 1969 on
Triumph TR2, TR3, TR3A 1952-62
Triumph TR4, TR4A 1961-67
Triumph TR5, TR250, TR6 1967 on
Triumph 1300, 1500 1965-73
Triumph 2000 Mk. 1, 2.5 PI Mk. 1 1963-69
Triumph 2000 Mk. 2, 2.5 PI Mk. 2 1969 on
Triumph Dolomite 1972 on
Triumph Herald 1959-68
Triumph Herald 1969-71
Triumph Spitfire, Vitesse 1962-68
Triumph Spitfire Mk. 3, 4 1969 on
Triumph GT6, Vitesse 2 Litre 1969 on
Triumph Stag 1970 on
Triumph Toledo 1970 on
Vauxhall Velox, Cresta 1957-72
Vauxhall Victor 1, 2, FB 1957-64
Vauxhall Victor 101 1964-67
Vauxhall Victor FD 1600, 2000 1967-72

Continued on following page

THE AUTOBOOK SERIES OF WORKSHOP MANUALS

Vauxhall Victor 3300, Ventora 1968-72
Vauxhall Victor FE Ventora 1972 on
Vauxhall Viva HA 1963-66
Vauxhall Viva HB 1966-70
Vauxhall Viva, HC Firenza 1971 on
Volkswagen Beetle 1954-67
Volkswagen Beetle 1968 on
Volkswagen 1500 1961-66
Volkswagen 1600 Fastback 1965-73
Volkswagen Transporter 1954-67
Volkswagen Transporter 1968 on
Volkswagen 411 1968-72
Volvo 120 series 1961-70
Volvo 140 series 1966 on
Volvo 160 series 1968 on
Volvo 1800 1960-73